The Top 10 Greatest Confederate Generals: Robert E. Lee, Stonewall Jackson, James Longstreet, JEB Stuart, A.P. Hill, Nathan Bedford Forrest, Joseph E. Johnston, Albert Sidney Johnston, P.G.T. Beauregard and Patrick Cleburne

By Charles River Editors

About Charles River Editors

Charles River Editors was founded by Harvard and MIT alumni to provide superior editing and original writing services, with the expertise to create digital content for publishers across a vast range of subject matter. In addition to providing original digital content for third party publishers, Charles River Editors republishes civilization's greatest literary works, bringing them to a new generation via ebooks.

Signup here to receive updates about free books as we publish them, and visit charlesrivereditors.com for more information.

Introduction

Robert E. Lee (1807-1870)

With the exception of George Washington, perhaps the most famous general in American history is **Robert E. Lee** (January 19, 1807 – October 12, 1870), despite the fact he led the Confederate Army of Northern Virginia against the Union in the Civil War. As the son of U.S. Revolutionary War hero Henry "Light Horse Harry" Lee III, and a relative of Martha Custis Washington, Lee was imbued with a strong sense of honor and duty from the beginning. And as a top graduate of West Point, Lee had distinguished himself so well before the Civil War that President Lincoln asked him to command the entire Union Army. Lee famously declined, serving his home state of Virginia instead after it seceded.

Lee is remembered today for constantly defeating the Union's Army of the Potomac in the Eastern theater from 1862-1865, considerably frustrating Lincoln and his generals. His leadership of his army led to him being deified after the war by some of his former subordinates, especially Virginians, and he came to personify the Lost Cause's ideal Southern soldier. His reputation was secured in the decades after the war as a general who brilliantly led his men to amazing victories against all odds.

Despite his successes and his legacy, Lee wasn't perfect. And of all the battles Lee fought in, he was most criticized for Gettysburg, particularly his order of Pickett's Charge on the third and final day of the war. Despite the fact his principle subordinate and corps leader, General James Longstreet, advised against the charge, Lee went ahead with it, ending the army's defeat at Gettysburg with a violent climax that left half of the men who charged killed or wounded.

Although the Civil War came to define Lee's legacy, he was involved in some of American history's other turning points, including the Mexican-American War and the capture of John Brown. This ebook closely examines Lee's war records, but it also humanizes the cheerful husband who was raised and strove to be dignified and dutiful.

Stonewall Jackson (1824-1863)

Thomas Jonathan Jackson is one of the most famous generals of the Civil War, but many of the people he continues to fascinate probably don't remember his whole name. That's because Jackson earned his famous "Stonewall" moniker at the First Battle of Manassas or Bull Run, when Brigadier-General Bee told his brigade to rally behind Jackson, whose men were standing like a stone wall. Ironically, it's still unclear whether that was a compliment for standing strong or an insult for not moving his brigade, but the nickname stuck for the brigade and the general itself.

Jackson would only enhance his legend over the next two years, first leading his army on one of the most incredible campaigns of the war in the Shenandoah Valley in 1862.. Known as the Valley Campaign, Jackson kept 3 Union armies occupied north of Richmond with less than 1/3 of the men, marching his army up and down the Valley 650 miles in three months. The impressive feat helped his men earn the nickname "foot cavalry."

He is equally known for his famous flank march and attack at Chancellorsville on May 2, 1863, which completely surprised the Army of the Potomac's XI Corps and rolled the Union line up. The attack would end up winning the battle for the Confederates, who were outnumbered by nearly 50,000 men at Chancellorsville. As fate would have it, Jackson was mortally wounded at the height of what may have been his finest hour, depriving the Confederacy of one of its best generals. Many still wonder how the outcome of Gettysburg or the Civil War itself may have changed if Jackson had lived.

Of all the Civil War generals, none have been mythologized like Stonewall Jackson, whose quirks and piety have made him a subject of study among military historians and Christians alike. This ebook closely examines Jackson's military career and discusses the legends and mystique that have since surrounded his legacy, but it also humanizes the devoutly religious and tender husband who humored his students at Virginia Military Institute, loved his family, never cursed, and treated strangers with the utmost respect.

James Longstreet (1821–1904)

One of the most important, and controversial, Confederate generals during the Civil War was Lieutenant General James Longstreet, the man Robert E. Lee called his "old war horse." Longstreet was Lee's principal subordinate for most of the war, ably managing a corps in the Army of Northern Virginia and being instrumental in Confederate victories at Second Bull Run, Fredericksburg, and Chickamauga. Longstreet was also effective at Antietam and the Battle of the Wilderness, where he was nearly killed by a shot through the neck.

Had Longstreet died on the field in early May 1864, he would almost certainly be considered one of the South's biggest heroes. However, it was his performance at Gettysburg and arguments with other Southern generals after the Civil War that tarnished his image. After the South lost the war and Gettysburg came to be viewed as one of its biggest turning points, former Confederate generals looked to that battle to find scapegoats to blame for losing the war. Longstreet was charged with being slow to attack on the second day of the Battle of Gettysburg, allowing the Union to man Little Round Top. He also resisted Lee's order for Pickett's Charge the next day, making his criticisms clear both that day and after the war through his rightings. The fact that he served in Republican administrations after the Civil War rubbed his former comrades the wrong way, and the Georgian Longstreet's criticism of Lee infuriated the Virginian Lost Cause advocates who idolized Lee.

Near the end of his life, Longstreet authored *From Manassas to Appomattox*, a Civil War memoirs that looked to rebut his critics. Longstreet didn't avoid his critics, facing them head on by fending off criticisms of his record for the most part, usually including letters written by other officers to his defense. Longstreet also didn't pull punches, which he does at times quite poignantly on Lee's mishaps, most notably of course at Gettysburg. In other instances, he defends himself by criticizing others. When Fitz Lee notes that R.E. Lee called Longstreet the hardest man to move in the Army (a comment that can't be confirmed or refuted), he comes to his own defense in part by criticizing Stonewall Jackson during the Seven Days campaign. Hindsight is 20/20, and Longstreet's arguments in the conduct of certain campaigns certainly benefited from the passing of 30 years. At a number of places, Longstreet believes that if his suggestions were followed, the results could have destroyed Union armies or won the War. Nobody will ever be sure if he's right or wrong on these matters, though historians typically consider those kinds of statements bluster.

This ebook looks at the life and career of one of the South's most important and controversial fighters, explaining his biggest accomplishments and discussing the biggest controversies. Along with pictures of Longstreet and other important people, places and events in his life, you will learn about Lee's Old War Horse like you never have before, in no time at all.

James Ewell Brown Stuart (1833–1864)

"Calm, firm, acute, active, and enterprising, I know no one more competent than [Stuart] to estimate the occurrences before him at their true value." – General Joseph E. Johnston, 1861

Alongside Lee, no one epitomized the chivalry and heroism celebrated by the Lost Cause more than JEB Stuart (1833-1864), the most famous cavalry officer of the Civil War. Stuart was equal parts great and grandiose, leading the cavalry for the Confederacy in Lee's Army of Northern Virginia until his death at the Battle of Yellow Tavern in May 1864. Stuart was a throwback to the past, colorfully dressing with capes, sashes, and an ostrich plumed hat, while sporting cologne and a heavy beard. But he was also brilliant in conducting reconnaissance, and he proved capable of leading both cavalry and infantry at battles like Chancellorsville. As the eyes and ears of Robert E. Lee's army, none were better, despite the fact that he was only in his late 20s and early 30s during the Civil War, far younger than most men of senior rank.

Nevertheless, Stuart's tough fighting was and still is eclipsed by his reputation for audacious cavalry movements. He embarrassed the Army of the Potomac by riding around it twice, making him famous and embarrassing Union generals like George McClellan. However, Stuart's role at Gettysburg was far more controversial. Given great discretion in his cavalry operations before the battle, Stuart's cavalry was too far removed from the Army of Northern Virginia to warn Lee of the Army of the Potomac's movements. Lee's army inadvertently stumbled into the Union army at Gettysburg, walking blindly into what became the largest battle of the war. Stuart has been heavily criticized ever since, and it is said Lee took him to task when he arrived on the second day, leading Stuart to offer his resignation. Lee didn't accept it, but he would later note in his after battle report that the cavalry had not updated him as to the Army of the Potomac's movements.

With his record and characteristics, it has proven almost impossible for Americans to hold a neutral view of Stuart, and it has been even harder to ignore him. This ebook addresses the controversies and battles that made Stuart famous, but it also humanizes the man who was courageous and cocky, yet self-conscious enough to hide what he considered to be a weak chin. Along with pictures of Stuart and other important people, places and events in his life, you will learn about the Confederacy's most famous cavalier like you never have before, in no time at all.

Nathan Bedford Forrest (1821–1877)

*"*I got there *first with the most* men. *"* – Nathan Bedford Forrest

When the war broke out, Nathan Bedford Forrest enlisted in the army and was instructed to raise a battalion of cavalry. A self-made man with no formal military training, Forrest spent the entire war fighting in the Western theater, becoming the only individual in the war to rise from the rank of Private to Lieutenant General. By the end of the war, Forrest was known throughout the South as the "Wizard of the Saddle," and anecdotes of his prowess in battle were legendary. In addition to being injured multiple times in battle, Forrest has been credited with having killed 30 Union soldiers in combat and having 29 horses shot out from under him. Northerners weren't the only ones who felt his wrath; Forrest famously feuded with several commanding officers and notoriously killed an artillery commander in his unit after a verbal confrontation spiraled out of control.

History has properly accorded Forrest his place as one of the most courageous soldiers of the Civil War, and Forrest attained a number of command successes in the Western theater of the war. But Forrest was also at the head of Confederate troops accused of massacring a Union garrison comprised mostly of black soldiers at Fort Pillow, and he was also a prominent slave trader, an overt racist, and likely a leader of the Ku Klux Klan after the Civil War. When he died in 1877, in part due to various war wounds, he was the nation's most notorious unreconstructed rebel. Ashdown and Caudill, authors of *The Myth of Nathan Bedford Forrest*, write that the story of Forrest "embraces violence, race, realism, sectionalism, politics, reconciliation, and repentance."

With these characteristics, it has proven almost impossible for any American to have a neutral view of Forrest, and it has been even harder to ignore him. Subsequently, Forrest's image has vacillated from celebrated to reviled, sometimes both at the same time, over the last 150 years, as the numerous and notable aspects of Forrest's life and legacy were considered by different people at different times.

This book traces his life and Civil War record in the first part, detailing both his wild successes and his biggest controversies. The second part looks at how Forrest's legacy has been interpreted in the North and South since the end of the war, and how it fits within the context of Civil War memory and historiography as a whole, showing how Americans' opinions of Forrest have changed over time in conjunction with how the war and its aftermath were viewed. Along with pictures of Forrest and other important people, places and events in his life, you will learn about the Wizard of the Saddle like you never have before.

Albert Sidney Johnston (1803-1862)

"The turning point of our fate." – Jefferson Davis on the death of Albert Sidney Johnston

Today Albert Sidney Johnston (1803- 1862) is one of the most overlooked generals of the Civil War, but in April 1862 he was widely considered the Confederacy's best general. After graduating from West Point, where he befriended classmates Jefferson Davis and Robert E. Lee, Johnston had a distinguished military career that ensured he would play a principal role in the Civil War. The fact that he was friends with Davis didn't hurt either, and near the beginning of the war Johnston was given command of the Western Department, which basically comprised the entire Western theater at the time.

The Confederates were served poorly in that theater by incompetent officers who Johnston and the South had been saddled with, and from the beginning of the Civil War the Confederates struggled to gain traction in the battlegrounds of Kentucky and Missouri. After critical Confederate setbacks at Fort Henry and Fort Donelson in early 1862, Johnston concentrated his forces in northern Georgia and prepared for a major offensive that culminated with the biggest battle of the war to that point, the Battle of Shiloh.

On the morning of April 6, Johnston directed an all out attack on Grant's army around Shiloh Church, and though Grant's men had been encamped there, they had failed to create defensive fortifications or earthworks. They were also badly caught by surprise. With nearly 45,000 Confederates attacking, Johnston's army began to steadily push Grant's men back toward the river.

As fate would have it, the Confederates may have been undone by friendly fire at Shiloh. Johnston advanced out ahead of his men on horseback while directing a charge near a peach orchard when he was hit in the lower leg by a bullet that historians now widely believe was fired by his own men. Nobody thought the wound was serious, including Johnston, who continued to aggressively lead his men and even sent his personal physician to treat wounded Union soldiers taken captive. But the bullet had clipped an artery, and shortly after being wounded Johnston began to feel faint in the saddle. With blood filling up his boot, Johnston unwittingly bled to death. The delay caused by his death, and the transfer of command to subordinate P.G.T. Beauregard, bought the Union defenders critical time on April 6, and the following day Grant's reinforced army struck back and pushed the Confederate army off the field.

This book chronicles the life and career of one of the Confederacy's most indispensable generals, and the most senior officer to die in battle during the war. Along with pictures of important people, places, and events in his life, you will learn about Albert Sidney Johnston like you never have before.

P.G.T. Beauregard (1818–1893)

On the refusal of Major Anderson to engage, in compliance with my demand, to designate the time when he would evacuate Fort Sumter, and to agree meanwhile not to use his guns against us, at 3.20 o'clock in the morning of the 12th instant I gave him formal notice that within one hour my batteries would open on him." – P.G.T. Beauregard's Official Report on Fort Sumter

Although Confederate generals like Robert E. Lee, Stonewall Jackson and JEB Stuart have long been the most celebrated men of the South, in April 1861 the man of the hour was P.G.T. Beauregard, the South's hero of Fort Sumter. Though Beauregard has never been considered one of the pantheon members of the South, it was he who was in command at Fort Sumter and responsible for the first shots of the Civil War.

Though Beauregard is remembered for his participation at Fort Sumter, the rest of his military career and personal life have been mostly relegated to the footnotes of history books. However, Beauregard was one of the most unique men of the war. A creole born in Louisiana, Beauregard's foreign appearance and demeanor were inescapable among his contemporaries, but he had a long and distinguished career at West Point and in the Mexican-American War even before the Civil War. Furthermore, Beauregard was one of the few who fought in crucial battles in both the East and West, commanding at the First Battle of Bull Run and later Shiloh, and his defense of Petersburg in 1864 saved the Confederacy for nearly another year.

This book looks at the life and career of one of the South's most unusual and important fighters. Along with pictures of Beauregard and other important people, places and events in his life, you will learn about the hero of Fort Sumter like you never have before.

Joseph E. Johnston (1807-1891)

"[The South's ranking of senior generals] seeks to tarnish my fair fame as a soldier and a man, earned by more than thirty years of laborious and perilous service. I had but this, the scars of many wounds, all honestly taken in my front and in the front of battle, and my father's Revolutionary sword. It was delivered to me from his venerated hand, without a stain of dishonor. Its blade is still unblemished as when it passed from his hand to mine. I drew it in the war, not for rank or fame, but to defend the sacred soil, the homes and hearths, the women and children; aye, and the men of my mother Virginia, my native South." – Joseph E. Johnston to Jefferson Davis, September 1861

During the Civil War, one of the tales that was often told among Confederate soldiers was that Joseph E. Johnston was a crack shot who was a better bird hunter than just about everyone else in the South. However, as the story went, Johnston would never take the shot when asked to, complaining that something was wrong with the situation that prevented him from being able to shoot the bird when it was time.

The story is almost certainly apocryphal, but it was aptly used to demonstrate the Confederates' frustration with a man who everyone regarded as a capable general. Johnston began the Civil War as one of the South's senior commanders, leading the ironically named Army of the Potomac to victory in the Battle of First Bull Run over Irvin McDowell's Union Army. But Johnston would become known more for losing by not winning. Johnston was never badly beaten in battle, but he had a habit of strategically withdrawing until he had nowhere left to retreat. When Johnston had retreated in the face of McClellan's army before Richmond in 1862, he finally launched a complex attack that not only failed but left him severely wounded, forcing him to turn over command of the Army of Northern Virginia to Robert E. Lee.

Johnston and Confederate President Jefferson Davis had a volatile relationship throughout the war, but Johnston was too valuable to leave out of service and at the beginning of 1864 he was given command of the Army of Tennessee. When Johnston gradually retreated in the face of Sherman's massive army (which outnumbered his 2-1) before Atlanta in 1864, Davis removed Johnston from command of the Army of Tennessee and gave it to John Bell Hood.

Johnston has never received the plaudits of many of the South's other generals; in fact, there are only a couple of monuments commemorating his service in the South. Yet Johnston was a competent general who fought in some of the most important campaigns of the Civil War, and it's often forgotten that it was his surrender to Sherman weeks after Appomattox that truly ended the Civil War. Johnston did so over Davis's command to keep fighting, incurring his wrath once more. Having dealt with each other, Sherman and Johnston became friends after the war, and when the elderly Johnston served as a pallbearer at Sherman's funeral, he contracted an illness that eventually killed him.

Given his prominent and controversial role in the Civil War, Johnston naturally took to writing memoirs, *Narrative of Military Operations During the Civil War*, which gives an extremely detailed account of the war, a defense of his actions, and criticism of Jefferson Davis and John Bell Hood. One of the most interesting parts of Johnston's memoirs come at the end, with his letters, telegrams, and even an anecdote about the origins of the Confederate Battle Flag.

This book examines Johnston's life, record in the war and legacy. Along with pictures of important people, places, and events in his life, you will learn about Johnston like you never have before.

A.P. Hill (1825-1865)

"Little Powell's got on his battle shirt!" – Hill's soldiers before a battle.

Of all the eccentric and enigmatic men who led during the Civil War, perhaps none had as mixed a record as Confederate Lieutenant General Ambrose Powell Hill, better known as A.P. Hill. Hill was a well known and highly respected general on both sides, particularly for his command of "Hill's Light Division" under Stonewall Jackson, which arrived just in time to save Lee's army during the Battle of Antietam. He continued to be Jackson's most capable subordinate until Jackson's death, when Lee gave him command of the III Corps of the Army of Northern Virginia just before the Pennsylvania campaign that climaxed at Gettysburg.

Known affectionately to his soldiers as Little Powell, Hill was considered courageous and courteous, a fitting representative of his native Virginia. But after the defeat at Gettysburg and in the wake of his death during the final week of the war, Hill's reputation was somewhat tarnished. Hill was frequently sick to the point of being unfit for command during crucial times like the final day of the Battle of Gettysburg, either because of nerves or the lingering effects of gonorrhea, which he contracted decades earlier around the time he became a West Point cadet in the fabled Class of 1846. He is perhaps best remembered for being engaged to Ellen B. Marcy, the future wife of Hill's West Point friend George B. McClellan, before her parents pressured her to break off the engagement.

This book profiles the famous general and examines his Civil War record, analyzing the legacy he's left behind. Along with pictures of important people, places, and events, you will learn about Hill like you never have before, in no time at all.

Patrick Cleburne (1828-1864)

"As between the loss of independence and the loss of slavery, we assume that every patriot will freely give up the latter..." – Patrick Cleburne, 1864

During the Civil War, the eyes of the nation usually stayed fixed to the Eastern theater, where Confederate General Robert E. Lee's Army of Northern Virginia constantly bedeviled the Union Army of the Potomac and its many commanders. Instrumental to that success at places like Second Manassas and Chancellorsville was Lee's corps commander Stonewall Jackson, who became one of the most popular and respected generals of the Civil War.

Despite the Confederates' success in holding off the Union's offensives in the East, however, the Union made steady progress in the Western theater, winning battles like Shiloh, capturing New Orleans, and sealing off the Mississippi River at Vicksburg. Like the Union generals in the East, Confederate generals in the West were either mortally wounded in battle (Albert Sidney Johnston) or proved ineffective (Braxton Bragg, John Pemberton). One of the only bright spots in the West for the Confederacy was Irish immigrant Patrick Cleburne, whose successes earned him the nickname "Stonewall of the West". Where so many Confederates were failing, Cleburne's strategic tactics and bold defensive fighting earned him fame and recognition throughout the South, even leading Lee to call him "a meteor shining from a clouded sky."

Unfortunately for Cleburne, he is also remembered today for reasons other than his battlefield successes. Cleburne was tasked with leading an assault that he heartily opposed during the Battle of Franklin near the end of 1864, but he obeyed the command and was killed in the assault within the Union lines. The general was so legendary even among Union soldiers that the valuables on his body were looted before his body came back to Confederate lines Upon hearing of his death, Cleburne's old corps commander noted, "Where this division defended, no odds broke its line; where it attacked, no numbers resisted its onslaught, save only once; and there is the grave of Cleburne."

Cleburne is also remembered for a bold and novel idea that he proposed to the Army of Tennessee in 1864. Realizing the Confederates' deficiency in manpower and resources, Cleburne suggested freeing the South's slaves so that they would fight for the Confederacy. It was such a radical idea that the Army buried it, and even when the Confederacy was on its last legs entering 1865, it could not muster the political support to emancipate some of their slaves to fight.

This book chronicles the life and career of the Stonewall of the West, analyzing his record in the war and assessing his legacy. Along with pictures of important people, places, and events in his life, you will learn about General Cleburne like you never have before, in no time at all.

Robert E. Lee, Stonewall Jackson, James Longstreet and JEB Stuart
Chapter 1: Robert E. Lee's Early Years

Robert Edward Lee was born on January 19, 1807, at Stratford Hall Plantation in Westmoreland County, Virginia, near Montross, the fifth child to Major General Henry "Light Horse Harry" Lee III (1756–1818) and his second wife, Anne Hill Carter (1773–1829). Though his year of birth has traditionally been recorded as 1807, historian Elizabeth Brown Pryor has noted Lee's writings indicate he may have been born the previous year. Lee's family had Norman-French lineage that could trace itself back to one of Virginia's pioneering families; Robert's great-great grandfather, Henry Lee I, was a prominent Virginian colonist originally arriving in Virginia from England in the early 1600s with Richard Lee I.

Light Horse Harry

Lee's well-regarded family also boasted his father's accomplishments. Lee's father had served with distinction as a cavalry officer under General George Washington in the American Revolution, and after the war Light Horse Harry served as a member of the Virginia legislature and as Governor of Virginia. His mother, daughter of Charles Carter (whose father Robert was one of the first wealthy men in America) and Anne Butler Moore, grew up in an idyllic life at Shirley Plantation, Tyler, one of the most elegant mansions in all Virginia. Both the Lees and Carters were prominent in Virginia's political affairs, with family members regularly sitting in the House of Burgesses, and serving as speakers and governors. Two Lees signed the Declaration of Independence.

The Shirley Plantation at the time of the Civil War

By the time of Robert's birth, Light Horse Harry, 17 years Anne's senior, was in deep financial trouble and scandal loomed over his family. Having retreated to Stratford Hall after failing as both a tobacco farmer and land speculator, Henry was aggressively hounded by creditors and subsequently stripped of property and servants to satisfy his mounting debts. Today "Light Horse Harry" is best remembered as Robert E. Lee's father, but at the time he was so absorbed in his own financial woes that he couldn't even be bothered to name his new son.

In 1809, Henry was arrested twice for debt and imprisoned in Westmoreland County jail, forcing Anne to deliver him food herself for lack of servants. Though offered asylum for herself and her children by her brother-in-law, husband of her late sister, Mildred, Anne refused to abandon her husband, choosing to maintain her home and family despite Henry's imprisonment. Upon his release, however, she insisted they move to Alexandria, Virginia, where she had numerous family members nearby and her children were assured an education at their neighboring plantations, and later, Alexandria Academy.

In 1813, Henry Lee's career and life in America came to a quiet (if not covert) end when he slipped off to Barbados in the West Indies after sustaining serious internal wounds--and by most reports, nearly killed--in a political riot in Baltimore, Maryland. Left to fend for herself, Anne spent her inheritance to provide for her children, writing infrequently to Henry, who was said to have spent little time at home even when things were going well. In 1818, when Robert was just 11, Anne was informed of her husband's death by a letter from her brother-in-law, two weeks after it occurred.

Though little has been written about Robert's boyhood, which was not something he discussed in his personal writings, by all accounts, Robert knew his father only as a shadowy, distant figure who had once been a great soldier and man of social standing. For Robert, it was Light Horse Harry's reputation as a man of apparent dignity, poise, and charm that could serve as a role model. And like any proud Virginian of the period, Light Horse Harry insisted that all his sons learn to swim, ride, shoot, box, dance, and use a sword--but only in self-defense--like every fine Virginia gentleman.

The tragedies of his father's later life, however--and the disgrace it brought his family-- invariably drew Robert close to his mother and in many ways shaped the man he became. It would not be unfair to say Robert was his mother's boy.

Young Robert began his formal education in Alexandria, Virginia, at a private school maintained by the wealthy Carter family for their numerous offspring on one of their numerous plantations, then transferred to nearby Alexandria Academy. Today Lee's letters are of great interest to historians and casual readers alike, but amazingly, Robert was only formally instructed in French, not English, resulting in a writing style that consistently utilized uncustomary spelling such as *honour* and *agreable*, with proper names like *french*, *english*, and *yankee* written in lowercase. These linguistic oddities would be well illustrated in countless letters sent to friends and family throughout his life.

Young Robert was also familiar with hard work at a young age. After his eldest brother, William, left for Harvard, brother Sidney Smith joined the U.S. Navy, and sister Anne was away most of the time seeking medical attention for a chronic illness (believed to be tuberculosis), it fell upon Robert as the eldest remaining sibling to assist his mother around the home, forcing him to develop a strong sense of responsibility while still very young.

Chapter 2: James Longstreet's Early Years

James (K.*) Longstreet was born on January 8, 1821 in Edgefield District, South Carolina (now part of North Augusta, Edgefield County), the fifth child and third son to James Longstreet (1783-1833) and Mary Ann Dent (1793-1855). Originally from New Jersey and Maryland respectively, the senior James owned a cotton plantation near the modern city of Gainesville in northeastern Georgia. James' ancestor, Dirck Stoffels Langestraet, immigrated to the Dutch colony of New Netherlands in 1657, with the "Longstreet" name becoming Anglicized over the generations.

*(All formal documents available list James Longstreet as his full name, while several informal papers included the "K" initial but no clarification of what it stands for.)

According to Longstreet's memoirs, which are still widely considered one of the most important memoirs written about the Civil War: "Grandfather William Longstreet first applied steam as a motive power, in 1787, to a small boat on the Savannah River at Augusta, and spent all of his private means upon that idea, asked aid of his friends in Augusta and elsewhere, had no encouragement, but, on the contrary, ridicule of his proposition to move a boat without a pulling or other external power, and especially did they ridicule the thought of expensive steam-boilers to be made of iron. To obviate costly outlay for this item, he built boilers of heavy oak timbers and strong iron bands, but the Augusta marines were incredulous…"

Of course, history does not credit William Longstreet for the discovery. What happened? According to Longstreet, "He failed to secure the necessary aid, and the discovery passed into the possession of certain New Yorkers, who found the means for practicable application, and now steam is the goddess that enlightens the world."

Though born in Edgefield District, South Carolina, James spent most of his youth in Augusta, Georgia (and later, some time in Somerville, Alabama). It is said that James' father was so impressed by his son's "rocklike" character that he nicknamed him "Peter" (as in "Peter the Rock" of the Bible), leading to him being known as "Pete" or "Old Pete" for much of his life.

Given his son's rocklike character, Longstreet's father charted a course for his son's future. According to Longstreet, "From my early boyhood he conceived that he would send me to West Point for army service." Early on, James' father chose the military life for his son but knew that the local educational system was much too inadequate to provide a good academic background. So in 1830, at the age of nine, James was sent to live with his aunt and uncle in Augusta; his uncle, Augustus Baldwin Longstreet, was a newspaper editor, educator, and Methodist minister. James spent the next eight years on his uncle's plantation, "Westover," while attending the Academy of Richmond County.

In 1833 when James was just twelve, his father died during a cholera epidemic while visiting Augusta. Although James' mother and the remainder of the family then moved to Somerville, Alabama, James remained with Uncle Augustus. While living and working on his Uncle Augustus' plantation in Augusta, Georgia, James spent eight years attending the Academy of Richmond County (and was no doubt greatly influenced by his uncle, who was himself an educator).

In his memoirs, however, Longstreet barely mentions his academic schooling, heading almost straight into a discussion about his West Point years in the first chapter of the memoirs. Some may take that as an indication he wasn't terribly interested in these early years, but it's just as likely that because he was writing the memoirs to rebut and attack his critics, he wanted to spend as little time as possible discussing pre-military life.

Though his father was gone, young James' resolve for a military life was not. In 1837, Augustus attempted to secure an appointment for James to the United States Military Academy at West Point, New York, but the vacancy for his congressional district had already been filled. A year later James got an appointment through another relative, Reuben Chapman, a Representative from the First District of Alabama (where his mother Mary lived).

Chapter 3: Stonewall Jackson's Early Years

Robert E. Lee and Stonewall Jackson have been the Confederacy's two most celebrated generals since 1862, and while both continue to be revered in the South for their military skills and successes, as men they are championed for very different reasons. For many Southerners, Lee continues to personify the essence of duty and dignity that all fine Southern gentlemen should possess, while Jackson is celebrated for being a more common man, a devout hard worker with quirks.

While 16 year old Robert E. Lee was receiving homeschooling on one of his family's many plantations, Thomas Jonathan Jackson was born on Jan 21, 1824, in Clarksburg, Virginia, an area that has since become part of the state of West Virginia. Young Thomas was the third child of attorney Jonathan Jackson (1790–1826) and Julia Beckwith Neale (1798–1831), both Virginia natives. But as far as family lineage was concerned, his most famous relatives were his great-grandparents, John Jackson (1715–1801) and Elizabeth Cummins [also known as Elizabeth Comings and Elizabeth Needles] (1723–1828).

Stonewall Jackson has come to personify integrity, but his great-grandfather, John Jackson, of Coleraine, County Londonderry, Ireland, had the dubious distinction of being convicted of larceny while living in London for stealing £170. He was subsequently sentenced to fulfill a seven-year indenture in America to work off the debt. Thomas' great-grandmother Elizabeth, a statuesque woman over six feet in height and born in London, was also convicted of larceny (in an unrelated case) for stealing nineteen pieces of jewelry, silver, and fine lace, receiving a similar sentence.

As fate would have it, John and Elizabeth were part of a group of 150 convicted criminals transported to Annapolis, Maryland in May 1749. The two met aboard their ship, and by the time their ship docked in America, they had begun a relationship. Although their indentures sent them to different areas of Maryland, the couple managed to remain in contact, going on to marry in July 1755 after fulfilling their legal obligations. After migrating west across the Blue Ridge Mountains to Moorefield, Virginia (now West Virginia) in 1758 with their two sons, and then to Tygart Valley in 1770, the couple somehow acquired large parcels of pristine farm land near present-day Buckhannon (near central West Virginia), including 3,000 acres Elizabeth apparently secured herself.

Like many Confederate generals, Stonewall Jackson had several relatives fight in the American Revolution. John and his two sons enlisted during the Revolution, subsequently fighting in the Battle of Kings Mountain on October 7, 1780, after which John was promoted to captain. While the men were away in the army, Elizabeth converted their home to a place she dubbed, "Jackson's Fort," which became a well-known haven for refugees from frontier Indian attacks.

In all, John and Elizabeth had eight children. Their second son was Edward Jackson (March 1, 1759– December 25, 1828), a county surveyor who sat in the Virginia legislature, and Edward's third son was Jonathan Jackson, a lawyer of Clarksburg, who was Stonewall's father. Thus, Thomas Jonathan Jackson was named for his maternal grandfather.

By the time Thomas was born, his parents already had two young children, Elizabeth (born in 1819) and Warren (born in 1821). His sister, however, died of typhoid fever on March 6, 1826 at just six years of age (with the two-year-old Thomas said to have remained at her bedside until the end). His father died of the same disease just twenty days later, on March 26. The day after his father died, Thomas' sister Laura Ann was born.

Now widowed at 28 years old and left with heavy debt and three young children to care for (including a newborn), Thomas' mother Julia sold the family's possessions to pay her debts and feed her family. Declining family charity, she moved her family into a small, one-room rented house where she taught school and took up sewing to support her three children for the next four years.

In 1830, Julia remarried, but her new husband, Blake Woodson, also an attorney, did not like his stepchildren and tended to ignore them. When Julia's health began to fail, Thomas and his sister Laura Ann were sent to live with their uncle, Cummins Jackson, who owned a grist mill in Jackson's Mill (near present-day Weston in Lewis County, West Virginia). Elder brother Warren went to live with other relatives on his mother's side of the family, dying of tuberculosis in 1841 at the age of 20.

Thomas and Laura Ann returned from Jackson's Mill briefly in November 1831 to be at their dying mother's bedside. On December 3, 1831, less than two months after giving birth to Thomas's half-brother, William Wirt Woodson, Julia died of complications in Fayette County, West Virginia, leaving her three eldest children orphaned. Julia was buried in an unmarked grave in a homemade coffin in Westlake Cemetery along the James River and Kanawha Turnpike in Fayette County near present-day Ansted, West Virginia.

After four years together at the Mill, Thomas and his sister were again separated, with Laura Ann sent to live with her mother's family while Thomas was sent to live with his Aunt Polly (his father's sister) and her husband, Isaac Brake, on a farm outside Clarksburg. After suffering constant verbal abuse from Brake for over a year, Thomas ran away, walking eighteen miles through the mountain wilderness to reach Jackson's Mill and the safety of his uncle Cummins Jackson. There he remained for the next 7 years tending sheep, driving teams of oxen, and helping harvest wheat and corn.

By all historic accounts, formal schools in this place and time in the United States were virtually non-existent, forcing most children to be taught "The Three Rs," *reading*, *writing* and '*rithmetic* by family or friends, if they themselves knew them. Thus, boys like young Thomas attended school when and where they could, but ultimately acquiring most of their education through self-teaching.

One account from this time describes Thomas as having once made a deal with one of his Uncle Cummins Jackson's slaves to trade pine knots for teaching the black man to read; pine knots Thomas would burn to provide light to stay awake all night reading borrowed books. Although Virginia law made it a serious crime to teach a slave, free Black, or Mulatto to read or write, Thomas nevertheless secretly taught the slave to write as promised. Once literate, the young slave fled to Canada via the Underground Railroad, the very thing the law intended to prevent. Regardless, it was not the last time Thomas would prove to be a successful teacher.

Chapter 4: JEB Stuart's Early Years

Young Stuart before the beard

JEB Stuart has long been viewed as one of the Confederacy's bravest soldiers, and a symbol of the perfect Christian, Virginian soldier that defeated Rebels turned to after the war. Stuart's destiny and legacy, of course, always centered around the Old Dominion.

James Ewell Brown "Jeb/J. E. B." Stuart was born at Laurel Hill plantation in Patrick County, Virginia, near the North Carolina border on February 6, 1833, the eighth of 11 children to Archibald Stuart and Elizabeth Letcher Pannill. His family ancestry in America began with Archibald and brother David Stuart who sought refuge from religious persecution (presumably in Ireland) by emigrating to Chester County, Pennsylvania in 1726, and subsequently moving again with his family (which included Judge John Stuart of Londonderry, Ireland) to Augusta County, Virginia about 1738.

Like Robert E. Lee, the superior he will always be associated with, Stuart was imbued with a sense of dignity and responsibility that was based in no small part on his family's military and political service. The first generation of American-born Stuarts was distinguished by the military services of Major Alexander Stuart (James' great grandfather), who nearly died of wounds sustained at the Battle of Guilford Court House during the American Revolution. Alexander's son, John, lived for a time in the West serving as a Federal judge in Illinois and Missouri, and as Speaker of the House of Representatives in Missouri.

John's son, Archibald was a veteran of the War of 1812, a slaveholder, an attorney, and a Democrat who represented Patrick County in both Houses of the Virginia General Assembly. Archibald married Elizabeth Pannill, who herself was a descendant of the prominent Letcher family, and and together produced 11 children, Jeb being their eighth. Elizabeth was known as a strict, religious woman, and in an unusual role for the time period, she essentially ran the family plantation.

In 1959, author Gertrude Hecker Winders published what was for many years considered a fair depiction of the boyhood life of "Jeb" Stuart, *Jeb Stuart: Boy in the Saddle*. In recent years, however, as part of an ongoing reexamination of Stuart's life, many critics and historians now believe it more a fanciful account based on urban legend, generalities, and supposition. While that was fittingly in keeping with the reputation and legacy Stuart would carve during the Civil War, the color of the stories has since been called heavily into question.

As a result, it seems that little verifiable information concerning Stuart's early life was written in his time, or it has yet to be uncovered. There are, however, a few well-documented events that can offer insight into the man who came to be known primarily by his various high-profile exploits during the Civil War.

Jeb was the youngest of the five sons who lived beyond childhood, and his father, Archibald, was a prominent politician and attorney who represented Patrick County in both Houses of the Virginia General Assembly and served one term in the U. S. House of Representatives. Jeb's mother, Elizabeth, was known as a stern, religious woman with a great love of nature who ran the family plantation. There can be little doubt that like most boys in this place and time in American history, young Jeb had his share of chores and responsibilities, and received a basic education as time permitted. By surviving accounts, Jeb enjoyed a "happy boyhood," loved his family home at Laurel Hill, displayed an enthusiasm for nature, and often said that one of his fondest dreams for adulthood was to one day own his family home and end his days there in quiet retirement.

The Stuart home has been described as "an unpretentious, comfortable farmhouse" which, tragically, was destroyed by fire in the winter of 1847-48, though no detailed description of the house remains. In a surviving letter, Jeb described the fire as "a sad disaster."

For a few years after the fire, Archibald and son John Dabney lived in the outbuilding that had served as the family kitchen; with Archibald apparently remaining there until his death in 1855. In 1859, Elizabeth Stuart sold the property to two men from Mt. Airy, North Carolina, and the Laurel Hill plantation passed out of the Stuart family's possession.

Although few personal anecdotes regarding the young Jeb survive, one incident that seems to foretell of the bravery and audacity he would later display as a Civil War officer occurred at about the age of ten. As the story is told, while walking through the woods one afternoon with an older brother, a swarm of hornets attacked the two, sending the elder brother running. Young

Jeb, however, is said to have "narrowed his eyes defiantly" and knocked the hornets' nest to the ground with a stick, defying the danger the bees posed. As would be seen repeatedly on the battlefield, James seems to have thrived on danger from a very early age.

Jeb received his earliest education at home, lessons presented by his mother and various relatives and neighbors, until 1845, when at the age of 12 he left Laurel Hill to be educated by a series of teachers in Wytheville, Virginia, and at the home of his aunt Anne (Archibald's sister) and her husband Judge James Ewell Brown (Stuart's namesake) at Danville. During the summer of 1848, Jeb became fascinated with military life and attempted to enlist in the U. S. Army, but the 15 year old teenager was rejected due to his age. That fall he entered Emory & Henry College, a private liberal arts school in Emory, Virginia where he studied for the next two years.

Finally, in 1850, Jeb gained entry into the military life he sought, appointed to the United States Military Academy at West Point, New York, by family friend, Representative Thomas Hamlet Averett, a man who had defeated James' father in the 1848 House election.

Chapter 5: West Point Years

Following his natural aptitude for mathematics, Robert applied for admission into the United States Military Academy at West Point in early 1825. Today West Point is considered the country's elite military academy, and Lee's fantastic academic record there is still the stuff of legends, but when Lee applied to West Point, it was a highly *unimpressive* school consisting of a few ugly buildings facing a desolate, barren parade ground. Accepted in March of that year, Robert began his formal career as a soldier in July at the age of 18.

Upon Robert's departure for West Point, his mother moved with her two remaining daughters, Elinor and Elizabeth, from Alexandria to Georgetown, Washington D.C. Later, as her health quickly deteriorated, she moved to the home of Henry Lee's grandson, William Henry Fitzhugh, at Ravensworth in Fairfax County, Virginia.

Quickly demonstrating his aptitude for leadership and devotion to duty, Robert ranked high among his West Point classmates from the very beginning of his stint. Never insubordinate, always impeccably dressed, and never receiving even a single demerit; he became the template for his fellow cadets, who referred to him as "The Marble Model." While studying there he made many life-long friends, including fellow Virginian Joseph E. Johnston, as well as Albert Sidney Johnston, Leonidas Polk, Jefferson Davis, John B. Magruder, and William N. Pendleton-- all of whom would come to play critical roles for the Confederacy during the Civil War.

Lee in his 20s

Excelling in both mathematics and military exercises (particularly tactics and strategy), Robert studied engineering, science, and drawing, among other subjects. In his free time, he was known to pore over Alexander Hamilton's autobiography, Napoleon's memoirs, and *Confessions* by the renowned 18th-century Genevan political philosopher and writer, Jean-Jacques Rousseau. Awarded the highest rank in the Corps--cadet adjunct--his senior year, Robert graduated with high honors in 1829, ranked first in his class in artillery and military tactics and second in overall standing. He was immediately commissioned brevet lieutenant in the U.S. Army Corps of Engineers, considered the elite of the army in 1829.

Immediately after graduation, Robert went to visit his mother who was by this time dying of advanced tuberculosis. Tending her to her final day, Anne passed away on June 29, 1829. Robert the boy then became Lee the military man.

In 1838, at the age of seventeen, James was appointed to West Point Military Academy in New York, where he proved to be a very poor student academically, as well as a disciplinary problem.

Longstreet explained why he had academic problems: "As cadet I had more interest in the school of the soldier, horsemanship, sword exercise, and the outside game of foot-ball than in the academic courses. The studies were successfully passed, however, until the third year, when I failed in mechanics. When I came to the problem of the pulleys, it seemed to my mind that a soldier could not find use for such appliances, and the pulleys were passed by. At the January examination I was called to the blackboard and given the problem of the pulleys. The drawing from memory of recitation of classmates was good enough, but the demonstration failed to satisfy the sages of the Academic Board. It was the custom, however, to give those who failed in the general examination a second hearing, after all of the classes were examined. This gave me two days to "cram" mechanics, and particularly on pulleys. But the professors were too wily to introduce them a second time, and took me through a searching examination of the six months course. The bridge was safely passed, however, and mechanics left behind. At the June examination, the end of the academic year, I was called to demonstrate the pulleys. The professor thought that I had forgotten my old friend the enemy, but I smiled, for he had become dear to me,--in waking hours and in dreams,--and the cadet passed easily enough for a maximum mark."

James also found other ways to earn scorn: "The cadets had their small joys and sometimes little troubles. On one occasion a cadet officer reported me for disobedience of orders. As the report was not true, I denied it and sent up witnesses of the occasion. Dick Garnett, who fell in the assault of the 3d, at Gettysburg, was one witness, and Cadet Baker, so handsome and lovable that he was called Betsy, was the other. Upon overlooking the records I found the report still there, and went to ask the superintendent if other evidence was necessary to show that the report was not true. He was satisfied of that, but said that the officer complained that I smiled contemptuously. As that could only be rated as a single demerit, I asked the benefit of the smile; but the report stands to this day, Disobedience of orders and three demerits. The cadet had his revenge, however, for the superintendent was afterwards known as The Punster."

Though popular with the other students (befriended by a number of future prominent Civil War figures, including George Henry Thomas, William S. Rosecrans, John Pope, D. H. Hill, Lafayette McLaws, George Pickett, and Ulysses S. Grant), the nearly 6' 2", 200 lb James racked up too many academic and disciplinary problems to receive high ranks. As a result, when he graduated in 1842, he finished third last in his class.

Upon graduation, James was commissioned brevet Second Lieutenant James Longstreet of the Fourth U.S. Infantry and sent to Jefferson Barracks, Missouri.

In his memoirs, Longstreet notes some of the West Point connections that were made by future Civil War generals, aside from his own. It was Longstreet's friendship with Grant that eventually allowed him to play a role in Grant's Republican administration after the war, which was viewed as almost treasonous by some of his former Confederate comrades.

Longstreet also points out that P.G.T. Beauregard and Irvin McDowell, the two commanding officers at the First Battle of Bull Run, went to West Point together. Beauregard's artillery instructor was Robert Anderson, who was in command of the garrison at Fort Sumter when Beauregard ordered the attack on it April 12, 1861, the first fighting of the Civil War.

Jackson as a cadet at West Point

In 1842, Thomas was accepted to the United States Military Academy at West Point, New York after being appointed by Congressman Samuel Hays, who chose Jackson as a replacement. As it turned out, Jackson was part of the most famous West Point class in history, the Class of 1846. Since his formal schooling had been so lacking up to that time, he had difficulty passing the entrance exams and was initially placed at the bottom of his class. Forced to work harder than most other cadets to absorb the lessons, despite his obvious shyness, he quickly began to display the tenacious determination that would come to characterize him for the remainder of his life. Becoming one of the hardest-working cadets in the academy, he moved steadily up the academic ladder, finally graduating 17th out of 59 students in the Class of 1846, and it was said by his peers that if he had stayed another year he would surely have graduated first in his class.

By the time Jackson and his peers attended West Point, they already had to deal with the legendary record of Robert E. Lee, who had finished first in his class without a single demerit over a decade earlier. Demerits were handed out for all kinds of infractions, from cleanliness to attire and tardiness. One Class of 1846 student had a very natural way of collecting demerits; George E. Pickett would often leave campus to drink, which helped him graduate last in the class. And if Jackson was to finish first, he would have had to beat out the young George B. McClellan, who finished second in the Class of 1846 and was considered a prodigy. Jackson went to school with future Civil War generals A.P. Hill (who was in love with McClellan's future wife), Darius Couch, and Cadmus Wilcox. Jackson's roommate in his junior year was the 6'4 George Stoneman, who led the Army of the Potomac's cavalry during the Battle of Chancellorsville and later became the Governor of California.

Stoneman

In 1850, Jeb entered the U. S. Military Academy at West Point and quickly adapted to military rigors, becoming a popular, happy student. Though not considered handsome during his teen years, and standing just five foot, nine inches tall, James' classmates began calling him "Beauty," which they explained as his "personal comeliness in inverse ratio to the term employed." He is said to have possessed a chin "so short and retiring as positively to disfigure his otherwise fine countenance." The weak chin did not escape his notice, and after graduation he would grow a beard that led a fellow officer to remark, "[He was] the only man I ever saw that [a] beard improved."

Today West Point is the country's elite military academy, but when Stuart entered the school in 1850, its importance in training the Civil War's greatest leaders was not yet known, and the campus hardly befitted a great institution. In 1852, Robert E. Lee, who had a legendary reputation at the Academy for finishing first in his class and not receiving a demerit nearly 20 years earlier, was appointed superintendent of the Academy, and Jeb soon became friends with the Lee family, seeing them socially on numerous occasions. Lee's nephew, Fitzhugh Lee (who would serve under Jeb during the Civil War as a lieutenant colonel of the First Virginia Cavalry beginning in August 1861), also arrived at the academy that year.

It was at West Point that Stuart proved to himself and others his cavalry talents. In his final year at West Point, in addition to achieving the cadet rank of second captain of the corps, he was one of only eight cadets designated "honorary cavalry officers" for his exceptional skills in horsemanship. In 1854, at the age of 21, Jeb graduated thirteenth in his class of forty-six, ranked tenth in his class in cavalry tactics. And although he enjoyed the civil engineering curriculum and did well in mathematics as well, his poor drawing skills hampered his engineering studies, so he finished 29th in that discipline. (A Stuart family legend insists that he deliberately slacked-off his academic studies his final year to avoid service in the elite--but dull--Army Corps of Engineers.)

In October of 1854, James was commissioned brevet Second Lieutenant James Ewell Brown Stuart, but he was already most often referred to as "Jeb." Of course, Stuart would be remembered as one of a handful of West Point men who became the greatest generals of the Civil War, and the future generals' years at West Point became a source of colorful stories about the men who would become Civil War legends. A clerical error by West Point administrators ensured that Hiram Ulysses Grant forever became known as Ulysses S. Grant. And years after Robert E. Lee met Albert Sidney Johnston and Jefferson Davis at West Point, William Tecumseh Sherman was roommates with George H. Thomas, who later became one of his principal subordinates and the "Rock of Chickamauga".

Chapter 6: Early Military Careers and the Mexican-American War

Although Lee's position in the U.S. Army Corps of Engineers was a prestigious one, Lee's first military assignment was at a remote army post at Fort Pulaski on Cockspur Island, Georgia (on the Savannah River). Though not yet receiving full lieutenant's pay, he was tasked with full responsibility for seeing to it that the groundwork for the construction of a new fort was laid--a job requiring him to spend much of his time immersed in mud up to his armpits.

Though he was now away from Virginia, Lee's time spent in Georgia also represented perhaps the most social period of his life. Lee managed to find sufficient distraction from his less-than-pleasant duties in the home of West Point friend, Jack Mackay, whose family home was located in Savanna and where Lee often spent time with Jack's two sisters Margaret and Eliza. Said to have enjoyed dancing, gossip, and parties, Lee, the Southern gentleman, was in his element, conversing and cavorting with Georgia's social elites. Still, even though Lee was often the charming "life of the party" and was sharing the company of many eligible women, he seems to have fancied few.

After serving 17 months at Fort Pulaski, Robert was transferred to Fort Monroe, Virginia, where he was made assistant to the chief of engineers. While stationed there, Lee met his second cousin, Mary Anna Randolph Custis. Mary was the pampered and frail daughter of Mary Lee Fitzhugh and famously wealthy but slovenly agriculturalist George Washington Parke Custis (grandson of Martha Washington). Although they outwardly had very little in common--he was elegant, admired stoicism, and relished social gatherings, while she was dull, complained incessantly, and loathed parties--Lee proposed marriage. Some historians believe the attraction was at least in part based on Mary's profession to having a religious epiphany the year before, damning the keeping of slaves. On July 5, 1831, the two were wed. The 3rd U.S. Artillery served as honor guard.

1862 map of Fort Monroe

In that Lee could scarcely support Mary in the style she'd been accustomed, he agreed to move into her family home, which still stands on a hill overlooking Washington, D.C. Even so, beginning in August of 1831, the couple shared Lee's cramped junior officer's quarters at the fort for a period of two years, during which Mary brought along one of her slaves, Cassy, to tend to her personal needs. A little more than a year later, Mary gave birth to their first child, George Washington Custis--who Lee nicknamed "Boo." In the years that followed, the Lees would produce six more children: Mary, William H. Fitzhugh, Eleanor Agnes, Annie, Robert Edward Jr., and Mildred. All three sons would serve in the Confederate Army under their father during the Civil War.

1854 engraving of Mary

From 1834 to 1837, Robert served as assistant engineer in Washington, but spent the summer of 1835 helping survey the boundary line between the states of Ohio and Michigan. In 1836 he was given his first solo project, that of finding a way to control the course of the "Mighty" Mississippi River, which was constantly threatening to destroy the burgeoning commerce of the city of St. Louis. Through the ingenious accomplishment of this daunting project involving the moving of 2,000 tons of rock to build strategically-placed dikes, an engineering feat in itself, Lee established once and for all his professional standing. Recognition for this monumental accomplishment came in the form of promotion to first lieutenant of engineers, assigned to supervise the engineering work for the St. Louis harbor, thus becoming a member of the board of engineers for U.S. Atlantic coast defenses. But while his professional life excelled during these years, his family life began to falter.

Shortly after giving birth to their second child, Mary Curtis, in 1835 (whom Lee would refer to simply as "Daughter"), his wife's health began a downward spiral that would plague her throughout her life. Chronic pelvic infection, abscesses of the groin, and rheumatism would come to define her day-to-day existence, and her physical limitations and mental state weighed heavily on Lee. In May 1837, Lee's third child, William Henry Fitzhugh was born, followed by Anne Carter in 1839, and Eleanor Agnes in 1841--with whom Lee kept in constant contact through letters while away performing his duties. That same year, he was promoted to captain and transferred to Fort Hamilton in New York Harbor, where he was put in charge of building fortifications. A short time later his family came to join him, and for the first time he was able to spend more than a few days at a time with them.

Ironically, as his family grew in size, despite his preference for spending his time close to home, Lee began hoping hostilities would erupt somewhere in the U.S. territories. Even on a captain's salary, soon the basic upkeep and education of his children would reach a critical point, and military men were seldom promoted above the rank of captain in peace time.

Lee with his son William, circa 1845

When the United States declared war on Mexico on May 13, 1846, Lee thought the opportunity to prove himself as a field officer had finally arrived. But the growing sentiment in the North was that the annexation of Texas was just a slaveholders' ploy to seize more territory for the further expansion of slavery. Ulysses S. Grant, one of the first American soldiers to cross the disputed border, believed the Army was being sent there just to provoke a fight, and a young Congressman from Illinois named Abraham Lincoln first gained national attention for sponsoring legislation demanding that President Polk show the spot where Mexicans had fired on American troops, believing that "President Polk's War" was full of deception.

Regardless, in September of 1846, Lee was sent to San Antonio de Bexar, Texas, with orders to report to Brigadier General John E. Wool. Considering that he might not return from this mission, Lee made out his will, leaving everything to his wife Mary, before setting off. There he was tasked with selecting travel routes for the troops and supervision of the construction of bridges for Wool's march toward Saltillo, the capital city of the northeastern Mexican state of

Coahuila, just south of Texas.

Daguerreotype of General John E. Wool

On January 16, 1847, Lee was then attached to General Winfield Scott's command at Brazos, Texas. Scott was planning to take the war deeper into Mexico, to Veracruz (in east-central Mexico) and then Mexico City. Immediately acknowledged for his excellent intuition as a scout, Lee became a member of Scott's staff and experienced his first active combat while taking part in the capture of Veracruz.

During the march to Mexico City, Lee was promoted to brevet major, receiving high praise for his insightful reconnaissance and choice of artillery placement that ultimately made the capture of Mexico's capital possible. It was also Lee's engineering skills that enabled American troops to cross the treacherous mountain passes leading to the capital. General Scott's official reports raved about Lee's war-time efforts, declaring that his "success in Mexico was largely due to the skill, valor, and undaunted courage of Robert E. Lee," calling him "the greatest military genius in America." Diaries of many of his fellow officers showed how impressed they all were with the brave "Virginian."

Winfield Scott was a military hero in the War of 1812 and the Mexican-American War

Brevet Second Lieutenant James Longstreet spent his first two years of military service at Jefferson Barracks, Missouri, where he was soon joined by his West Point friend, Lieutenant Ulysses S. Grant. Longstreet pointed out in his memoirs that he loved his assignment, but not for military reasons. "I was fortunate in the assignment to Jefferson Barracks, for in those days the young officers were usually sent off among the Indians or as near the borders as they could find habitable places. In the autumn of 1842 I reported to the company commander, Captain Bradford R. Alden, a most exemplary man, who proved a lasting, valued friend. Eight companies of the Third Infantry were added to the garrison during the spring of 1843, which made garrison life and society gay for the young people and interesting for the older classes. All of the troops were recently from service in the swamps and Everglades of Florida, well prepared to enjoy the change from the war-dance of the braves to the hospitable city of St. Louis; and the graceful step of its charming belles became a joy forever."

Longstreet even recalls being with Grant when he met his wife Julia, writing, "Of the class of 1843, Ulysses S. Grant joined the Fourth Regiment as brevet lieutenant, and I had the pleasure to ride with him on our first visit to Mr. Frederick Dent's home, a few miles from the garrison, where we first met Miss Julia Dent, the charming woman who, five years later, became Mrs. Grant. Miss Dent was a frequent visitor at the garrison balls and hops, where Lieutenant Hoskins, who was something of a tease, would inquire of her if she could tell where he might find "the small lieutenant with the large epaulettes."

Grant

In 1847, while serving in the Mexican-American War, Major Longstreet met Maria Louisa Garland (called "Louise" by her family), the daughter of Longstreet's regimental commander, Lt. Colonel John Garland.

Married in March of 1848 (one month after the conclusion of the war), the couple had ten children together (only five of whom lived to adulthood): John G. (1848-1918), Augustus Baldwin (1850-1862), William Dent (1853-1854), James (1857-1862), Mary Anne (1860-1862), Robert Lee (1863-1940), James (1865-1922), Fitz Randolph (1869-1951), Louise Longstreet Whelchel (1872-1957), and an unnamed child presumed to have died at birth.

Although their marriage would last over 40 years, Longstreet never mentioned Louise in his memoirs, and most of what is known today about their relationship came from the writings of his second wife, Helen Dortch Longstreet.

At about the same time that Longstreet began courting Maria Louisa Garland, Longstreet's West Point friend and fellow Jefferson Barracks comrade Ulysses S. Grant met and began a relationship with Longstreet's fourth cousin, Julia Dent, with the couple marrying on August 22, 1848 in St. Louis, Missouri. While historians agree that Longstreet attended the Grant-Dent wedding, his specific role during the ceremony remains unclear. Grant biographer Jean Edward Smith asserts that Longstreet served as Grant's Best Man, while John Y. Simon, editor of Julia Grant's memoirs, states that Longstreet "may have been a groomsman." But as Longstreet biographer Donald Brigman Sanger points out, neither Grant nor Longstreet mentioned the role of "Best Man" in either of their memoirs or other personal writings.

Sent into the action sometime in 1846, Second Lieutenant Longstreet served with distinction in the Mexican-American War with the Eighth U. S. Infantry, receiving brevet promotions to captain for the battles at Contreras and Churubusco, and major for the action at Molino del Rey-- having been cited for gallant and meritorious conduct numerous times.

In the Battle of Chapultepec, September 12-13, 1847, Major Longstreet was severely wounded in the thigh with a musket ball while charging up the hill carrying his regimental colors. Naturally, the color bearer who holds the flag marches front and center and is unarmed, making it the most dangerous position in 19th century warfare, and one that requires incredible bravery. As the incident is recorded, upon falling, Longstreet handed the flag to his friend, a young Lieutenant who finished last in his West Point class of 1846, George E. Pickett. Pickett earned distinction for reaching the summit during the battle, and both men earned reputations at Mexico that would allow them to command brigades early in the Civil War.

Longstreet and General Winfield Scott Hancock (whose performance at Gettysburg during Pickett's Charge on Day 3 was crucial for the Union's success) fought together in the Battle of Churubusco.

There is no question that Longstreet made a name for himself in Mexico, and it was a reputation that would help earn him command over a brigade right at the outset of the Civil War. Yet Longstreet barely mentions his actual service during the Mexican-American war in his memoirs, instead recalling the politics behind the war and two heroic vignettes about other men he fought with in battle. Again, readers can quickly get the sense that he considered Mexico cursory to his life and legacy.

The Class of 1846 graduated at a fortuitous time for military men. At the age of 22, Thomas received his first commission, officially becoming Thomas Jonathan Jackson, Second Lieutenant of artillery. Jackson was immediately assigned to various posts around New York, but by the time the men had graduated tensions were brewing between the United States and Mexico. The growing sentiment in the North was that the annexation of Texas was just a slaveholders' ploy to seize more territory for the further expansion of slavery. Ulysses S. Grant, one of the first American soldiers to cross the disputed border, believed the Army was being sent there just to provoke a fight, and a young Congressman from Illinois named Abraham Lincoln first gained national attention for sponsoring legislation demanding that President Polk show the spot where Mexicans had fired on American troops, believing that "President Polk's War" was full of deception.

For members of the Class of 1846, however, the Mexican-American War provided a chance for much needed combat experience. As the war geared up, Jackson was sent to serve in the

Mexican-American War, joining the Third Assault Group where he was assigned command of the First and Fourth Artillery, designated as infantry to strengthen the forces of General Emanuel Twigg at Veracruz.

Becoming part of a major siege at Veracruz that lasted from March 7-27, 1847, (when the city surrendered to the U. S. Army), Jackson got his first taste of commanding in battle, and the notoriety that followed. Then moving on to Contreras and Chapultepec, over the next year he rose to the temporary rank of major by demonstrating the doggedness, coolness under pressure, and fearlessness he would later become known for. It was in Mexico that he first met the formidable Robert E. Lee, who was serving as part of General Winfield Scott's staff and whose reputation was already start to grow. George McClellan was also distinguishing himself in Mexico, conducting reconnaissance for Scott and serving as an engineering officer at Chapultepec.

After the war ended, Jackson served at a series of forts before his company was sent to Florida to deal with the Seminole Native American uprising. But, like many career military officers, Jackson found army life during peacetime tedious and unrewarding. In 1851, Jackson resigned his army commission and joined the faculty of the Virginia Military Institute at Lexington, Virginia, becoming a professor of artillery tactics and natural philosophy.

Among Lee and his principle subordinates in the Army of Northern Virginia, JEB Stuart was the only one who didn't fight in the Mexican-American War.

On January 28, 1855, brevet Second Lieutenant James "Jeb" Stuart was assigned to the U. S. Mounted Rifles Cavalry at Fort Davis, Texas (in what is today Jeff Davis County), becoming a leader on scouting missions over the San Antonio to El Paso Road, where for the next three months he fought the Apaches. He was then transferred to the newly formed First Cavalry

Regiment at Fort Leavenworth, Kansas Territory, where he became regimental quartermaster and commissary officer under the command of Colonel Edwin V. Sumner. His organizational and logistical talents quickly becoming apparent, he was promoted to first lieutenant later that same year.

Edwin "Bull" Sumner would lead a corps for the Army of the Potomac in the major campaigns of 1862

In an attempt to organize the center of North America – Kansas and Nebraska – without offsetting the slave-free balance, Senator Stephen Douglas of Illinois proposed the Kansas-Nebraska Act. The Kansas-Nebraska Act eliminated the Missouri Compromise line of 1820, which the Compromise of 1850 had maintained. The Missouri Compromise had stipulated that states north of the boundary line determined in that bill would be free, and that states south of it *could* have slavery. This was essential to maintaining the balance of slave and free states in the Union. The Kansas-Nebraska Act, however, ignored the line completely and proposed that all new territories be organized by popular sovereignty. Settlers could vote whether they wanted their state to be slave or free.

When popular sovereignty became the standard in Kansas and Nebraska, the primary result was that thousands of zealous pro-slavery and anti-slavery advocates both moved to Kansas to influence the vote, creating a dangerous (and ultimately deadly) mix. Numerous attacks took place between the two sides, and many pro-slavery Missourians organized attacks on Kansas towns just across the border.

The best known abolitionist in Bleeding Kansas was a middle aged man named John Brown. A radical abolitionist, Brown organized a small band of like-minded followers and fought with the armed groups of pro-slavery men in Kansas for several months, including a notorious incident known as the Pottawatomie Massacre, in which Brown's supporters murdered five men. Over 56 people died until John Brown left the territory, which ultimately entered the Union as a free state in 1859.

John Brown

Now a veteran of the Native American frontier conflicts, from 1855 to 1861 First Lieutenant Stuart was given a leadership position in defusing "Bleeding Kansas" (or the "Border War"), the violent political confrontations between anti-slavery "Free-Staters" (like John Brown) and pro-slavery "Border Ruffians" that took place in the Kansas Territory and neighboring towns of Missouri, and ended with the "Pottawatomie Massacre."

On July 29, 1857, Stuart demonstrated his knack for initiative and bravery during the Cheyenne uprising known as the Battle of Solomon's River in present day Kansas. According to reports, after his commander, Colonel Sumner, ordered a "drawn sabers" charge against a band of Cheyenne who were firing a barrage of arrows, Stuart and three other lieutenants chased one Cheyenne down, who Stuart then shot in the thigh. The Native American, however, turned and fired at Stuart with a flintlock, striking him directly in the chest, but doing little actual damage. By the time Stuart returned to Fort Leavenworth that September to reunite with his family, word of his courage and exceptional leadership abilities preceded him.

Chapter 7: Life Before the War, 1850-1859

When the Mexican-American War ended in 1848, Lee returned to service with the U.S. Army Corps of Engineers. After spending three years at Fort Carroll in Baltimore harbor, Lee was made superintendent of West Point in 1852, a tribute to both his exemplary military record and his natural ability to lead. Although he voiced his preference for field duty rather than a desk job, he assumed his new position with zeal. Lee made numerous improvements to the buildings, revamped the curriculum, and was known to spend a great deal of time with the cadets, gaining him a reputation as a fair and kind superintendent.

Lee had proven himself at West Point a second time, but his destiny was not to remain there. With dissension mounting between the North and South, exacerbated by the Mexican-American War, it wasn't long before Lee would find himself in the middle of an insurgence.

In early 1855, Lee was promoted to lieutenant colonel of the newly organized 2nd Cavalry and stationed at Jefferson Barracks in St. Louis, Missouri. Much of his time spent during the next few years at his new post were spent in court-martial service or with the 2nd Cavalry on the Texas frontier, where local Native American tribes posed an ongoing threat to settlers.

During this time, Lee continued to demonstrate his talent as both soldier and organizer, but as would later be revealed in his letters, these were not happy years for Lee. He disliked being separated from his family and felt guilty for not being available to his wife, who by now had become a chronically-ill invalid. Indeed, for nearly two decades, Lee found himself constantly being pulled in opposite directions by his wife's needful requests and his sense of duty to the job he was assigned. In one famous letter in 1834, Lee responded to one of Mary's requests to return by writing to her, "But why do you urge my immediate return, & tempt one in the strongest manner... I rather require to be strengthened & encouraged to the full performance of what I am called on to execute."

Lee in 1850

Although Lee returned to Washington at every opportunity, it was the death of his father-in-law in October of 1857 that would ultimately lead him to request an extended leave from the Army. Having to deal with the settlement of her father's estate exacerbated Mary's already frail condition, prompting Lee to find a way to remain at her side. And as it would happen, Lee was home in 1859 tending to family matters when he received orders from Washington to hurry to Harpers Ferry, West Virginia.

After the Mexican-American War and his recovery from the wound sustained at Chapultepec, Longstreet served on routine frontier duty in Texas, primarily at Forts Martin Scott (near Fredericksburg) and Bliss (in El Paso). During this time, Longstreet advanced to the rank of major, mostly performing scouting missions.

Beginning in July of 1858, he began serving as paymaster for the Eighth Infantry. Author Kevin Phillips of *The Cousins' Wars* claims that during this period, Longstreet was involved in a plot to draw the Mexican state of Chihuahua into the Union as a slave state.

As Longstreet put it, "I was stationed at Albuquerque, New Mexico, as paymaster in the United States army when the war-cloud appeared in the East. Officers of the Northern and Southern States were anxious to see the portending storm pass by or disperse, and on many occasions we, too, were assured, by those who claimed to look into the future, that the statesman would yet show himself equal to the occasion, and restore confidence among the people." Clearly Longstreet at the time was hoping for some sort of grand compromise that would avert war.

By the time Jackson assumed his position at Virginia Military Institute in the Spring 1851, he'd already acquired many of the "idiosyncrasies" that would come to identify him for the remainder of his life. And though he is said to have worked hard to be an effective educator, by all accounts, he never became a popular or successful teacher, instead becoming the butt of ongoing jokes mocking his stern, religious demeanor and peculiar interests.

Having discovered *hydropathology*, the form of alternative medicine widely known as the "water cure," which advocated the practice of bathing in various types of minerals springs as a preventative healing agent, Jackson was known to have spent considerable time at spas on Lake Ontario, as well as Warm Springs, Rockbridge Alum Springs, and Bath Alum Springs in Virginia.

During this time, Jackson also became increasingly more involved with religion, with God not only coming to dominate his thoughts, but his teaching. To a greater and greater degree, religion became intertwined in the lessons he presented his cadets; Jackson even began finding a way to incorporate God into artillery courses. Although known as a thorough instructor, he had a reputation for only allowing students to reach conclusions based on his orthodox views, with no variations.

An indication of his single-mindedness is reflected in a letter written to his sister Laura Ann during this time: "We are all children of suffering and sorrow in this world. No earthly calamity can shake my hope in the future so long as God is my friend." He even established a Sunday School for blacks, which he compelled his own slaves to attend, writing, "My heavenly father has condescended to use me for setting up a large Sabbath-school for the Negroes here."

His students mocked him frequently, but they were not without cause. Instead of wearing a standard military uniform, Jackson wore the uniform he'd worn in the Mexico Campaign, topped with a tight-fitting cadet's cap that he would sport to his final day. As the most rigid teacher by far, he displayed what would be characterized today as neurotic, obsessive-compulsive behavior: leaving and returning home, beginning and ending each class, eating each meal, and reciting prayers, each at the same *exact* moment each day. Jackson would not alter these habits under any circumstance. And though he was inherently quite shy, Jackson spoke in a screeching voice and was known to stutter when compelled to speak unexpectedly, yet he still insisted on leading church meetings and even joined the village debating society, "The Franklin", making members quite uncomfortable with what they considered his absurd points of views.

Sometime in 1883, Jackson surprised his sister Laura Ann with the announcement that not only had he met a woman he intended to marry, but that there had already been a brief courtship and a wedding date set. Jackson had met Eleanor, the daughter of Rev. George Junkin, president of Washington College in Virginia. Eleanor (or Elinor) and Jackson were married sometime in mid-1883, with their wedding attended by just a few close family members, including Dr. Junkin and

Eleanor's sister Margaret.

Although Margaret was several years older than Eleanor, the sisters were seldom seen apart and dressed identically. They were, in fact, so inseparable that Margaret went along on the couple's honeymoon, a trip to New York City, Niagara Falls, Canada, Boston, and West Point. An entry in Margaret's diary from this trip provides some interesting insight into Jackson's mind and perhaps the type of man he aspired to be. As the three stood on the battlefield in Quebec where the Battle of the Plains of Abraham had taken place during the French and Indian War, Jackson approached the statue of General Wolfe, took off his cap reverently, and quoted Wolfe in a quivering voice, "'I die content!'" Then he said, "To die as he died, who would not die content!"

After returning from a stagecoach ride to visit Jackson's relatives in western Virginia in November of 1854, the now-pregnant Eleanor (who Jackson referred to as "my sister") immediately took to her bed. Just days later, she died in childbirth at the age of thirty, delivering a stillborn. Jackson went into grim but stoic mourning.

In July of 1856, with little word to those around him, Jackson decided to take advantage of a vacation offered by the Institute and set off for Europe. His passport described him as 5 feet 9 ¾ inches in stature with grey eyes, an aquiline nose, small mouth, oval chin, dark brown hair, oval face, dark complexion, and a weight of about 175 pounds.

During his time abroad, Jackson developed an ever-increasing sense of duty and moral righteousness, coupled with his great religious conviction, which he now saw as "the cause". This steadfastness earned him the mocking title "Deacon Jackson," with some comparing him with Oliver Cromwell (April 25 1599–September 3 1658), the zealous English military and political leader. As Lord Protector and England's first Puritan ruler, Cromwell believed that individuals' religious beliefs should be respected, yet he permitted people who opposed popular 17th century English beliefs to be tortured and imprisoned. While in Europe, Jackson visited Waterloo, site of perhaps the most famous battle in history, where the Imperial French Army under Napoleon was defeated. Picking up a bit of French, he began his mornings by reading Scriptures from the French New Testament.

Upon his return, Jackson went back to his teaching duties and within a very short time announced that he again planned to marry. He'd actually met the future Mrs. Jackson, Mary Anna Morrison, shortly before his marriage to his first wife, Eleanor, while visiting his friend (and future Confederate general) D. H. Hill. Also the daughter of a minister and college president (this one from Davidson College in North Carolina), Jackson approached her father with his intentions and then requested a leave of absence from the Institute--right in the middle in the academic term--even before informing "Anna" of his plan, which he delivered by letter. In July of 1857 they were married at Cottage Home, the Morrison house in North Carolina.

Presenting her with a gold watch and a set of seed pearls, they honeymooned in Richmond, Baltimore, Philadelphia, New York, Saratoga, and Niagara. And as Anna noted in her diary, they also visited several spas "for the health of the groom."

Upon retuning to his teaching duties at the Institute, Anna immediately became aware of Jackson's strict regimen. Up at 6:00 a.m., cold bath, brisk walk (rain or shine); 7:00 am, family prayers (which she and their servants were required to attend), followed by breakfast and his walk to campus during which he would perform mental exercises while following the same precise route each day, without any deviation. Home at 11:00 a.m., he then stood at a high table (with no chair) where he studied the Bible, followed by lunch. At 12:30 p.m., he shared a half hour of leisure time with Anna, during which she would sit beneath a shade tree while he worked in the fields with a slave field hand. In the evening he would often sit facing the wall while he finished some mental task of his design, asking Anna not to disturb him. He would finish off the evening by having Anna read to him.

Early in 1858, Anna bore a daughter, Mary Graham, who died just a few weeks later of jaundice on May 25. A short time later, Jackson began displaying serious signs of hypochondria, continually suffering various vague ailments. Inflammations of the ear and throat (during which he claimed to have lost the hearing in his right ear though doctors could find no cause) led to neuralgia; inflamed tonsils led to complications of the lungs and bronchitis. Additionally, he began to think the right side of his body was heavier than his left so he would periodically raise his right arm to allow the blood to flow downward--thus lightening that arm.

Meanwhile, his daily routine became even more obsessive-compulsive. The colonel of the Institute reported that on more than one occasion he had witnessed Jackson pacing back and forth outside the Institute office because he'd arrived a few minutes earlier than his customary time to present his weekly report; Jackson refused to enter until the precise moment he was supposed to. And when he spoke, every comment became a statement about God.

In July of 1855 while stationed at Fort Leavenworth, Kansas Territory, Stuart met Flora Cooke, daughter of Lieutenant Colonel Philip St. George Cooke, commander of the Second U. S. Dragoon Regiment. (Cooke is noted for his authorship of the standard Army Cavalry Manual and is sometimes called the "Father of the U. S. Cavalry.") Biographer and historian Burke Davis described Flora as "an accomplished horsewoman, and though not pretty, an effective charmer," to whom "Stuart succumbed with hardly a struggle."

In September of that year, less than two months after meeting, Stuart proposed marriage. In a clever play off another famous general's words, Stuart wrote of his whirlwind courtship, "*Veni, Vidi, Victus sum,*" Latin for "I came, I saw, I was conquered". Although the couple had planned a gala wedding at Fort Riley, Kansas, the death of Stuart's father on September 20, 1855, brought a change of plans, with the wedding subsequently held on November 14, attended only by family members.

In 1856 the couple's first child, a girl, was born, but died the same day. Then on November 14, 1857, Flora gave birth to a second daughter whom they named Flora. In early 1858 the Stuart's relocated to Fort Riley, Kansas with their two slaves--one inherited from his father's estate, one purchased to help around the Stuart household--where they remained until 1859.

In October of 1859, while still in service to the U. S. Army, Stuart developed a new saber hook, "an improved method of attaching sabers to belts"--for which the U. S. government paid him $5,000 for a "right to use" license. It was while he was in Washington discussing the contract (and applying for an appointment to the quartermaster department) that Stuart heard about John Brown's raid on the U. S. Arsenal at Harpers Ferry and volunteered to be Colonel Lee's *aide-de-camp*.

On June 26, 1860, wife Flora gave birth to a son who would at first be named Philip St. George Cooke Stuart, after Jeb's well known father in law.

Chapter 8: Harpers Ferry

After his activities in Kansas, John Brown spent the next few years raising money in New England, which would bring him into direct contact with important abolitionist leaders, including Frederick Douglass. Brown had previously organized a small raiding party that succeeded in raiding a Missouri farm and freeing 11 slaves, but he set his sights on far larger objectives. In 1859, Brown began to set a new plan in motion that he hoped would create a full scale slave uprising in the South. Brown's plan relied on raiding Harpers Ferry, a strategically located armory in western Virginia that had been the main federal arms depot after the Revolution. Given its proximity to the South, Brown hoped to seize thousands of rifles and move them south, gathering slaves and swelling his numbers as he went. The slaves would then be armed and ready to help free more slaves, inevitably fighting Southern militias along the way.

In recognition of how important Douglass had become among abolitionists, Brown attempted to enlist the support of Douglass by informing him of the plans. While Douglass didn't blow the whistle on Brown, he told Brown that violence would only further enrage the South, and slaveholders might only retaliate further against slaves with devastating consequences. Instead of helping Brown, Douglass dissuaded freed blacks from joining Brown's group because he believed it was doomed to fail.

In July 1859, Brown traveled to Harper's Ferry under an assumed name and waited for his recruits, but he struggled to get even 20 people to join him. Rather than call off the plan, however, Brown went ahead with it. That fall, Brown and his men used hundreds of rifles to seize the armory at Harper's Ferry, but the plan went haywire from the start, and word of his attack quickly spread. Local pro-slavery men formed a militia and pinned Brown and his men down while they were still at the armory.

After being called to Harpers Ferry, Lee took decisive command of a troop of marines stationed there, surrounded the arsenal, and gave Brown the opportunity to surrender peaceably. When Brown refused, Lee ordered the doors be broken down and Brown taken captive, an affair that reportedly lasted just three minutes. A few of Brown's men were killed, but Brown was taken alive. Acknowledged for accomplishing this task so quickly and efficiently, Lee was sent back to resume his duties in Texas. By most accounts, Lee already knew what was on the wind.

Young JEB Stuart played an active role in opposing the raid at Harpers Ferry. In October of 1859, while conducting business in Washington, D.C., Stuart volunteered to carry secret instructions to Lieutenant Colonel Robert E. Lee and then accompany him and a squad of U. S. Military Militia to Harpers Ferry, where Brown had staged a raid on the armory. While delivering Lee's written ultimatum to the leader of the raid, who was going by the pseudonym Isaac Smith, Stuart remembered "Old Ossawatomie Brown" from the events at Bleeding Kansas, and ultimately assisted in his arrest.

The fallout from John Brown's raid on Harpers Ferry was intense. Southerners had long suspected that abolitionists hoped to arm the slaves and use violence to abolish slavery, and Brown's raid seemed to confirm that. Meanwhile, much of the northern press praised Brown for his actions. In the South, conspiracy theories ran wild about who had supported the raid, and many believed prominent abolitionist Republicans had been behind the raid as well. On the day of his execution, Brown wrote, "I, John Brown, am now quite *certain* that the crimes of this *guilty land* will never be purged away but with *blood.* I had, as I now think vainly, flattered myself that without very much bloodshed it might be done."

The man in command of the troops present at Brown's hanging was none other than Thomas Jonathan Jackson, who was ordered to Charlestown in November 1859. After Brown's hanging, Jackson began to believe war was inevitable, but he wrote his aunt, "I think we have great reason for alarm, but my trust is in God; and I cannot think that He will permit the madness of men to interfere so materially with the Christian labors of this country at home and abroad."

Chapter 9: The War Cloud and Choosing Sides

By the Fall of 1860, however, everyone could see the "war-cloud" on the horizon. Despite having virtually zero support in the slave states, Abraham Lincoln ascended to the presidency at the head of a party that was not yet 10 years old, and one whose stated goal was to end the expansion of slavery. Although Lincoln did not vow to abolish slavery altogether, southerners believed Lincoln's presidency constituted a direct threat to the South's economy and political power, both of which were fueled by the slave system. Southerners also perceived the end of the expansion of slavery as a threat to their constitutional rights, and the rights of their states, frequently invoking northern states' refusals to abide by the Fugitive Slave Act. With the election of Republican candidate Abraham Lincoln as president on November 6, 1860, many Southerners considered it the final straw. Someone they knew as a "Black Republican" was now set to be inaugurated as President in March.

Throughout the fall and winter of 1860, Southern calls for secession became increasingly serious. In a last-ditched effort to save the Union, Kentucky's Senator John Crittenden tried to assume the stateliness of his predecessor Henry Clay. Crittenden, however, proved to be no Henry Clay: his proposal that a Constitutional Amendment reinstate the Missouri Compromise line and extend it to the Pacific failed. President Buchanan supported the measure, but President-Elect Lincoln said he refused to allow the further expansion of slavery under any conditions.

The Crittenden Compromise failed on December 18. Two days later, South Carolina seceded from the Union. President Buchanan sat on his hands, believing the Southern states had no right to secede, but that the Federal government had no effective power to prevent secession. In January, Mississippi, Florida, Alabama, Georgia, Louisiana and Kansas followed South Carolina's lead. The Confederacy was formed on February 4th, in Montgomery, Alabama, with former Secretary of War Jefferson Davis as its President. On February 23rd, Texas joined the Confederacy.

Jefferson Davis

When Texas seceded from the Union in 1861, Lee was recalled to Washington to await orders while an appropriate response was formulated. A devout admirer of George Washington and the monumental self-sacrifice he'd made to establish the Union, Lee hated the idea of a divided nation. Thus, he began to see his destiny as protecting the freedom, liberty, and legal principles for which Washington had so gallantly risked his life. Even so, he suffered great trepidation in choosing between standing with his native Virginia and the Northern Union, should it come down to a civil war, especially when President Lincoln would offer Lee command of the United States Army.

In a letter to his sister Lee wrote, " ...in my own person I had to meet the question whether I should take part against my native state...with all my devotion to the Union, and the feeling of loyalty and duty of an American citizen, I have not been able to make up my mind to raise my hand against my relatives, my children, my home. I have therefore resigned my commission in the army, and, save in defense of my native state--with the sincere hope I may never be called upon to draw my sword."

Lee grieved his choice to break with his men, and particularly General Scott, whom he considered a close, personal friend. Ultimately, however, just as Washington had chosen to separate himself from the British Empire, Lee chose to separate from the Union to fight what the South regarded a second war of independence. And once he chose sides, Lee never looked back.

Although Major James Longstreet was not enthusiastic about the idea of states' secession from the Union, he had learned from his uncle Augustus about the doctrine of states' rights early in his life and seen his uncle's passion for it.

Historically-speaking, there are two quite divergent accounts of Longstreet's entry into the Confederate Army at the start of the War. One states that although born in South Carolina and reared in Georgia, Longstreet offered his services to the state of Alabama (which had appointed him to West Point and where his mother had lived). Thus, as the senior West Point graduate from that state, he was automatically commissioned a rank commensurate with that state's policy. Other accounts, however, assert that Longstreet deliberately traveled to Richmond, Virginia - not Alabama - and offered his services as a paymaster of the new Confederate army. Perhaps, both scenarios are somehow true.

Here's how Longstreet remembered the early days of the Civil War in his memoirs: "When mail-day came the officers usually assembled on the flat roof of the quartermaster's office to look for the dust that in that arid climate announced the coming mail-wagon when five or ten miles away; but affairs continued to grow gloomy, and eventually came information of the attack upon and capture of Fort Sumter by the Confederate forces, which put down speculation and drew the long-dreaded line. A number of officers of the post called to persuade me to remain in the Union service. Captain Gibbs, of the Mounted Rifles, was the principal talker, and after a long but pleasant discussion, I asked him what course he would pursue if his State should pass ordinances of secession and call him to its defence. He confessed that he would obey the call. It was a sad day when we took leave of lifetime comrades and gave up a service of twenty years. Neither Union officers nor their families made efforts to conceal feelings of deepest regret. When we drove out from the post, a number of officers rode with us, which only made the last farewell more trying."

In any regard, on June 17 1861, Major Longstreet resigned from the U. S. Army and on June 22 he met with Confederate President Jefferson Davis at the executive mansion, where he was informed that he had been appointed a brigadier general, a commission he accepted on June 25.

Lee and Longstreet, having been veterans of the United States longer, struggled with their personal choices, but Jackson and Stuart knew from the start which side they'd choose.

Even before Virginia's Succession Convention, held on February 13, 1861 after seven seceding states had formed the Confederacy on February 4, an incident occurred at Virginia Military Institute that threatened to lead to bloodshed. In their patriotic zeal, a group of cadets had fired on a United States flag in the village, ripped it down, and replaced it with a Virginia State flag. The town's volunteer militia responded by driving off the cadets and then re-hoisting the U. S. flag, per protocol. Someone then sounded the drums across the Institute campus, bringing most of the cadets running out of the barracks ready for a confrontation. Halted by their commanding officer, Colonel Smith, the boys were quickly corralled back into their barracks, at which time they all began to call out for Jackson. When he arrived, he spoke for the first time as a man who could inspire troops: "I admire the spirit you have in rushing to the defense of your comrades; and I commend the way in which you obeyed the commands of your superior officer. The time may come, young gentlemen, when your state will need your services, and if that time comes, draw your swords and throw away your scabbards!"

On April 22, 1861, First Lieutenant Stuart received a commission as captain in the U. S. Army, but this came 10 days after the assault on Fort Sumter, recognized as the beginning of the Civil War. After Abraham Lincoln's election in 1860, a handful of Southern states had already seceded, and Virginia would join them after Sumter. By the time Stuart received the promotion, he was already determined to fight with Virginia, and thus the Confederacy, in the civil conflict. A little over a week later, in early May, he tendered his resignation from the Federal army.

Moving his family to Virginia, on May 10, 1861, "Jeb" was commissioned a lieutenant colonel of the Virginia Infantry. Meanwhile, his father-in-law, Philip St. George Cooke, chose not to resign his Army commission, prompting Stuart to write his wife that it would "do irreparable injury to our only son" to have him named after Cooke. "Jeb" wrote to his brother-in-law (future Confederate Brig. General John Rogers Cooke) saying, "[Philip] will regret it but once, and that will be continuously." After consideration, "Jeb" and Flora renamed the boy, James Ewell Brown Stuart, Jr., an obvious indicator of his disgust with his father-in-law's political views.

Colonel Cooke

Once Jeb left for Richmond to join the fighting, Flora settled in at Wytheville, Virginia, arranging to sometimes stay at or near her husband's camp where they could share meals, music, and conversation. Even so, their frequent separations strained their relationship, and it didn't help that in addition to writing frequently to his wife, "Jeb" also carried on correspondences with other women attracted to his fame. Although the couple acknowledged these exchanges as "insubstantial flirtations," Flora detested the photographs and gifts the women sent, and wrote of feeling laughed at for her husband's fondness for society and the ladies. But by all other accounts, "Jeb" was a thoughtful and romantic husband who always carried his wife's photograph in a silver frame near his heart.

On November 3, 1862, while "Jeb" was with the Army of Northern Virginia during the early stages of what would become the Fredericksburg campaign, their daughter Flora died of typhoid fever. In the following weeks, Stuart wrote that his wife was "not herself since the loss of her little companion." The following October, their daughter Virginia Pelham was born--both easing the pain and intensifying the loss. Flora wrote, "She is said to be like Little Flora. I hope she is."

Chapter 10: Fort Sumter

Lincoln's predecessor was among those who could see the potential conflict coming from a mile away. As the Confederacy continued to grow during his last months in office, President James Buchanan instructed the federal army to permit the Confederacy to take control of forts in its territory, hoping to avoid a war. Conveniently, this also allowed Southern forces to take control of important forts and land ahead of a potential war, which would make secession and/or a victory in a military conflict easier. Many Southern partisans within the federal government at the end of 1860 took advantage of these opportunities to help Southern states ahead of time.

One of the forts in the South was Fort Sumter, an important but undermanned and undersupplied fort in the harbor of Charleston, South Carolina. Buchanan attempted to resupply Fort Sumter in the first few months of 1860, but the attempt failed when Southern sympathizers in the harbor fired on the resupply ship.

In his Inauguration Speech, President Lincoln struck a moderate tone. Unlike most Inauguration Addresses, which are typically followed by balls and a "honeymoon" period, Lincoln's came amid a major political crisis. To reassure the South, he reiterated his belief in the legal status of slavery in the South, but that its expansion into the Western territories was to be restricted. He outlined the illegality of secession and refused to acknowledge the South's secession, and promised to continue to deliver U.S. mail in the seceded states. Most importantly, he pledged to not use force unless his obligation to protect Federal property was restricted: "In doing this there needs to be no bloodshed or violence, and there shall be none unless it be forced upon the national authority. The power confided to me will be used to hold, occupy, and posess the property and places belonging to the Government and to collect the duties and imposts; but beyond what may be necessary for these objects, there will be no invasion, no using of force against or among the people anywhere."

Lincoln had promised that it would not be the North that started a potential war, but he was also aware of the possibility of the South initiating conflict. After he was sworn in, Lincoln sent word to the Governor of South Carolina that he was sending ships to resupply Fort Sumter, to which the governor replied demanding that federal forces evacuate it.

Although he vowed not to fire the first shot, Lincoln was likely aware that his attempt to resupply Fort Sumter in Charleston Harbor would draw Southern fire; it had already happened under Buchanan's watch. After his inauguration, President Lincoln informed South Carolina governor Francis Pickens that he was sending supplies to the undermanned garrison at Fort Sumter. When Lincoln made clear that he would attempt to resupply the fort, Davis ordered Beauregard to demand its surrender and prevent the resupplying of the garrison.

In early April, the ship Lincoln sent to resupply the fort was fired upon and turned around. On April 9, Confederate President Davis sent word to General Beauregard to demand the fort's evacuation. At the time, the federal garrison consisted of Major Robert Anderson, Beauregard's artillery instructor from West Point, and 76 troops. Even before the bombardment, upon learning that he was opposed by Beauregard, Anderson remarked that the Southern forces in Charleston harbor would be exercised with "skill and sound judgment". Beauregard also remembered his former superior, and before the bombardment, he sent brandy, whiskey and cigars to Anderson and his garrison, gifts the Major refused.

At 4:30 a.m. on the morning of April 12, 1861, Beauregard ordered the first shots to be fired at Fort Sumter, effectively igniting the Civil War. After nearly 34 hours and thousands of rounds fired from 47 artillery guns and mortars ringing the harbor, on April 14, 1861, Major Anderson surrendered Fort Sumter, marking the first Confederate victory. No casualties were suffered on either side during the dueling bombardments across Charleston harbor, but, ironically, two Union soldiers were killed by an accidental explosion during the surrender ceremonies.

Beauregard

After the attack on Fort Sumter, support for both the northern and southern cause rose. Two days later, Lincoln issued a *call-to-arms* asking for 75,000 volunteers. That led to the secession of Virginia, Tennessee, North Carolina, and Arkansas, with the loyalty of border states like Kentucky, Maryland, and Missouri still somewhat up in the air. The large number of southern sympathizers in these states buoyed the Confederates' hopes that those too would soon join the South. Moreover, the loss of these border states, especially Virginia, all deeply depressed Lincoln. Just weeks before, prominent Virginians had reassured Lincoln that the state's historic place in American history made its citizens eager to save the Union. But as soon as Lincoln made any assertive moves to save the Union, Virginia seceded. This greatly concerned Lincoln, who worried Virginia's secession made it more likely other border states and/or Maryland would secede as well.

Despite the loss of Fort Sumter, the North expected a relatively quick victory. Their expectations weren't unrealistic, due to the Union's overwhelming economic advantages over the South. At the start of the war, the Union had a population of over 22 million. The South had a population of 9 million, nearly 4 million of whom were slaves. Union states contained 90% of the manufacturing capacity of the country and 97% of the weapon manufacturing capacity. Union states also possessed over 70% of the total railroads in the pre-war United States at the start of the war, and the Union also controlled 80% of the shipbuilding capacity of the pre-war United States.

However, like William Tecumseh Sherman, Longstreet was among the few who thought the

Civil War would last a long time. "Speaking of the impending struggle, I was asked as to the length of the war, and said, 'At least three years, and if it holds for five you may begin to look for a dictator,' at which Lieutenant Ryan, of the Seventh Infantry, said, 'If we are to have a dictator, I hope that you may be the man.'"

Although the North blockaded the South throughout the Civil War and eventually controlled the entire Mississippi River by 1863, the war could not be won without land battles, which doomed hundreds of thousands of soldiers on each side. This is because the Civil War generals began the war employing tactics from the Napoleonic Era, which saw Napoleon dominate the European continent and win crushing victories against large armies. However, the weapons available in 1861 were far more accurate than they had been 50 years earlier. In particular, new rifled barrels created common infantry weapons with deadly accuracy of up to 100 yards, at a time when generals were still leading massed infantry charges with fixed bayonets and attempting to march their men close enough to engage in hand-to-hand combat.

Chapter 11: The First Battle of Bull Run or Manassas

Although Lee, Jackson, Stuart, and Longstreet were destined to become the 4 most famous soldiers of the Confederates' most famous army, they all took different paths to get there. Ironically, of the 4, it was Robert E. Lee who wasn't part of the first major battle of the war, the First Battle of Bull Run or Manassas.

On May 10, 1861, Stuart was commissioned a lieutenant colonel of the Virginia Infantry and ordered by Maj. General Robert E. Lee to report to Colonel Thomas J. Jackson at Harpers Ferry. Stuart's reputation had clearly made the rounds, because when he reported to the man who would months later become Stonewall Jackson, Jackson ignored Stuart's infantry designation and instead assigned him command of all the cavalry companies of the Army of the Shenandoah, organized as the First Virginia Cavalry Regiment. Thus, on July 4, 1861, Jeb Stuart began his service in the Confederate cavalry, less than 3 weeks before the First Battle of Bull Run.

Although Stuart would soon appear in his trademark flamboyant line attire--a scarlet-lined gray cape, yellow sash, hat cocked to the side displaying a peacock plume, jack boots, gauntlets, red flower in his lapel, and full red beard doused with cologne (reminiscent of commanders of the Napoleonic era)--when he accepted his Confederate commission, he was still wearing his Federal uniform and would do so even as he fought at Falling Waters, Virginia, on July 2, 1861. And while most Confederate officers were somehow distinguishable on the battlefield, Stuart--whose horse "Highfly" soon became as famous as his extraordinary rider--became one of the most visually stunning.

Quickly becoming one of the most dominant commanders in the field, on July 16, Stuart was promoted to Full Colonel of the First Virginia Cavalry.

Though Jackson fundamentally opposed secession from the Union, upon the outbreak of the Civil War, he went with his native state of Virginia when it seceded, offering his services to the Confederacy. Bringing the cadets he'd trained to Richmond, he was promoted to colonel and in a short time gained attention and further promotion.

His first assignment was the small command at Harpers Ferry, Virginia (current-day West Virginia), at the confluence of the Shenandoah and Potomac Rivers. Already familiar with the area as a result of John Brown, Harpers Ferry was in an ideally placed location, touching the tips of multiple states. Jackson was first tasked with holding the line, until General Joseph E. Johnson assumed command of the Confederate forces in the Shenandoah Valley, at which point Jackson was given command of a brigade. Jackson and his men then withdrew to a more defensible position at Winchester in the Valley.

Ordered to report to Brig. General P.G.T. Beauregard at Manassas, Brig. General Longstreet was given command of a brigade of three regiments—the First, Eleventh, and Seventeenth Virginia Infantry. Immediately assembling his staff, Longstreet trained his brigade incessantly and within just a few weeks had trained his "green" recruits in close-order drill and battlefield maneuvers. Though considered a dogged combat trainer and able defensive commander, ultimately, his field tactics would make him the object of great controversy before the War's end.

After Fort Sumter, the Lincoln Administration pushed for a quick invasion of Virginia, with the intent of defeating Confederate forces and marching toward the Confederate capitol of Richmond. Lincoln pressed Irvin McDowell to push forward. Despite the fact that McDowell knew his troops were inexperienced and unready, pressure from the Washington politicians forced him to launch a premature offensive against Confederate forces in Northern Virginia. His strategy during the First Battle of Bull Run was grand, but it proved far too difficult for his inexperienced troops to carry out effectively.

McDowell

In late Spring 1861, Davis ordered Beauregard to northern Virginia as second-in-command to General Joseph E. Johnston, where he was to oppose the federal forces building up under McDowell. Though Johnston was the superior in rank, he ceded authority to Beauregard near Manassas Junction, leaving Beauregard in command there. At Manassas, Beauregard took charge of the Confederate forces assembling near the rail junction at Manassas and had his men construct defenses along a 14 mile front along Bull Run Creek. Meanwhile, Johnston was gathering and training additional troops in the Shenandoah Valley.

Joseph E. Johnston

McDowell's strategy during the First Battle of Bull Run was grand, and in many ways it was the forerunner of a tactic Lee and Jackson executed brilliantly on nearly the same field during the Second Battle of Bull Run or Manassas in August 1862. McDowell's plan called for parts of his army to pin down Beauregard's Confederate soldiers in front while marching another wing of his army around the flank and into the enemy's rear, rolling up the line. McDowell assumed the Confederates would be forced to abandon Manassas Junction and fall back to the next defensible line, the Rappahannock River. In July 1861, however, this proved far too difficult for his inexperienced troops to carry out effectively.

On July 18, Union General Irwin McDowell set out with two divisions on a twelve-mile circuitous march west from Centreville, Virginia to cross Bull Run at Sudley Springs Ford, intending to strike Beauregard's troops at Manassas-Sudley Road in an effort to turn the Southern left flank. Meanwhile, another division was set to drive directly west along the turnpike and across Stone Bridge, while back at Centreville, another division stayed in reserve. The remaining division, scattered along the lines of communication all the way back to Washington but would ultimately take no part in the ensuing battle, made a total of 32,000 men at McDowell's disposal.

Longstreet's new recruits achieved one of the first Confederate victories, seeing action at Blackburn's Ford on July 18 and successfully stopping the lead Union division in its march towards Manassas. And unbeknownst to McDowell, several days earlier, General Beauregard had received advance warning of troop movement from a civilian and had forwarded a coded message to Jefferson Davis along with a request to move General Joseph E. Johnston and his 12,000 men from the Shenandoah Valley to Manassas, via rail. Beauregard's intelligence placed the Union Army within attack position by July 17.

The First Battle of Bull Run made history in several ways. McDowell's army met Fort Sumter hero P.G.T. Beauregard's Confederate army near the railroad junction at Manassas on July 21, 1861. Located just 25 miles away from Washington D.C., many civilians from Washington came to watch what they expected to be a rout of Confederate forces. And for awhile, it appeared as though that might be the case.

McDowell's strategy fell apart though, thanks to railroads. Confederate reinforcements under General Joseph E. Johnston's Army, including JEB Stuart's cavalrymen and a brigade led by Thomas Jonathan Jackson, arrived by train in the middle of the day, a first in the history of American warfare. With Johnston's army arriving midday on July 21, it evened up the numbers between Union and Confederate. Shoring up the Confederates' left flank, some of Johnston's troops, led by Jackson's brigade, helped reverse the Union's momentum and ultimately turn the tide. As the battle's momentum switched, the inexperienced Union troops were routed and retreated in disorder back toward Washington in an unorganized mass. With over 350 killed on each side, it was the deadliest battle in American history to date, and both the Confederacy and the Union were quickly served notice that the war would be much more costly than either side had believed.

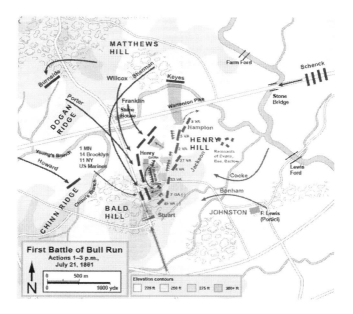

First Battle of Bull Run
Actions 1–3 p.m.,
July 21, 1861

N

0   500 m
0   1000 yds

Elevation contours
225 ft   250 ft   275 ft   300+ ft

Ironically, McDowell commanded the Army of Northeastern Virginia and Joseph E. Johnston commanded the Army of the Potomac at First Bull Run. A little over a year later it would be Lee's Army of Northern Virginia fighting elements of the Union Army of the Potomac at Second Bull Run, on nearly the same ground.

It was also during First Manassas or Bull Run that Jackson earned the famous nickname "Stonewall", but there is an enduring mystery over the origin of his nickname. What is known is that during the battle, Jackson's brigade arrived as reinforcements at a crucial part of the battlefield on the Confederate left. Confederate Brigadier General Barnard Bee, commanding a nearby brigade, commanded his men to reestablish their battle line next to Jackson's brigade, shouting, "There is Jackson standing like a stone wall. Rally behind the Virginians." General Bee was mortally wounded shortly after that command and died the following day. Thus, it remains unclear whether Bee was complimenting Jackson's brigade for standing firm or whether he was criticizing Jackson's brigade for inaction. Without Bee around to explain his command, nobody will ever know for certain. However, that has not stopped people from debating Bee's comment. Regardless, the nickname Stonewall stuck, and Jackson was henceforth known as Stonewall Jackson. His brigade also inherited the title, known throughout the war as the Stonewall brigade.

Longstreet's brigade played almost no role in the fighting on July 21, other than having to sustain artillery fire for several hours. But when the Union army was routed and began fleeing in a disorganized panic, Longstreet was incensed that his commanders did not attempt to pursue the disorganized federal troops running back toward Washington. Longstreet's staff officer, Moxley Sorrel, later wrote that Longstreet "dashed his hat furiously to the ground, stamped, and bitter words escaped him."

Jackson eventually emerged as the man who gained the most fame during the battle, but others at the time thought the man of the hour was Jeb Stuart. When Jackson's brigade turned the tide, Stuart then executed a highly-aggressive charge during which, "[the] Confederate cavalry-men were armed with costly English shot guns, which they held at the breast and fired (both barrels at once) as they approached . . . ." In a panic, many of McDowell's men ran frantically toward Washington, with Stuart's cavalry among the units pursuing them some 12 miles, and subsequently taking the Union headquarters on Munson's hill (within sight of Washington). Of this remarkable Confederate victory, General Jubal Early, who served under Stonewall Jackson, wrote: "Stuart did as much toward saving the Battle of First Manassas as any subordinate who participated in it."

From this point on, Stuart's celebrity grew, and he became known as Stuart "the brash," Stuart "the fearless," Stuart the *beau sabreur* of mounted infantry."

Chapter 12: Earning Promotions

Today Lee is remembered as the Civil War's greatest general, and George B. McClellan is often derided as one of the Union's most ineffective generals. And most associate Lee with the Army of Northern Virginia, which he came to command in the summer of 1862 and defeat McClellan in the Seven Days Battles. However, in 1861, it was McClellan that got the best of Lee.

Though Lee took no direct part in the first battle at Manassas (Bull Run) in July of 1861, he was tasked with saving western Virginia from Union forces under General George B. McClellan who'd defeated Confederate troops in Kanawha Valley. Bad weather, poorly trained men, and lack of cooperation among his officers, however, ultimately led to a dismal defeat for Lee. With the Union taking control of western Virginia, Lee considered the campaign a miserable, personal failure, and western Virginia would formally become the new state of West Virginia and part of the Union in 1863.

Given such a crushing defeat at the beginning of the war, that might have been the end of Lee's Civil War career. However, Jefferson Davis's faith in Lee's abilities ensured it was just the beginning. It's quite possible that Lee was saved by his past association with Davis at West

Point. History has accorded Abraham Lincoln a spot in the pantheon of American politics for the manner in which he steered the Union to victory and into the Reconstruction period after the war. In turn, Davis has been heavily criticized. While Jefferson Davis had personal favorites like Lee and Albert Sidney Johnston, Davis constantly clashed with other Confederate generals like Joseph Johnston, which led to often discombobulated war strategy. At the same time, part of the Confederacy's raison d'etre was that the federal government was too centralized, so the decentralized nature of the Southern states hampered Davis's ability to manage and coordinate the war effort.

Though only a few months into the war, by August 1861, things were already going badly for the South. Although eyes remained intently focused on the Eastern theater, with the two capitals (Washington D.C. and Richmond) located within 100 miles of each other, several forts to the west had fallen to General Ulysses S. Grant, most of Kentucky and a large portion of Tennessee were all but abandoned, and Confederate general Joseph E. Johnson was planning a draw back from Manassas after the battle there. Equally disheartening, European recognition didn't come as expected, and supplies were already running dangerously low.

At this point, Jefferson Davis put Lee in command of the southeastern coast of the Confederacy, an area under imminent threat from a Union unit out of Hampton Roads near Norfolk. Mustering what was becoming Lee's trademark determination, he took decisive action by enlisting more troops, establishing blockades at all access points, and establishing an inner line of defense beyond the reach of Union naval guns. Lee quickly and decisively brought an abrupt halt to the advance of Union forces.

On October 7, 1861, Longstreet was promoted to major general and assumed command of a division in the newly reorganized Confederate Army of Northern Virginia. He was now in command of 4 infantry brigades and Hampton's Legion.

Though he had attained personal success thus far, he suffered personal tragedy in January 1862 due to a scarlet fever epidemic in Richmond that killed his one-year-old daughter Mary Anne, his four-year-old son James, and six-year-old son Augustus ("Gus"), all in the span of a week. Understandably depressed, Longstreet became personally withdrawn and melancholy, turning to religion. Those close to him and who served under him noted the change in camp around him after January 1862. What had once been a boisterous headquarters that tolerated partying and poker games had become a solemn, somber and more devout one.

After commanding the Confederate Army's outposts along the upper Potomac River at Fairfax Court House and Munson's Hill, Stuart was given command of the cavalry of the ironically named Army of the Potomac, which eventually became the Army of Northern Virginia. On September 24, 1861, Stuart was promoted to Brigadier General. Among those advocating his promotion was General Joseph E. Johnston, who in August wrote to Confederate President

Jefferson Davis saying: "[Stuart] is a rare man, wonderfully endowed by nature with the qualities necessary for an officer of light cavalry. Calm, firm, acute, active, and enterprising, I know no one more competent than he to estimate the occurrences before him at their true value. If you add to this army a real brigade of cavalry, you can find no better brigadier-general to command it."

Chapter 13: Jackson's Valley Campaign of 1862

After the defeat at the First Battle of Bull Run, at Manassas, it became clear that the Civil War would be a prolonged conflict. In fact, the same battle lines remained for the next several months, with Confederate forces stationed near Manassas Junction while the Union licked its wounds and reorganized a large army, eventually the Army of the Potomac, in heavily fortified Washington D.C.

Jackson had been a virtual unknown upon his arrival at the front line of First Bull Run, but by the spring of 1862, "Stonewall" was already becoming known across the battlefields. It would be the Valley Campaign of 1862 that made him a legend.

In the early months of 1862, Jackson was given command of an army numbering about 17,000 in the Shenandoah Valley. His task was daunting. The loss at Bull Run prompted a changing of the guard, with George B. McClellan, the "Young Napoleon", put in charge of reorganizing and leading the Army of the Potomac. That spring, the Army of the Potomac conducted an ambitious amphibious invasion of Virginia's peninsula, circumventing the Confederate defenses to the north of Richmond by attacking Richmond from the southeast.

General Johnston's outnumbered army headed toward Richmond to confront McClellan, but the Union still had three armies totaling another 50,000 around the Shenandoah Valley, which represented a threat to Richmond from the north. It was these armies that Jackson would be tasked with stopping.

Jackson would go on to lead his undermanned army through what military strategists and historians consider the most incredible campaign of the Civil War. From late March to early June, Jackson kept all 3 Union armies bottled up and separated from each other in the Shenandoah Valley by marching up and down the Valley about 650 miles in 50 days, earning his army the nickname "foot cavalry."

Beginning in March, Jackson used his intimate knowledge of the Valley to begin moving his forces to meet individual Union armies separately, which kept the odds even in terms of manpower. First he engaged a Union division at the First Battle of Kernstown on March 23, mistakenly thinking it was smaller and vulnerable than it was. His men, outnumbered two to one, were repulsed, but he had spooked the Union, and instead of reinforcing McClellan on the Peninsula, the Union troops were left in the Valley to protect Washington D.C. from Jackson.

Although Jackson is revered today as an almost ideal commander, a lot of his subordinates bristled under his leadership, believing not only that he asked too much but that he was too strict. One of the first to feel Jackson's wrath was General Richard B. Garnett, who led the Stonewall Brigade at First Kernstown. When Garnett retreated from a bad position without orders during the battle, while running low on ammunition, Jackson had him arrested, and he was later court martialed. Jackson had essentially questioned Garnett's manhood, humiliating him. For the rest of the war, Garnett would try to prove his courage. Although he could not walk after being kicked by a horse in the days before the Battle of Gettysburg, Garnett famously insisted on riding a horse at the head of his brigade during Pickett's Charge, which made him a very conspicuous target. Garnett was killed during the Charge.

Garnett

After the defeat at First Kernstown, the only tactical defeat Jackson suffered during the war, he marched his army south (which, idiosyncratically, was referred to as marching "up" the Valley) over the next 30 days until engaging 6,000 Union soldiers at the Battle of McDowell on May 8. Over the next two weeks, to keep Union forces under Generals Banks and McDowell from linking up, Jackson marched north through the Valley, engaging McDowell at Front Royal on May 23 and then Banks at Winchester on May 25.

Once Jackson kept the two from linking, the Union armies tried to pin Jackson down in the Valley, but once again his men evaded them by quickly marching south "up" the entire Valley. Near the southern end of the Valley, Jackson's forces successfully engaged General John Fremont at Cross Keys on June 8 and then attacked General Erastus Tyler's men at Port Republic the next day.

Jackson's diversionary tactics had been remarkably successful in preventing reinforcements from being sent to the Army of the Potomac.

Chapter 14: The Peninsula Campaign

Called to Richmond in March 1862, Lee became part of Jefferson Davis's inner circle. At this time, his primary job was to mediate between feuding generals. While some Southern generals, including Lee, believed troops should be shifted as needed to meet new threats, General Johnston insisted that all troops should be concentrated around Richmond as preparation for a final showdown.

Despite Union successes in the Western theater, the focus of the Lincoln Administration remained concentrated on Richmond. The loss at Bull Run prompted a changing of the guard, with George McClellan, the "Young Napoleon", put in charge of reorganizing and leading the Army of the Potomac. McClellan had finished second in his class at West Point and was a well-regarded engineer, not to mention a foreign observer at the siege of Sevastopol during the Crimean War. This experience made him fit for commanding an army, but it also colored his military ideology in a way that was at odds with a Lincoln Administration that was eager for aggressive action and movement toward Richmond.

Under McClellan, and at Lincoln's urging, the Army of the Potomac conducted an ambitious amphibious invasion of Virginia in the spring of 1862. McClellan hoped to circumvent Confederate defenses to the north of Richmond by attacking Richmond from the southeast, landing his giant army on the Virginian peninsula. McClellan originally surprised the Confederates with his movement, but the narrow peninsula made it easier for Confederate forces to defend. One heavily outnumbered force led by John Magruder famously held out under siege at Yorktown for nearly an entire month, slowing the Army of the Potomac down. Magruder used a tactic of marching his men up and down the siege lines repeatedly to give the appearance he had several times more men than he actually had.

General Magruder

Commanding Confederate forces opposing McClellan was General Joseph E. Johnston. During the Civil War, one of the tales that was often told among Confederate soldiers was that Joseph E.

Johnston was a crack shot who was a better bird hunter than just about everyone else in the South. However, as the story went, Johnston would never take the shot when asked to, complaining that something was wrong with the situation that prevented him from being able to shoot the bird when it was time. The story is almost certainly apocryphal, used to demonstrate the Confederates' frustration with a man who everyone regarded as a capable general. Johnston began the Civil War as one of the senior commanders, leading (ironically) the Army of the Potomac to victory in the Battle of First Bull Run over Irvin McDowell's Union Army. But Johnston would become known more for losing by not winning. Johnston was never badly beaten in battle, but he had a habit of "strategically withdrawing" until he had nowhere else to go.

Johnston gradually pulled his troops back to a line of defense nearer Richmond as McClellan advanced. Several weeks later, after word of General Stonewall Jackson's startling victories in the Shenandoah Valley were received, Johnston learned that McClellan was moving along the Chickahominy River. McClellan's Army of the Potomac got close enough to Richmond that they could see the city's church steeples.

It was at this point that Johnston got uncharacteristically aggressive. Johnston had run out of breathing space for his army, and he believed McCellan was seeking to link up with McDowell's forces. Therefore he drew up a very complex plan of attack for different wings of his army, and struck at the Army of the Potomac at the Battle of Seven Pines on May 31, 1862. Like McDowell's plan for First Bull Run, the plan proved too complicated for Johnston's army to execute, and after a day of bloody fighting little was accomplished from a technical standpoint. However, McClellan was rattled by the attack, and Johnston was seriously wounded during the fighting, resulting in military advisor Robert E. Lee being sent to assume command of the Army of Northern Virginia. Longstreet had done well as a rear guard commander at Yorktown and Williamsburg, successfully delaying the advance of Union Maj. General George B. McClellan's army toward Richmond, but during the Battle of Seven Pines, he marched his men in the wrong direction down the wrong road, causing congestion and confusion among other Confederate units and ultimately weakening the effectiveness of the massive Confederate counterattack launched against McClellan. In his official report, Longstreet blamed fellow Maj. General Benjamin Huger for the logistical confusion, an indication of the contention that would follow his personal and military life from that time on.

From his first day in command, Lee faced a daunting, seemingly impossible challenge. McClellan had maneuvered nearly 100,000 troops to within seven miles of Richmond, three Union units were closing in on General Jackson's Confederates in Virginia's Shenandoah Valley, and a fourth Union army was camped on the Rappahannock River ostensibly ready to come to McClellan's aid. On June 12, as McClellan sat on Richmond's eastern outskirts waiting for reinforcements, Lee began to ring the city with troop entrenchments. Realizing that McClellan's flank appeared to be exposed, Lee tasked Stuart with assessing whether the Union army had any real protection north and west of the exposed flank. Stuart suggested that his men circumnavigate McClellan's army, to which Lee responded with deference that would become his trademark and a symbol of his trust in his subordinates. Lee gave Stuart unspecifically vague orders:

> "You will return as soon as the object of your expedition is accomplished, and you must bear constantly in mind, while endeavoring to execute the general purpose of your mission, not to hazard unnecessarily your command or to attempt what your judgment may not approve; but be content to accomplish all the good you can without feeling it necessary to obtain all that might be desired. I recommend that you take only such men as can stand the expedition, and that you take every means in your power to save and cherish those you take. You must leave sufficient cavalry here for the service of this army, and remember that one of the chief objects of your expedition is to gain intelligence for the guidance of future operations."

With that, Stuart embarked with 1200 troopers on a spectacular three-day, 150 mile ride in the rear of and around the entire Army of the Potomac, a mission that would require him to keep just ahead of pursuing horsemen led by Union Brig. General Philip St. George Cooke, Stuart's father-in-law. Though daunting and dangerous, Stuart and his men successfully completed the historic ride, with Stuart returning to Richmond to report to Lee on June 14 and most of his cavalry returning the following day. Stuart was able not only to report that McClellan's flank was indeed completely unguarded, he delivered 165 captured Union soldiers, 260 horses and mules, and a collection of quartermaster and ordinance supplies as well. The "ride around McClellan" proved to be a public relations sensation for Stuart, resulting in dramatic newspaper accounts, hordes of women cheering and strewing flower petals in his path when he rode through the streets of Richmond, and his face appearing on the front pages of most newspapers in both the North and South. The flamboyant officer relished every second of his ride, later writing, "There was something of the sublime in the implicit confidence and unquestioning trust of the rank and file in a leader guiding them straight, apparently, into the very jaws of the enemy, every step appearing to them to diminish the faintest hope of extrication."

Stuart also knew how to cultivate his newfound glory. When Stuart reported to General Lee, he also gave a verbal report to Virginia's governor, who rewarded him with a sword. During one visit to the governor, Stuart gave an impromptu address on the steps of the executive mansion to an assembling crowd, playfully telling them he "had been to the Chickahominy to visit some of his old friends of the United States Army, but they, very uncivilly, turned their backs upon him." The man who wrote the account of that speech also noted Stuart very conspicuously galloped off as the crowd cheered.

Although it was this kind of bombast that would come to color Stuart's legacy and in some ways eclipse his solid work, his men realized just how capable he was. In his 1887 memoirs, Colonel John Singleton Mosby (assigned as a first lieutenant to Stuart's cavalry scouts) wrote: "In his work on the outposts Stuart soon showed that he possessed the qualities of a great leader of cavalry. He never had an equal in such service. He discarded the old maxims and soon discovered that in the conditions of modern war the chief functions of cavalry are to learn the designs and to watch and report the movements of the enemy." And for his own part, Stuart always reported which of his subordinates had distinguished themselves in post-battle reports.

In a series of confrontations known as the Seven Days' Battle, Lee instructed Jackson to move as if to advance back through the Shenandoah Valley but then secretly bring his entire force by train back to the Richmond sector as reinforcements. Jackson had successfully tied up the Union armies in the Valley before returning to Richmond. Lee immediately took the offensive, attacking the Army of the Potomac repeatedly in a flurry of battles known as the Seven Days Battles. Fearing he was heavily outnumbered, McClellan began a strategic retreat, and despite badly defeating the Confederates at the Battle of Malvern Hill, the last battle of the Seven Days Battles and the Peninsula Campaign, it was clear that the Army of the Potomac was quitting the campaign. The failure of McClellan's campaign devastated the morale of the North, as McClellan had failed to advance despite originally having almost double the manpower.

In a characteristically audacious manner that came to define his generalship, Lee's bold offensive tactics had seen his army engage in bloody hand-to-hand combat that ranged from Mechanicsville to Fraser's Farm to Malvern Hill. By themselves, none of the battles could be called pivotal or even tactical victories for the Confederates, and Malvern Hill was a debacle, but from a strategic standpoint Lee succeeded in forcing McClellan and his back-up forces to retreat, while Jackson's tactics proved effective in the Shenandoah. Lee had prevented McClellan from capturing Richmond.

During the Seven Days Battles, Longstreet was more effective. In command of an entire wing of Lee's army, Longstreet aggressively attacked at Gaines' Mill and Glendale. Historians have credited Longstreet for those battles and criticized Stonewall Jackson for being unusually lethargic during the Seven Days Battles, ultimately contributing to Lee's inability to do more damage or capture McClellan's Army of the Potomac. Jackson's performance was not lost on Longstreet, who pointed out that he performed poorly at the Seven Days Battles to defend charges that he was slow at Gettysburg. By the end of the campaign, Longstreet was one of the most popular and praised men in the army. Like Longstreet's father, Sorrel considered him a "rock in steadiness when sometimes in battle the world seemed flying to pieces." General Lee himself called Old Pete "the staff in my right hand." Though it is often forgotten, Longstreet was now Lee's principle subordinate, not Stonewall Jackson.

The Seven Days Battles were a strategic success for Lee, but they are often pointed to as Jackson's worst week of the war. Although Jackson's men were successful during their fighting,

Stonewall was uncharacteristically unaggressive and seemingly fatigued. At the Battle of Mechanicsville, Jackson halted his men within earshot of the fighting, and he was late to bring his men up in the battles that followed. It is generally assumed that he was exhausted by the Valley Campaign and the quick movements to a new front, although General James Longstreet, while defending accusations after the war that he was slow at Gettysburg, would later point out Jackson's slowness during the Seven Days and argue that "General Jackson never showed his genius when under the immediate command of General Lee."

At Richmond, Lee reorganized the Army of Northern Virginia into the structure with which it is most remembered. Jackson now took command of a force consisting of his own division (now commanded by Brig. General Charles S. Winder) and those of Maj. General Richard S. Ewell, Brig. General William H. C. Whiting, and Maj. General D. H. Hill. The other wing of Lee's army was commanded by James Longstreet. On July 25, 1862, after the conclusion of the Seven Days Battles had brought the Peninsula Campaign to an end, Stuart was promoted to Major General, his command upgraded to Cavalry Division.

Longstreet in 1862

Chapter 15: The Second Battle of Bull Run or Manassas

Even before McClellan had completely withdrawn his troops, Lee sent Jackson northward to intercept the new army Abraham Lincoln had placed under Maj. General John Pope, formed out of the scattered troops in the Virginia area. Pope had found success in the Western theater, and he was uncommonly brash, instructing the previously defeated men now under his command that his soldiers in the West were accustomed to seeing the backs of the enemy. Pope's arrogance turned off his own men, and it also caught the notice of Lee.

On June 26, General Pope deployed his forces in an arc across Northern Virginia; its right flank under Maj. General Franz Sigel positioned at Sperryville on the Blue Ridge Mountains, its center columns under Maj. General Nathaniel P. Banks at Little Washington, and its left flank under Maj. General Irvin McDowell at Falmouth on the Rappahannock River. On July 13, Lee responded by sending Jackson with 14,000 men to Gordonsville, with Maj. General A. P. Hill's division of 10,000 men set to join him by July 27. This would set off one of the most significant battles of Jackson's military career.

On August 6, Pope marched his forces south into Culpeper County intending to capture the rail junction at Gordonsville in an attempt to draw Confederate attention away from General McClellan's withdrawal from the Virginia Peninsula. In response, Jackson went on the offensive, attacking Banks' center division, which proved precisely the right move. Jackson's larger intention was to then move on to Culpeper Court House, 26 miles north of Gordonsville-- the focal point of the Union arc--and then take on each of the Union armies separately. It was an ambitious plan to say the least.

Setting out on August 7, Jackson's march was immediately hampered by a severe heat wave, worsened by his now characteristic secrecy about his strategy. His field officers were so confused as to the exact route they were to follow that his column only progressed 8 miles over the next twenty-four hours. This slow progress allowed the Union cavalry to alert Pope of Confederate movement, and he countered by sending General Sigel to meet up with General Banks at Culpeper Court House and maintain a defensive line on a ridge above Cedar Run, seven miles to the south.

On the morning of August 9, Jackson's army crossed the Rapidan River into Culpeper County, led by Maj. General Richard S. Ewell's division, followed by Brig. General Charles S. Winder's division, with Maj. General A. P. Hill's troops picking up the rear. Just before noon, Brig. General Jubal Early's brigade, the front line of Ewell's division, came upon Union cavalry and artillery occupying the ridge above Cedar Run. Winder's division quickly formed to Early's left (on the west side of the Turnpike), with Brig. General William Taliaferro's brigade positioned closest to Early, and Col. Thomas S. Garnett's units forming on the far Confederate left. Then, Winder's artillery filled the gap on the road between the two divisions, the "Stonewall" Brigade, led by Col. Charles R. Ronald were brought up as support behind the cannons, while A. P Hill's division stood in reserve on the Confederate left. Meanwhile, the Union formed a line joining the armies of Brig. Generals Crawford, Auger, Geary, and Prince, while Brig. General George S. Greene's brigade was kept in reserve in the rear.

A little before 5:00 p.m., Confederate General Winder was mortally wounded while standing in the open attempting to direct his troops. As a result, command of his division fell to General Taliaferro, who was completely ignorant of Jackson's battle plan. Meanwhile, the "Stonewall Brigade," which was supposed to come up to support Garnett's brigade should they become separated from the main Confederate line, remained a half mile behind instead. Then before leadership could be reestablished, Union forces attacked again. When Jackson's brigade finally advanced, they were quickly dispended of by Crawford's troops--with Jackson ordering the batteries withdrawn before they could be captured. At this point, Taliaferro and Early's left were hit hard by the Union advance and were nearly broken.

As the story is told, determined to inspire his men to take the offensive, Jackson suddenly rode into the battlefield and attempted to brandish his sword, but the man who had once warned his VMI cadets to be ready to throw the scabbards of their swords away found that due to the infrequency with which he had drawn it, it had rusted in its scabbard. Undaunted, he unbuckled the sword from his belt--scabbard and all--and waved it over his head. Then he grabbed a battle flag from a retreating standard bearer and called for his men to rally around him. Heartened by their commander's zeal, the Stonewall Brigade set fiercely into the Union troops, quickly driving them back. And although Union forces were subsequently able to regroup and attack, the Stonewall Brigade had given the Confederate front line time to reform and A. P Hill's troops time to come up and fill in the gaps.

Almost immediately, the Union forces collapsed and went in full retreat. Confederate infantry and General William E. Jones' 7th Virginia Cavalry chased in hot pursuit, nearly capturing Banks and Pope at their headquarters a mile behind the Union line). But with darkness setting in, Jackson decided to give up the pursuit because he was unsure of where the rest of Pope's army was positioned. For the next two days, Jackson maintained his position south of Cedar Run, waiting for a Union attack that never came. Finally, after receiving news that Pope's entire army had arrived at Culpeper Court House, on August 12, Jackson fell back to a more defensive position behind the Rapidan River.

Though steeped in difficulties and a series of errors, the Battle at Cedar Mountain was deemed an unqualified victory for the Confederacy and for Stonewall Jackson himself. He'd wreaked such havoc against the Northern forces (Union casualties numbered at over 2300) that Union General-in-Chief Henry W. Halleck called off Pope's planned advance on Gordonsville, thereby giving Lee the initiative in the Northern Virginia Campaign and effectively shifting the fighting in Virginia from the Virginia Peninsula into northern Virginia--essentially a Union retreat.

Once certain McClellan was in full retreat, Lee joined Jackson, planning to strike Pope before McClellan's troops could arrive as reinforcements. In August 1862, Stuart completed yet another ride around the Union army, though this one was not as historic or memorable. On August 21, while conducting a series of highly-effective raids against Union forces, Stuart was nearly captured (and did lose his signature peacock plumed hat and cloak), but the following day managed to overrun Union commander Maj. General John Pope's headquarters during a raid on Catlett's Station, Virginia, not only capturing Pope's full uniform, but several staff officers and secret orders that provided Lee invaluable intelligence concerning troop reinforcements for Pope's army.

In late August 1862, in a "daring and unorthodox" move, Lee divided his forces and sent Jackson northward to flank them, ultimately bringing Jackson directly behind Pope's army and supply base. This forced Pope to fall back to Manassas to protect his flank and maintain his lines of communication. Recognizing Lee's genius for military strategy, General Jackson quickly became Lee's most trusted commander, and he would later say that he so trusted Lee's military instincts that he would even follow him into battle blindfolded.

When Pope's army fell back to Manassas to confront Jackson, his wing of Lee's army dug in along a railroad trench and took a defensive stance. The Second Battle of Manassas or Bull Run was fought August 28-30, beginning with the Union army throwing itself at Jackson the first two days. But the concentration on Stonewall's men opened up the Union army's left flank for Longstreet's wing, which marched 30 miles in 24 hours to reach the battlefield by the late afternoon of August 29. When Longstreet's men finally arrived around noon on August 29, Lee informed Longstreet of his plan to attack the Union flank--which was at that time concentrating its efforts on General Jackson. Longstreet initially rejected Lee's suggestion to attack, recommending instead that a reconnaissance be conducted to survey the field. And although Longstreet's artillery was ultimately a major factor in helping Jackson resist the Union attack on August 29, his performance that day was described by some Lost Cause advocates as slow, and they considered his disobedience of General Lee insubordination. Lee's most famous biographer, Douglas Southall Freeman, later wrote: "The seeds of much of the disaster on July 2, 1863, at the Battle of Gettysburg were sown in that instant—when Lee yielded to Longstreet and Longstreet discovered that he would."

Nevertheless, the Second Battle of Bull Run or Manassas is considered one of Longstreet's most successful. While Jackson's men defended themselves the first two days, Lee used Longstreet's wing on August 30 to deliver a devastating flank attack before reinforcements from the retreating Army of the Potomac could reach the field. With over 25,000 men, Longstreet's attack lasted several hours, while he and Lee were in the thick of things directing brigades and artillery batteries while coming under fire themselves. Eventually, Longstreet's attack swept Pope's army off the field. Fought on the same ground as the First Battle of Manassas nearly a year earlier, the result was the same: a decisive Confederate victory that sent Union soldiers scrambling back to the safety of Washington. Longstreet called Lee's campaign "clever and brilliant", and it helped reinforce the belief that using offensive marching and defensive battle tactics (like having Jackson's wing flank Pope's army and forcing Pope to attack it) was the key to success.

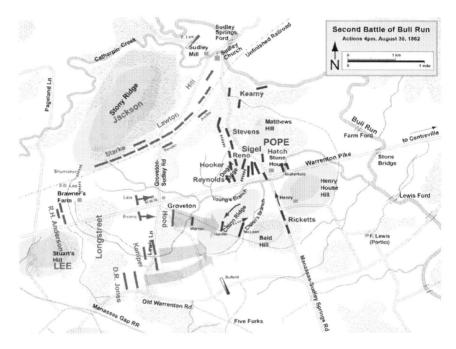

After the battle, General Lafayette McLaws (who had joined Longstreet's First Corps as First Division Commander and subsequently stayed with Longstreet for most of the War) assessed Longstreet unapologetically, saying, "James Longstreet is a humbug--a man of small capacity who is very obstinate, not at all chivalrous, exceedingly conceited, and entirely selfish!" Thus it seems that Longstreet's propensity for friction was apparent long before that fateful day at Gettysburg.

Chapter 16: The Maryland Campaign

After two days' fighting, Lee had achieved another major victory, and he now stood unopposed 12 miles away from Washington D.C. While Johnston and Beauregard had stayed in this position in the months after the first battle, Lee determined upon a more aggressive course: taking the fighting to the North.

In early September, convinced that the best way to defend Richmond was to divert attention to Washington, Lee had decided to invade Maryland after obtaining Jefferson Davis's permission. Today the decision is remembered through the prism of Lee hoping to win a major battle in the North that would bring about European recognition of the Confederacy, potential intervention, and possible capitulation by the North, whose anti-war Democrats were picking up political momentum. However, Lee also hoped that the fighting in Maryland would relieve Virginia's resources, especially the Shenandoah Valley, which served as the state's "breadbasket". And though largely forgotten today, Lee's move was controversial among his own men. Confederate soldiers, including Lee, took up arms to defend their homes, but now they were being asked to invade a Northern state. An untold number of Confederate soldiers refused to cross the Potomac River into Maryland.

Despite that, Longstreet also held the same view as Lee, believing an invasion of Maryland had plenty of advantages. He wrote in his memoirs, "The Army of Northern Virginia was afield without a foe. Its once grand adversary, discomfited under two commanders, had crept into cover of the bulwarks about the national capital. The commercial, social, and blood ties of Maryland inclined her people to the Southern cause. A little way north of the Potomac were inviting fields of food and supplies more plentiful than on the southern side; and the fields for march and manoeuvre, strategy and tactics, were even more inviting than the broad fields of grain and comfortable pasture-lands. Propitious also was the prospect of swelling our ranks by Maryland recruits."

In the summer of 1862, the Union suffered more than 20,000 casualties, and Northern Democrats, who had been split into pro-war and anti-war factions from the beginning, increasingly began to question the war. As of September 1862, no progress had been made on Richmond; in fact, a Confederate army was now in Maryland. And with the election of 1862 was approaching, Lincoln feared the Republicans might suffer losses in the congressional midterms that would harm the war effort. Thus, he restored General McClellan and removed General Pope after the second disaster at Bull Run. McClellan was still immensely popular among the Army of the Potomac, and with a mixture of men from his Army of the Potomac and Pope's Army of Virginia, he began a cautious pursuit of Lee into Maryland.

McClellan

Historians believe that Lee's entire Army of Northern Virginia had perhaps 50,000 men at most and possibly closer to 30,000 during the Maryland campaign. However, Lee sized up George McClellan, figured he was a cautious general, and decided once again to divide his forces throughout Maryland. In early September, he ordered Jackson to capture Harpers Ferry while he and Longstreet maneuvered his troops toward Frederick. With McClellan now assuming command of the Northern forces, Lee expected to have plenty of time to assemble his troops and bring his battle plan to fruition.

However, the North was about to have one of the greatest strokes of luck during the Civil War. For reasons that are still unclear, Union troops in camp at Frederick came across a copy of Special Order 191, wrapped up among three cigars. The order contained Lee's entire marching plans for Maryland, making it clear that the Army of Northern Virginia had been divided into multiple parts, which, if faced by overpowering strength, could be entirely defeated and bagged. The "Lost Order" quickly made its way to General McClellan, who took several hours to debate whether or not it was intentional misinformation or actually real. Once he decided it was accurate, McClellan is said to have famously boasted, "Here is a paper with which if I cannot whip Bobby Lee, I will be willing to go home."

The North's luck was helped by Stuart, who had no clue orders had been lost and was busy handling public relations instead of reconnaissance. Now officially designated the "Eyes of the Army," in September of 1862, Stuart committed what many military historians deem his first tactical error when, for a five-day period at the beginning of the Maryland Campaign, he rested his men and entertained local civilians at a gala ball at Urbana, Maryland rather than keep the Union enemy under surveillance. With no incoming intelligence, Lee was unaware of Union General McClellan's location and the speed at which his forces approached.

The Confederates were completely unaware of the North's luck as they began to carry out Lee's plans. To Jackson's advantage, Col. Dixon S. Miles, Union commander at Harpers Ferry, had insisted on keeping most of his troops near the town instead of taking up commanding positions on the most important position, Maryland Heights. On September 12, Confederate forces engaged the Union's marginal defenses on the heights, but only a brief skirmish ensued. Then on September 13, two Confederate brigades arrived and easily drove the Union troops from the heights--but the critical positions to the west and south of town remained heavily defended.

By September 14, Jackson had methodically positioned his artillery around Harpers Ferry and ordered Maj. Gen. A. P. Hill to move down the west bank of the Shenandoah River in preparation for a flank attack on the Union left the next morning. By the following morning, Jackson had positioned nearly fifty guns on Maryland Heights and at the base of Loudoun Heights. Then he began a fierce artillery barrage from all sides, followed by a full-out infantry assault. Realizing the hopelessness of the situation, Col. Miles raised the white flag of surrender.

Eventually, the Confederates figured out where McClellan was, and to Lee's great surprise, McClellan's army began moving at an uncharacteristically quick pace, pushing in on his Confederate forces at several mountain passes at South Mountain, including at Turner's Gap and Crampton's Gap. While Jackson's wing was forcing the Harpers Ferry garrison to surrender, Lee regathered his other scattered units around Sharpsburg near Antietam Creek. McClellan's army, which may have outnumbered Lee's forces by about 50,000 men, confronted the Confederates around the night of September 16.

Longstreet described the scene before the battle commenced: "The blue uniforms of the federals appeared among the trees that crowned the heights on the eastern bank of the Antietam. The number increased, and larger and larger grew the field of blue until is seemed to stretch as far as the eye could see, and from the tops of the mountains down to the edge of the stream gathered the great army of McClellan."

As fate would have it, the bloodiest day in the history of the United States took place on the 75th anniversary of the signing of the Constitution. On September 17, 1862, Lee's Army of Northern Virginia fought McClellan's Army of the Potomac outside Sharpsburg along Antietam Creek. That day, nearly 25,000 would become casualties, and Lee's army barely survived fighting the much bigger Northern army. The fighting that morning started with savage fighting on the Confederate left flank near Dunker church, in a corn field and forests. The Confederates barely held the field in the north sector.

Lee's army may have been saved by the Northern army's inability to cross the creek near "Burnside's Bridge". Ambrose Burnside had been given command of the "Right Wing" of the Army of the Potomac (the I Corps and IX Corps) at the start of the Maryland Campaign for the

Battle of South Mountain, but McClellan separated the two corps at the Battle of Antietam, placing them on opposite ends of the Union battle line. However, Burnside continued to act as though he was a wing commander instead of a corps commander, so instead of ordering the IX corps, he funneled orders through General Jacob D. Cox. This poor organization contributed to the corps's hours-long delay in attacking and crossing what is now called "Burnside's Bridge" on the right flank of the Confederate line.

General Burnside

Making matters worse, Burnside did not perform adequate reconnaissance of the area, which afforded several easy fording sites of the creek out of range of the Army of Northern Virginia. Instead of unopposed crossings, his troops were forced into repeated assaults across the narrow bridge which was dominated by Confederate sharpshooters on high ground across the bridge. The delay allowed General A.P. Hill's Confederate division to reach the battlefield from Harpers Ferry in time to save Lee's right flank that afternoon. Fearing that his army was badly bloodied and figuring Lee had many more men than he did, McClellan refused to commit his reserves to continue the attacks. The day ended in a tactical stalemate.

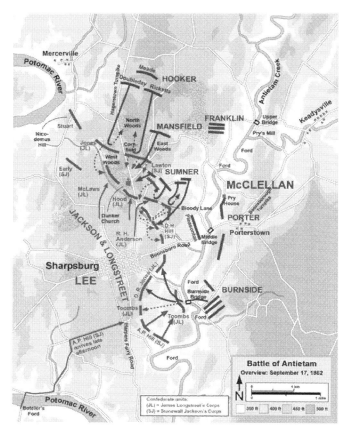

On the morning of September 18, Lee's army prepared to defend against a Union assault that ultimately never came. Finally, an improvised truce was declared to allow both sides to exchange their wounded. That evening, Lee's forces began withdrawing across the Potomac to return to Virginia, with McClellan, surprisingly, opting not to pursue, citing shortages of equipment and the fear of overextending his forces. Nevertheless, Antietam is now widely considered a turning point in the war. Although the battle was tactically a draw, it resulted in forcing Lee's army out of Maryland and back into Virginia, making it a strategic victory for the North and an opportune time for President Abraham Lincoln to issue the Emancipation Proclamation.

Dead soldiers along the turnpike at Antietam. Antietam was the first battle in which war dead were photographed and made publicly available, stunning Americans.

Although Lee and Jackson would ultimately receive the lion's share of credit for stopping McClellan's advance, it had been Longstreet's men who had held Lee's position long enough on the left and middle for Jackson to arrive and administer damage. One account describes Longstreet as coming upon an abandoned piece of artillery during one of the assaults, jumping off his horse, and then manning the gun himself for a half hour as his men kept reloading.

The same day as the Battle of Antietam, the *Washington Star* erroneously reported, "At the latest advices everything was favorable. Gen. Longstreet was reported killed and [General] Daniel Harvey Hill taken prisoner." Later that same day, the *Star* dispatched, "Gen. Longstreet was wounded and is a prisoner." All of that was incorrect.

Once the Army of Northern Virginia was safely back in Virginia, Stuart executed another of his daring circumnavigations of the Army of the Potomac, this time traveling 120 miles in under 60 hours. Once again he had embarrassed his Union opponents while seizing horses and supplies. Afterwards, Stuart gifted "Stonewall" Jackson a fine, new officer's tunic, trimmed with gold lace, commissioned from a Richmond tailor, which he thought would give Jackson more of a "proper" general appearance--a gift to which Jackson was famously indifferent and almost always refuse to wore (with the exception of his last official portrait, which was taken less than two weeks before Chancellorsville). And while these exploits proved only marginally significant (resulting in little military advantage), when word reached the newspapers, they did much to boost Southern morale.

Even then, it did not escape the notice of observers that Stuart and Jackson were an odd couple, and Jackson biographer James Robertson Jr. later wrote, "Stuart and Jackson were an unlikely pair: one outgoing, the other introverted; one flashily uniformed, the other plainly dressed; one Prince Rupert and the other Cromwell. Yet Stuart's self-confidence, penchant for action, deep love of Virginia, and total abstinence from such vices as alcohol, tobacco, and pessimism endeared him to Jackson... Stuart was the only man in the Confederacy who could make Jackson laugh—and who dared to do so."

Despite heavily outnumbering the Southern army and badly damaging it during the battle of Antietam, McClellan never did pursue Lee across the Potomac, citing shortages of equipment and the fear of overextending his forces. General-in-Chief Henry W. Halleck wrote in his official report, "The long inactivity of so large an army in the face of a defeated foe, and during the most favorable season for rapid movements and a vigorous campaign, was a matter of great disappointment and regret." Lincoln had also had enough of McClellan's "slows", and his constant excuses for not taking forward action. Lincoln relieved McClellan of his command of the Army of the Potomac on November 7, 1862, effectively ending the general's military career.

Chapter 17: The Fredericksburg Campaign

In place of McClellan, Lincoln appointed Burnside, who had just failed at Antietam. Burnside didn't believe he was competent to command the entire army, a very honest (and accurate) judgment. However, Burnside also didn't want the command to fall upon Joe Hooker, who had been injured while aggressively fighting with his I Corps at Antietam in the morning. Thus, he accepted. Around that same time, Jackson learned that he had become a father, receiving a letter informing him of the birth of his daughter, Julia Laura Jackson, on November 23.

Under pressure from Lincoln to be aggressive, Burnside laid out a difficult plan to cross the Rappahannock and attack the Confederates near Fredericksburg. The plan was doomed from the very beginning. On December 12, Burnside's army struggled to cross the river under fire from Confederate sharpshooters in the town.

The majority of the fighting took place the next day, and the most contested fighting found

Stuart and his men in the thick of it on the Confederates' right flank. Maj General Stuart and his cavalry—more specifically, his horse artillery under Major John Pelham—protected Stonewall Jackson's flank when it came under attack from General William B. Franklin. Franklin's "grand division" was able to penetrate General Jackson's defensive line to the south, but it was ultimately driven back. After the battle, General Lee commended Stuart's cavalry which, in his words, "effectually guarded our right, annoying the enemy and embarrassing his movements by hanging on his flank and attacking when the opportunity occurred."

However, the battle is mostly remembered however for the piecemeal attacks the Union army made on heavily fortified positions Longstreet's men took up on Marye's Heights. With the massacre at Antietam still fresh in his mind (partially caused by the Confederates having not constructed defensive works), Longstreet ordered trenches, abatis (obstacles formed by felled trees with sharpened branches), and fieldworks to be constructed - which to Longstreet's credit, set a precedent for all future defensive battles of the Army of Northern Virginia. To his thinking, if the artillery didn't keep Union forces at bay, the twenty-five hundred Confederates lined up four-deep behind a quarter-mile long four-foot stone wall would deter even the most foolhardy. Thus when it was learned that General Burnside was planning a direct assault on "the Heights," even the other Union generals couldn't believe it.

As they threw themselves at Longstreet's heavily fortified position along the high ground, the Northern soldiers were mowed down again and again. General Longstreet compared the near continuous fall of soldiers on the battlefield to "the stead dripping of rain from the eaves of a house." Still, Burnside sent wave after wave up the hill, with the Union injured (or those just cowering in the field) trying to stop the advancing men by grabbing at their legs and feet-- begging them to turn back. In the end, a recorded 14 assaults were made on Marye's Heights, all of which failed, with over 12,650 Union soldiers killed, wounded, or gone missing. Despite all their efforts, not one Union soldier got within 100 feet of the wall at Marye's Heights before being shot or forced to withdraw. And although General Longstreet is credited with assuring a Confederate victory, many historians characterize the battle as "murder, not warfare."

As men lay dying on the field that night, the Northern Lights made a rare appearance. Southern soldiers took it as a divine omen and wrote about it frequently in their diaries. The Union soldiers saw less divine inspiration in the Northern Lights and mentioned it less in their own. The Battle of Fredericksburg also spawned one of Lee's most memorable quotes. During the battle, Lee turned to Longstreet and commented, "It is well that war is so terrible, otherwise we would grow too fond of it."

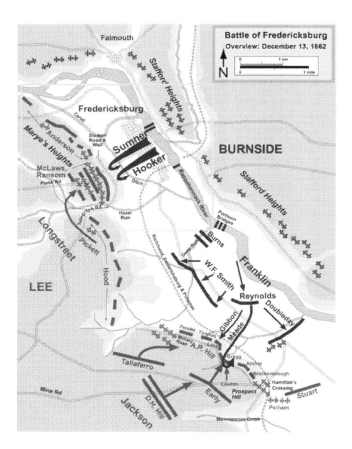

After the virtual slaughter (with the dead said to have been stacked up in rows), the Union army retreated across the river in defeat. Although Lee had accomplished a decisive victory over Burnside's forces, the Union general had positioned his reserves and supply line so strategically that he could easily fall back without breaking lines of communication--while Lee had no such reserves or supplies. And since Lee didn't have the men to pursue and completely wipe out Burnside's army (and simply holding them would ultimately prove too costly), Lee chose not to give chase. Some military strategists contend this was a military blunder, but either way, the fighting in 1862 was done.

Chapter 18: The Chancellorsville

Campaign

In a sense, the Battle of Chancellorsville was a defining moment in the careers of three of the four leaders of the Army of Northern Virginia. After the Confederate victory at Fredericksburg, Lee dispatched Longstreet and his corps back to the Virginia Peninsula to protect Richmond and gather food and other much-needed supplies. Although Longstreet accomplished both missions, he was later criticized for having not taken advantage of the opportunity to attack Union positions in the area. As had now become Longstreet's *modus operandi*, to deflect responsibility, he simply responded that he didn't think they could afford the "powder and ball"--an assertion many historians fully doubt. In May of 1863, General Lee ordered Longstreet to rejoin his Army of Northern Virginia in time for a potential battle, but Longstreet's men would not reach Chancellorsville in time.

As it turned out, Longstreet's corps wasn't needed. Lee had concluded an incredibly successful year for the Confederates in the East, but the South was still struggling. The Confederate forces in the West had failed to win a major battle, suffering defeat at places like Shiloh in Tennessee and across the Mississippi River. As the war continued into 1863, the southern economy continued to deteriorate. Southern armies were suffering serious deficiencies of nearly all supplies as the Union blockade continued to be effective as stopping most international commerce with the Confederacy. Moreover, the prospect of Great Britain or France recognizing the Confederacy had been all but eliminated by the Emancipation Proclamation.

Given the unlikelihood of forcing the North's capitulation, the Confederacy's main hope for victory was to win some decisive victory or hope that Abraham Lincoln would lose his reelection bid in 1864, and that the new president would want to negotiate peace with the Confederacy. Understandably, this colored Confederate war strategy, and unquestionably Lee's.

After the Fredericksburg debacle and the "Mud March" fiasco that left a Union advance literally dead in its tracks, Lincoln fired Burnside and replaced him with "Fighting Joe" Hooker. Hooker had gotten his nickname from a clerical error in a newspaper's description of fighting, but the nickname stuck, and Lee would later playfully refer to him as F.J. Hooker. Hooker had stood out for his zealous fighting at Antietam, and the battle may very well have turned out differently if he hadn't been injured at the head of the I Corps. Now he was in command of a 100,000 man Army of the Potomac, and he devised a complex plan to cross the Rappahannock River with part of his force near Fredericksburg to pin down Lee while using the other bulk to turn Lee's left, which would allow his forces to reach the Confederate rear.

Hooker's plan initially worked perfectly, with the division of his army surprising Lee. Lee was outnumbered two to one and now had to worry about threats on two fronts. Incredibly, Lee once again decided to divide his forces in the face of the enemy, sending Stonewall Jackson to turn the Union army's right flank while the rest of the army maintained positions near Fredericksburg. The Battle of Chancellorsville is one of the most famous of the Civil War, and the most famous part of the battle was Stonewall Jackson's daring march across the Army of the Potomac's flank, surprising the XI Corps with an attack on May 2, 1863. Having ignored warnings of Jackson's march, the XI Corps was quickly routed.

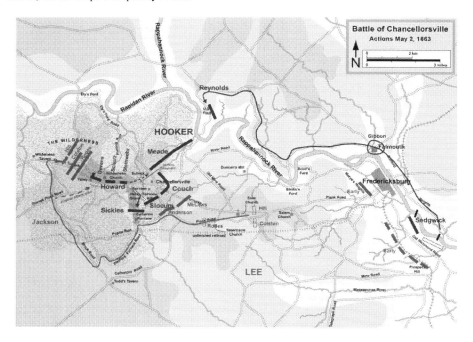

The surprise was a costly success however. Jackson scouted out ahead of his lines later that night and was mistakenly fired upon by his own men, badly wounding him. Jackson's natural replacement, A.P. Hill, was also injured.

Bypassing the next most-senior infantry general in the corps, Brig. General Robert E. Rodes directed Stuart himself to take temporary command of the Second Infantry Corps, a decision Lee seconded when news reached him. Although this change in command effectively ended the flanking attack underway, Stuart proved to be a remarkably adaptive leader and very effective infantry commander, launching a successful, well-coordinated assault against the Union right flank at Chancellorsville the following day. Meanwhile on the other flank, the Confederates evacuated from Fredericksburg but ultimately held the line. Hooker began to lose his nerve, and he was injured during the battle when a cannonball nearly killed him. Historians now believe that Hooker may have commanded part of the battle while suffering from a concussion.

On May 4, as Hooker abandoned the high ground at Hazel Grove in favor of Fairview, Stuart showed particular acumen by immediately taking control of the position and ordering thirty pieces of artillery to bombard the Union positions, not only forcing General Hooker's troops from Fairview (which Stuart then captured for the Confederacy), but essentially decimating the Union lines while destroying Hooker's headquarters at Chancellor House. Of this well-played turn of events, Stuart wrote: "As the sun lifted the mist that shrouded the field, it was discovered that the ridge on the extreme right was a fine position for concentrating artillery. I immediately ordered thirty pieces to that point, and, under the happy effects of the battalion system, it was done quickly. The effect of this fire upon the enemy's batteries was superb."

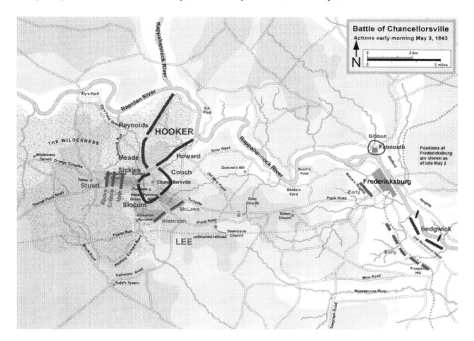

Stuart's effective utilization of a mere 20,000 men to snatch victory from a Union force numbering over 80,000 prompted Confederate General Porter Alexander to comment, "Altogether, I do not think there was a more brilliant thing done in the war than Stuart's extricating that command from the extremely critical position in which he found it." Some historians have speculated that Stuart's success at Hazel Grove was what induced Dan Sickles to disobey George Meade's orders on Day 2 at Gettysburg and advance his III Corps a mile out in front of the rest of the Union line to occupy high ground. Perhaps fearful of a replay like Chancellorsville, that fateful decision would dominate the fighting on the second day of the war's greatest battle.

The spot where Jackson was shot

By the end of the battle, the Army of the Potomac had once again been defeated, retreating across the river. But Lee would also lose his "right hand". Jackson had been shot multiple times, twice in the left arm. After being painfully carried back behind the Confederate lines, Jackson had his left arm amputated. When Lee heard of Jackson's injuries, he sent his religious leader Chaplain Lacy to Stonewall with the message, "Give him my affectionate regards, and tell him to make haste and get well, and come back to me as soon as he can. He has lost his left arm, but I have lost my right arm."

After the amputation, Stonewall was transported to Thomas C. Chandler's plantation, well behind the battle lines, to convalesce. He seemed to be recovering, and his wife and newborn daughter joined him at the plantation, but his doctors were unaware Jackson was exhibiting common symptoms that indicated oncoming pneumonia. Jackson lay dying in the Chandler plantation outbuilding on Sunday, May 10, 1863 with his wife Anna at his side. He comforted his wife, telling her, "It is the Lord's Day...my wish is fulfilled. I always wanted to die on Sunday." Near the end, a delirious Jackson seemed to have his mind on war, blurting out, "Tell

A. P. Hill to prepare for actions! Pass the infantry to the front! Tell Major Hawks..." His final words were "Let us cross over the river, and rest under the shade of the trees."

Although the Confederate Army had won the Battle at Chancellorsville, the loss of "Stonewall" not only diminished the victory but caused a general malaise to befall his men; as well as General Lee.

Jackson's tomb

Chapter 19: The Pennsylvania Campaign

In the spring of 1863, General Lee discovered that McClellan had known of his plans and was able to force a battle at Antietam before all of General Lee's forces had arrived. General Lee now believed that he could successfully invade the North again, and that his defeat before was due in great measure to a stroke of bad luck. In addition, General Lee hoped to supply his army on the unscathed fields and towns of the North, while giving war ravaged northern Virginia a rest. After Chancellorsville, Longstreet and Lee met to discuss options for the Confederate Army's summer campaign. Longstreet advocated detachment of all or part of his corps to be sent to Tennessee, citing Union Maj. General Ulysses S. Grant's advance on Vicksburg, the critical Confederate stronghold on the Mississippi River. Longstreet argued that a reinforced army under Bragg could defeat Rosecrans and drive toward the Ohio River, compelling Grant to release his hold on Vicksburg. Lee, however, was opposed to a division of his army and instead advocated a large-scale offensive (and raid) into Pennsylvania. In addition, General Lee hoped to supply his army on the unscathed fields and towns of the North, while giving war ravaged northern Virginia a rest.

Knowing that victories on Virginia soil meant little to an enemy that could simply retreat, regroup, and then return with more men and more advanced equipment, Lee set his sights on a Northern invasion, aiming to turn Northern opinion against the war and against President Lincoln. With his men already half-starved from dwindling provisions, Lee intended to confiscate food, horses, and equipment as they pushed north--and hopefully influence Northern politicians into giving up their support of the war by penetrating into Harrisburg or even Philadelphia. Given the right circumstances, Lee's army might even be able to capture either Baltimore or Philadelphia and use the city as leverage in peace negotiations.

In early June, the Army of Northern Virginia occupied Culpeper, Virginia. After their victories at Fredericksburg and Chancellorsville against armies twice their size, Confederate troops felt invincible and anxious to carry the war north into Pennsylvania. Assuming his role as Lee's "Eyes of the Army" for the Pennsylvania Campaign, Stuart bivouacked his men near the Rappahannock River, screening the Confederate Army against surprise Union attacks. Taken with his recent successes, Stuart requested a full field review of his units by General Lee, and on June 8, paraded his nearly 9,000 mounted troops and four batteries of horse artillery for review, also charging in simulated battle at Inlet Station about two miles southwest of Brandy Station. While Lee himself was unavailable to attend the review, some of the cavalrymen and newspaper reporters at the scene complained that all Stuart was doing was "feeding his ego and exhausting the horses." He began to be referred to as a "headline-hunting show-off."

Despite the critics, Stuart basked in the glory. Renowned Civil War historian Stephen Sears described the scene, "The grand review of June 5 was surely the proudest day of Jeb Stuart's thirty years. As he led a cavalcade of resplendent staff officers to the reviewing stand, trumpeters heralded his coming and women and girls strewed his path with flowers. Before all of the spectators the assembled cavalry brigade stretched a mile and a half. After Stuart and his entourage galloped past the line in review, the troopers in their turn saluted the reviewing stand in columns of squadrons. In performing a second "march past," the squadrons started off at a trot, then spurred to a gallop. Drawing sabers and breaking into the Rebel yell, the troopers rush toward the horse artillery drawn up in battery. The gunners responded defiantly, firing blank charges. Amidst this tumult of cannon fire and thundering hooves, a number of ladies swooned in their escorts' arms."

However much Stuart enjoyed "horsing around", there was serious work to be done. The following day, Lee ordered Stuart to cross the Rappahannock and raid Union forward positions, shielding the Confederate Army from observation or interference as it moved north. Already anticipating this imminent offensive move, Stuart had ordered his troops back into formation around Brandy Station. Here, Stuart would endure the first of two low points in his military career: the Battle of Brandy Station, the largest predominantly cavalry engagement of the Civil War.

Union Maj. General Joseph Hooker interpreted Stuart's presence around Culpeper as a precursor to a raid on his army's supply lines. In response, he ordered his cavalry commander, Maj. General Alfred Pleasonton, to take a combined force of 8,000 cavalry and 3,000 infantry on a raid to "disperse and destroy" the 9,500 Confederates. Crossing the Rappahannock River in two columns on June 9,1863 at Beverly's Ford and Kelly's Ford, the first infantry unit caught Stuart completely off-guard, and the second surprised him yet again. Suddenly the Confederates were being battered both front and rear by mounted Union troops.

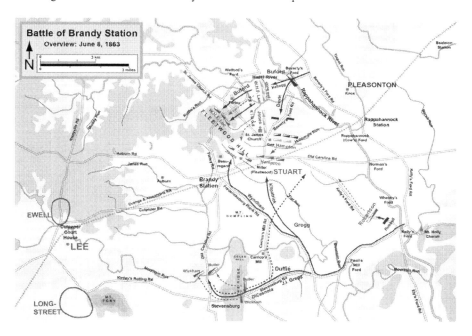

In addition to being the largest cavalry battle of the war, the chaos and confusion that ensued across the battlefield also made Brandy Station unique in that most of the fighting was done while mounted and using sabers. One account of the battle noted, "Of the bodies that littered the field that day, the vast majority were found to have perished by the sword."

After ten hours of charges and countercharges that swept back and forth across Fleetwood Hill (where Stuart had headquartered the night before) involving drawn sabers and revolvers, Pleasonton decided to withdraw his exhausted men across the Rappahannock River. Stuart immediately claimed a Confederate victory because his men had managed to hold the field and inflicted more casualties on the enemy while forcing Pleasonton to withdraw before locating

Lee's infantry. But Stuart was trying to save face, and nobody else, including Lee, took his view of the battle. The fact was, the Southern cavalry under Stuart had not detected the movement of two large columns of Union cavalry and had fallen prey to not one but *two* surprise attacks. Two days later the Richmond *Enquirer* reported: "If Gen. Stuart is to be the eyes and ears of the army we advise him to see more, and be seen less. Gen. Stuart has suffered no little in public estimation by the late enterprises of the enemy."

Lee was now painfully aware of the increased competency of the Union cavalry, as well as the decline of the seemingly once-invincible Southern mounted armed forces under Stuart.

In the wake of Jackson's death, Lee reorganized his army, creating three Corps out of the previous two, with A.P. Hill and Richard S. Ewell "replacing" Stonewall. Hill had been a successful division commander, but he was constantly battling bouts of sickness that left him disabled, which would occur at Gettysburg. Ewell had distinguished himself during the Peninsula Campaign, suffering a serious injury that historians often credit as making him more cautious in command upon his return.

With Stuart's cavalry screening his movements, Lee marched his army into Pennsylvania, once again dividing his forces to take different objectives. This time, however, they mostly stayed within a day's marching distance of each other. Meanwhile, the loss at Chancellorsville led to Lincoln relieving Hooker as he was leading the Army of the Potomac in pursuit of Lee. George Meade assumed command of the Army of the Potomac just a few days before the Battle of Gettysburg.

During the first weeks of summer of 1863, as Stuart screened the army and completed several well-executed offenses against Union cavalry, many historians think it likely that he had already planned to remove the negative effect of Brandy Station by duplicating one of his now famous circumnavigating rides around the enemy army. But as Lee began his march north through the Shenandoah Valley in western Virginia, it is highly unlikely that is what he wanted or expected.

Before setting out on June 22, the methodical Lee gave Stuart specific instructions as to the role he was to play in the Pennsylvania offensive: as the "Eyes of the Army" he was to guard the mountain passes with part of his force while the Army of Northern Virginia was still south of the Potomac River, and then cross the river with the remainder of his army and screen the right flank of Confederate general Richard Stoddert Ewell's Second Corps as it moved down the Shenandoah Valley, maintaining contact with Ewell's army as it advanced towards Harrisburg.

But instead of taking the most direct route north near the Blue Ridge Mountains, Stuart chose a much more ambitious course of action.

Stuart decided to march his three best brigades (under Generals Hampton and Fitzhugh Lee, and Col. John R. Chambliss) between the Union army and Washington, north through Rockville to Westminster, and then into Pennsylvania--a route that would allow them to capture supplies along the way and wreak havoc as they skirted Washington. In the aftermath, the *Washington Star* would write: "The cavalry chief [Stuart] interpreted his marching orders in a way that best suited his nature, and detached his 9000 troopers from their task of screening the main army and keeping tabs on the Federals. When Lee was in Pennsylvania anxiously looking for him, Stuart crossed the Potomac above Washington and captured a fine prize of Federal supply wagons . . . ."

But to complicate matters even more, as Stuart set out on June 25 on what was probably a glory-seeking mission, he was unaware that his intended path was blocked by columns of Union infantry that would invariably force him to veer farther east than he or Lee had anticipated. Ultimately, his decision would prevent him from linking up with Ewell as ordered and deprive Lee of his primary cavalry force as he advanced deeper and deeper into unfamiliar enemy territory. According to Halsey Wigfall (son of Confederate States Senator Louis Wigfall) who was in Stuart's infantry, "Stuart and his cavalry left [Lee's] army on June 24 and did not contact [his] army again until the afternoon of July 2, the second day of the [Gettysburg] battle."

According to Stuart's own account, on June 29 his men clashed briefly with two companies of Union cavalry in Westminster, Maryland, overwhelming and chasing them "a long distance on the Baltimore road," causing a "great panic" in the city of Baltimore. On June 30, the head of Stuart's column then encountered Union Brig. General Judson Kilpatrick's cavalry as it passed through Hanover--reportedly capturing a wagon train and scattering the Union army--after which Kilpatrick's men were able to regroup and drive Stuart and his men out of town. Then after a twenty-mile trek in the dark, Stuart's exhausted men reached Dover, Pennsylvania, on the morning of July 1 (which they briefly occupied).

Late on the second day of the battle, Stuart finally arrived, bringing with him the caravan of captured Union supply wagons, and he was immediately reprimanded by Lee. One account describes Lee as "visibly angry" raising his hand "as if to strike the tardy cavalry commander." While that does not sound like Lee's style, Stuart has been heavily criticized ever since, and it has been speculated Lee took him to task harshly enough that Stuart offered his resignation. Lee didn't accept it, but he would later note in his after battle report that the cavalry had not updated him as to the Army of the Potomac's movements.

Given great discretion in his cavalry operations before the battle, Stuart's cavalry was too far removed from the Army of Northern Virginia to warn Lee of the Army of the Potomac's movements. As it would turn out, Lee's army inadvertently stumbled into Union cavalry and then the Union army at Gettysburg on the morning of July 1, 1863, walking blindly into what became the largest battle of the war.

It is believed that one of the first notices Lee got about the Army of the Potomac's movements actually came from a spy named "Harrison", a man who apparently worked undercover for Longstreet but of whom little is known. Harrison reported that General George G. Meade was now in command of the Union Army and was at that very moment marching north to meet Lee's army. According to Longstreet, he and Lee were supposedly on the same page at the beginning of the campaign. "His plan or wishes announced, it became useless and improper to offer suggestions leading to a different course. All that I could ask was that the policy of the campaign should be one of defensive tactics; that we should work so as to force the enemy to attack us, in such good position as we might find in our own country, so well adapted to that purpose—which might assure us of a grand triumph. To this he readily assented as an important and material adjunct to his general plan." Lee later claimed he "had never made any such promise, and had never thought of doing any such thing," but in his official report after the battle, Lee also noted, "It had not been intended to fight a general battle at such a distance from our base, unless attacked by the enemy.

Without question, the most famous battle of the Civil War took place outside of the small town of Gettysburg, Pennsylvania, which happened to be a transporation hub, serving as the center of a wheel with several roads leading out to other Pennsylvanian towns. Lee was unaware of Meade's position when an advanced division of Hill's Corps marched toward Gettysburg on the morning of July 1. The battle began with John Buford's Union cavalry forces skirmishing against the advancing division of Heth's just outside of town. Buford's actions allowed the I Corps of the Army of the Potomac to reach Gettysburg and engage the Confederates, eventually setting the stage for the biggest and most well known battle of the war.

Day 1 by itself would have been one of the 20 biggest battles of the Civil War, and it was a tactical Confederate victory. While the Army of the Potomac's I and XI Corps engaged in heavy fighting, they were eventually flanked from the north by Ewell's Corps, which was returning toward Gettysburg from its previous objective. After a disorderly retreat through the town itself, the Union men began to dig in on high ground to the southeast of the town.

It was at this point that Lee arrived on the field and saw the importance of this position. He sent discretionary orders to Ewell that Cemetery Hill be taken "if practicable." Ewell chose not to attempt the assault. Lee's order has been criticized because it left too much discretion to Ewell, leaving historians to speculate on how the more aggressive Stonewall Jackson would have acted on this order if he had lived to command this wing of Lee's army, and how differently the second day of battle would have proceeded with Confederate possession of Culp's Hill or Cemetery Hill. Discretionary orders were customary for General Lee because Jackson and Longstreet, his other principal subordinate, usually reacted to them aggressively and used their initiative to act quickly and forcefully. Ewell's decision not to attack, whether justified or not, may have ultimately cost the Confederates the battle.

General Ewell

With so many men engaged and now taking refuge on the high ground, Meade, who was an engineer like Lee, abandoned his previous plan to draw up a defensive line around Emmittsburg a few miles to the South. After a council of war, the Army of the Potomac determined to defend at Gettysburg.

July 2, 1863, Day 2 of the Battle of Gettysburg, may have been the most important day of James Longstreet's career, and it is certainly the most important day of James Longstreet's legacy. The actions of Longstreet's corps that day have affected all the post-war charges, defenses, and historians' opinions about Longstreet ever since.

On the morning of Day 2, Lee decided to attempt attacks on both Union flanks, ordering Ewell's corps to attack Culp's Hill on the Union right while Longstreet's corps would attack on the Union left.

As it turned out, both attacks would come too late. Though there was a controversy over when Lee ordered Longstreet's attack, Longstreet's march got tangled up and caused several hours of delay. Lost Cause advocates attacking Longstreet would later claim his attack was supposed to take place as early as possible, although no official Confederate orders gave a time for the attack. Lee gave the order for the attack around 11:00 a.m., and it is known that Longstreet was reluctant about making it; he still wanted to slide around the Union flank, interpose the Confederate army between Washington D.C. and the Army of the Potomac, and force Meade to attack them. Between Longstreet's delays and the mixup in the march that forced parts of his corps to double back and make a winding march, Longstreet's men weren't ready to attack until about 4:00 p.m.

Longstreet's biographer, Jeffrey Wert, wrote, "Longstreet deserves censure for his performance on the morning of July 2. He allowed his disagreement with Lee's decision to affect his conduct. Once the commanding general determined to assail the enemy, duty required Longstreet to comply with the vigor and thoroughness that had previously characterized his generalship. The concern for detail, the regard for timely information, and the need for preparation were absent." Edwin Coddington, whose history of the Gettysburg Campaign still continues to be considered the best ever written, described Longstreet's march as "a comedy of errors such as one might expect of inexperienced commanders and raw militia, but not of Lee's ' War Horse' and his veteran troops." Coddington considered it "a dark moment in Longstreet's career as a general."

Writing about Day 2, Longstreet criticized Lee, insisting once again that the right move was to move around the Union flank. "The opportunity for our right was in the air. General Halleck saw it from Washington. General Meade saw and was apprehensive of it. Even General Pendleton refers to it in favorable mention in his official report. Failing to adopt it, General Lee should have gone with us to his right. He had seen and carefully examined the left of his line, and only gave us a guide to show the way to the right, leaving the battle to be adjusted to formidable and difficult grounds without his assistance. If he had been with us, General Hood's messengers could have been referred to general Headquarters, but to delay and send messengers five miles in favor of a move that he had rejected would have been contumacious. The opportunity was with the Confederates from the assembling on Cemetery Hill. It was inviting of their preconceived plans. It was the object of and excuse for the invasion as a substitute for more direct efforts for the relief of Vicksburg. Confederate writers and talkers claim that General Meade could have escaped without making aggressive battle, but that is equivalent to confession of the inertia that failed to grasp the opportunity."

The delay would ultimately allow the Army of the Potomac to move men onto Little Round Top, high ground that commanded much of the field. Though there were delays in his corps' movement, Longstreet's men delivered a ferocious attack. Longstreet's and Hill's men smashed the Union soldiers, particularly the III Corps, which commander Dan Sickles had moved forward nearly a mile against Meade's orders. The salient in the Union army's line led to much of the effort of the attack taking place there, and the North was able to hold off the attacks against Little Round Top.

Meanwhile, Ewell's attack against Culp's Hill on the other end of the field met with some success in pushing the Army of the Potomac back. However, the attack started so late in the day that nightfall made it impossible for the Confederates to capitalize on their success. Ewell's men would spend the night at the base of Culp's Hill and partially up the hill, but it would fall upon them to pick up the attack the next morning.

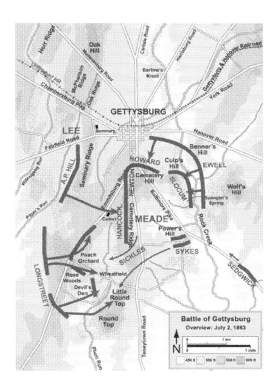

That night, Meade held another council of war. Having been attacked on both flanks, Meade and his top officers correctly surmised that Lee would attempt an attack on the center of the line the next day. Moreover, captured Confederates and the fighting and intelligence of Day 2 let it be known that the only Confederate unit that had not yet seen action during the fighting was George Pickett's division of Longstreet's corps.

General Meade

If Day 2 was Longstreet's worst day of the Civil War, Day 3 was almost certainly Robert E. Lee's. After the attack on Day 2, Longstreet spent the night continuing to plot potential movements around Little Round Top and Big Round Top, thinking that would again get the Confederate army around the Union's flank. Longstreet himself did not realize that a reserve corps of the Union army was poised to block that maneuver.

Longstreet did not meet with Lee on the night of July 2, so when Lee met with him the following morning he found Longstreet's men were not ready to conduct an early morning attack, which Lee had wanted to attempt just as he was on the other side of the lines against Culp's Hill. With Pickett's men not up, however, Longstreet's corps couldn't make such an attack. Lee later wrote that Longstreet's "dispositions were not completed as early as was expected."

On the morning of July 3, the Confederate attack against Culp's Hill fizzled out, but by then Lee had already planned a massive attack on the Union center, combined with having Stuart's cavalry attack the Union army's lines in the rear. A successful attack would split the Army of the Potomac at the same time its communication and supply lines were severed by Stuart, which would make it possible to capture the entire army in detail.

There was just one problem with the plan, as Longstreet told Lee that morning: no 15,000 men who ever existed could successfully execute the attack. The charge required marching across an open field for about a mile, with the Union artillery holding high ground on all sides of the incoming Confederates. Longstreet ardently opposed the attack, but, already two days into the battle, Lee explained that because the Army of the Potomac was here on the field, he must strike at it. Longstreet later wrote that he said, "General Lee, I have been a soldier all my life. It is my opinion that no fifteen thousand men ever arrayed for battle can take that position." Longstreet proposed instead that their men should slip around the Union forces and occupy the high ground, forcing Northern commanders to attack them, rather than *vice versa.*

Realizing the insanity of sending 15,000 men hurtling into all the Union artillery, Lee planned to use the Confederate artillery to try to knock out the Union artillery ahead of time. Although old friend William Pendleton was the artillery chief, the artillery cannonade would be supervised by Edward Porter Alexander, Longstreet's chief artillerist, who would have to give the go-ahead to the charging infantry because they were falling under Longstreet's command. Alexander later noted that Longstreet was so disturbed and dejected about ordering the attack that at one point he tried to make Alexander order the infantry forward, essentially doing Longstreet's dirty work for him.

As Longstreet had predicted, from the beginning the plan was an abject failure. Stuart's men did not defeat the Union cavalry and thus had no success. Just after 1:00 p.m. 150 Confederate guns began to fire from Seminary Ridge, hoping to incapacitate the Union center before launching an infantry attack, but they mostly overshot their mark. The artillery duel could be heard from dozens of miles away, and all the smoke led to Confederate artillery constantly overshooting their targets. Eventually, Union artillery chief Henry Hunt cleverly figured that if the Union cannons stopped firing back, the Confederates might think they successfully knocked out the Union batteries. On top of that, the Union would be preserving its ammunition for the impending charge that everyone now knew was coming. When they stopped, Lee, Alexander, and others mistakenly concluded that they'd knocked out the Union artillery.

A short time later, Confederate General George Pickett, commander of one of the three divisions under General Longstreet, prepared for the *Lee-designed* charge (henceforth known as "Pickett's Charge") aimed at the Union center. With his men in position, Pickett asked Longstreet to give the order to advance, but Longstreet would only nod, fearing that "to verbalize the order may reveal his utter lack of confidence in the plan." And while most of the men participating in that charge had been led to believe that the battle was nearly over and that all that remained was to march unopposed to Cemetery Hill, in actually, those men were unwittingly walking into a virtual massacre.

As the Confederate line advanced, Union cannon on Cemetery Ridge and Little Round Top began blasting away, with Confederate soldiers continuing to march forward. One Union soldier later wrote, "We could not help hitting them with every shot . . . a dozen men might be felled by one single bursting shell." By the time Longstreet's men reached Emmitsburg Road, Union artillery switched to firing canister (tin cans filled with iron and lead balls), and as the

Confederate troops continued to approach the Union center, Union troops positioned behind the wall cut down the oncoming Confederates, easily decimating both flanks. And while some of the men did mange to advance to the Union line and engage in hand-to-hand combat, it was of little consequence.

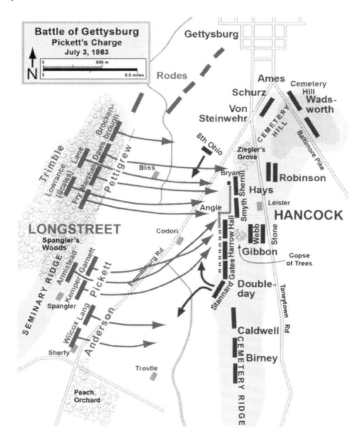

In about an hour, nearly 6,500 Confederates were dead or wounded, five times that of the Union, with all 13 regimental commanders in Pickett's division killed or wounded. In the aftermath of the defeat, General Longstreet stated, "General Lee came up as our troops were falling back and encouraged them as well as he could; begged them to reform their ranks and reorganize their forces . . . and it was then he used the expression . . . 'It was all my fault; get together, and let us do the best we can toward saving which is left to us.'" Longstreet never resisted an opportunity to distance himself from failure and direct it towards someone else, even Lee.

Today Pickett's Charge is remembered as the American version of the Charge of the Light Brigade, a heroic but completely futile march that had no chance of success. In fact, it's remembered as Pickett's Charge because Pickett's Virginians wanted to claim the glory of getting the furthest during the attack in the years after the war. The charge consisted of about 15,000 men under the command of James Longstreet, with three divisions spearheaded by Pickett, Trimble, and Pettigrew. Trimble and Pettigrew were leading men from A.P. Hill's corps, and Hill was too disabled by illness that day to choose the men from his corps to make the charge. As a result, some of the men who charged that day had already engaged in heavy fighting.

Longstreet was so sure of disaster that he could barely take it upon himself to order the men ahead. He was right. The charge suffered about a 50% casualty rate, as the Confederates marched into hell. The men barely made a dent in the Union line before retreating in disorder back across the field, where Lee met them in an effort to regroup them in case the Union counterattacked. At one point, Lee ordered Pickett to reform his division, to which Pickett reportedly cried, "I have no division!"

Pickett

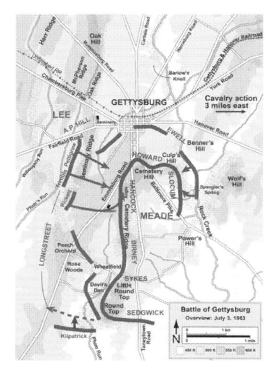

Coincidentally, Gettysburg was the second battle in which Longstreet was incorrectly reported killed. On Saturday, July 4, the *Washington Star* reported that prisoners of the final battle "assert that [in addition to Confederate General William] Barksdale, Longstreet was also killed." On Monday, July 6, the *Star* reported, "Longstreet was mortally wounded and captured. He is reported to have died an hour afterward." Yet again, these reports were incorrect.

After the South had lost the war, the importance of Gettysburg as one of the "high tide" marks of the Confederacy became apparent to everyone, making the battle all the more important in the years after it had been fought. Former Confederate comrades like Longstreet and Jubal Early would go on to argue who was responsible for the loss at Gettysburg (and thus the war) in the following decades. Much of the debate was fueled by those who wanted to protect Lee's legacy, especially because Lee was dead and could not defend himself in writing anymore. However, on July 3, Lee insisted on taking full blame for what occurred at Gettysburg, telling his retreating men, "It's all my fault." Historians have mostly agreed, placing the blame for the disastrous Day 3 on Lee's shoulders. Porter Alexander would later call it Lee's "worst day" of the war.

However, after the war, former Confederates would not accept criticism of Lee, and blame for the loss at Gettysburg was placed upon other scapegoats. Although it was not immediately apparent where the blame rested for such a devastating loss, not long after the Battle of Gettysburg two names kept surfacing: cavalry leader General "Jeb" Stuart and General James Longstreet; Stuart blamed for robbing Lee of the "eyes" he needed to know of Union movement, and Longstreet for delaying his attack on Round Top Hills the second day and acting too slowly in executing the assault on the Union left flank.

Though credited with devoting his full attention to the Confederate cause upon his arrival, many historians attribute the catastrophic loss to the absence of Stuart and his cavalry. Immediately becoming the most devastating event of Stuart's military career, in his official report General Lee's wrote, " . . . the absence of the cavalry rendered it impossible to obtain accurate information. By the route [we] pursued, the Federal Army was interposed between [my] command and our main body, preventing any communication with [Stuart] until his arrival at Carlisle. The march toward Gettysburg was conducted more slowly than it would have been had the movements of the Federal Army been known." Some of Stuart's subordinates would come to his defense after the war, and Lee deserves some blame for allowing his subordinates so much discretion, which may have worked with Stonewall Jackson but backfired spectacularly with Ewell and Stuart. After the war, Stuart's subordinate, General Thomas L. Rosser stated what many were already convinced of, "On this campaign, [Stuart] undoubtedly, make the fatal blunder which lost us the battle of Gettysburg."

Chapter 20: The End of 1863

By September 9, 1863, General Lee had reorganized his cavalry, creating a cavalry corps for Stuart with two divisions of three brigades each. In the Bristoe Campaign (in Virginia), Stuart was assigned to lead a broad turning movement in an attempt to access General Meade's rear, but Meade skillfully withdrew his army without providing the opportunity. On October 13, Stuart stumbled into the rear guard of the Union III Corps near Warrenton, resulting in Lee having to send General Ewell's corps to rescue him; Stuart managed to hide his troopers in a wooded ravine until the unsuspecting III Corps moved on. And then on October 14, as Meade withdrew towards Manassas Junction, brigades from the Union II Corps fought a rearguard action against Stuart's cavalry and a division of Brig. General Harry Hays near Auburn, with Stuart's cavalry effectively bluffing Union General Gouverneur K. Warren's infantry and narrowly evading disaster.

After the Confederate debacle at Bristoe Station and an aborted advance on Centreville, Virginia, Stuart's cavalry shielded the withdrawal of Lee's army from Manassas Junction, after which Union General Judson Kilpatrick's cavalry pursued Stuart's cavalry along the Warrenton Turnpike--but were lured into an ambush near Chestnut Hill and routed. Kilpatrick was the one

Civil War officer who may have been even more flamboyant than Stuart.

And in a confrontation fought on October 19, 1863 that became known as the "Buckland Races" (and likened to a fox hunt), Stuart and Maj. General Wade Hampton's cavalry succeeded in not only routing Kilpatrick's cavalry, they pursued it at full-gallop for five miles to Haymarket and Gainesville, eventually forcing it to scatter. At this point, the Southern press began to reconsider its harsh criticism of Stuart.

In June of 1863, Union general William Rosecrans marched southeast toward Chattanooga, Tennessee, in pursuit of Confederate general Braxton Bragg, intending to "drive him into the sea." By this point, both the Union and Confederates had realized how uniquely important Chattanooga was as the rail and road gateway to all points south of the Ohio River and east of the Mississippi River.

In mid-September, the Union Army under General Rosecrans had taken Chattanooga, but rather than be pushed out of the action, Bragg decided to stop with his 60,000 men and prepare a counterattack south of Chattanooga at a creek named Chickamauga. To bolster his fire-power, Confederate President Jefferson Davis sent 12,000 additional troops (some sources say as many as 60,000) under the command of Lieutenant General Longstreet. In only nine days, Longstreet had successfully moved his entire corps by rail to come to Bragg's aid.

On the morning of September 19, 1863, Bragg's men assaulted the Union line, which was established in a wooded area thick with underbrush along the river. That day and the morning of the next, Bragg continue to pummel Union forces, with the battle devolving from an organized succession of coordinated assaults into what one Union soldier described as "a mad, irregular battle, very much resembling guerilla warfare on a vast scale in which one army was bushwhacking the other, and wherein all the science and the art of war went for nothing."

Late that second morning, Rosecrans was misinformed that a gap was forming in his front line, so he responded by moving several units forward to shore it up. What Rosecrans didn't realize, however, was that in doing so he accidentally created a quarter-mile gap in the Union center, directly in the path of an eight-brigade (15,000 man) force led by Longstreet. Described by one of Rosecrans' own men as "an angry flood," Longstreet's attack, which historians are split on whether it was skill or luck, was successful in driving one-third of the Union Army to the crossroads of Rossville, five miles north, with Rosecrans himself running all the way to Chattanooga where he was later found weeping and seeking solace from a staff priest.

The destruction of the entire army was prevented by General George H. Thomas, who rallied the remaining parts of the army and formed a defensive stand on Horseshoe Ridge. Union units spontaneously rallied to create a defensive line on their fall-back point at Horseshoe Ridge--

forming a new right wing for the line of Maj. General George H. Thomas, who had now assumed overall command of the remaining forces. And although the Confederates launched a series of well-executed (albeit costly) assaults, Thomas and his men managed to hold until nightfall, when they made an orderly retreat to Chattanooga while the Confederates occupied the surrounding heights, ultimately besieging the city. Dubbed "The Rock of Chickamauga", Thomas's heroics ensured that Rosecrans' army was able to successfully retreat back to Chattanooga.

In the aftermath of the Battle of Chickamauga, Longstreet blamed the number of men lost during what would be the bloodiest battle of the Western Theater on Bragg's incompetence, also criticizing him for refusing to pursue the escaping Union army. He later stated to Jefferson Davis, "Nothing but the hand of God can help as long as we have our present commander." Bragg owed his position to being a close friend of Jefferson Davis's, and one of the criticisms often lodged at Davis by historians is that he played favorites to the detriment of the South's chances. Even after he reluctantly removed Bragg from command out West, he would bring Bragg to Richmond to serve as a military advisor.

Bragg

Following the victory at Chickamauga, Longstreet departed on an independent mission to expel the Union army from Knoxville, Tennessee--operations that would fail due to what Longstreet explained away as "weakened forces and disagreeable subordinates." Longstreet then took a position at Gordonsville, Virginia where he was poised to protect against Union invasion via the Shenandoah Valley, or quickly reunite with the main body of Lee's Army of Northern Virginia should the main thrust of Union movement advance towards Fredericksburg. On May 4, 1864, upon finding out that his long-time friend General Ulysses S. Grant was now in command of the

Union Army, Longstreet confided to his fellow officers, "He will fight us every day and every hour until the end of the war."

Chapter 21: The Overland Campaign

Although the Army of the Potomac had been victorious at Gettysburg, Lincoln was still upset at what he perceived to be General George Meade's failure to trap Robert E. Lee's Army of Northern Virginia in Pennsylvania. When Lee retreated from Pennsylvania without much fight from the Army of the Potomac, Lincoln was again discouraged, believing Meade had a chance to end the war if he had been bolder. Though historians dispute that, and the Confederates actually invited attack during their retreat, Lincoln was constantly looking for more aggressive fighters to lead his men.

With Lee continuing to hold off the Army of the Potomac in a stalemate along the same battle lines at the end of 1863, Lincoln shook things up. In March 1864, Grant was promoted to lieutenant general and given command of all the armies of the United States. His first acts of command were to keep General Halleck in position to serve as a liaison between Lincoln and Secretary of War Edwin Stanton. And though it's mostly forgotten today, Grant technically kept General Meade in command of the Army of the Potomac, even though Grant attached himself to that army before the Overland Campaign in 1864 and thus served as its commander for all intents and purposes.

In May 1864, with Grant now attached to the Army of the Potomac, the Civil War's two most famous generals met each other on the battlefield for the first time. Lee had won stunning victories at battles like Chancellorsville and Second Bull Run by going on the offensive and taking the strategic initiative, but Grant and Lincoln had no intention of letting him do so anymore. Grant ordered General Meade, "Lee's army is your objective point. Wherever Lee goes, there you will go also."

By 1864, things were looking so bleak for the South that the Confederate war strategy was simply to ensure Lincoln lost reelection that November, with the hope that a new Democratic president would end the war and recognize the South's independence. With that, and given the shortage in manpower, Lee's strategic objective was to continue defending Richmond, while hoping that Grant would commit some blunder that would allow him a chance to seize an opportunity.

On May 4, 1864, Grant launched the Overland Campaign, crossing the Rapidan River near Fredericksburg with the 100,000 strong Army of the Potomac, which almost doubled Lee's hardened but battered Army of Northern Virginia. It was a similar position to the one George McClellan had in 1862 and Joe Hooker had in 1863, and Grant's first attack, at the Battle of the

Wilderness, followed a similar pattern. Nevertheless, Lee proved more than capable on the defensive.

From May 5-6, Lee's men won a tactical victory at the Battle of the Wilderness, which was fought so close to where the Battle of Chancellorsville took place a year earlier that soldiers encountered skeletons that had been buried in (too) shallow graves in 1863. Both armies sustained heavy casualties while Grant kept attempting to move the fighting to a setting more to his advantage, but the heavy forest made coordinated movements almost impossible.

On the second day, the aggressive Lee used General Longstreet's corps to counterattack on the second day. In his first confrontation since rejoining Lee's army, Longstreet launched a powerful flanking attack along the Orange Plank Road against the Union II Corps and nearly drove it off the field. Then instituting what are recognized as innovative tactics to deal with difficult terrain, Longstreet ordered the advance of six brigades by heavy skirmish lines--four to flank the Union right and two against the front--which allowed his men to deliver continuous fire into the enemy while proving elusive targets themselves.

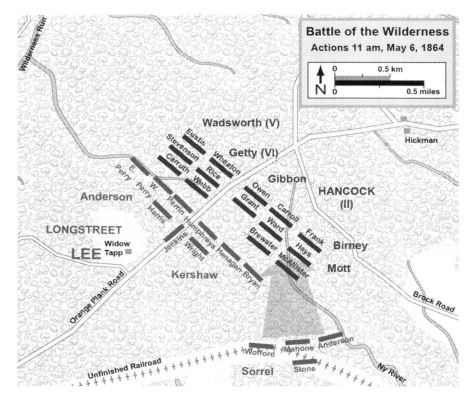

Battle of the Wilderness

Actions 11 am, May 6, 1864

Almost exactly a year earlier, just miles away from where the Battle of the Wilderness was fought, Stonewall Jackson was mortally wounded by fire from his own men. Longstreet nearly suffered the same fate. During the assault, Longstreet was himself wounded — accidentally shot by one of his own men – with the ball passing through the base of his neck and lodging in his shoulder. To assure his men, Longstreet raised his hat as he was being carried off the field, but with Longstreet incapacitated, the momentum of the attack was lost, forcing General Lee to delay further action until units could be realigned. This setback gave Union defenders sufficient time to reorganize.

By the end of the day, the battle ended at virtually the same place it had started that morning-- except that now, thousands of men lied dead. Confederate General Edward Porter Alexander later spoke of the loss of Longstreet at the critical juncture of the battle, saying, "I have always believed that, but for Longstreet's fall, the panic which was fairly underway in Hancock's Corps would have been extended and have resulted in Grant's being forced to retreat back across the

Rapidan."

During the Battle of the Wilderness, Stuart's pushing of Confederate General Thomas L. Rosser's "Laurel Brigade" into a fight with the better-armed "Michigan Brigade" under General George Custer resulted in significant loss of life. And when Grant continued to maneuver his men toward Richmond, Lee continued to parry, with Stuart receiving some credit for success in delaying the advance of the Union forces.

In early May of 1864, Union cavalry commander Maj. General Philip Sheridan organized a massive raid against Confederate supply and railroad lines near Richmond. Moving aggressively, he crossed the North Anna River and seized Beaver Dam Station on the Virginia Central Railroad. Anticipating their arrival, the Confederate troops had already destroyed most of the critical military supplies, so Sheridan's men destroyed railroad cars, ripped out telegraph lines, and rescued several hundred (some estimates are in the thousands) Union captives.

On May 9, the largest cavalry force ever seen in the Eastern Theater, over 10,000 with 32 artillery pieces, arched southeast intending to slip behind Lee's army with three goals: to disrupt Lee's supply lines by destroying railroad tracks and supplies; to threaten the Confederate capital of Richmond; and most significantly for Sheridan, to take Stuart out of the war.

As expected, Stuart dispatched a force of about 3,000-4,500 cavalrymen to intercept Sheridan's cavalry. As Stuart rode to meet the enemy, accompanied by his aide, Maj. Andrew R. Venable, they stopped briefly to see Stuart's wife, Flora, and his children, Jimmie and Virginia. Venable later wrote, "He told me he never expected to live through the war, and that if we were conquered, that he did not want to live."

At noon on May 11, 1864, the two forces met at Yellow Tavern, an abandoned inn six miles north of Richmond, Virginia. Not only did the Union outnumber the Confederates (ten to one by some estimates), it had superior firepower--armed with newly-developed rapid-firing Spencer carbine rifles.

After a spirited resistance by Confederate troops from the low ridge bordering the road to Richmond that lasted over three hours, the First Virginia Cavalry pushed the advancing Union soldiers back from the hilltop as Stuart, mounted on horseback in his conspicuous attire, rallied his men and encouraged them to keep pushing forward. While Union men of the Fifth Michigan Cavalry were steadily retreating, one of them, 48 year old sharpshooter John A. Huff, found himself only about 20 yards away from the vaunted and easily recognizable Stuart. Huff turned and shot Stuart with his .44-caliber pistol, sending a bullet slicing through his stomach and exiting his back, just right of his spine. In excruciating pain, an ambulance took Stuart to the home of his brother-in-law Dr. Charles Brewer, in Richmond, to await his wife's arrival.

The following day, before his wife could reach his side, at 7:38 p.m., Stuart died. In his final moments, Stuart ordered his sword and spurs be given to his son. His dying words were: "I am resigned; God's will be done." He was just 31 years old.

The death of Stuart brought a cloud of gloom to the South, second only to that following the death of Stonewall Jackson. Having known Stuart well before the war, Lee took the news of his death very hard, and witnesses observed him break down upon learning of Stuart's fate. Lee himself noted, "Among the gallant soldiers who have fallen in this war, General Stuart was second to none in valor, in zeal, and in unfaltering devotion to his country. To military capacity of a high order and all the nobler virtues of the soldier he added the brighter graces of a pure life, guided and sustained by the Christian's faith and hope. The mysterious hand of an all-wise God has removed him from the scene of his usefulness and fame. His grateful countrymen will mourn his loss and cherish his memory. To his comrades in arms he has left the proud recollection of his deeds and his inspiring influence of his example."

With Stuart dead and Longstreet forced to rest and convalesce during the rest of the Overland Campaign, Grant continued to maneuver his men toward Richmond, and Lee continued to parry. The next major battle took place at Spotsylvania Court House, where a salient in the Confederate line nearly spelled disaster. Fighting raged around the "Bloody Angle" for hours, with soldiers fighting hand to hand before the Confederates finally dislodged the Union soldiers."

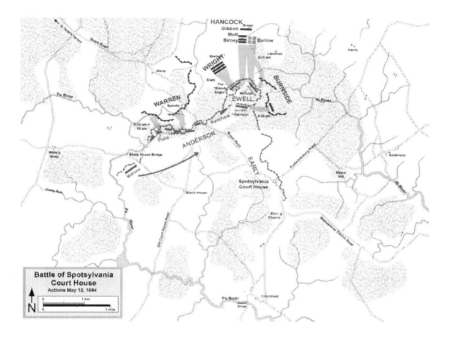

Lee's army continued to stoutly defend against several attacks by the Army of the Potomac, but massive casualties were inflicted on both sides. After Spotsylvania, Grant had already incurred about 35,000 casualties while inflicting nearly 25,000 casualties on Lee's army. Grant, of course, had the advantage of a steady supply of manpower, so he could afford to fight the war of attrition. It was a fact greatly lost on the people of the North, however, who knew Grant's track record from Shiloh and saw massive casualty numbers during the Overland Campaign. Grant was routinely criticized as a butcher.

As fate would have it, the only time during the Overland Campaign Lee had a chance to take the initiative was after Spotsylvania. During the fighting that came to be known as the Battle of North Anna, Lee was heavily debilitated with illness. Grant nearly fell into Lee's trap by splitting his army in two along the North Anna before avoiding it.

By the time the two armies reached Cold Harbor near the end of May 1864, Grant incorrectly thought that Lee's army was on the verge of collapse. Though his frontal assaults had failed spectacularly at places like Vicksburg, Grant believed that Lee's army was on the ropes and could be knocked out with a strong attack. The problem was that Lee's men were now masterful at quickly constructing defensive fortifications, including earthworks and trenches, making their positions impregnable. While Civil War generals kept employing Napoleonic tactics, Civil War soldiers were building the types of defensive works that would be the harbinger of World War I's trench warfare.

At Cold Harbor, Grant decided to order a massive frontal assault against Lee's well fortified and entrenched lines. His decision was dead wrong, literally. Although the story of Union soldiers pinning their names on the back of their uniforms in anticipation of death at Cold Harbor is apocryphal, the frontal assault on June 3 inflicted thousands of Union casualties in about half an hour. With another 12,000 casualties at Cold Harbor, Grant had suffered about as many casualties in a month as Lee had in his entire army at the start of the campaign. Grant later admitted, ""I have always regretted that the last assault at Cold Harbor was ever made...No advantage whatever was gained to compensate for the heavy loss we sustained."

Chapter 22: The Siege of Petersburg

After the Confederate victory at Cold Harbor on June 12, 1864, General P.G.T. Beauregard attempted in vain to convince his superiors that Grant's next move would be to cross the James River and attempt to seize Petersburg, the main railroad hub of the Confederacy situated just miles away from Richmond. Beauregard proved prophetic; after Cold Harbor, Grant managed to successfully steal an entire day's march on Lee and crossed the James River, moving on the Confederacy's primary railroad hub at Petersburg with two Union Army corps totaling 16,000 men on June 15.

Incredibly, the war was saved right then and there by the quick and skillful defense of Petersburg organized by Beauregard and his 5,400 men, outnumbered 3 to 1 by the Union attackers. With Union forces breathing down their necks, Beauregard sent urgent messages to both Lee and the War Department asking for immediate reinforcements, despite serious doubts they could reach him in time. After the war, when the back and forth messages were publicly published, one historian noted, "Nothing illustrates better the fundamental weakness of the Confederate command system than the weary series of telegrams exchanged in May and early June between Davis, Bragg, Beauregard, and Lee. Beauregard evaded his responsibility for determining what help he could give Lee; Davis and Bragg shirked their responsibility to decide, when he refused. The strangest feature of the whole affair was that, in the face of Lee's repeated requests, nobody in the high command thought to order Beauregard to join Lee."

Meanwhile, for three days Union General William "Baldy" Smith seized Confederate artillery and occupied Confederate trenches, winning key positions that gave him and his troops unobstructed entrance into Petersburg. With each passing day, Beauregard assumed retreat was inevitable. But then just as events reached the critical point, Smith lost his nerve and decided to wait for reinforcements before launching his main attack, giving Confederate troops ample time to arrive and successfully fend off a series of assaults characterized as "poorly coordinated" and "driven home without vigor." Ultimately, Lee managed to get his Army of Northern Virginia to Beauregard before the Union could muster a proper attack.

By June 20, Grant had called off all attacks and opted to make a siege of Petersburg. And while Beauregard was credited with preventing a Union occupation -- the saving of Petersburg deemed his greatest military achievement -- Grant had nonetheless succeeded in occupying a fixed position that would greatly limit Lee's movement and give Grant the upper hand. Although Beauregard's actions had saved Petersburg from occupation -- and probable destruction -- they resulted in a ten-month siege of the city that ultimately proved successful for the North anyway.

The siege lines of Petersburg kept Lee completely pinned down and stretched his army. As Lee continued to maintain a tenuous grip there, Sherman's men in the West defeated Joseph E. Johnston and John Bell Hood in the Atlanta Campaign and then marched to sea, capturing Savannah by Christmas. Sherman's successes helped ensure Lincoln was reelected, ensuring the war would go on. Although he'd lost the use of his right arm and could not speak above a whisper, in October of 1864, Longstreet reassumed command of his corps and joined Lee's forces at Petersburg, Virginia. At Cedar Creek on October 19, Union General Philip Sheridan executed a stunning victory over Longstreet, capturing 43 pieces of Confederate artillery and taking numerous prisoners--including Confederate general Stephan Dodson.

Lee had almost no initiative, at one point futilely sending Jubal Early with a contingent through the Shenandoah Valley and toward Washington D.C. in an effort to peel off some of Grant's men. Though Early made it to the outskirts of Washington D.C. and Lincoln famously became the only president to come under enemy fire at Fort Stevens, the Union's "Little Phil" Sheridan pushed Early back through the Valley and scorched it.

Petersburg dragged on through the winter of 1864 as Grant continually advanced his frontline, slowly exhausting Lee's resources. The most famous battle during this time took place when Union engineers burrowed underneath the Confederate siege lines and lit the fuse on a massive amount of ammunition, creating a "crater" in the field. But even then, the Battle of the Crater ended with a Union debacle.

Entering 1865, the Confederacy was in utter disarray. Lee's Army of Northern Virginia had tenuously defended against Grant's siege at Petersburg for nearly six months. The main Confederate army in the West had been nearly destroyed at the Battle of Franklin weeks earlier. And Sherman's army faced little resistance as it marched through the Carolinas. By the time Lincoln delivered his Second Inaugural Address in March 1865, the end of the war was in sight.

Although Confederate leaders remained optimistic, by the summer of 1864 they had begun to consider desperate measures in an effort to turn around the war. From 1863-1865, Confederate leaders had even debated whether to conscript black slaves and enlist them as soldiers. Even as their fortunes looked bleak, the Confederates refused to issue an official policy to enlist blacks. It was likely too late to save the Confederacy anyway.

Lee's siege lines at Petersburg were finally broken on April 1 at the Battle of Five Forks, which is best remembered for Pickett enjoying a cod bake lunch while his men were being defeated. Historians have attributed it to unusual environmental acoustics that prevented Pickett and his staff from hearing the battle despite their close proximity, not that it mattered to the Confederates at the time. Between that and Gettysburg, Pickett and Lee were alleged to have held very poor opinions of each other by the end of the war, and there is still debate as to whether Lee had ordered Pickett out of the army during the Appomattox campaign.

After fighting raged all along the lines on April 2, the Army of Northern Virginia was finally forced to quit Petersburg, and with it Richmond.

Chapter 23: The Appomattox Campaign

Having retreated from Petersburg, Lee's battered army began stumbling toward a rail depot in the hopes of avoiding being surrounded by Union forces and picking up much needed food rations. While Grant's army continued to chase Lee's retreating army westward, the Confederate government sought to escape across the Deep South. On April 4, President Lincoln entered Richmond and toured the home of Confederate President Jefferson Davis.

Fittingly, the food rations did not arrive as anticipated. On April 7, 1865, Grant sent Lee the first official letter demanding Lee's surrender. In it Grant wrote, "The results of the last week must convince you of the hopelessness of further resistance on the part of the Army of Northern Virginia in this struggle. I feel it is so, and regret it as my duty to shift myself from the responsibility of any further effusion of blood by asking of you the surrender of that portion of the Confederate States army known as the Army of Northern Virginia." Passing the note to General Longstreet, now his only advisor, Longstreet said, "Not yet." But by the following evening during what would be the final Confederate Council of War (and after one final attempt had been made to break through Union lines), Lee finally succumbed, stating regretfully, "There is nothing left me but to go and see General Grant, and I had rather die a thousand deaths."

Communications continued until April 9, at which point Lee and Grant two met at Appomattox Court House. When Lee and Grant met, the styles in dress captured the personality differences perfectly. Lee was in full military attire, while Grant showed up casually in a muddy uniform. The Civil War's two most celebrated generals were meeting for the first time since the Mexican-American War.

The McLean Parlor in Appomattox Court House. McLean's house was famously fought around during the First Battle of Bull Run, leading him to move to Appomattox.

The Confederate soldiers had continued fighting while Lee worked out the terms of surrender, and they were understandably devastated to learn that they had surrendered. Some of his men had famously suggested to Lee that they continue to fight on. Porter Alexander would later rue the fact that he suggested to Lee that they engage in guerrilla warfare, which earned him a stern rebuke from Lee. As a choked-up Lee rode down the troop line on his famous horse Traveller that day, he addressed his defeated army, saying, "Men, we have fought through the war together. I have done my best for you; my heart is too full to say more." After surrendering, Lee wrote one last order to his army and a report to Confederate President Jefferson Davis, before heading home to Virginia to live out the rest of his days.

Appomattox is frequently cited as the end of the Civil War, but there still remained several Confederate armies across the country, mostly under the command of General Joseph E. Johnston, who Lee had replaced nearly 3 years earlier. On April 26, Johnston surrendered all of his forces to General Sherman. Over the next month, the remaining Confederate forces would surrender or quit. The last skirmish between the two sides took place May 12-13, ending ironically with a Confederate victory at the Battle of Palmito Ranch in Texas. Two days earlier, Jefferson Davis had been captured in Georgia.

Although the surrender of the Army of Northern Virginia to General Ulysses S. Grant and the Army of the Potomac at Appomattox Courthouse did not officially end the long and bloody Civil

War, the surrender is often considered the final chapter of the war. For that reason, Appomattox has captured the popular imagination of Americans ever since Lee's surrender there on April 9, 1865.

Lee on Traveller

Chapter 24: The Post-War Years

As a civilian for the first time in 40 years, the Proclamation of Amnesty and Reconstruction of 1865 prevented citizen Lee from holding public office even though he was many times encouraged to enter politics; he was, after all, a celebrity.

Even so, he applied for a complete personal pardon as provided for by the proclamation, hoping to set an example for other leading Southerners. In a paperwork snafu involving the required Oath of Allegiance, however, Lee did not receive his pardon in his lifetime, but a general amnesty did restore his right to vote. It wasn't until 1975 that a National Archive employee ran across Lee's sworn oath and Congress retroactively restored his American citizenship.

Although offered many prestigious positions, Lee opted to spend his final years as president of Washington College in Lexington, Virginia. While there, he raised the school's level of scholarship and established schools of commerce and journalism. With a growing fan club of sorts, young men from all across the South flocked to what became known as "General Lee's school," later christened Washington and Lee University.

While many statesmen of the South remained "unreconstructed" and spread bitterness, resentment, and hatred after the Confederacy's defeat, Lee openly urged his students and friends to maintain the peace and accept the outcome of the war. As a true "Washingtonian" and believer in what America represented as a whole, he spent his final years doing what he could to restore the political, economic, and social life of the South, urging all to "Make your sons Americans."

Lee had frequently been ill during the Civil War, and though he began collecting papers and records with which to write memoirs about the Civil War, his health began to quickly fail in early 1870. Lee died on October 12, 1870 of a stroke, outlived by his frail wife Mary, who died November 5, 1873. Lee was buried in the chapel he built on campus in Lexington, Virginia, along with his other family members; a building often referred to as "The Shrine of the South," a spot visited by thousands each year.

Lee's home has been preserved in Arlington National Cemetery, near Washington, D.C. Lee's birthday, January 19, is observed as a legal holiday in most Southern states. Lee represents Virginia in Statuary Hall in the Capitol in Washington.

Lee's Arlington House

Shortly after the end of the Civil War, James Longstreet was appointed the Adjutant General of the Louisiana State Militia by the Republican Governor of that state, and by 1872 became Major General in command of all New Orleans militia and state police forces.

In 1874, one of his most controversial post-War incidents occurred during protests of election irregularities, when an armed force of 8,400 "White League" members advanced on the State

House. Longstreet, in command of a 3,600 man force comprised of Metropolitan Police, city police, and African-American militia troops armed with two Gatling guns and a battery of artillery, foolishly rode into the crowd of protesters and was promptly pulled from his horse, shot, and taken prisoner. Emboldened by his capture, the 'White League' then charged, causing many of Longstreet's men to flee or surrender, with 38 men ultimately killed and 79 wounded, prompting Federal troops to be called in to restore order.

Longstreet's use of black troops during this disturbance increased his denunciations by anti-Reconstructionists.

Longstreet in later years

During the post-War Reconstruction, Longstreet fell drastically out of public favor. His political attitudes, criticism of Lee at Gettysburg (who Longstreet referred to as "Marse Robert," a term of endearment reserved for friends), and outspoken admiration for Radical Republican and former Union commander Ulysses S. Grant (who became the 18th President of the United States in 1869) only amplified the ire and resentment of the Southern people.

Moving to New Orleans, Longstreet took a position as an insurance company president but was soon ousted. Having joined the Republican Party, "Lincoln's Party", directly after the War, he found that all his employment (and personal) opportunities were limited to Republican prospects, which dried up after the Democrats assumed control. Thus he was forced to accept positions as postmaster, U. S. Marshall, and in 1880, Ambassador to Turkey (an appointment provided by President Grant). Then from 1896 (or 1898) until his death in 1904, he served as U. S. Commissioner of Railroads.

In June of 1867, Longstreet was asked by a reporter from a local newspaper how Louisiana should respond to the new Federal mandate that required former Confederate states to give Blacks the vote. Longstreet responded that the South should obey; that *might makes right*. "The ideas that divided political parties before the war, upon the rights of the States, were thoroughly discussed by our wisest statesmen, and eventually appealed to the arbitrament of the sword. The decision was in favor of the North . . . and should be accepted." Longstreet was immediately denounced as a traitor by many Southerners; some speculating that he had been a traitor all along. In his 1896 memoirs, he wrote that the day after he made that statement, "old comrades passed me on the streets without speaking."

In 1884, Longstreet relocated to Gainesville, Georgia, where he went into semi-retirement on a 65 acre farm his neighbors referred to mockingly as "Gettysburg," where he raised turkeys, grew orchards, and set up vineyards on terraced ground, all while writing his memoirs.

On April 9, 1889 (the 24th anniversary of Lee's surrender at Appomattox), a devastating fire occurred (which many saw simply as *come-uppance*) that destroyed Longstreet's house and most of his personal possessions, including his personal Civil War documents and memorabilia (which partly explains why so little written about his youth still exists). Then in December of that year, Maria Louise Garland, his wife of 40 years, died.

On September 8, 1897, the 76 year old Longstreet married his second wife, the 34 year old Helen Dortch of Atlanta, Georgia. Although Longstreet's children are said to have reacted poorly to the marriage, by all accounts, Helen was a devoted wife and avid supporter of James' legacy after his death. Helen would outlive James by 58 years, dying in 1962 at the age of 99.

In his final years, the American people, for the most part, seems to have forgotten about the post-War controversies and once again recognized Longstreet as a principal leader during the Civil War; once again recognizing him as the field commander who had once warranted the designation of Lee's "War Horse", even though it was a term he personally despised. He and General George Pickett remained friends to his final days.

In 1896, James Longstreet published his memoirs, *From Manassas to Appomattox*. While considered overtly defensive in tone and containing numerable inconsistencies, contradictions, half-truths, and outright lies, it is nonetheless viewed today as an important source of insight into the Civil War, this portion of American history, and of course, James Longstreet himself.

On January 2, 1904 at the age of nearly 83, Longstreet died while visiting Gainesville. He was buried in Alta Vista Cemetery, Hall County, Georgia.

An indication of how long it has taken for Longstreet to get the credit he deserved for his participation in the war can be found in the fact that only recently was a monument to Longstreet constructed at Gettysburg. There is no special recognition at Hollywood Cemetery in Richmond, Virginia (although there are for George Pickett and "Jeb" Stuart), and most, if not all, Confederate Generals are buried in Hollywood rather than Gettysburg National Cemetery.

According to *The Confederate Image: Prints of the Lost Cause*, "There [is] nothing mysterious about the scarcity of portraits of General Longstreet . . . it seems a near-miracle that two survive," (a lithograph by J. L. Giles and an engraving made in France by Goupil et cie.) As this text explains, the production of such prints "was determined by postwar myth as much as wartime performance, and there was good reason to shunt Longstreet aside for other heroes."

While it is true that for a brief period of time after Stonewall Jackson's death, General Longstreet held a command of great importance that *could* have led to assuming Jackson's former status as unequivocal champion of the South -- second only to Robert E. Lee -- immediately following the War, he quickly embraced what he termed "practical reconstruction and reconciliation," stating, "The sword has decided in favor of the North . . . [and Northern principles] cease to be principles and become law." After becoming an avowed Republican and Grant supporter in 1869 (as well as devout Catholic), the vast majority of Southerners shunned him. (It is most likely that the Giles lithograph was made before that date, before he was widely deemed a traitor.)

Chapter 25: The Legacy of Robert E. Lee

Although Lee saw war as a disintegrating and largely unnecessary response to social disapproval - an act of disloyalty that fundamentally undermines a society's stability - as a military man, Lee spent most of his mature life waiting for the next war and the next battle.

Lee hadn't chosen a career in law or politics or even farming (as he'd often said he'd prefer), he'd chosen the life of a soldier; a military strategist whose job it was to enable his side to overcome the opposition through cunning, ingenuity, and deception. And for all his moral and ethical aversion to armed dissention, in reality, his natural abilities and formidable training in accomplishing these goals weren't fully utilized in times of peace, only in times of war.

As a practical man who as a boy had watched his family suffer and disintegrate due to his father's irresponsibility, Lee had vowed never to subject his family to the same financial embarrassment and social indignation. And although history records Lee as a man of principles, more to the heart it seems, he was a man of duty. A man of peace who relied upon conflict. And it seems likely that he was torn between these two principles for most of his life.

Modern history describes Lee as a man who gave his loyalty, his industry, to the causes of the South although fundamentally, he opposed the enslavement of his fellow man. More flattering accounts emphasize that he'd actually given up his slaves long before the Civil War began.

More accurately, however, it wasn't so much that he'd "given up" his slaves as participated in slave-rental. And while Lee was never known to refer to human chattel as "slaves" or even the more popular, "darkies" (preferring instead, "the people"), Lee is quoted as saying, "The best men of the South have long desired to do away with the institution [of slavery] and were quite willing to see it abolished. But the question has ever been, 'What will you do with the freed people?'"

As records show, in late 1857, Lee inherited 63 slaves from his father-in-law, George Washington Parke Curtis. Though technically the property of his wife, Mary, responsibility for their care and maintenance ultimately fell to Lee as Master of the plantation. And while the principled Lee may have been repulsed by the idea of further subjugating these men, woman, and children under his charge, the pragmatic Lee, the dutiful Lee, knew that he could never provide for his family in the true Southern spirit--the way his wife Mary had long been accustomed-- without supplementing his officer's pay.

He needed to not only make certain that his wife and children wouldn't be left to their own devices should he die or be killed, but consider the immediate issues at hand: by the time his son Curtis started boarding school, tuition cost three hundred dollars a year; nearly a fourth of a captain's pay. Thus, as his family grew in size, so too did the necessity to compromise his principles. But as one story from his younger days demonstrates, for Lee, the issue couldn't have been nearly that cut and dry.

As the account is told, following the passing of his mother Anne, Lee's sister Mildred inherited responsibility for Nat, an elderly house servant and coachman, who in his old age, apparently suffered tuberculosis. On the advise that warmer climate might make Nat's final days more pleasant, the twenty-two year old Lee took Nat along with him to his post on Cockspur Island, where he is said to have nursed him with all the tenderness of a son through his final days. Thus, it seems that Lee's sense of responsibility and humanity rose far beyond simply supporting or opposing slavery. He genuinely saw his charges as *people*.

In the end, while the principled Lee may have seen slavery as an abomination against mankind--something he'd put an end to and something that would have pleased his wife who by this time had become an anti-slavery advocate--the practical Lee saw it as a necessary evil; a means to an end. The dutiful Lee found a way to compromise.

Ironically, though he had no use for post-war politics, Lee's legacy was crafted and embroiled in it. Though Lee accepted the South's loss, unreconstructed rebels continued to "fight" the Civil War with the pen, aiming to influence how the war was remembered. Much of this was accomplished by the Southern Historical Society, whose stated aim was the homogenization of Southern white males. But longstanding feuds between former generals found their way into the papers, and the feuds were frequently based on regional differences. These former Confederates looked to their idealized war heroes as symbols of their suffering and struggle. Based in Richmond, the Society's ideal Southern white male embodied the "Virginian" essence of aristocracy, morality and chivalry. The Society's ideal male, of course, was Robert E. Lee. David Blight credits the Society for creating a "Lee cult" that dominates public perception to this day. Writing about this perception of Lee, Charles Osbourne described the perception as "an edifice of myth built on the foundation of truth…the image became an icon."

With Lee being pushed forward as the quintessential Southern man, he began to be treated as the ideal man and ideal leader. This sentiment eventually began to influence Northern views of the man as well. An equestrian statue of Lee that was unveiled in Richmond in 1890 sparked an outburst of sentimentality that affected the North as well as the South. Reporting on the unveiling of the Lee statue, the *New York Times* referred to the memory of Lee as a "possession of the American people" and called the monument a "National possession." As far west as Minnesota, it was noted that the "Lee cult" was "in vogue." Not all Northerners shared the sentimental appreciation of the Lee cult. Frederick Douglass found that he could "scarcely take up a newspaper…that is not filled with nauseating flatteries of the late Robert E. Lee."

Few men in American history--perhaps, General George Armstrong Custer, General Douglas MacArthur, and General George S. Patton--can be so clearly defined by their military accomplishments as Robert E. Lee. Though by most accounts he was a loving and attentive husband and father, a family man with tiny feet who loved to have his children tickle them, that part of him pales in comparison to his demonstration of duty. Even as the leader of a failed cause, his sense of humility and selflessness gives him an extraordinarily unique and unparalleled place in American history.

As a soldier, Lee's strongest attribute was his natural ability to access a military situation and quickly devise an effective strategy. He excelled in his capacity to anticipate an opponent's moves and then outmaneuver them--often with inferior numbers and resources at his dispose. Never did he settle to meet the enemy on even tactical terms, and by most measure, he was unparalleled in American military history as a battlefield strategist.

Although field entrenchments had been used as a method of defense long before the founding of America, Lee refined this ancient science into a fine, fluid, and adaptive art--one that's studied today on university campuses across the land. He was a guerilla fighter with the mental agility of a ballerina; the optimal warrior in this place and time in American history when that was precisely what was called for. This, added to his power to arouse unparalleled devotion in his men, provided--quite handily--the South's greatest chance to end their war victoriously. Quite remarkable for a man who'd often remarked that all he really ever wanted to be was a farmer.

Still, Lee was far from perfect, despite the attempts of the Southern Historical Society to defend his war record as fault free, at the expense of some of his subordinates. Given that the Confederacy lost the war, some historians have pointed out that Lee was often too eager to engage in offensive warfare. After all, Lee scored large and smashing victories at places like Chancellorsville that deprived him of more manpower against opponents that could afford casualties more than he could. Moreover, for the engineer who used tactics to successfully defend against typical Civil War tactics, he all too often engaged in the same futile offensive tactics himself, none more costly than Pickett's Charge.

More objective analysts, including those among Lee's contemporaries like Longstreet and Porter Alexander, pointed out that despite these kinds of criticisms, it was Lee's daring tactics and successes that extended the Civil War so many years. Pointing out how many more casualties Lee's armies inflicted compared to those he lost, many of his subordinates compared him favorably to Napoleon, even if Lee never won the necessary complete victory.

Much of what we know today about the Civil War comes from letters, government correspondences, and journal entries made by the soldiers involved, both Confederate and Union. Although Lee was never able to write memoirs, he was prolific letter writer, contributed abundantly to all three. Even in the heat of battle, it seems, his first impulse was to document his thoughts; express in words the complexities of his emotional state, mental reasoning, and assessment of the situation as he saw it. These correspondences provide invaluable insight not just into Lee the man, Lee the soldier, and Lee the husband and father, but insight into a period of American history which for the most part only received serious, unbiased reporting years after the fact.

Described by biographer Roy Blount, Jr. as "a sort of precursor-cross between England's Cary Grant and Virginia's Randolph Scott"--and perhaps the most beautiful person in America-- Robert E. Lee is perhaps the most written-about character of the Civil War era next to President Lincoln himself. Depicted as a handsome war hero, unifying national figure in the aftermath of a war-torn country, and a symbol of what is noble and just in the American spirit, Lee's image has evolved over time.

After Lee's death, former Maryland slave, writer, and statesman Frederick Douglass wrote, "[I]t would seem . . . that the soldier who kills the most men in battle--even in a bad cause--is the greatest Christian and entitled to the highest place in heaven." Some 37 years later on the eve of the Celebration of the Hundredth Anniversary of Lee's birth, President Theodore Roosevelt wrote, "[Lee] stood that hardest of all strains, the strain of bearing himself well through the gray evening of failure; and therefore out of what seemed failure he helped to build the wonderful and mighty triumph of our national life, in which all his countrymen, north and south, share." And now approaching a century and a half after his death, history has shown an iconic evolution from mere post-war personality to what biographer Thomas L. Connelly terms a man considered a "military genius and a spiritual leader, the nearest thing to a saint that the white South has possessed."

There can be no doubt that Lee's lasting legend is a combination of both fact and fiction; myth and understatement. As was common in 19th century America, heroes weren't always born--they were sometimes made. And it seems likely that what we now know of Lee was a carefully constructed conglomeration of both. In fact, immediately following his death, a group of Virginians led by general Jubal Early began a campaign to make Lee a national idol, a campaign that undoubtedly flavored 19th century biographies attempting to paint a fair yet colorful portrait of the iconic war hero. Immediately after the war, Grant was initially the most *popular* Civil War figure, but he was soon eclipsed.

As someone once astutely observed, 'Desperate times call for desperate measures,' and for many, America suffered no more desperate times than when brothers were called upon to take arms against bothers. And if survival of such an unnatural ordeal required the glorification--even exaggeration--of one who seemed to do it best, then we can hardly condemn those who may have sought to assure their success. But by any measure, Robert E. Lee was indeed an extraordinary individual who demonstrated through actions what we have come to define as the "American Spirit." In the face of unprecedented adversity, he repeatedly stood up, stepped forward, and sacrificed himself for the greater good. And that's why he holds the place in American history that he does.

Chapter 26: The Legacy of Stonewall Jackson

Jackson's death on the battlefield in May 1863 brought him instant hero status. Following a nationwide outpouring of grief, the *Atlanta Southern Confederacy* posed, "Who will rise to fill his place? Who will be the future great and renowned chief to fill the place of Stonewall Jackson?" Similarly, the *Atlanta Daily Intelligencer* called him "the idol of the people and army." And when the editor of the Richmond *Sentinel* learned of his battlefield death, he is said to have lamented, "No life is dearer to the people. Oh, who can take the place in our armies. Who can fill his place in our hearts?"

A few months before the battle that took "Stonewall's" life, Virginia novelist-turned-war-correspondent John Esten Cooke published one of the first highly flattering Jackson biographies, a three-part series published in *Southern Illustrated News* entitled, "Stonewall Jackson and the Old Stonewall Brigade," in which the author writes, "Greatest of the Generals is General Stonewall Jackson. No soldier of the war has been more uniformly successful in his undertakings. [Jackson's victories] left behind the great funeral procession of whipped generals--dead reputations."

While by and large, Jackson was seen as essentially, Robert E. Lee's right hand man--the brawn behind Lee's formidable brains--a growing contingency portrayed Jackson as an impressive field strategist. A man who had often followed his own instincts to the Confederate Army's benefit. But, from 1870 and 1885, he was slowly transformed from astute strategist to "able but eccentric subordinate whose successes were mainly due to his ability to carry out Lee's plans"--with Lee himself have unwittingly helped initiate the rewriting--the demotion, as it were--of Jackson's image.

In mid-1863, John Esten Cooke approached the Jackson family with *Life of Stonewall Jackson, the Hero of the Present War for Independence*, his flattering treatment of Jackson's life. He was certain that the fawning account published earlier in the *Southern Illustrated News* would garner him preferential treatment as the Jackson family official biographer. The Jackson family, however, had already chosen Stonewall's former chief of staff, the Presbyterian chaplain Robert L. Dabney (March 5, 1820 – January 3, 1898), as the *official* "Stonewall" biographer. Ignoring the Jackson family's wishes, Cooke quickly published his *unauthorized* biography, which Dabney quickly countered with *True Courage: A Discourse Commemorative of Lieutenant General Thomas J. Jackson*. A flood of other unauthorized biographies then hit the market including sensationalist writer Catherine Hopley's *"Stonewall" Jackson*, Georgia poet H. M.

Thompson's *The Death of Jackson*, and even a children's book glorifying his exploits.

In late 1865, Stonewall's widow asked Robert E. Lee to read *Life of General Thomas J. Jackson,* Robert Lewis Dabney's new manuscript (which would be published in 1866), and give his candid opinion of the account Dabney intended to present as fact. Upon reading the manuscript, Lee referred to "some errors into which the author has no doubt inadvertently fallen." In early 1866, Mrs. Jackson implored Lee to provide a list of the errors so that Dabney could correct them, unaware that Lee had thought Jackson was being given far too much credit for the army's successes and that officers of the other corps might reasonably think, "less weight than was due had been given to the effect they produce" in battle.

Additionally, Dabney's account of the Seven Days' Battle did not fault Jackson's performance on the battlefield, claiming, that "Jackson's arrival on the Peninsula brought a strength 'beyond that of his numbers'"--which Lee knew was wholly untrue. And while Lee did not wish to detract from his most loyal general's fame, as more and more erroneous accounts began to circulate, he felt it his duty to set the historic record straight.

In late 1867, an article describing the events of the Campaign of Chancellorsville--the battle in which Lee had taken on and defeated Union Army Maj. General Joseph Hooker's Army with an army less than half the size--appeared in the *Southern Review,* crediting Jackson with masterminding the choice to divide the troops to outflank the enemy; the decisive strategy that ultimately brought a Confederate victory. When asked by *Review* editor Albert Bledsoe for a response, Lee wrote back "every move of an army must be properly ordered [so] there was no question as to who was responsible for the operations of the Confederates, or whom any failure would have been charged." Thus began a concerted campaign to set things straight--to credit Lee where credit was due, and to credit Jackson where credit was due.

Among the first to come to Lee's defense was former Confederate general Jubal Early, who'd served under both Jackson and Lee and was the Confederate commander in several key battles of the Valley Campaigns of 1864 including a daring raid on the outskirts of Washington, D.C., who in the late 1860s made a formal address in Washington, giving full credit to Lee for Chancellorsville.

Then in 1874, the "Fighting Parson" Baptist evangelist J. William Jones, who'd ministered to troops under both Jackson and Lee, published *Personal Reminiscences* in which he reprinted the Bledsoe letter, stating "it is due alike to General Lee and to the truth of history." Three years later, Colonel Walter Taylor in his *Four Years with General Lee,* agreed that Lee had devised the strategy for Jackson's most effective flank attack. But by and large, history credits Fitzhugh Lee and his "Southern Tours," with recasting history and ultimately setting the "Stonewall" Jackson story straight.

Fitzhugh Lee (November 19, 1835–April 28, 1905), nephew of Robert E. Lee, was a Confederate cavalry general in the Civil War who'd served at Bull Run, the Northern Virginia Campaign, the Maryland Campaign of 1862, and in the Battle of Chancellorsville. It had been Fitzhugh Lee's reconnaissance that discovered that the Union Army's right flank was open, allowing Jackson to successfully outmaneuver Hooker--a movement led by Lee's cavalry.

In 1879, Fitzhugh Lee addressed a meeting of the Army of Northern Virginia Association, announcing that he was determined to settle any remaining questions regarding who had conceived the now "famed" flanking maneuver that had taken place at Chancellorsville. Denying that his uncle "had been fooled by Hooker's march across the Rappahannock River"--as several Jackson supporters had insisted in the years following the war, he emphasized Robert's "almost superhuman intelligence," describing Jackson as "overconfident and convinced that Hooker would retreat"--which he did not. "[Robert E. Lee] was the only one who wisely knew that a battle must be fought at Chancellorsville. Consequently, Lee ordered Jackson to make the flanking march around Hooker's right wing." Continuing his "Southern Tours" until 1882, Fitzhugh Lee travelled throughout the South, reiterating that beneath Jackson's success was the genius of Robert E. Lee.

Unfortunately, however, as word spread and public perception shifted, it became difficult to know Jackson's true role in not only Chancellorsville--but other battles. Although it had long been accepted that Robert E. Lee had found Jackson a very competent general whose loyalty and valor were unquestioned, suddenly his accomplishments became buried beneath uncertainty and relentless scrutiny (something, by all known accounts, Robert E. Lee would not have wanted).

In a series of articles appearing in the Southern Historical Society's *Papers*, Jackson's performance at Seven Days' Battles (which took place June 25 to July 1, 1862, near Richmond) was attacked--now holding him responsible for General McClellan's defeat. This was followed by a new accounting of the battle of Mechanicsville in which "Jackson's men were too late . . . to get into the fight or help their comrades" and details about battles at Gaines' Mill and Frazier's Farm in which "other Rebel units had to bear the brunt because Jackson had been delayed" and Jackson "made a great blunder [by his] feeble effort to cross the White Swamps and remained an idle spectator of the gallant fight." Well into the next century, historians and the American public continued to speculate as to what Jackson had actually done in the war.

Despite the arguments among Confederate veterans in the years after the war, Stonewall Jackson continues to be considered one of the greatest generals of the Civil War and American history. Jackson possessed a strong military background even before the outbreak of the Civil War. His training in the U.S. Military Academy at West Point, recognition as a man of fearless resolve in the Mexican-American War, and his experience as an instructor at the Virginia

Military Institute, easily justified his rank of brigadier general at the first major battle of the Civil War near Manassas, Virginia. What he ever lacked in experience, he more than made up for in loyalty and resolve.

However, Jackson's untimely death just two years into the Civil War cut him down at the height of what most military historians believe might have been a gloriously successful career, leaving behind a string of unanswered questions regarding his ability to command independently; the reliability of his decision-making skills in the field.

While recognized as among the ablest of General Robert E. Lee's generals--*yes*, he obeyed and carried out his orders to the letter--after his death, a closer examination of his military actions called into question the results he'd produced and been credited for. Though a recognized master of rapid deployment and surprise attacks, his intentions were so veiled in secrecy--his "stonewall" visage--that even his own officers seldom knew his battle plans until instructed to execute them--and sometimes, not even then. So, which results were by design; which by happenstance?

There can be no denying that not only did Stonewall Jackson make unilateral decisions that affected his army--and his army's effectiveness in battle--but that Lee's contention that 'every move of an army must be properly ordered [so] there was no question as to who was responsible for the operations of the Confederates, or whom any failure would have been charged' seems slightly disingenuous, especially because Lee often gave discretionary orders to his principal subordinates.

Never was this more clear than during the Gettysburg campaign, when JEB Stuart interpreted Lee's orders as giving him latitude to make a circuitous cavalry raid around the Army of the Potomac that left Lee's army stumbling blindly into Day 1 of the Battle of Gettysburg. And on the first day of that battle, Richard S. Ewell's Corps flanked the Army of the Potomac's I and XI Corps and pushed them back through the town until they began to dig in on high ground to the southeast of the town. It was at this point that Lee arrived on the field and saw the importance of this position. He sent discretionary orders to Ewell that Cemetery Hill be taken "if practicable." Ewell chose not to attempt the assault. Lee's order has been criticized because it left too much discretion to Ewell (who succeeded Jackson to corps command), leaving historians to speculate on how the more aggressive Stonewall Jackson would have acted on this order if he had lived to command this wing of Lee's army, and how differently the second day of battle would have proceeded with Confederate possession of Culp's Hill or Cemetery Hill. Discretionary orders were customary for General Lee because Jackson and Longstreet, his other principal subordinate, usually reacted to them aggressively and used their initiative to act quickly and forcefully. Ewell's decision not to attack, whether justified or not, may have ultimately cost the Confederates the battle.

Indeed, history reflects that Jackson did indeed take it upon himself to make critical decisions; some that benefited the Confederate cause, some that worked against them.

Today, the "Stonewall" Jackson Shrine is the plantation office building where General Jackson died, now part of Fredericksburg & Spotsylvania National Military Park. The office was one of several outbuildings on Thomas C. Chandler's 740-acre plantation named "Fairfield." This typical frame structure saw use primarily by the men for recreation, but for work as well. Chandler kept records in the office and one of his sons once practiced medicine there, but with three of the Chandler boys away serving in the Confederate Army, the building no longer witnessed its ante-bellum level of activity after Jackson's demise.

The Chandler Plantation

Chapter 27: The Legacy of James Longstreet

For decades after his death, Longstreet, who was called "Old Pete" by his troops and "Old War Horse" by Lee, was viewed primarily through his arguments with other Confederate generals, his own analyses, and his memoirs. In sum, he was viewed very unflatteringly. To an extent this continues. As historians have since discovered, once weighted against known historical facts,

Longstreet's descriptions not only contain flights of fantasy and self-aggrandizing (as autobiographical accounts are prone to do), they contain gross inaccuracies, distortions, and outright lies. Many of his descriptions of events simply did not, *could* not, have occurred as he states. He exaggerates his combat record, grossly overrates his reputation as a corps leader, and boasts of a level of confidence with Lee that simply did not exist. Thus as is academically prudent in such cases, Longstreet's version of history in the memoirs is largely discounted.

Some continue to assert that Longstreet was too selfish and had too high an opinion of himself. To these people, a cursory evaluation of Longstreet's service record makes it clear that whether or not one holds him responsible for the South's defeat at Gettysburg, his behavior there was not an isolated--or even *out-of-character*--incident. It was, in fact, just another episode in a long pattern of behavior at odds with a man entrusted with the second-highest position in the Confederate Army. Even as early as the Battle of Seven Pines on May 31, 1862, though not a particularly significant battle for Longstreet, he'd already begun to reveal ambitions that far exceeded his limitations. Though initially appearing to be a simple unwillingness to cooperate, the underlying disconnect manifested again at Second Manassas (where he responded dangerously slow and was reluctant to attack), his attempted siege of Suffolk (which weighed heavily against him until Lee and Jackson's victory at Chancellorsville overshadowed his lack of good judgment), and then at Knoxville (where his failure was categorically written off as just "one of the winter of 1863-1864 disasters").

Long before Gettysburg, Longstreet was characterized by his men and commanders as "congenitally resistant to hurry himself," resistant to change of orders (even from his supreme commander, Lee), and disliked to overextend his men (once bivouacked, he allowed his men to prepare three-days' rations before breaking camp, even when they were supposed to stick to a timetable). In fact, his designation as Lee's "old reliable" appears to have been bestowed by someone who had never actually worked with him or had to rely upon him.

Similarly, Longstreet's clash with A. P. Hill, then Jackson, Hood and Toombs, were indicative of his unwillingness to accept that he was not the center of attention; not the one destined for greatness. And, of course, as the War progressed, Longstreet's propensity to find fault (and start feuds) with Lafayette McLaws (who he tried to have court-martialed), Evander Law (who he tried to have arrested), Charles Field, and ultimately, Lee himself, was highly indicative of the self-possessed illusion Longstreet was living (and fighting) under. While always quick to reprimand any subordinate who questioned his orders, he clearly hesitated to resist orders from his superiors on occasions. In his Gettysburg account, Longstreet had the impudence to blame Lee for "not changing his plans" based on Longstreet's "want of confidence in them."

On the surface, it's easy to assume that Longstreet paid his dues and earned his advancement in the Confederate Army. And in that he was one of the final hold-outs who resisted surrender to the Union until the South was out of options, it's also easy to assume that his loyalty--at least during the conflict--was to the Southern cause. But many historians believe that assumption may be ill-conceived.

As a captain in the U. S. Army, Longstreet transferred to the paymaster department in order to achieve a higher rank and pay, that of major, having "denounced all dreams of military glory." Subsequently, (by the majority of accounts), when he enlisted in the Confederate Army, he did not join the troop complement of any particular state--as most soldiers loyal to their state did--he applied directly for the paymaster post, thus securing for himself rank and privilege.

In that Longstreet arrived at Richmond from a New Mexican garrison *via* Texas, arriving later than most officers who came from various army outposts, he *coincidentally* arrived in the War Office at precisely the time a brigadier general was being selected for three regiments of Virginia volunteers. The result of this *coincidence* was that Longstreet started as a brigadier general when most of his peers (some of whom were better experienced) were starting as colonels. This meant that at promotion time, he made major general while they were only making brigadier. Thus, when Lee took control and was forming his two corps, Longstreet's seniority made him next in line for command (alongside "Stonewall" Jackson). But from several military historians' perspectives, he was not the best qualified--just *coincidentally* in the right place at the right time.

After General Robert E. Lee died in October of 1870, a group of ex-Confederates led by General Jubal Early (who had led a division in Ewell's corps at Gettysburg) publicly criticized Longstreet for ignoring orders and delaying his attack on the second day of the Battle on July 2, 1863. But while many former Confederates held Longstreet accountable for not following orders, Early took it one step further, arguing that Longstreet -- not Lee -- was responsible for the Confederate defeat (deemed a "tactical disaster" by most) that by most accounts was the beginning of the end for the Confederacy.

Early

In his memoirs, however, Longstreet defended himself, saying that the blistering post-War attacks concerning Gettysburg were merely "payback for supporting Black suffrage", thus shifting the blame back to Lee. He wrote, "[Lee] knew that I did not believe that success was possible . . . he should have put an officer in charge who had more confidence in his plan." He went on to say that Lee should have given the responsibility to Early, thus justifying his insubordination.

It's also important to note that Lee himself never made any post-War statements to suggest that he held Longstreet responsible for the Confederacy's demise.

Despite what many considered to be some critical military and personal failures and shortcomings, General James Longstreet is regarded by many today as one of the best, if not *the* best, tactical commanders on either side of the War, even though he did not do well in independent command. Although his emphatic belief that the Confederacy should fight a "strategic offensive-tactical defensive" war was in direct conflict with his commanders (including General Lee), some historians (including Jeffry D. Wert) believe that had Lee followed Longstreet's advice, it is quite likely that not only would the Southern army have endured longer, it possibly would have won the war.

While historians and scholars will continue to disagree on Longstreet's ultimate level of negligence (or incompetence), everyone agrees that he did have a profound effect on the War. And even those who have criticized him have pointed out how thoroughly competent he was when battle was actually joined. Biographer Jeffry Wert wrote "Longstreet ... was the finest corps commander in the Army of Northern Virginia; in fact, he was arguably the best corps commander in the conflict on either side." Richard L. DiNardo wrote, "Even Longstreet's most virulent critics have conceded that he put together the best staff employed by any commander, and that his de facto chief of staff, Lieutenant Colonel G. Moxley Sorrel, was the best staff officer in the Confederacy."

Longstreet's reputation has also been on the upswing in the past few decades, due in no small part to Michael Shaara's 1974 novel *The Killer Angels*, which portrayed Longstreet in a more flattering light. That novel was the basis for the 1993 film *Gettysburg*, which has also helped rehabilitate Longstreet's legacy and helped make clear to the public how instrumental he was during the war. In 1982, Thomas L. Connolly and Barbara L. Bellows published *God and General Longstreet*, which took the Lost Cause proponents like Early to task for their blatant fabrications (such as the one that Lee ordered Longstreet to attack in the early morning of Day 2 of Gettysburg), helping make clear the extent of historical revision propagated by the Lost Cause. In doing so, they cast Longstreet as a sympathetic victim of circumstances and sectional and political hostility.

No analysis of Longstreet's contribution to the Civil War would be just or complete without first recognizing the leadership methodology Lee used in guiding his commanders. As many historians point out, in that Lee had not personally trained his field commanders, he was forced to accept these men as they came. Accordingly, Lee's leadership style was designed to promote the individual man's initiative (which most cite as a weakness in his leadership), encouraging them to explore their fullest potential through independent thought.

Thus, Lee did not dictate precise orders (which by his reasoning would have denied each leader's creative participation and sharing of responsibility) but offered what was generally perceived as suggestions or *discretionary* orders. This loose approach to leadership obliged Lee to depend heavily upon each of his field commander's judgment, which, as it turned out, was often in conflict with his own. While some commanders, like "Stonewall" Jackson, urged aggressive and quick movements, others, like Longstreet, preferred defensive tactics. In fact, many historians believe the only reason Longstreet may have blundered during Day 2 of Gettysburg is because Lee gave a discretionary order to a conservative general (Ewell), who refused to take the initiative and attack Culp's Hill on the first night of the battle. Had Jackson survived Chancellorsville and received the same order, he might have made the attack, and if it succeeded there never would have been a 3 day battle at Gettysburg.

For that reason, many military historians contend that as supreme field commander of the Confederate forces, Lee should have adapted his leadership style to best serve the Southern interests, or removed Longstreet at the first sign that he could not be depended upon to follow Lee's lead.

Lee Bibliography

Freeman, Douglas Southall. *R.E. Lee: A Biography*, 1934-5.

Blount, Jr., Roy. *Robert E. Lee*. New York: Penguin Books, 2003.

Connelly, Thomas L. *The Marble Man: Robert E. Lee and His Image in American Society*. New York: Alfred A. Knopf, 1977.

Dowdey, Clifford (editor). *The Wartime Papers of R. E. Lee*. New York: Bramhall House, 1961.

Fellman, Michael. *The Making of Robert E. Lee*. New York: Random House, 2000.

Flood, Charles. *Lee: The Last Years*. New York: Houghton, 1981.

Horn, Stanley F. (editor). *The Robert E. Lee Reader*. New York: Konecky & Konecky, 1949.

Nagel, Paul C. *The Lee's of Virginia*. New York: Oxford University Press, 1990.

Pryor, Elizabeth Brown (October 29, 2009). "Robert Edward Lee (ca. 1806-1870)," *Encyclopedia Virginia*. Retrieved March 11, 2012.

Thomas, Emory M. *Robert E. Lee: A Biography*. New York: W. W. Norton & Company, 1995.

Van Doren Stern, Philip. *Robert E. Lee: The Man and the Soldier*. New York: Bonanza Books, 1963.

Jackson Bibliography

Biel, Timothy L. *The Civil War*. San Diego: Lucent Books, 1991.

Connelly, Thomas L. *The Marble Man: Robert E. Lee and His Image in American Society*. New York: Alfred A. Knopf, 1977.

Davis, Burke. *They Called Him Stonewall: A Life of Lieutenant General T. J. Jackson, C. S. A.*

New York: Holt, Rinehart and Winston, 1968.

Dupuy, Trevor. *The Military History of the Civil War*. New York: Franklin Watts Inc., 1961.

Fellman, Michael. *The Making of Robert E. Lee*. New York: Random House, 2000.

Horn, Stanley F. (editor). *The Robert E. Lee Reader*. New York: Konecky & Konecky, 1949.

Vandiver, Frank E. *Mighty Stonewall*. New York: McGraw-Hill, 1957.

Virginia Military Institute website: http://www.vmi.edu/archives.aspx?id=4933

The American Civil War, Battle of Antietam: http://www.brotherswar.com/Antietam-14.htm

Handy Timeline Reference: http://www.americancivilwar.com/south/stonewall_jackson.html

Longstreet Bibliography

Alexander, Edward P. (Gary W. Gallagher, editor). *Fighting for the Confederacy: The Personal Recollections of General Edward Porter Alexander*. Chapel Hill: University of North Carolina Press, 1989.

Catton, Bruce. *This Hallowed Ground*. New York: Doubleday & Company, Inc., 1956.

Davis, Kenneth C. *The Civil War: Everything You Need to Know About America's Greatest Conflict but Never Learned*. New York: William Morrow and Company, Inc., 1996.

Dowdey, Clifford. *Lee's Last Campaign: The Story of Lee & His Men against Grant--1864*. Lincoln: University of Nebraska Press, 1988.

Gaffney, P., and D. Gaffney. *The Civil War: Exploring History One Week at a Time*. New York: Hyperion, 2011.

Garrison, Webb. *Civil War Curiosities*. Nashville: Rutledge Hill Press, 1994.

Lanning, Michael Lee. *The Civil War 100*. Illinois: Sourcebooks, Inc., 2006.

Neely, Mark E., Holzer, Harold & Boritt, Gabor S. *The Confederate Image*. Chapel Hill: The

University of North Carolina Press, 1987.

Phillips, Kevin. *The Cousins' Wars*. New York: Basic Books, 1999.

Rhea, Gordon C. *The Battle of the Wilderness May 5–6, 1864*. Baton Rouge: Louisiana State University Press, 1994.

Sanger, Donald B., & Thomas Robson Hay. *James Longstreet, I: Soldier*. Baton Rouge: Louisiana State University Press, 1952.

Sell, Bill. *Civil War Chronicles: Leaders of the North and South*. New York: MetroBooks, 1996.

Stepp, John, W. and Hill, William I. (editors). *Mirror of War, The Washington Star Reports the Civil War*. The Evening Star Newspaper Co., 1961.

Tagg, Larry. *The Generals of Gettysburg*. CA: Savas Publishing, 1998.

Wert, Jeffry D. *General James Longstreet: The Confederacy's Most Controversial Soldier: A Biography*. New York: Simon & Schuster, 1993.

Patrick Cleburne
Chapter 1: Cleburne's Early Years

Patrick Ronayne Cleburne was born on March 16 or 17, 1828 in Ovens, County Cork, Ireland, at Bride Park Cottage, the third child and second son born to prominent middle-class doctor Joseph Cleburne and his wife Mary Anne Ronayne. Despite the uncertainty over his birthday, it is commonly believed that Patrick was born on St. Patrick's Day, thus accounting for his given name. Among Patrick's siblings were sister Anne, and brothers William and Joseph.

In 1829 when Patrick was just 18 months old, his mother died. A short time later, his father married Isabella Stewart, resulting in three half-siblings: Isabella, Robert, and Christopher.

In 1836 when Patrick (whom his family called "Ronayne") was 8 years of age, his family moved to Grange Farm near Ballincollig, a little town about six miles west of Cork City in County Cork, Ireland. While there, Patrick attended Church of Ireland Reverend William Spedding's boarding school, in addition to being home-educated.

In November of 1843, Patrick's father Joseph contracted typhus from a patient and died suddenly, unexpectedly orphaning his children. The 15 year old "Ronayne" was now expected to carry on the family profession of medicine, an ironic career path considering his ultimate fate.

With plans to enroll in Apothecary Hall, an association of apothecaries founded in 1791 in Dublin, Ireland, Patrick apprenticed for two years but then failed the language portion of the entrance exam in February of 1846. An alternate account describes Patrick as having failed the entrance exam to Trinity College of Medicine [the sole residential college of the University of Dublin in Ireland] which may or may not be one and the same. Too ashamed to return home, he enlisted in Her Majesty's Forty-First Regiment of Foot of the British Army, expecting to be sent to British-occupied India. Coincidentally enough, the 41st Regiment had served with distinction during the War of 1812, where it was the most decorated unit and participated in the capture of Detroit.

Although Cleburne had anticipated he would be sent to India, his regiment was instead assigned to a post in Mullingar, located in County Westmeath, Ireland, for civil duties related to the nationwide crisis surrounding the Great Irish Famine. For three and a half years, Private Cleburne was posted at various barracks around famine-stricken Ireland.

After serving during the violent months of the 1848 Young Ireland Rebellion, a failed Irish nationalist uprising led by the Young Ireland Movement on July 29, 1848 in the village of Ballingarry, County Tipperary, Private Cleburne was promoted to corporal on July 1, 1849. A short time later, however, he bought his discharge from the British Army.

After three years in the British Army, Patrick Cleburne was once again a civilian, but rather than being greeted by the warm welcome he'd expected upon returning home, he arrived to discover that the family farm was six months in arrears in rent. His stepmother suggested that the four eldest children (Patrick, his older sister Anne, and two brothers William and Joseph) immigrate to America. Thus, on November 5, 1849, Patrick and his siblings boarded the ship at Bridgetown, bound for America and an incredibly uncertain future.

Chapter 2: Antebellum Years

Arriving in New Orleans, Louisiana, on Christmas Day, 1849, employment naturally became the siblings' first priority, with Patrick, Anne, William, and Joseph heading up the Mississippi River in search of work. Separating a short time later, Patrick spent a short time in Cincinnati, Ohio where he worked as a pharmacist, then moved on to Helena, Arkansas, where in April of 1850 he became a druggist and business partner at *Nash and Grant's Drugstore*.

Despite being a young immigrant, Patrick quickly became part of Helena's social scene, and a short time later Patrick became close friends with attorney (and future Confederate Major General) Thomas C. Hindman, who encouraged Patrick to study law. In December of 1855, Patrick and Thomas Hindman formed a business partnership with a man named William Weatherly to buy the local newspaper, the *Democratic Star*. The following year, shortly after achieving his American citizenship through the 5 year naturalization process, Patrick sat and passed the Arkansas bar examination, subsequently becoming a partner in Hindman's law firm. Joining numerous social clubs and affiliations, Patrick quickly grew to love his new community, taking part in many civic projects, and even becoming one of the few to volunteer to care for the sick during a yellow fever outbreak.

Hindman

As Cleburne was starting to settle in, the United States was trying to sort out its intractable issues. In an attempt to organize the center of North America – Kansas and Nebraska – without offsetting the slave-free balance, Senator Stephen Douglas of Illinois proposed the Kansas-Nebraska Act. The Kansas-Nebraska Act eliminated the Missouri Compromise line of 1820, which the Compromise of 1850 had maintained. The Missouri Compromise had stipulated that states north of the boundary line determined in that bill would be free, and that states south of it *could* have slavery. This was essential to maintaining the balance of slave and free states in the Union. The Kansas-Nebraska Act, however, ignored the line completely and proposed that all new territories be organized by popular sovereignty. Settlers could vote whether they wanted their state to be slave or free.

Stephen Douglas, "The Little Giant"

After becoming an American citizen, Patrick Cleburne joined the Democratic Party, the completely dominant party across the South. However, while the Democrats were the power in the future Confederate states because of their support of the extension of slavery, Cleburne had no position on the nation's most divisive issue. Cleburne never owned slaves, and he had actually voiced his opposition to the South's "peculiar institution", but he felt an unswerving loyalty to the community that had welcomed him so openly.

When popular sovereignty became the standard in Kansas and Nebraska, the primary result was that thousands of zealous pro-slavery and anti-slavery advocates both moved to Kansas to influence the vote, creating a dangerous (and ultimately deadly) mix. Numerous attacks took place between the two sides, and many pro-slavery Missourians organized attacks on Kansas towns just across the border.

The best known abolitionist in Bleeding Kansas was a middle aged man named John Brown. A radical abolitionist, Brown organized a small band of like-minded followers and fought with the armed groups of pro-slavery men in Kansas for several months, including a notorious incident known as the Pottawatomie Massacre, in which Brown's supporters murdered five men. Over 50 people died before John Brown left the territory, which ultimately entered the Union as a free state in 1859.

John Brown

As a Democrat, Cleburne naturally supported his friend and law partner Thomas Hindman in Hindman's bid for a Senate seat against the controversial anti-immigrant, anti-Catholic *Know-Nothing Party* (American Party) candidate, W. D. Rice in the 1856 elections. One night, following a Hindman-Rice debate, both Cleburne and Hindman were wounded when Rice and unknown accomplices ambushed the two on a dark Helena street. Shot in the back, Patrick turned around and shot one of his assailants dead before collapsing on the street.

After Cleburne and Hindman recovered from their injuries they appeared before a grand jury to address a series of charges lodged against them, including murder. Ultimately they were exonerated, and the two men spent time recuperating at Hindman's parents' house in Mississippi.

A few years later, things began to come to a head for the nation. After his activities in Kansas, John Brown spent the next few years raising money in New England, which would bring him into direct contact with important abolitionist leaders, including Frederick Douglass. Brown had previously organized a small raiding party that succeeded in raiding a Missouri farm and freeing 11 slaves, but he set his sights on far larger objectives. In 1859, Brown began to set a new plan in motion that he hoped would create a full scale slave uprising in the South. Brown's plan relied on raiding Harpers Ferry, a strategically located armory in western Virginia that had been the main federal arms depot after the Revolution. Given its proximity to the South, Brown hoped to seize thousands of rifles and move them south, gathering slaves and swelling his numbers as he went. The slaves would then be armed and ready to help free more slaves, inevitably fighting Southern militias along the way.

In July 1859, Brown traveled to Harper's Ferry under an assumed name and waited for his recruits, but he struggled to get even 20 people to join him. Rather than call off the plan, however, Brown went ahead with it. That fall, Brown and his men used hundreds of rifles to seize the armory at Harper's Ferry, but the plan went haywire from the start, and word of his attack quickly spread. Local pro-slavery men formed a militia and pinned Brown and his men down while they were still at the armory.

After being called to Harpers Ferry, Robert E. Lee took decisive command of a troop of marines stationed there, surrounded the arsenal, and gave Brown the opportunity to surrender peaceably. When Brown refused, Lee ordered the doors be broken down and Brown taken captive, an affair that reportedly lasted just three minutes. A few of Brown's men were killed, but Brown was taken alive. Lee earned acclaim for accomplishing this task so quickly and efficiently.

The fallout from John Brown's raid on Harpers Ferry was intense. Southerners had long suspected that abolitionists hoped to arm the slaves and use violence to abolish slavery, and Brown's raid seemed to confirm that. Meanwhile, much of the northern press praised Brown for his actions. In the South, conspiracy theories ran wild about who had supported the raid, and many believed prominent abolitionist Republicans had been behind the raid as well. On the day of his execution, Brown wrote, "I, John Brown, am now quite *certain* that the crimes of this *guilty land* will never be purged away but with *blood.* I had, as I now think vainly, flattered myself that without very much bloodshed it might be done."

By the Fall of 1860, everyone could see the "war-cloud" on the horizon. With the election of Republican candidate Abraham Lincoln as president on November 6, 1860, many Southerners considered it the final straw. Someone they knew as a "Black Republican", leader of a party whose central platform was to stop the spread of slavery to new states, was now set to be inaugurated as President in March.

Throughout the fall and winter of 1860, Southern calls for secession became increasingly serious. In a last-ditched effort to save the Union, Kentucky's Senator John Crittenden tried to assume the stateliness of his predecessor Henry Clay. Crittenden, however, proved to be no Henry Clay: his proposal that a Constitutional Amendment reinstate the Missouri Compromise line and extend it to the Pacific failed. President Buchanan supported the measure, but President-Elect Lincoln said he refused to allow the further expansion of slavery under any conditions.

The Crittenden Compromise failed on December 18. Two days later, South Carolina seceded from the Union. President Buchanan sat on his hands, believing the Southern states had no right to secede, but that the Federal government had no effective power to prevent secession. In January, Mississippi, Florida, Alabama, Georgia, Louisiana and Kansas followed South Carolina's lead. The Confederacy was formed on February 4th, in Montgomery, Alabama, with former Secretary of War Jefferson Davis as its President. On February 23rd, Texas joined the Confederacy.

By 1860, Patrick Cleburne had become a naturalized American citizen, a wealthy lawyer, and was very popular with the local residents of Helena, Arkansas. Despite his aversion to slavery, he supported the rights and desires of the portion of the country now seeking to self-govern itself, and no doubt he drew a parallel between the fledgling Confederacy and his native Ireland after what he'd witnessed in the Irish fight for independence. At the same time, Cleburne's support of Southern values endeared him to the people of Arkansas whom he would later lead in battle.

Chapter 3: The Yell Rifles

In early 1861, local plantation owners and citizens of Helena, Arkansas formed a militia they called the "Yell Rifles," named after local war hero and Arkansas governor Archibald Yell, who had been killed in action at the Battle of Buena Vista in the Mexican War. Of course, his death ensured Yell was celebrated as a war hero even though his cavalry unit was best known for its insubordination. By some accounts, Patrick himself had organized the militia. Either way, the group elected Cleburne captain, and he quickly set out to instruct the company in drilling and other military skills he'd learned in the British Army. On April 8, 1861, the "Rifles" joined with other independent volunteer companies of the area to force the surrender of the U. S. Federal Arsenal at Little Rock--with Federal troops subsequently abandoning the arsenal without a fight on February 8.

Archibald Yell

On May 14, eight days after Arkansas seceded from the Union to join the Confederate States of America, the Yell Rifles became Company F of the First Infantry Regiment, Arkansas State Troops, organized at Mound City, six miles above Memphis on the Mississippi River. Captain Patrick Ronayne Cleburne was immediately appointed colonel of the regiment.

Chapter 4: The Battle of Shiloh

Although Cleburne was not involved in any major battle during 1861, he was still promoted in March 1862, when Colonel Cleburne became Brigadier General Patrick Ronayne Cleburne of the Fifteenth Arkansas Infantry. As it turned out, it came just a month before the biggest battle in American history at the time would be fought.

The battle of Shiloh came about after Ulysses S. Grant had captured Fort Henry and Fort Donelson in the first two months of 1862, which secured the Union precious control over much of the Mississippi River and much of Kentucky and Tennessee. After the victories at Fort Henry and Fort Donelson, Grant was now at the head of the Army of the Tennessee, which was nearly 50,000 strong and firmly encamped at Pittsburg Landing on the western side of the Tennessee River. The losses had dismayed the Confederates, who quickly launched an offensive in an attempt to wrest control of Tennessee from the Union.

At the head of the Confederate army was Albert Sidney Johnston, President Jefferson Davis's favorite general, and widely considered the South's best general. On the morning of April 6, Johnston directed an all out attack on Grant's army around Shiloh Church, intending to drive Union forces away from the Tennessee River Valley and into the swamps of Owl Creek to the west before Grant's army could link up with Maj. General Don Carlos Buell's Army of the Ohio. Though Grant's men had been encamped there, they had failed to create defensive fortifications or earthworks and were caught so badly by surprise that the battle began with Grant several miles away from the battlefield.

With nearly 45,000 Confederates attacking, Johnston's army began to steadily push Grant's men back toward the river. Displaying "extraordinary personal valor and obvious command ability", Cleburne's brigade in Hardee's corps was on the Confederate left, driving back William Tecumseh Sherman's troops near Shiloh Church. Cleburne and the rest of Hardee's corps continued to advance, but Hardee's command got so mixed with General Braxton Bragg's divisions that as they kept moving forward they became too intermingled to effectively control. With the Union soldiers retreating and making temporary stands, the Confederates continued to be unable to breakthrough the line on their left.

Cleburne would describe the action in his post-battle report:

"[S]oon after daylight, I advanced with the division against the enemy, keeping the proper distance from and regulating my movements by those of General Wood's brigade, which was on my right. I remained myself near the right of my brigade so as to preserve, as far as possible, my connection with the division. Trigg's battery followed near the right of my brigade, but was under the control of the chief of artillery, and left me after the first encounter. I advanced some distance through the woods without opposition. The enemy first showed himself about 400 yards off towards my left flank. I ordered Captain Trigg to send a howitzer in this direction and wake him up with a few shells. Continuing to move forward, the Fifteenth Arkansas engaged the enemy's skirmishers and drove them in on their first line of battle. My skirmishers then fell back on their reserve.

I was soon in sight of the enemy's encampments, behind the first of which he had formed his line of battle. He was very advantageously posted and overlapped my left flank by at least half a brigade. His line was lying down behind the rising ground on which his tents were pitched, and opposite my right he had made a breastwork of logs and bales of hay. Everywhere his musketry and artillery at short range swept the open spaces between the tents in his front with an iron storm that threatened certain destruction to every living thing that would dare to cross them. An almost impassable morass, jutting out from the foot of the height on which the enemy's tents stood, impeded the advance of my center, and finally caused a wide opening in my line. The Fifth Tennessee and the regiments on its left kept to the left of this swamp, and the Sixth Mississippi and Twenty-third Tennessee advanced on its right. My own horse bogged down in it and threw me, and it was with great difficulty I got out. My brigade was soon on the verge of the encampments and the battle began in earnest. Trigg's battery, posted on some high ground in the woods in my rear, opened over the heads of my men, but so thick were the leaves, he could only see in one direction, while the enemy were playing on him from several. The result was he was unable to accomplish much, and was ordered to a new position. I had no artillery under my command from this time forward."

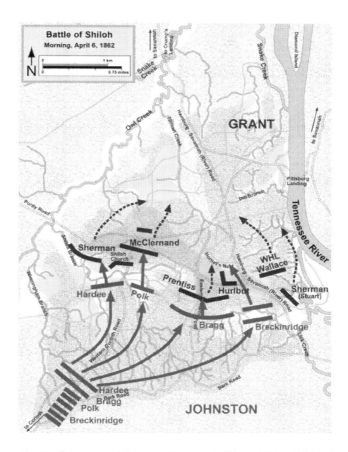

Battle of Shiloh
Morning, April 6, 1862

By 9:00 a.m., the Confederate attack began to focus on the Hornet's Nest right in the middle of the Union line, as Hardee's corps continued its assault on the left. However, as the Confederates failed to break the line in the Hornet's Nest despite anywhere from 8-14 charges, the offensive got bogged down.

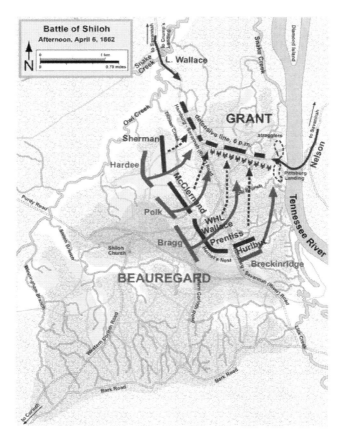

As fate would have it, the Confederates may have been undone by friendly fire at Shiloh. Johnston advanced out ahead of his men on horseback while directing a charge near a peach orchard when he was hit in the lower leg by a bullet that historians now widely believe was fired by his own men. Nobody thought the wound was serious, including Johnston, who continued to aggressively lead his men and even sent his personal physician to treat wounded Union soldiers taken captive. But the bullet had hit an artery, and Johnston began to feel faint in the saddle. With blood filling up his boot, Johnston unwittingly bled to death.

Johnston

Johnston's death was hidden from his men, and command fell upon P.G.T. Beauregard, who was the South's hero at Fort Sumter and at the First Battle of Bull Run. General Beauregard was competent, but Johnston's death naturally caused a delay in the Confederate command. It was precious time that Grant and General Sherman used to rally their troops into a tight defensive position around Pittsburg Landing.

The evening brought a lull in the fighting, and the Confederates were ultimately unable to achieve a breakthrough anywhere. That night, soldiers from Buell's army began linking up with Grant's battered army, and reconnaissance by cavalry officer Nathan Bedford Forrest learned of it. Though Forrest's reports would be disregarded by Beauregard, Forrest told Cleburne that night, "If the enemy comes on us in the morning, we'll be whipped like hell." Meanwhile, Beauregard sent a telegram to Confederate President Jefferson Davis that claimed "A COMPLETE VICTORY".

Beauregard was dead wrong. The following morning, Grant's army, now reinforced by Don Carlos Buell's 20,000 strong Army of the Ohio, launched a successful counterattack that drove the Confederates off the field and back to Corinth, Mississippi. Cleburne described the harrowing second day:

> "It rained heavily during the night. Every fifteen minutes the enemy threw two shells from his gunboats, some of which burst close around my men, banishing sleep from the eyes of a few, but falling chiefly among their own wounded, who were strewn thickly between my camp and the river. History records few instances of more reckless

inhumanity than this.

Soon after daylight on Monday morning I received notice that the enemy were pushing forward and driving in our cavalry pickets. It now became plain Buell had arrived and we had a fresh army to fight. In a few moments I received orders from General Hardee to advance on the Bark road. I reformed my brigade and fired off my wet guns.

My brigade was sadly reduced. From near 2,700 I now numbered about 800. Two regiments, the Second Tennessee and Sixth Mississippi, were absent altogether. Hundreds of my best men were dead or in the hospitals, and, I blush to add, hundreds of others had run off early in the fight of the day before--some through cowardice and some loaded with plunder from the Yankee encampments.

With the gallant few still with me I advanced about a mile to a place where I found a line of battle. It was halted, and, I was informed, was a part of General Breckinridge's command. I formed on the left of this line, halted, and ordered my men to lie down. I could plainly see the enemy's line in my front and that it stretched beyond my left as far as the eye could see.

At this time a battery of six guns came up in my rear and offered its assistance. I think it was the Washington Battery.

About half a mile to my left, in a neck of woods, I could see troops moving from the direction of the enemy and passing far in rear of my line. Soon a heavy fight commenced in this direction. I endeavored to discover the character of these troops, but could not. Finally Colonel Kelly, of your division, rode up, and informed me they were enemies. The battery immediately opened on their flanks and soon cleared them out of the woods.

An officer now bore me an order from General Breckinridge to move forward with his line and attack the force in our front. I sent back word that I was completely without support and outflanked on the left and would be destroyed if I advanced. I received for answer that the order was from General Bragg, that it was positive, and I must immediately advance. I did so, but had not gotten far before a battery on the left of General Breckinridge's line commenced firing across my front, obliging me to halt.

The enemy soon replied with rifled guns. This duel was carried on diagonally across the line of my proposed advance. I moved my line forward into a valley that separated me from the enemy, so as to prevent the Washington Battery to take part in the fight by firing over my line. The enemy brought up another battery, and for half an hour an artillery fight was carried on over my line the fiercest I saw during the day. The whole line of infantry on my right had halted and were merely spectators of the fight.

Here I had some men killed by limbs cut from the trees by our own artillery. It soon became apparent that our artillery was overmatched. It ceased firing, and the whole line of infantry charged the enemy. There was a very thick undergrowth here of young trees, which prevented my men from seeing any distance, yet offered them no protection from the storm of bullets and grape shot that swept through it. I could not see what was going on to my right or left, but my men were dropping all around before the fire of an unseen foe."

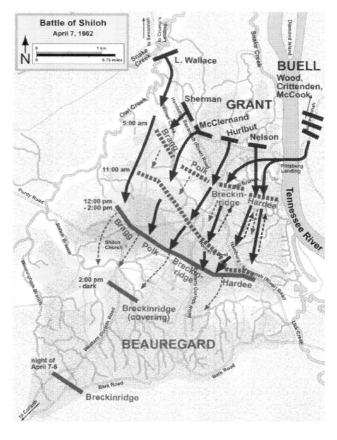

Grant's army had just won the biggest battle in the history of North America, with nearly

24,000 combined casualties among the Union and Confederate forces. Usually the winner of a major battle is hailed as a hero, but Grant was hardly a winner at Shiloh. The Battle of Shiloh took place before costlier battles at places like Antietam and Gettysburg, so the extent of the casualties at Shiloh shocked the nation. Moreover, at Shiloh the casualties were viewed as needless; Grant was pilloried for allowing the Confederates to take his forces by surprise, as well as the failure to build defensive earthworks and fortifications, which nearly resulted in a rout of his army. Speculation again arose that Grant had a drinking problem, and some even assumed he was drunk during the battle. Though the Union won, it was largely viewed that their success owed to the heroics of General Sherman in rallying the men and Don Carlos Buell arriving with his army, and General Buell was happy to receive the credit at Grant's expense.

Grant himself was not above playing the blame game. Miscommunication between Grant and division commander Lew Wallace resulted in Wallace failing to properly march his men into the fight while the Confederates were advancing on the first day. For the rest of his life, Grant blamed Wallace for the failure, but historians do not believe the miscommunication was actually his fault. Nevertheless, with Grant and Halleck heaping the blame Wallace for the near loss at Shiloh, it permanently tarnished Wallace's military career, and he was removed from his command in June 1862. Still, it's likely that any military accomplishments Lew Wallace may have lost out on during the Civil War would have been eclipsed by his authorship in 1880 of the classic *Ben-Hur* anyway.

Although Halleck agreed with Grant that Lew Wallace deserved the blame Grant was giving him, Grant was ultimately the fall guy. As a result of the Battle of Shiloh, General Halleck demoted Grant to second-in-command of all armies in his department, an utterly powerless position. And when word of what many considered a "colossal blunder" reached Washington, several congressmen insisted that Lincoln replace Grant in the field. Lincoln famously defended Grant, telling critics, "I can't spare this man. He fights."

Lincoln may have defended Grant, but he found precious few supporters, and the negative attention bothered Grant so much that it is widely believed he turned to alcohol again. While historians still debate that, what is known is that he considered resigning his commission, only to be dissuaded from doing so by General Sherman. Sherman had experienced the same career path as Grant, with failed business ventures, a stint in the Mexican-American War, early success in the Civil War and then a failure that nearly cost him his career (in Sherman's case, a nervous breakdown). As Sherman would later note, he supported Grant when Grant was drunk, and Grant supported him when he was crazy.

Sherman

Chapter 5: The Siege of Corinth

Following the Union victory at the Battle of Shiloh, Union armies under Maj. General Henry W. Halleck advanced on the vital rail center of Corinth, Mississippi. Employing what many consider an overly-cautious method of advance (moving only five miles in three weeks due to entrenching after each skirmish), by May 25, 1862, Halleck was finally in position to establish a blockade of the city. Thus began what would become known as the Siege of Corinth (or First Battle of Corinth).

Why were they moving so slowly? In the weeks following the Battle of Shiloh, a stream of intelligence reports began rolling in to Union General Halleck's headquarters that the Confederates were amassing troops at Corinth, Mississippi. Assistant Secretary of War Thomas A. Scott, who was traveling with Halleck as a War Department observer, wired Washington in mid-May, stating, "The enemy are concentrating a powerful army [at Corinth]." According to their intelligence, General Beauregard had 60,000 "fresh troops" (by one report), with another saying that 100,000 troops were waiting at Corinth--with more arriving daily. A captured army surgeon assured Grant that reinforcements would soon raise the number of Confederates to 200,000. With a Beauregard-led attack considered imminent, the Union Army was kept poised to take the defensive at a moment's notice.

Little did they know they were victims of a ruse initiated in part by the deceptive Beauregard.

Although Union troops had moved slowly and cautiously toward Corinth (averaging less than one mile a day), a month after Shiloh, Halleck -- who had taken to the field for the first time to personally take command of his troops -- and his 100,000 found themselves approaching the rebel lines. But despite what they'd been led to believe, Beauregard had just over 50,000 men. Recognizing that he didn't have the manpower to stand up to Halleck's much larger and better rested army, as Union troops moved into position, Beauregard abruptly moved his forces under the cover of darkness, but not before arranging one final deception: he had steam engines come puffing and whistling into town at regular intervals, accompanied by the sound of loud cheers, thus giving the impression of arriving troops.

Finally, on May 30, 1862, as the last few Confederate troops blew up the remaining supplies to keep them from Union hands, General Pope led his regiments slowly into town, only to find it abandoned. Leaving Halleck and Pope feeling like fools, Beauregard kept his troops, including Cleburne's men, on the move until they were well out of danger, some 50 miles south at Tupelo, Mississippi.

Chapter 6: The Kentucky Campaign

Despite the setbacks at Shiloh and Corinth, the Confederates still looked to press the offensive, and armies under Braxton Bragg and Kirby Smith launched a campaign that aimed to bring Kentucky back into the Confederate fold. The stakes were high; as Lincoln once famously said, "I hope to have God on my side, but I must have Kentucky."

The first major battle of that campaign was the Battle of Richmond, fought August 29–30, precisely the same time Lee's Army of Northern Virginia was inflicting a decisive defeat upon John Pope's Union Army at Second Manassas. At Richmond, Brigadier General Cleburne led the advance forces of Maj. General Edmund Kirby Smith's Army of Kentucky, marching north through Kingston and pushing aside Union skirmishers in the area. As Cleburne's men and Confederate cavalry headed toward Union General Mahlon Dickerson Manson's battle line near Zion Church, both sides braced for a fight on the morning of the second day of the battle, with Smith ordering Cleburne to attack and promising reinforcements would be up in time.

Following a mutual artillery barrage exchange and a concerted Confederate assault on the Union right flank, Union troops finally retreated into Rogersville--but not before the Confederates captured over 4,300 Union troops (including General Manson). Shelby Foote would later note that it was one of the most decisive battles of the Civil War in terms of the % of an army captured in battle. During the fighting, Cleburne suffered a serious shrapnel wound to the face and lost several teeth. Unable to speak, he temporarily relinquished his command following the battle. Cleburne would require 6 weeks to recover, but he'd be back in time for the grand battle of the campaign.

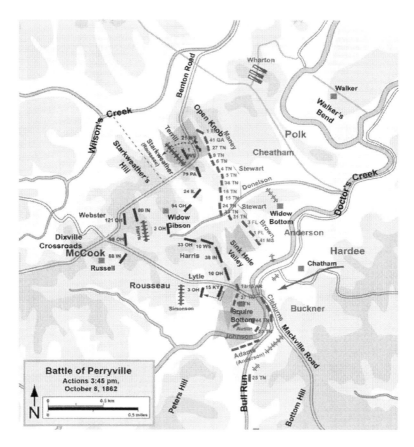

The largest battle in the state of Kentucky and the climactic battle of the Kentucky campaign took place at the Battle of Perryville, Kentucky, fought on October 8, 1862 in Chaplin Hills (west of Perryville). Confederate General Braxton Bragg's Army of Mississippi launched a full-out assault against a corps under the command of Maj. General Don Carlos Buell.

Though Cleburne's brigade was among the first units to arrive in the vicinity, it was not ordered to enter the fray until about 3:40 p.m., hours after the battle had started. They came up at a critical time, however, arriving just as Brig. General Bushrod R. Johnson's troops were running out of ammunition.

Though Cleburne's horse, Dixie, was immediately killed by artillery fire, which also injured Cleburne's ankle, he kept his troops moving forward and maintained command of his brigade throughout the ensuing battle. The first deadly opponent he faced happened to be Confederate artillery, as his men came under friendly fire because they were wearing blue uniform trousers captured from Union soldiers at Richmond. The assault that was spearheaded by Cleburne drove the Union men in their front back further than a mile, and the battle continued to rage elsewhere to the north and west. The colonel of the 17th Ohio would later note, "What soldier under Buell will forget the horrible affair at Perryville, where 30,000 men stood idly by to see and hear the needless slaughter in McCook's unaided, neglected and even abandoned command, without firing a shot or moving a step in its relief?"

After a day of bloody fighting, Union casualties totaled more than 4,000 and the Confederates suffered aout 3,500. Braxton Bragg's Army of Mississippi had won a tactical victory against what was primarily a single corps of Maj. General Don Carlos Buell's Union Army of the Ohio. However, since Bragg withdrew to Tennessee soon after the battle and the Union Army was able to retain control of the critical border state for the remainder of the war, the battle was considered a victory for the Union strategically speaking.

Cleburne had been injured twice during the battle but stuck it out, continuing to lead his men until the end of the battle. For his bravery and successes, he would be promoted to Major General on December 13, 1862.

Chapter 7: The Battle of Stones River (Murfreesboro)

Following the Battle of Perryville, Kentucky on October 8, 1862 and the devastating Union defeat at the Battle of Fredericksburg, Virginia from December 11--15, the Union turned its attention to Middle Tennessee, with Maj. General William S. Rosecrans marching his Army of the Cumberland from Nashville, Tennessee on December 26 to challenge Confederate General Braxton Bragg's Army of Tennessee at Murfreesboro. Two of the war's most incompetent commanding generals were about to face off for the first time, but not the last.

Rosecrans

On the morning of December 31, 1862, Cleburne's infantry was part of a silent, fixed-bayonet vanguard in an assault comprised of his troops and those of Major General John McCown. Moving through the woods in two long, solid lines, the only thing that alerted the groggy Union soldiers was the "slapping of knapsacks, the creak of cartridge boxes, and the muffled thud of shoes." The Union army was caught off-guard just like at Shiloh, but this time a breakthrough occurred almost immediately. As Hardee's other division began drifting to the left during the attack, Cleburne's division (which had been in the rear) came up and filled the gap seamlessly. The two divisions swept the Union line aside, capturing several artillery batteries before they could even fire a shot at the Confederates. Half of Union General Richard Johnson's division was killed, wounded or captured in just a few minutes.

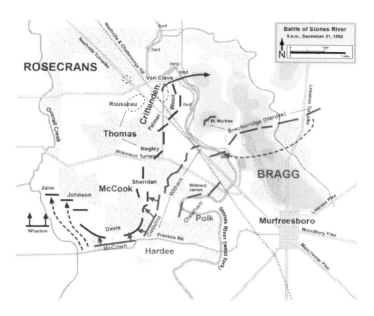

Major General Cleburne's division advanced three miles as it routed the Union right flank and drove it back to the Nashville Pike, its final line of defense. Unfortunately for the Confederates, their aim had been to drive the Union away from the Pike and divide their lines of communication, but the Confederate assault only managed to create a tighter defensive line for Rosencrans' army.

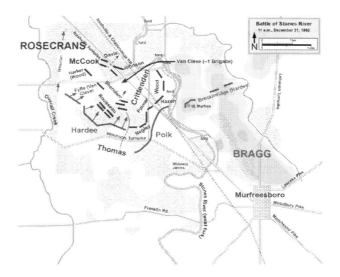

Meanwhile, the Confederates only stretched their line during the assaults, and though Bragg thought he had won a victory after the fighting that day, Rosecrans had his army dig in and prepare to continue fighting in the next few days. When Rosecrans refused to retreat, Bragg struck at the Union army again on January 2, only to be sharply repulsed. Now believing that the Union army would severely outman his army, Bragg began a strategic withdrawal on the night of January 3.

In terms of the percentage of casualties, the Battle of Stones River had the highest percentage of casualties on both sides of any major battle in the Civil War. Rosecrans' Union army suffered over 30% casualties, and Bragg's Confederate army suffered about 28% casualties. Cleburne had been successful in yet another Confederate defeat, and Confederate aspirations of controlling Middle Tennessee were gone.

Chapter 8: The Battle of Chickamauga

On July 4, 1863, Confederate General Pemberton surrendered Vicksburg and its nearly 35,000 man garrison to Ulysses S. Grant. Coincidentally, the surrender of Vicksburg came a day after the Army of the Potomac scored a critical victory at the Battle of Gettysburg in the East, which has widely overshadowed the Vicksburg campaign in Civil War history. Despite the dazzle of Gettysburg, what Grant had accomplished in the span of two and a half months not only cut the Confederacy in half, it made him the most important field general in the Union Army.

The Union had little time to celebrate Vicksburg. In June 1863, Union general William Rosecrans marched southeast toward Chattanooga, Tennessee, in pursuit of Confederate general Braxton Bragg, intending to "drive him into the sea." By this point, both the Union and Confederates had realized how uniquely important Chattanooga was as the rail and road gateway to all points south of the Ohio River and east of the Mississippi River.

In mid-September, the Union Army under General Rosecrans had taken Chattanooga, but rather than be pushed out of the action, Bragg decided to stop with his 60,000 men and prepare a counterattack south of Chattanooga at a creek named Chickamauga. To bolster his fire-power, Confederate President Jefferson Davis sent 12,000 additional troops under the command of Lieutenant General James Longstreet, whose corps had just recently fought at Gettysburg in July. In only nine days, Longstreet had successfully moved his entire corps by rail to come to Bragg's aid.

On the morning of September 19, 1863, Bragg's men assaulted the Union line, which was established in a wooded area thick with underbrush along the river. That day, Bragg continued to pummel Union forces, with the battle devolving from an organized succession of coordinated assaults into what one Union soldier described as "a mad, irregular battle, very much resembling guerilla warfare on a vast scale in which one army was bushwhacking the other, and wherein all the science and the art of war went for nothing." By 6 p.m., as it was getting dark, Bragg ordered Cleburne's division to shore up the Confederate army's right flank. Though there hadn't been fighting in that sector, with the fighting taking place to the south, Cleburne now launched an attack that was hampered by the night and the heavily wooded underbrush. Cleburne called off the attack at 9:00 p.m., having incurred about 30% casualties in his division.

On the morning of September 20, both armies braced for the battle to resume. Before the fighting resumed, Bragg ordered the right wing, which included Cleburne's division, to attack the Union army's left flank. Having already expended men and energy the previous day, the assault by the right wing of the Confederate army was badly repulsed in the morning, and the assault had fizzled out by noon. However, the sheer size of the assault had also forced the Union command to try to scramble units as reinforcements, causing one of the greatest blunders of the entire war.

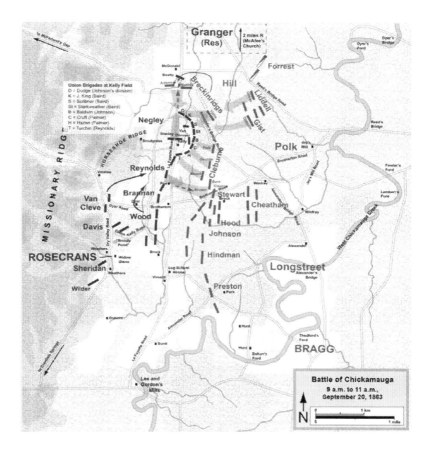

Rosecrans and his staff were misinformed that a gap was forming in his front line, and the exhausted Union commander did not realize at one point that his subordinates had issued contradictory orders meant to shore up a gap that didn't exist. When Union General Wood's brigade pulled out of the line to go support General Joseph Reynolds' division, he accidentally created a quarter-mile gap in the Union center, directly in the path of an eight-brigade (15,000 man) force led by Longstreet. Described by one of Rosecrans' own men as "an angry flood," Longstreet's attack was successful in driving one-third of the Union Army to the crossroads of Rossville five miles north, with Rosecrans himself running all the way to Chattanooga, where he was later found weeping and seeking solace from a staff priest.

George H. Thomas

The time had come for General George H. Thomas to play his greatest role in the Civil War. As the Confederate assault continued, Thomas led the Union left wing against heavy Confederate attack even after nearly half of the Union army abandoned their defenses and retreated from the battlefield, racing toward Chattanooga. The destruction of the entire army was prevented by Thomas as he rallied the remaining parts of the army and formed a defensive stand on Horseshoe Ridge. Union units spontaneously rallied to create a defensive line on their fall-back point at Horseshoe Ridge, forming a new right wing for the line of General Thomas, who had now assumed overall command of the remaining forces. And although the Confederates launched a series of well-executed (albeit costly) assaults, Thomas and his men managed to hold until nightfall, when they made an orderly retreat to Chattanooga while the Confederates occupied the surrounding heights, ultimately besieging the city. Dubbed "The Rock of Chickamauga", Thomas's heroics ensured that Rosecrans' army was able to successfully retreat back to Chattanooga.

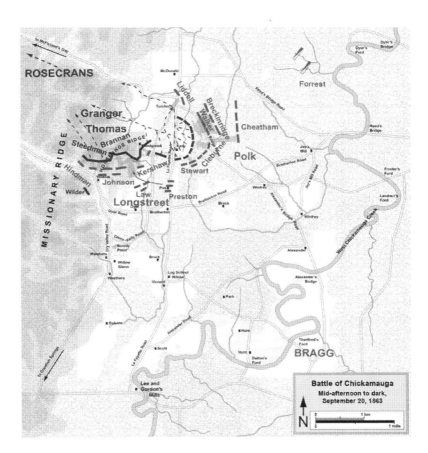

In the aftermath of the Battle of Chickamauga, several Confederate generals blamed the number of men lost during what would be the bloodiest battle of the Western Theater on Bragg's incompetence, also criticizing him for refusing to pursue the escaping Union army. General Longstreet later stated to Jefferson Davis, "Nothing but the hand of God can help as long as we have our present commander." Bragg owed his position to being a close friend of Jefferson Davis's, and one of the criticisms often lodged at Davis by historians is that he played favorites to the detriment of the South's chances. Even after he reluctantly removed Bragg from command out West, he would bring Bragg to Richmond to serve as a military advisor.

Bragg

Following the battle, General Cleburne continued to remain a presence even as Confederate forces advanced, prompting Union General Sheridan to mount a follow-up offensive hoping to isolate Cleburne from the main body of the Confederate Army. Cleburne and his men, however, were able to resist Sheridan on their own before making a clean getaway.

Chapter 9: The Chattanooga Campaign

Following the devastating Union defeat at the Battle of Chickamauga in mid-September of 1863, the disheartened Union Army retreated to Chattanooga, Tennessee. While Union General William S. Rosecrans put the men to work digging defensive entrenchment's around the city and waiting for Washington to send reinforcements, on September 23, the Confederate Army under General Braxton Bragg arrived at the outskirts of Chattanooga and proceeded to seize control of the surrounding heights: Missionary Ridge (to the east), Lookout Mountain (to the southwest), and Raccoon Mountain (to the west). From these key vantage points, the Confederates could not only lob long-range artillery onto the Union entrenchments, they could sweep the rail and river routes that supplied the Union army. Bragg planned to lay siege to the city and starve the Union forces into surrendering.

On September 29, U. S. Secretary of War Edwin M. Stanton ordered Union general Ulysses S. Grant, commander of the newly-created Military Division of the Mississippi, to go to Chattanooga to bring all the territory from the Appalachian Mountains to the Mississippi River (including a portion of Arkansas) under a single command for the first time. Considering General Rosecrans' spotty record, Grant was given the option of replacing him with Brigadier

General Thomas, who to date had never failed to deliver--even under the gravest of conditions.

Hearing an inaccurate report that Rosecrans was preparing to abandon Chattanooga, Grant relieved Rosecrans of command and installed Thomas as commander of the Army of the Cumberland, telegraphing Thomas saying, "Hold Chattanooga at all hazards. I will be there as soon as possible." Without hesitation, Thomas replied, "We will hold the town till we starve."

During the Battle of Wauhatchie, fought from October 28–29, 1863 in Hamilton and Marion Counties, Tennessee, and Dade County, Georgia, the Union seized Brown's Ferry on the Tennessee River, successfully opening a supply line to the Union Army stranded in Chattanooga without supplies. Though it was a small battle, especially compared to what would come later in the campaign, the battle was notable because it was one of the few pitched battles fought at night. As the Union opened up the supply line, Confederate forces attempted to overpower the Union forces defending the ferry by mounting an unexpected night assault, which was led by Major General Cleburne and his men. Despite their efforts, the Union was able to maintain control of the ferry and keep a supply line open.

As Grant relieved Rosecrans and placed General Thomas in charge of reorganizing the Army of the Cumberland, Lincoln detached General Hooker and two divisions from the Army of the Potomac and sent them west to reinforce the garrison at Chattanooga. During a maneuver in which General Hooker had moved three divisions into Chattanooga Valley hoping to occupy Rossville Gap, Hooker's first obstacle was to bypass an artillery line the Confederates had established to block the movement of Union supplies. Initially, Grant merely used Hooker's men to establish the "Cracker Line", a makeshift supply line that moved food and resources into Chattanooga from Hooker's position on Lookout Mountain.

In November 1863, the situation at Chattanooga was dire enough that Grant took the offensive in an attempt to lift the siege. By now the Confederates were holding important high ground at positions like Lookout Mountain and Missionary Ridge. On November 24, 1863 Maj. Gen. Hooker captured Lookout Mountain in order to divert some of Bragg's men away from their commanding position on Missionary Ridge. That was supposed to allow General Sherman and four divisions of his Army of the Tennessee to attack Bragg's right flank the following morning and assault Missionary Ridge. At the same time, Grant had ordered General Thomas to support Sherman's assault simultaneously and "either carry the rifle pits and ridge directly in front of them or move to the left, as the presence of the enemy may require."

Sherman's attack would come against Cleburne's well dug-in defenders, pitting nearly 17,000 Union soldiers against Cleburne's 4,000. However, Sherman's assault went wrong from the start, and he delayed it when he discovered he was on the wrong terrain. Sherman had mistakenly occupied the wrong hill, and instead of assaulting Missionary Ridge, Sherman's men found themselves on ground completely detached from Missionary Ridge and separated by a deep valley with steep sides. Far from reaching the "ideal" spot to attack Bragg's right flank, he had put himself in a position forcing his men to fight an interim battle with Confederates just to reach Missionary Ridge.

Cleburne had anticipated a morning attack, but by 7:00 a.m. Sherman's attack had still not materialized, allowing Bragg to move additional troops to Cleburne's position. Cleburne used these reinforcements to form a dense defensive line that ran from the railroad tunnel northward several hundred yards along the spine of Tunnel Hill to its summit, then doglegged to the east atop a steep, tree-covered spur. Cleburne described the terrain in his post-battle report, "The right of Missionary Ridge, to which I was ordered, runs nearly north and south, parallel to the Tennessee River, which is about 1 miles west of it. From the tunnel north along the ridge it is about a mile to the Chickamauga River, which bounds the ridge on that side, flowing thence westwardly into the Tennessee River. To simplify the description, the two rivers and the ridge may be said to form three sides of a square. The Tennessee Valley, between the rivers and the ridge, is mostly level, with a continuation of cleared fields bordering the ridge, but immediately in front of the center of my position, about 1,200 yards north and 600 yards west of the railroad tunnel, was a high detached ridge, which in a military point of view dominated over every point within cannon range."

Choosing to move forward before more reinforcements could arrive, Sherman began his advance, only to be met by vicious artillery and infantry fire that sent many Union soldiers tumbling down the hillside. A Confederate solder later said, "It looked like a lot of the boys had been sliding down the hillside, for when a line of the enemy would be repulsed they would start down the hill and soon the whole line would be rolling down like a ball it was so steep a hillside." This began a four-hour gun battle while Cleburne's men defended the position against Sherman, with Grant ordering Major General George H. Thomas to move forward and seize the Confederate line of rifle pits at the base of the ridge to Sherman's right and Cleburne's left. Cleburne continued to deliver punishing artillery fire, refusing to yield.

At the height of the fighting, Cleburne's overextended line was in danger of breaking, but Sherman never committed his entire force, no doubt due to his lingering confusion over the terrain. After Cleburne was reinforced by yet another division, he sensed the opportunity to order a counterattack around 4:00 p.m. With his Confederates charging down the hill, Cleburne at the front, the Confederates routed Sherman's attackers, who were exhausted and low on ammunition at that point. By the time Sherman's assault had ended, Cleburne had inflicted 2,000 casualties and Sherman's men had nothing to show for it. Historian Steven E. Woodworth would write, "Cleburne was in fine form today, deftly shifting troops around his hilltop position and skillfully judging when and where to launch limited counterattacks—often leading them himself."

Cleburne described the final charge by his men: "In the meantime, General Cumming, having placed the Fifty-sixth Georgia in line for the charge, and supported it by placing the Thirty-sixth

Georgia 10 paces in rear, moved forward to the charge; twice he was checked and had to reform. Warfield's (Arkansas) regiment with empty guns, and the gallant First and Twenty-seventh Tennessee prepared to share his next effort. At the command the whole rushed forward with a cheer, Lieutenant-Colonel Sanders, simultaneously leading the left of Mills' (Texas) regiment on the enemy's flank. The enemy, completely surprised, fled down the foot, the Texas troops on the left pursuing him beyond the foot and nearly across the open ground in front. Our charging columns returned with many prisoners and stand of colors; a fresh force of the enemy, attempting to follow us as we returned from this charge, was quickly met and routed by the Fiftieth Tennessee and with troops of my division. Immediately on his last repulse the enemy opened a rapid and revengeful artillery fire on Tunnel Hill from his batteries on the detached hill, and under cover of this fire he went to work felling trees and fortifying his position."

Sherman's attack had failed, but the Union was about to have one of the most amazing days of the war. As Thomas's men reached the base of the Missionary Ridge, they found that it had not afforded them protection from the Confederate defenders in their front. As a result, they began making impromptu charges up the hill. The advance actually defied Grant's orders, since Grant, initially upset, had only ordered them to take the rifle pits at the base of Missionary Ridge, figuring that a frontal assault on that position would be futile and fatal. As the Union soldiers stormed ahead, General Grant caught the advance from a distance and asked General Thomas why he had ordered the attack. Thomas informed Grant that he hadn't; his army had taken it upon itself to charge up the entire ridge.

As it turned out, historians have often criticized Grant's orders, with acclaimed historian Peter Cozzens noting, "Grant's order to halt at the rifle pits at the base of the ridge was misunderstood by far too many of the generals charged with executing it. Some doubted the order because they thought it absurd to stop an attack at the instant when the attackers would be most vulnerable to fire from the crest and to a counterattack. Others apparently received garbled versions of the order." Sheridan later wrote, "Seeing the enemy thus strengthening himself, it was plain that we would have to act quickly if we expected to accomplish much, and I already began to doubt the feasibility of our remaining in the first line of rifle-pits when we should have carried them. I discussed the order with Wagner, Harker, and Sherman, and they were similarly impressed, so while anxiously awaiting the signal I sent Captain Ransom of my staff to Granger, who was at Fort Wood, to ascertain if we were to carry the first line or the ridge beyond. Shortly after Ransom started the signal guns were fired, and I told my brigade commanders to go for the ridge."

Eventually finding their way to safe spots, Union soldiers, though quite disorganized, were able to slowly advance against the Confederate line; finally overwhelming Confederate defenders on the right. As it turned out, the Confederate left flank, anchored by a brigade of less-experienced Alabamians, had not put nearly as much thought into their formation as

Cleburne had, resulting in poor positioning that easily collapsed under Hooker's advance. When Confederate General Breckinridge rode the front line and saw the destruction the left flank had sustained, he screamed, "Boys, get away the best you can!" and barely escaped with his life. Within minutes, the Alabama unit was completely surrounded: those who had not managed to escape (679 of them) were taken prisoner.

To the amazement of Grant and the officers watching, the men making the attack scrambled up Missionary Ridge in a series of unconcerted, disorganized attacks that somehow managed to send the Confederates into a rout, thereby lifting the siege on Chattanooga. With that, the Army of the Cumberland had essentially conducted the most successful frontal assault of the war spontaneously. While Pickett's Charge, still the most famous attack of the war, was one unsuccessful charge, the Army of the Cumberland made over a dozen charges up Missionary Ridge and ultimately succeeded. In his post-battle report, Cleburne describes the moment he heard the shocking news. "Soon after the final defeat of the enemy in front of Smith's position. I received a dispatch from General Hardee to send to the center all the troops I could spare, as the enemy were pressing us in that quarter. I immediately ordered Generals Cumming and Maney, with their respective brigades, to report accordingly, and went myself to push them forward. Before I had gone far, however, a dispatch from General Hardee reached me, with the appalling news that the enemy had pierced our center, and were on Missionary Ridge, directing me to take command of my own, Walker's, and Stevenson's divisions and form a line across the ridge, so as to meet an attack upon my flank, and take all other necessary measures for the safety of the right wing."

With that, Bragg's army was routed and forced to retreat to Dalton, Georgia, and effectively ending the siege of Union forces in Chattanooga, Tennessee. Cleburne had once again been a bright spot in the battle of Missionary Ridge, but the disastrous Confederate rout was a devastating blow, and it forced the exhausted army into a retreat into northwest Georgia through Ringgold Gap. To give his troops, artillery, and wagon trains sufficient time to pass through the narrow gap, General Braxton Bragg sent orders to Cleburne, whose division was pulling up the rear, to defend the pass "at all hazards."

On the morning of November 27, Cleburne's division set up its defense in the pass and waited until Joe Hooker's three divisions confronted them. Cleburne's troops opened up on the advancing Union soldiers with a blaze of artillery and rifle fire, taking them by surprise. Hooker attempted to use his large manpower advantage to flank Cleburne's division on both flanks, but Cleburne's men stoutly defended their positions for five hours, despite being outnumbered 3:1. Continuing to hold Hooker at bay, Cleburne's division gave Bragg's plenty of time to escape the pursuing Federals, and at noon Cleburne managed to safely extricate his own men and retreat. Cleburne would receive an official Thanks from the Confederate Congress for his defense of Ringgold Gap.

Chapter 10: Cleburne's Radical Plan for Reinforcements

By 1864, things were looking so bleak for the South that the Confederate war strategy was simply to ensure Lincoln lost reelection that November, with the hope that a new Democratic president would end the war and recognize the South's independence. With that, and given the shortage in manpower, Lee's strategic objective was to continue defending Richmond, while hoping that Grant would commit some blunder that would allow him a chance to seize an opportunity.

Although many Southern leaders continued to blindly delude themselves, and the Southern people in general still believed success was on the horizon, it was obvious to many that the Confederacy was in trouble. One of those concerned was Cleburne, who knew full well the Confederacy was losing the war because of the North's advantage in resources and manpower. With most of the South now overrun with increasingly more aggressive Union forces, their economy near ruin, and remaining Confederate armies battered and disintegrating, Confederate options were few.

On December 31, 1863, General Cleburne stunned fellow officers (as well as much of the South when they caught wind) when he wrote a memorandum proposing what he saw as a viable solution to the problem of insufficient troops. With a handful of subordinate generals signing his letter, Cleburne made one of the boldest suggestions of the Civil War to Joseph Johnston, the new commander of the Army of Tennesee:

GENERAL: Moved by the exigency in which our country is now placed, we take the liberty of laying before you, unofficially, our views on the present state of affairs. The subject is so grave, and our views so new, we feel it a duty both to you and the cause that before going further we should submit them for your judgment and receive your suggestions in regard to them. We therefore respectfully ask you to give us an expression of your views in the premises. We have now been fighting for nearly three years, have spilled much of our best blood, and lost, consumed, or thrown to the flames an amount of property equal in value to the specie currency of the world. Through some lack in our system the fruits of our struggles and sacrifices have invariably slipped away from us and left us nothing but long lists of dead and mangled. Instead of standing defiantly on the borders of our territory or harassing those of the enemy, we are hemmed in today into less than two-thirds of it, and still the enemy menacingly confronts us at every point with superior forces. Our soldiers can see no end to this state of affairs except in our own exhaustion; hence, instead of rising to the occasion, they are sinking into a fatal apathy, growing weary of hardships and slaughters which promise no results. In this state of things it is easy to understand why there is a growing belief that some black catastrophe is not far ahead of us, and that unless some extraordinary change is soon made in our condition we must overtake it. The consequences of this condition are showing themselves more plainly every day; restlessness of morals spreading everywhere, manifesting itself in the army in a growing disregard for private rights; desertion spreading to a class of soldiers it never dared to tamper with before; military commissions sinking in the estimation of the soldier; our supplies failing; our firesides in ruins. If this state continues much longer we must be subjugated. Every man should endeavor to understand the meaning of subjugation before it is too late. We can give but a faint idea when we say it means the loss of all we now hold most sacred--slaves and all other personal property, lands, homesteads, liberty, justice, safety, pride, manhood. It means that the history of this heroic struggle will be written by the enemy; that our youth will be trained by Northern school teachers; will learn from Northern school books their version of the war; will be impressed by all the influences of history and education to regard our gallant dead as traitors, our maimed veterans as fit objects for derision. It means the crushing of Southern manhood, the hatred of our former slaves, who will, on a spy system, be our secret police. The conqueror's policy is to divide the conquered into factions and stir up animosity among them, and in training an army of negroes the North no doubt holds this thought in perspective. We can see three great causes operating to destroy us: First, the inferiority of our armies to those of the enemy in point of numbers; second, the poverty of our single source of supply in comparison with his several sources; third, the fact that slavery, from being one of our chief sources of strength at the commencement of the war, has now become, in a military point of view, one of our chief sources of weakness.

The enemy already opposes us at every point with superior numbers, and is endeavoring to make the preponderance irresistible. President Davis, in his recent message, says the enemy "has recently ordered a large conscription and made a subsequent call for volunteers, to be followed, if ineffectual, by a still further draft." In addition, the President of the United States announces that "he has already in training an army of 100,000 negroes as good as any troops," and every fresh raid he makes and new slice of territory he wrests from us will add to this force. Every soldier in our army already knows and feels our numerical inferiority to the enemy. Want of men in the field has prevented him from reaping the fruits of his victories, and has prevented him from having the furlough he expected after the last reorganization,, and when he turns from the wasting armies in the field to look at the source of supply, he finds nothing in the prospect to encourage him. Our single source of supply is that portion of our white men fit for duty and not now in the ranks. The enemy has three sources of supply: First, his own motley population; secondly, our slaves; and thirdly, Europeans whose hearts are fired into a crusade against us by fictitious pictures of the atrocities of slavery, and who meet no hindrance from their Governments in such enterprise, because these Governments are equally antagonistic to the institution. In touching the third cause, the fact that slavery has become a military weakness, we may rouse prejudice and passion, but the time has come when it would be madness not to look at our danger from every point of view, and to probe it to the bottom. Apart from the assistance that home and foreign prejudice against slavery has given to the North, slavery is a source of great strength to the enemy in a purely military point of view, by supplying him with an army from our granaries; but it is our most vulnerable point, a continued embarrassment, and in some respects an insidious weakness. Wherever slavery is once seriously disturbed, whether by the actual presence or the approach of the enemy, or even by a cavalry raid, the whites can no longer with safety to their property openly sympathize with our cause. The fear of their slaves is continually haunting them, and from silence and apprehension many of these soon learn to wish the war stopped on any terms. The next stage is to take the oath to save property, and they become dead to us, if not open enemies. To prevent raids we are forced to scatter our forces, and are not free to move and strike like the enemy; his vulnerable points are carefully selected and fortified depots. Ours are found in every point where there is a slave to set free. All along the lines slavery is comparatively valueless to ns for labor, but of great and increasing worth to the enemy for information. It is an omnipresent spy system, pointing out our valuable men to the enemy, revealing our positions, purposes, and resources, and yet acting so safely and secretly that there is no means to guard against it. Even in the heart of our country, where our hold upon this secret espionage is firmest, it waits but the opening fire of the enemy's battle line to wake it, like a torpid serpent, into venomous activity.

In view of the state of affairs what does our country propose to do? In the words of President Davis "no effort must be spared to add largely to our effective force as promptly as possible. The sources of supply are to be found in restoring to the army all who are improperly absent, putting an end to substitution, modifying the exemption law, restricting details, and placing in the ranks such of the able-bodied men now employed as wagoners, nurses, cooks, and other employés, as are doing service for which the negroes may be found competent." Most of the men improperly absent, together with many of the exempts and men having substitutes, are now without the Confederate lines and cannot be calculated on. If all the exempts capable of bearing arms were enrolled, it will give us the boys below eighteen, the men above forty-five, and those persons who are left at home to meet the wants of the country and the army, but this modification of the exemption law will remove from the fields and manufactories most of the skill that directed agricultural and mechanical labor, and, as stated by the President, "details will have to be made to meet the wants of the country," thus sending many of the men to be derived from this source back to their homes again. Independently of this, experience proves that striplings and men above conscript age break down and swell the sick lists more than they do the ranks. The portion now in our lines of the class who have substitutes is not on the whole a hopeful element, for the motives that created it must have been stronger than patriotism, and these motives added to what many of them will call breach of faith, will cause some to be not forthcoming, and others to be unwilling and discontented soldiers. The remaining sources mentioned by the President have been so closely pruned in the Army of Tennessee that they will be found not to yield largely. The supply from all these sources, together with what we now have in the field, will exhaust the white race, and though it should greatly exceed expectations and put us on an equality with the enemy, or even give us temporary advantages, still we have no reserve to meet unexpected disaster or to supply a protracted struggle. Like past years, 1864 will diminish our ranks by the casualties of war, and what source of repair is there left us? We therefore see in the recommendations of the President only a temporary expedient, which at the best will leave us twelve months hence in the same predicament we are in now. The President attempts to meet only one of the depressing causes mentioned; for the other two he has proposed no remedy. They remain to generate lack of confidence in our final success, and to keep us moving down hill as heretofore. Adequately to meet the causes which are now threatening ruin to our country, we propose, in addition to a modification of the President's plans, that we retain in service for the war all troops now in service, and that we immediately commence training a large reserve of the most courageous of our slaves, and further that we guarantee freedom within a reasonable time to every slave in the South who shall remain true to the Confederacy in this war. As between the loss of independence and the loss of slavery, we assume that every patriot will freely give up the latter--give up the negro slave rather than be a slave himself. If we are correct in this assumption it only remains to show how this great national sacrifice is, in all human probabilities, to change the current of success and sweep the invader from our country.

Our country has already some friends in England and France, and there are strong motives to induce these nations to recognize and assist us, but they cannot assist us without helping slavery, and to do this would be in conflict with their policy for the last quarter of a century. England has paid hundreds of millions to emancipate her West India slaves and break up the slave trade. Could she now consistently spend her treasure to reinstate slavery in this country? But this barrier once removed, the sympathy and the interests of these and other nations will accord with our own, and we may expect from them both moral support and material aid. One thing is certain, as soon as the great sacrifice to independence is made and known in foreign countries there will be a complete change of front in our favor of the sympathies of the world. This measure will deprive the North of the moral and material aid which it now derives from the bitter prejudices with which foreigners view the institution, and its war, if continued, will henceforth be so despicable in their eyes that the source of recruiting will be dried up. It will leave the enemy's negro army no motive to fight for, and will exhaust the source from which it has been recruited. The idea that it is their special mission to war against slavery has held growing sway over the Northern people for many years, and has at length ripened into an armed and bloody crusade against it. This baleful superstition has so far supplied them with a courage and constancy not their own. It is the most powerful and honestly entertained plank in their war platform. Knock this away and what is left? A bloody ambition for more territory, a pretended veneration for the Union, which one of their own most distinguished orators (Doctor Beecher in his Liverpool speech) openly avowed was only used as a stimulus to stir up the anti-slavery crusade, and lastly the poisonous and selfish interests which are the fungus growth of the war itself. Mankind may fancy it a great duty to destroy slavery, but what interest can mankind have in upholding this remainder of the Northern war platform? Their interests and feelings will be diametrically opposed to it. The measure we propose will strike dead all John Brown fanaticism, and will compel the enemy to draw off altogether or in the eyes of the world to swallow the Declaration of Independence without the sauce and disguise of philanthropy. This delusion of fanaticism at an end, thousands of Northern people will have leisure to look at home and to see the gulf of despotism into which they themselves are rushing.

The measure will at one blow strip the enemy of foreign sympathy and assistance, and transfer them to the South; it will dry up two of his three sources of recruiting; it will take from his negro army the only motive it could have to fight against the South, and will probably cause much of it to desert over to us; it will deprive his cause of the powerful stimulus of fanaticism, and will enable him to see the rock on which his so called friends are now piloting him. The immediate effect of the emancipation and enrollment of negroes on the military strength of the South would be: To enable us to have armies numerically superior to those of the North, and a reserve of any size we might think necessary; to enable us to take the offensive, move forward, and forage on the enemy. It would open to us in prospective another and almost untouched source of supply, and furnish us with the means of preventing temporary disaster, and carrying on a protracted struggle. It would instantly remove all the vulnerability, embarrassment, and inherent weakness which result from slavery. The approach of the enemy would no longer find every household surrounded by spies; the fear that sealed the master's lips and the avarice that has, in so many cases, tempted him practically to desert us would alike be removed. There would be no recruits awaiting the enemy with open arms, no complete history of every neighborhood with ready guides, no fear of insurrection in the rear, or anxieties for the fate of loved ones when our armies moved forward. The chronic irritation of hope deferred would be joyfully ended with the negro, and the sympathies of his whole race would be due to his native South. It would restore confidence in an early termination of the war with all its inspiring consequences, and even if contrary to all expectations the enemy should succeed in overrunning the South, instead of finding a cheap, ready-made means of holding it down, he would find a common hatred and thirst for vengeance, which would break into acts at every favorable opportunity, would prevent him from settling on our lands, and render the South a very unprofitable conquest. It would remove forever all selfish taint from our cause and place independence above every question of property. The very magnitude of the sacrifice itself, such as no nation has ever voluntarily made before, would appal our enemies, destroy his spirit and his finances, and fill our hearts with a pride and singleness of purpose which would clothe us with new strength in battle. Apart from all other aspects of the question, the necessity for more fighting men is upon us. We can only get a sufficiency by making the negro share the danger and hardships of the war. If we arm and train him and make him fight for the country in her hour of dire distress, every consideration of principle and policy demand that we should set him and his whole race who side with us free. It is a first principle with mankind that he who offers his life in defense of the State should receive from her in return his freedom and his happiness, and we believe in acknowledgment of this principle. The Constitution of the Southern States has reserved to their respective governments the power to free slaves for meritorious services to the State. It is politic besides. For many years, ever since the agitation of the subject of slavery commenced, the negro has been dreaming of freedom, and his vivid imagination has surrounded that condition with so many gratifications that it has become the paradise of his hopes. To attain it he will tempt dangers and difficulties not exceeded by the bravest soldier in the field. The hope of freedom is perhaps the only moral incentive that can be applied to him in his present condition. It would be preposterous then to expect him to fight against it with any degree of enthusiasm, therefore we must bind him to our cause by no doubtful bonds; we must leave no possible loophole for treachery to creep in. The slaves are dangerous now, but armed, trained, and collected in an army they would be a thousand fold more dangerous: therefore when we make soldiers of them we must make free men of them beyond all question, and thus enlist their sympathies also. We can do this more effectually than the North can now do, for we can give the negro not only his own freedom, but that of his wife and child, and can secure it to him in his old home. To do this, we must immediately make his marriage and parental relations sacred in the eyes of the law and forbid their sale. The past legislation of the South concedes that large free middle class of negro blood, between the master and slave, must sooner or later destroy the institution. If, then, we touch the institution at all, we would do best to make the most of it, and by emancipating the whole race upon reasonable terms, and within such reasonable time as will prepare both races for the change, secure to ourselves all the advantages, and to our enemies all the disadvantages that can arise, both at home and abroad, from such a sacrifice. Satisfy the negro that if he faithfully adheres to our standard during the war he shall receive his freedom and that of his race. Give him as an earnest of our intentions such immediate immunities as will impress him with our sincerity and be in keeping with his new condition, enroll a portion of his class as soldiers of the Confederacy, and we change the race from a dreaded weakness to a position of strength.

Will the slaves fight? The helots of Sparta stood their masters good stead in battle. In the great sea fight of Lepanto where the Christians checked forever the spread of Mohammedanism over Europe, the galley slaves of portions of the fleet were promised freedom, and called on to fight at a critical moment of the battle. They fought well, and civilization owes much to those brave galley slaves. The negro slaves of Saint Domingo, fighting for freedom, defeated their white masters and the French troops sent against them. The negro slaves of Jamaica revolted, and under the name of Maroons held the mountains against their masters for 150 years; and the experience of this war has been so far that half-trained negroes have fought as bravely as many other half-trained Yankees. If, contrary to the training of a lifetime, they can be made to face and fight bravely against their former masters, how much more probable is it that with the allurement of a higher reward, and led by those masters, they would submit to discipline and face dangers.

We will briefly notice a few arguments against this course. It is said Republicanism cannot exist without the institution. Even were this true, we prefer any form of government of which the Southern people may have the molding, to one forced upon us by a conqueror. It is said the white man cannot perform agricultural labor in the South. The experience of this army during the heat of summer from Bowling Green, Ky., to Tupelo, Miss., is that the white man is healthier when doing reasonable work in the open field than at any other time. It is said an army of negroes cannot be spared from the fields. A sufficient number of slaves is now administering to luxury alone to supply the place of all we need, and we believe it would be better to take half the able bodied men off a plantation than to take the one master mind that economically regulated its operations. Leave some of the skill at home and take some of the muscle to fight with. It is said slaves will not work after they are freed. We think necessity and a wise legislation will compel them to labor for a living. It is said it will cause terrible excitement and some disaffection from our cause. Excitement is far preferable to the apathy which now exists, and disaffection will not be among the fighting men. It is said slavery is all we are fighting for, and if we give it up we give up all. Even if this were true, which we deny, slavery is not all our enemies are fighting for. It is merely the pretense to establish sectional superiority and a more centralized form of government, and to deprive us of our rights and liberties. We have now briefly proposed a plan which we believe will save our country. It may be imperfect, but in all human probability it would give us our independence. No objection ought to outweigh it which is not weightier than independence. If it is worthy of being put in practice it ought to be mooted quickly before the people, and urged earnestly by every man who believes in its efficacy. Negroes will require much training; training will require time, and there is danger that this concession to common sense may come too late.

P. R. Cleburne, major-general, commanding division
D. C. Govan, brigadier-general
John E. Murray, colonel, Fifth Arkansas
G. F. Baucum, colonel, Eighth Arkansas
Peter Snyder, lieutenant-colonel, commanding Sixth and Seventh Arkansas
E. Warfield, lieutenant-colonel, Second Arkansas
M. P. Lowrey, brigadier-general
A. B. Hardcastle, colonel, Thirty-second and Forty-fifth Mississippi
F. A. Ashford, major, Sixteenth Alabama
John W. Colquitt, colonel, First Arkansas
Rich. J. Person, major, Third and Fifth Confederate
G. S. Deakins, major, Thirty-fifth and Eighth Tennessee
J. H. Collett, captain, commanding Seventh Texas
J. H. Kelly, brigadier-general, commanding Cavalry Division"

Knowing that his suggestion was highly controversial and would undoubtedly meet with considerable opposition, Cleburne believed his colleagues could, nonetheless, be persuaded to support it. He could not have been more wrong. When Cleburne's suggestion was presented to fellow officers at a meeting of the Army of Tennessee on January 2, 1864, his proposal was met with polite silence, if not outright awe. Although news of Cleburne's suggestion to free the slaves made its way across the South, the Army of Tennessee officially had no response and did not act upon it. Fittingly, by the spring of 1864, the Union forces would occupy Dalton, and many runaway slaves from northwest Georgia made their way to Chattanooga, eventually being mustered into the 14th and 44th United States Colored Infantry.

Not only did Confederate President Jefferson Davis give no consideration to Cleburne's idea, historians believe Cleburne's suggestion most likely undermined his almost-assured promotion to lieutenant general. While Cleburne understood the military necessities, Davis almost certainly was aware of the political ramifications. In his famous "Cornerstone" speech, delivered in March 1861, the Confederacy's Vice President, Alexander Stephens, explained the reason for secession.

Claiming that the Founding Fathers' assumption that the races were equal was wrong, Stephens explained, "Our new government is founded upon exactly the opposite idea; its foundations are laid, its corner–stone rests, upon the great truth that the negro is not equal to the white man; that slavery — subordination to the superior race — is his natural and normal condition."

The Union had recognized the potential value of including blacks among their ranks as early as mid-1862, and several Union commanders formed all-black units even before Secretary of War Edwin Stanton issued the official orders to do so in August of 1862. Additionally, when black soldiers fighting for the Union were captured in battle, Confederate soldiers routinely treated them far more severely than their White counterparts--threatening to execute them on the spot or put them in irons. At the Battle of Fort Pillow fought on April 12, 1864, Confederate Major General Nathan Bedford Forrest and his men have been widely accused of massacring black soldiers garrisoning the fort by shooting them after they had surrendered. Forrest would later write of Fort Pillow, "The approximate loss was upward of five hundred killed, but few of the officers escaping. My loss was about twenty killed. It is hoped that these facts will demonstrate to the Northern people that negro soldiers cannot cope with Southerners." As a man who was apathetic about slavery and was realistic about the fact that properly trained black soldiers would fight just as well as properly trained white soldiers, Cleburne seems to have had perspective few Southerners would allow themselves to entertain.

Due to Southern prejudice and the Confederates' lingering doubts regarding the fighting abilities of blacks, Confederate President Jefferson Davis refused to even consider the idea of conscripting black soldiers until over a year after Cleburne had floated the idea. In early 1865, when Confederate President Jefferson Davis told his generals, "We are reduced to choosing whether the negros shall fight for or against us," leading secessionist Thomas Howell Cobb responded pointedly, "Gentlemen, if slaves make good soldiers our whole theory of slavery is wrong."

Ultimately it would require Robert E. Lee to come out in support of a plan similar to the one Cleburne brought before the Army of Tennessee. With Lee's support, on March 13, 1865, the Confederate Congress voted by a very narrow margin to pass the Negro Soldier Bill, designed to arm slaves and grant them freedom after the war for their service and loyalty to the Confederacy. Even then, the scope of freeing slaves envisioned by Southern politicians was drastically more limited than Cleburne's proposal, which would have freed more than merely the slaves that were armed and fought. In support of the bill, General Robert E. Lee stated that arming blacks was "not only expedient but necessary." It was already past necessary; Lee would surrender at Appomattox less than a month later, and the Civil War would be all but over by the end of April.

Given the way the war ended, and the belated manner in which the Confederates began to warm up to Cleburne's suggestion, Cleburne is often given credit for being a visionary in this regard. However, it's only fair to note that the Confederates had serious concerns regarding the loyalty of freed slaves. Though Southerners often portrayed slavery as a benign institution that benefited blacks, if only for propaganda purposes, they were fully aware of the possibility that freed slaves might turn their guns upon their former masters.

Chapter 11: The Atlanta Campaign

Sherman united the armies for the Atlanta Campaign, which in essence formed the biggest army in American history. Sherman set his sights on the Confederacy's last major industrial city in the West and the General Joseph E. Johnston's Army of Tennessee, which aimed to protect it.

Joseph E. Johnston

After detaching troops for essential garrisons and minor operations, Sherman assembled his nearly 100,000 men and in May 1864 began his invasion of Georgia from Chattanooga, Tennessee, where his forces now spanned a line roughly 500 miles wide. The right wing and the cavalry, under General Oliver O. Howard, was directed to Jonesboro, Milledgeville, and then Atlanta; the left wing under General Henry W. Slocum was sent to Stone Mountain and then on to threaten Augusta, and ultimately meeting up with Howard's forces. The 60,000 strong Army of the Cumberland, under General Thomas, formed the backbone of Sherman's forces.

Throughout May 1864, Lee skillfully stalemated Grant in a series of battles known as the

Overland Campaign, inflicting nearly 50,000 casualties on the Army of the Potomac. The casualties were so staggering that Grant was constantly derided as a butcher, and his lack of progress ensured that anti-war criticism of the Lincoln Administration continued into the summer before the election. The Democrats nominated George McClellan, the former leader of the Army of the Potomac. McClellan had not been as aggressive as Lincoln hoped, but he was still exceedingly popular with Northern soldiers despite being fired twice, and the Democrats assumed that would make him a tough candidate against Lincoln. At the same time, Radical Republicans were still unsure of their support for Lincoln, and many begun running their own campaign against Lincoln for not prosecuting the war vigorously enough, urging Lincoln to withdraw from the campaign. It would fall upon Sherman's forces in the West to deliver the necessary victory.

During the Civil War, one of the tales that was often told among Confederate soldiers was that Joseph E. Johnston was a crack shot who was a better bird hunter than just about everyone else in the South. However, as the story went, Johnston would never take a shot when asked to, complaining that something was wrong with the conditions that prevented him from being able to shoot the bird when it was time. The story is almost certainly apocryphal, but it aptly demonstrated the South's frustration with a man who everyone regarded as a capable general but seemed ever reluctant to take a chance or take the fight to the enemy. Johnston was never badly beaten in battle, but he had a habit of "strategically withdrawing" until he had nowhere else to go. In 1862, Johnston had retreated in the face of McClellan's Army of the Potomac until it was less than 10 miles from Richmond. A wound to Johnston led to his replacement by Robert E. Lee over the Army of Northern Virginia, and the salvation of Richmond.

Two years later, Johnston's army of 50,000 now found itself confronted by almost double its numbers, and General Johnston began gradually retreating in the face of Sherman's forces, despite repulsing them in initial skirmishes at Resaca and Kennesaw Mountain. Cleburne's division was engaged in these relatively small battles, but aside from Kennesaw Mountain, where a frontal assault incurred a few thousand casualties, Sherman continued to eschew full-scale attacks in favor of strategic movements designed to continue moving toward Atlanta.

Johnston continued to retreat toward Atlanta throughout May and June, which greatly worried President Davis. Davis and Johnson already had a rocky relationship, and when Johnston retreated to within 3 miles of Atlanta, Davis replaced him with John Bell Hood, an aggressive general who had served as a division commander under Longstreet at places like Gettysburg and

Chickamauga.

Taking command in early July 1864, Hood lashed out at Sherman's armies with several frontal assaults on various portions of Sherman's line, but the assaults were repulsed, particularly at Peachtree Creek on July 20, where Thomas's defenses hammered Hood's attack. At the same time, Sherman was unable to gain any tactical advantages when attacking north and east of Atlanta.

After Peachtree Creek, Cleburne participated in the Battle of Atlanta when Hood ordered Lt. Gen. William J. Hardee's corps to march around the Union left flank while Maj. Gen. Benjamin Cheatham's corps assaulted the front. The mismanaged coordination resulted in Hardee not getting his troops in position in time, allowing General James Birdseye McPherson to reinforce his left. Despite hours of fighting, some of it hand-to-hand, and the death of McPherson, the only Union commanding general to die in battle, the Union managed to repulse the Confederate assault and inflict nearly 8,500 casualties on Hood's army, damage the Southerners could ill afford.

In August, Sherman moved his forces west across Atlanta and then south of it, positioning his men to cut off Atlanta's supply lines and railroads. When the Confederate attempts to stop the maneuvering failed, the writing was on the wall. On September 1, 1864, Hood and the Army of Tennessee evacuated Atlanta and torched everything of military value.

On September 3, 1864, Sherman famously telegramed Lincoln, "Atlanta is ours and fairly won." Two months later, so was Lincoln's reelection.

Sherman has earned fame and infamy for being the one to bring total war to the South, and it started at Atlanta. Once his men entered the city, Sherman ordered the 1,600 citizens remaining in Atlanta to evacuate the city as he, in Grant's words, set out to "destroy [Atlanta] so far as to render it worthless for military purposes," with Sherman himself remaining a day longer to supervise the destruction himself "and see that it was well done." Then on November 14, 1864, Sherman abandoned the ravaged city, taking with him thirteen thousand mules and horses and all the supplies the animals could carry.

One of the most famous movies of all time, *Gone With The Wind*, depicts the burning of Atlanta after Sherman occupied it in 1864. Over time, history came to view Sherman as a harbinger of total war, and in the South, Sherman is still viewed as a brutal warmonger. Considerable parts of Atlanta and Columbia did burn when Sherman occupied them in 1864 and 1865 respectively, but how responsible was Sherman for the initial fires? The answer is unclear.

As part of its retreat out of Atlanta, Confederate forces were ordered to burn anything of military value to keep it from falling into the hands of Sherman's army. Inevitably, those fires did not stay contained, damaging more than their intended targets. In November, preparing for the March to the Sea, Sherman similarly ordered everything of military value burned. Those fires also spread, eventually burning much of Atlanta to the ground. When Sherman's men left, only 400 buildings were left standing in the city.

Chapter 12: Cleburne's Engagement

Prior to the Franklin-Nashville Campaign of 1864, Cleburne was serving as Best Man at the wedding of friend and fellow officer General William Hardee, when he met Susan Tarleton, the bride's Maid of Honor. Instantly "smitten," he convinced her to allow him to "call upon her" the following day and subsequently accompanied her (along with the rest of the wedding party) to her hometown of Mobile, Alabama, where the Hardee wedding celebration continued. From there, Patrick and Susan became inseparable.

Hardee

Upon arriving in Mobile, Alabama state officials organized a military review in General Cleburne's honor. Impressed with her new suitor's celebrity and apparent popularity, she spent the remainder of Patrick's two-week furlough with him until it was time for him to report back to his command. Asking her to marry before he returned to the front, she responded neither yes or no, suggesting that they write to each other, thus beginning a long-distance romance via mail currier. A month later, Patrick scheduled another leave of absence, only his second since he entered the war, and awaited Susan's consent. Two weeks later, a giddy Patrick confided to a fellow officer that after six weeks, Susan had finally agreed to marry him.

It was a marriage destined to never take place.

Chapter 13: The Battle of Franklin

"If this that is so dear to my heart is doomed to fail, I pray heaven may let me fall with it, while my face is toward the enemy and my arm battling for that which I know to be right." – Patrick Cleburne, October 1864

Sherman's march to the sea is one of the best known campaigns of the Civil War, and when he successfully took Savannah, he telegraphed Lincoln to offer the city as a "Christmas gift". Lincoln responded, "Many, many thanks for your Christmas gift – the capture of Savannah. When you were leaving Atlanta for the Atlantic coast, I was anxious, if not fearful; but feeling that you were the better judge, and remembering that 'nothing risked, nothing gained' I did not interfere. Now, the undertaking being a success, the honour is all yours; for I believe none of us went farther than to acquiesce. And taking the work of Gen. Thomas into the count, as it should be taken, it is indeed a great success."

Lincoln's reference to "the work of Gen. Thomas" was alluding to arguably the most decisive battle of the entire Civil War. Sherman's Atlanta Campaign and March to the Sea will forever overshadow what Thomas accomplished at the end of 1864, but the Franklin-Nashville campaign may have been the most lopsided of the war.

As Sherman began his infamous march, Lincoln instructed General Grant to redirect General Thomas' efforts back to Tennessee to protect Union supply lines and stop the offensive mounted by Confederate general John Bell Hood. Hood had broken away from Atlanta, Georgia, and was endeavoring to force Sherman to follow him, thus diverting him from his intended path of destruction. With Sherman marching east toward the sea, he directed Thomas to try to block Hood around Nashville.

Hood

In late November, Thomas's men, being led by his principal subordinate John Schofield, all but blindly stumbled into Hood's forces, and it was only through luck that some of them had not been bottled up before they could regroup together. Receiving word of Union troop movement in the Nashville area, General Hood sent for his generals while attempting to hold off Schofield's advance. Hood knew that if Schofield reached Thomas' position, their combined armies would number more than twice his. Though the Confederates successfully blocked Schofield's route to Nashville, the Union general managed to execute an all-night maneuver that brought him to Franklin, about 18 miles south of Nashville.

As Major General Patrick Cleburne led his men toward Franklin to join Hood, he passed St. John's Episcopal Church, commending as he gazed at the quaint, ivy-covered Gothic-style church with its well-maintained cemetery, that no spot he'd seen in America reminded him so much of his native Ireland. "Almost worth dying for, to be buried in such a beautiful spot," he said. Several of his men would be haunted by that uncanny remark for years to follow.

On November 29, the Union army began digging in around Columbia, and late the following afternoon Hood ordered a frontal assault on the dug in Union army, which upset his own officers. Hood stressed the necessity of defeating Schofield's forces before Thomas could arrive, though some historians believe his decision to mount a frontal attack was a rash decision made out of fury at the fact Schofield had escaped his grasp. Cleburne, perhaps the most vocally outspoken opponent of the plan, suggested a counter-proposal: a plan to flank the Union position. Hood refused to consider it, and as Cleburne mounted his horse and acknowledged his duty, Cleburne rallied his men and promised Hood, "We will take the works or fall in the attempt!" In a more private remark to one of his brigadier generals, Daniel Gowan, Cleburne said, "Well, Govan, if we are to die, let us die like men."

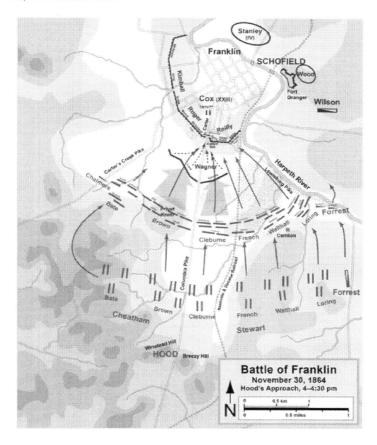

When the fighting began at 4:00 pm that afternoon, the sun was already starting to set as Cleburne's division was chosen to lead what would later be recognized as one of the most "ill-conceived and futile" assaults of the Western Theatre; an open-field charge against a heavily-fortified Union position that could only result in heavy casualties. In typical Cleburne fashion, the general led the charge, and after he had his first mount shot out from under him, he quickly called for another. His second mount was almost instantly killed as well.

Now deciding to proceed on foot, Cleburne removed his trademark French military kepi, set it atop his sword, thrust it high into the air so that his troops could follow his lead, and then disappeared into the thick, black smoke rolling across the battlefield. Though the exact details of his death are unknown, he was last seen advancing on foot toward the Union line with his sword still in the air. He no doubt made himself one of the most conspicuous targets on the field in his attempt to make himself visible to his men. Later accounts report that he was found just inside the Union line, with his body later carried back to an aid station along the Columbia Turnpike. Confederate war records list the cause of death as a shot to the abdomen or possibly a bullet to the heart. When Cleburne's body was found, it was missing his boots, sword, watch, and everything else of value.

Often referred to as the "Pickett's Charge of the West", the assault of 20,000 men famously resulted in the death or wounding of 14 of the Confederacy's generals, most famously Patrick Cleburne, the "Stonewall of the West". In *The Army of Tennessee*, historian Stanley F. Horn described the Battle of Franklin:

> "The annals of war may long be searched for a parallel to the desperate valor of the charge of the Army of Tennessee at Franklin, a charge which has been called "the greatest drama in American history." Perhaps its only rival for macabre distinction would be Pickett's Charge at Gettysburg. A comparison of the two may be of interest. Pickett's total loss at Gettysburg was 1,354; at Franklin the Army of Tennessee lost over 6,000 dead and wounded. Pickett's charge was made after a volcanic artillery preparation of two hours had battered the defending line. Hood's army charged without any preparation. Pickett's charge was across an open space of perhaps a mile. The advance at Franklin was for two miles in the open, in full view of the enemy's works, and exposed to their fire. The defenders at Gettysburg were protected only by a stone wall. Schofield's men at Franklin had carefully constructed works, with trench and parapet. Pickett's charge was totally repulsed. The charge of Brown and Cleburne penetrated deep into the breastworks, to part of which they clung until the enemy retired. Pickett, once repelled, retired from the field. The Army of Tennessee renewed their charge, time after time. Pickett survived his charge unscathed. Cleburne was killed, and eleven other general officers were killed, wounded or captured. "Pickett's charge at Gettysburg" has come to be a synonym for unflinching courage in the raw. The slaughter-pen at Franklin even more deserves the gory honor."

After repeated frontal assaults failed to create a gap in the Union lines, Schofield withdrew his men across the river on the night of November 30, successfully escaping Hood's army. Meanwhile, Hood had inflicted nearly 8,000 casualties upon his army, men the Confederacy could ill afford to lose, while the Union lost about a quarter of that.

Despite practically wrecking his army, which was now only about 25,000 strong, Hood marched his battered army to a position outside Nashville, Tennessee, where he took up defensive positions while awaiting reinforcements from Texas. About two weeks later, at the Battle of Nashville (December 15–16, 1864), Thomas effectively destroyed Hood's command, inflicting over 6,000 more Confederate casualties while losing less than half that. Upon reaching his headquarters at Tupelo, Mississippi, General Hood requested to be relieved of command, rather than be removed in disgrace.

Chapter 14: Cleburne's Legacy

The death of Major General Patrick Ronayne Cleburne was a heavy blow to the Confederacy and to his would-be bride. It is said that Susan learned of Patrick's death five days after the battle while working in her garden, when a small boy delivering the daily newspaper approached and said: "Read all about it . . . big battle near Franklin, Tennessee! General Cleburne killed! Read all about it!"

Susan eventually accepted the marriage proposal of Hugh Laign Cole, a former Confederate officer of the Second North Carolina Infantry and staff officer to Generals G. B. Anderson and Braxton Bragg. Married in 1867, the couple was awaiting the birth of their first child when on June 30, 1868 Susan died from a cerebral hemorrhage.

Major General Patrick Ronayne Cleburne's body was initially laid to rest at St. John's Episcopal Church near Mount Pleasant, Tennessee, where it remained for six years. It was the very church Cleburne had first noticed during the campaign leading to the Battle of Franklin. In 1870, for reasons unknown, General Cleburne was disinterred and moved to his adopted hometown of Helena, Arkansas, buried with much fanfare in Maple Hill Cemetery, overlooking the Mississippi River.

Patrick Ronayne Cleburne became the highest-ranking Irish-born officer in American military history, ultimately attaining the rank of major general. Though there were celebrated Irish officers and Irish brigades on both sides of the fighting, Cleburne was the only Irishman to be promoted so loftily during the Civil War.

Despite the fact that Patrick Ronayne Cleburne can not be credited with winning any great battles and had no apparent effect on the outcome of the Civil War, Cleburne, referred to by many in his time as the "Stonewall of the West", was one of the most popular Confederate division commanders of the War. His British military training, discipline, and charm earned him the loyalty and respect of his men, and he was held in singular high esteem by the public at large. And like Stonewall Jackson's untimely demise at Chancellorsville, a victim of friendly fire, Cleburne's death at the Battle of Franklin was widely viewed as a needless loss to the Confederate Army and to the Southern cause as well. Cleburne was mourned throughout the

Confederacy; and his men grieved over his death for months.

As many historians and students of military strategy readily acknowledge, Cleburne was quite unlike most other combat officers, who seemingly used one general template regarding the positioning of men on the battlefield and would make minor tweaks depending on the terrain. Cleburne, on the other hand, tended to assess the terrain as the determining factor in positioning his men, instead of vice-versa. That versatility no doubt accounted for his uncanny ability to establish nearly-impenetrable lines of defense on both the front line and in rear guard actions, and it was a key to his men's ability to resist much larger forces opposing them. More than just a simple offense vs. defense perspective, Cleburne had apparently developed a rather unique method of assessment and deployment of the men under his command not typical for the Civil War.

There was another important way Cleburne distinguished himself from many of his contemporaries. While it can truthfully be said that the characteristics of the prominent generals of the Civil War ran the full gamut of personality types, generally many Civil War commanders were self-promoters, aloof, arrogant, inept, and fundamentally unfriendly individuals. This was especially the case with Confederate leaders in the West, where politics and friendship with Jefferson Davis trumped merit. While there are certainly numerous exceptions to this assessment, none seems to fall less within this dubious category than Patrick Ronayne Cleburne, particularly in his capacity as a Civil War field commander.

One often told story illustrating Cleburne's singular sense of humanity occurred in the fall of 1864 after his division had found itself cut off from supply trains while crossing the mountains of north Georgia and was forced to live off the land. Though many commanders, both Union and Confederate, thought nothing of appropriating food, livestock, and even personal possessions from the farms they encountered, Cleburne had given his men specific orders not to intrude on private property. In that apple, chestnut, and persimmon trees were abundant in the area, he thought it unnecessary to steal from the very people they had sworn to protect. Five or six of his men, however, chose to disobey his orders, proceeding to raid a nearby private apple orchard.

A short time later, Confederate forces under General Hiram Granbury approached Cleburne's position, finding the general sitting on a split-rail fence smoking his corn cob pipe. At his feet sat six bushel baskets of apples, and nearby stood two of his personal aides and the six men who had disobeyed orders, who according to Granbury were looking "mean as they well could look." As Granbury approached, he saluted Cleburne, who smiled and said, "General Granbury, I am peddling apples today. These gentlemen [he pointed to the men apparently under arrest] have been very kind. They have gathered the apples for me and charged nothing! Now, you get down and take an apple, and have each of your men pass by and take one -- only one, mind you -- until they are gone!" Understanding full-well Cleburne's motivation, Granbury smiled, took an apple, and ordered his men to line up and follow suit. With the guilty parties now thoroughly embarrassed by having to see the condemning face of each man as they approached, Cleburne then made each man carry a fence rail two miles as punishment. While the punished men probably resented Cleburne for being stringent regarding the taking of apples in the area, they also had to understand that a commander who led strictly "by-the-book" would have handled the situation much differently, and no doubt more harshly.

Another incident, which speaks to his humanity and sense of fairness occurred a short time later near Atlanta, Georgia after a company out on patrol encountered a stray cow and, being out of fresh meat, decided the opportunity was just too good to pass up. Killing and dragging it a quarter mile back to camp, the men, expecting their bivouac to break at any moment, quickly set out to slaughter the animal, cut it into transportable chunks, and cook it on a scaffold over an open fire. But before they could execute their plan, General Cleburne came riding up on an inspection of his troops.

Fearing they would be disciplined for their unauthorized actions, one man in the company quickly ran up to the general and said, "General, we have some nice, fat beef cooking, and it is about done; come and eat dinner with us!" Quickly realizing what they had done, Cleburne smiled and said, "Well, it does smell good! I believe I will!" Instead of punishing his men for their indiscretion, he applauded their resourcefulness and took the opportunity to share a meal with them, never questioning the source of the beef.

Several physical locations are named after Patrick Ronayne Cleburne including Cleburne County in Alabama and Arkansas, and the city of Cleburne, Texas.

The spot where General Cleburne was killed in Franklin, Tennessee was reclaimed by preservationists and is now designated "Cleburne Park."

The Patrick R. Cleburne Confederate Cemetery is a memorial cemetery in Jonesboro, Georgia named in honor of General Cleburne.

Major General Patrick Cleburne's Civil War frock coat and horse bridle are on display at the Museum of the Confederacy at Appomattox, Virginia.

Bibliography

Catton, Bruce. *Grant Takes Command.* New York: Little, Brown and Company, 1968.
    This Hallowed Ground. Great Britain: Wordsworth, 1998.

Davis, Kenneth C. *The Civil War: Everything You Need to Know About America's Greatest Conflict but Never Learned*. New York: William Morrow and Company, Inc., 1996.

Encyclopedia of Arkansas History & Culture, "Patrick Ronayne Cleburne (1828–1864)." Accessed via: http://encyclopediaofarkansas.net/encyclopedia/entry-detail.aspx?entryID=339 07.27.2012.

Find a Grave website: Susan Tarleton Cole, http://www.findagrave.com/cgi-bin/fg.cgi?page=gr&GRid=10516356

Gaffney, P., and D. Gaffney. *The Civil War: Exploring History One Week at a Time*. New York: Hyperion, 2011.

Gragg, Rod. *The Illustrated Confederate Reader*. New York: Gramercy Books, 1989.

Lanning, Michael Lee. *The Civil War 100*. Illinois: Sourcebooks, Inc., 2006.

McPherson, James M. *Ordeal by Fire: The Civil War and Reconstruction*. New York: McGraw-Hill, 2001.

Rand, Clayton. *Sons of the South*. New York: Holt, Rinehart and Winston, 1961.

Stevens, Joseph E. *1863: The Rebirth of a Nation*. New York: Bantam Books, 1999.

A.P. Hill
Chapter 1: Early Years

Ambrose Powell Hill, Jr. was born on November 9, 1825, fourth of eight children born to Major Thomas and Fannie (or Frances) Russell Baptist Hill, at "Greenland," the Hill family estate, ten miles west of Culpeper, Virginia.

He was named for his uncle, Ambrose Powell Hill (1785–1858), who served in both houses of the Virginia legislature, and Captain Ambrose Powell, an Indian fighter, explorer, sheriff, legislator, and close friend of President James Madison. Hill's family and friends began calling him "Powell" or "Little Powell" from a very early age, and the nickname would stick.

The last of four sons, "Powell" had three older brothers: John Henry, Edwin Baptist, and Thomas Theophilius, who were followed by four younger sisters: Evelyn, Ann, Margret Ann, and Lucy. Despite their age difference (eight years apart), Powell was closest to sister Lucy, who he often referred to as "Lute."

When "Powell" was still a boy, his father Thomas moved the family from "Greenland" into the town of Culpeper Court House, taking up residence in a large brick home which still stands at the corner of Main and Davis Streets.

Hill's boyhood home

From his father, young "Powell" learned the skills of horsemanship and enjoyed hunting and fishing with his father and older brothers. If surviving accounts can be trusted, even from a young age he and his father shared many a discussion over the validity of "Southern states rights", but given his death during the Civil War, most of what has been written about him was secondhand and mostly came after the war, with accounts invariably taking his record and perceived characteristics into account.

As his mother's youngest son, Powell and Fannie grew particularly close. Fannie was said to have been particularly sensitive regarding her mental illness, though other members of the family commented on her "real or imaginary" maladies, but Powell enjoyed reading with her. Eventually this habit resulted in Powell becoming an avid reader, and he is said to have devoured everything from Shakespeare to the Bible to the historical accounts of French military and political leader Napoleon Bonaparte.

While few details of "Powell's" early education survive, his early schooling has been traced to the town of Culpeper Court House, Virginia, where he was apparently educated at a number of local schools, then to the Black Hills Seminary, a boarding school where fellow classmates are said to have noted that his devotion to studying exceeded that of all the other students.

While attending various Culpeper Court House schools, "Powell" developed friendships with a number of local residents, among them future Confederate general and Virginia governor James Kemper, who later described Powell as "self reliant, forceful, and bright." As fate would have it, Kemper would lead a regiment in Hill's brigade in early 1862 and take Hill's brigade after Powell was promoted to command of a division. And though Powell also attended Black Hills Seminary, he remained enamored with the exploits of history's legendary military leaders, especially Napoleon.

Kemper

When "Powell" was about 15, his mother joined the "New Light" Baptist revival movement then sweeping across central Virginia, and in her newfound zeal for religion she banned card-playing and dancing in the Hill household, resulting in the young boy developing a rebellious nature regarding religion. Hill's aversion to religion left him at odds with future West Point classmate Thomas Jonathan Jackson, and later in his professional life he would exhibit what has been described as *somewhat irreligious* tendencies that would rub several overtly religious commanders serving in the Confederate Army the wrong way during the Civil War.

When "Powell" announced to his family that he'd decided to follow the military path and become a soldier, his family immediately set their efforts (and social clout) toward securing him a place at West Point; his father pushing him towards the field of arms. To secure an appointment to the Academy, a prospective cadet needed to obtain a formal recommendation from a Congressman or political official, so family and friends petitioned their Congressmen and Secretary of War John Spencer on Powell's behalf.

Their concerted efforts paid off on April 26, 1842, when the 16-year-old "Powell" accepted a conditional appointment to West Point Military Academy as a member of the Class of 1846.

Chapter 2: West Point

At the age of 16, one year younger than the mandated 17, "Powell" (or "A. P." as some of his classmates would soon begin to refer to him) embarked on the career in which he would spend the remainder of his life: professional soldier. Southern journalist Edward Pollard, whose voluminous *Lost Cause* helped set the course of Civil War historiography upon its publication in the late 1860s, would later write of Hill, "He had made arms not only his profession, but an enthusiastic study, to which he was prompted by the natural tastes and dispositions of his mind." Commissioned to enter the United States Military Academy at West Point, New York in 1842, he became one of 85 hopeful cadets; an appointment did not guarantee that a cadet could stay, only that he would be given the chance to demonstrate his academic prowess.

Upon arrival, "A. P." was assigned to Room 36, becoming the roommate of the highly intelligent son of a prominent Philadelphian doctor and founder of Jefferson Medical College, George B. McClellan. During their years together, McClellan and Hill would become exceptionally close friends, with the remarkably brilliant McClellan assumed to have helped A. P. with his studies. Though a bright and studious cadet, Hill found West Point a challenging environment. Its coursework, which included mathematics, engineering, military tactics, natural philosophy, geology, drawing, astronomy, rhetoric, mineralogy, chemistry, French, geography, history, ethics, and law, was rigorous and difficult.

McClellan

In their strict and Spartan living quarters, "A. P." and McClellan became fast friends with future Civil War generals Darius N. Couch, George E. Pickett, Jesse L. Reno, George Stoneman, Truman Seymour, and Cadmus M. Wilcox. As Union generals, McClellan, Couch, Reno, Stoneman, and Seymour would all find themselves fighting against Hill's men on Civil War battlefields. Hill's class also included his future Confederate commander, Thomas Stonewall Jackson , but Hill and the other native Virginians did not initially get along with the silent and more reserved Jackson. Additionally, by the time Jackson arrived at West Point on June 20, 1842, the final day to report to campus, Hill, Dabney Maury, George Pickett, and Birkett Fry had already formed their own clique. The four Virginians quickly determined "Jackson is a jackass" and made no attempts to befriend him.

Jackson as a cadet at West Point

By the end of his first year at West Point (1842-1843), Hill was positioned 39th of 83 cadets in his class, ranked 38th in French and 39th in mathematics. On the Conduct Roll, he was ranked 142nd in conduct of 223 cadets in all classes, with 53 demerits. By the end of his second year (1843-1844), Hill had improved his overall class rank to 23rd of 78th, standing 30th in mathematics, 19th in French, 18th in English grammar, and 13th in drawing/drafting. He completed his second year at 129th of 211 cadets, with 70 demerits on the Conduct Roll.

Like all the other cadets completing their second year at West Point, Hill looked forward to visiting home during the summer break of 1844. Now almost 19 years-of-age, the young cadet returned to Culpeper, enjoying all the attention and notoriety his town typically afforded returning cadets parading the town streets in dress uniform. On his way back to the Academy, however, Hill made a mistake that would haunt him for the remainder of his life and ultimately cost him a year at West Point. Returning from furlough with a case of gonorrhea, consequent medical complications caused him to miss so many classes that he was required to repeat his third year and was nearly dismissed altogether. Though many historians continue to consider him part of the now-famous "Class of '46", Hill was reassigned to the Class of 1847 and thus made new friendships with several future Civil War generals, including Ambrose Burnside and Henry Heth. Hill's men would fight Burnside's men in the final hours of the Battle of Antietam, and it would be Heth's division in Hill's corps that would begin the Battle of Gettysburg.

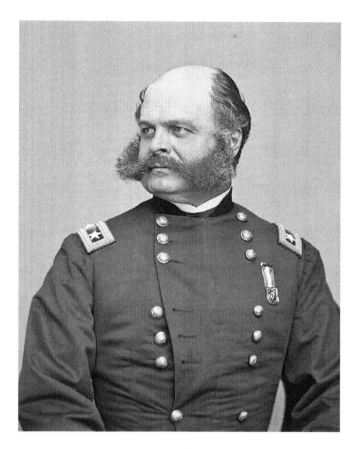

Burnside

In 1847, Hill graduated 15th in his class of 38, and he was appointed brevet Second Lieutenant Ambrose Powell Hill, Jr. of the First U. S. Army Artillery.

Chapter 3: Life Before the Civil War

Despite having been given the brevet rank of second lieutenant in the First U. S. Army Artillery upon graduation from West Point in 1847, Hill was attached to a cavalry company and sent to Mexico to fight in the Mexican-American War. However, Hill saw no major combat during the war, even while classmates like McClellan and Pickett distinguished themselves during the fighting. At the conclusion of the Mexican-American War, Hill was assigned garrison duties on the Atlantic coast before being transferred to Florida in the 1850s to assist in the forced relocation of the Seminoles

In 1855, Hill was sent to fight in the Seminole War, but in a harbinger of things to come, he missed the worst of the fighting due to various illnesses. He served in Florida and along the Texas frontier for approximately a year, but once again his military accomplishments during this period were relatively undistinguished.

Hill ultimately contracted an illness that was probably a mild case of yellow fever, though some historians contend he had begun to display "imaginary" illnesses as his mother had. Whatever the case, he requested permission from Secretary of War (and future Confederate President) Jefferson Davis to be transferred to Washington, D. C., and in response Davis complied by having him appointed to the Coast Survey Office from 1855-1860.

In the years before the war, the most memorable aspect of his personal life was his engagement to the future wife of his close friend George McClellan during the 1850s. When McClellan returned from observing the Crimean War in 1856, he began courting Ellen Marcy, the daughter of his former commander Captain Randolph Barnes Marcy, who had been in charge of the Red River expedition and had promoted McClellan to brevet captain. But Ellen, or "Nelly," as she was referred to, refused McClellan's first proposal of marriage; by then, she had already received nine marriage proposals from a variety of prominent suitors, most notably one from A. P. Hill. In fact, if Ellen could have had her way, it would have been Hill who she married. Hill and Ellen were in love, and later in 1856 Ellen accepted Hill's proposal of marriage, but he ultimately withdrew the proposal because her family disapproved of him. Hill and McClellan remained friendly, but those familiar with their history often claimed that Hill would fight more tenaciously when opposing McClellan's army because of Ellen, an almost certainly apocryphal tale.

George and Ellen McClellan

Spurned by his lover's parents, on July 18, 1859 Hill married a young widow named Kitty ("Dolly") Morgan McClung, making him the brother-in-law of future Confederate cavalry generals John Hunt Morgan (Hill's best man) and Basil W. Duke.

Chapter 4: The Start of the Civil War

While Hill was in Florida and on the frontier, the United States was trying to sort out its intractable issues. In an attempt to organize the center of North America – Kansas and Nebraska

– without offsetting the slave-free balance, Senator Stephen Douglas of Illinois proposed the Kansas-Nebraska Act. The Kansas-Nebraska Act eliminated the Missouri Compromise line of 1820, which the Compromise of 1850 had maintained. The Missouri Compromise had stipulated that states north of the boundary line determined in that bill would be free, and that states south of it *could* have slavery. This was essential to maintaining the balance of slave and free states in the Union. The Kansas-Nebraska Act, however, ignored the line completely and proposed that all new territories be organized by popular sovereignty. Settlers could vote whether they wanted their state to be slave or free.

When popular sovereignty became the standard in Kansas and Nebraska, the primary result was that thousands of zealous pro-slavery and anti-slavery advocates both moved to Kansas to influence the vote, creating a dangerous (and ultimately deadly) mix. Numerous attacks took place between the two sides, and many pro-slavery Missourians organized attacks on Kansas towns just across the border.

The best known abolitionist in Bleeding Kansas was a middle aged man named John Brown. A radical abolitionist, Brown organized a small band of like-minded followers and fought with the armed groups of pro-slavery men in Kansas for several months, including a notorious incident known as the Pottawatomie Massacre, in which Brown's supporters murdered five men. Over 50 people died before John Brown left the territory, which ultimately entered the Union as a free state in 1859.

After his activities in Kansas, John Brown spent the next few years raising money in New England, which would bring him into direct contact with important abolitionist leaders, including Frederick Douglass. Brown had previously organized a small raiding party that succeeded in raiding a Missouri farm and freeing 11 slaves, but he set his sights on far larger objectives. In 1859, Brown began to set a new plan in motion that he hoped would create a full scale slave uprising in the South. Brown's plan relied on raiding Harpers Ferry, a strategically located armory in western Virginia that had been the main federal arms depot after the Revolution. Given its proximity to the South, Brown hoped to seize thousands of rifles and move them south, gathering slaves and swelling his numbers as he went. The slaves would then be armed and ready to help free more slaves, inevitably fighting Southern militias along the way.

In recognition of how important escaped slave Frederick Douglass had become among abolitionists, Brown attempted to enlist the support of Douglass by informing him of the plans. While Douglass didn't blow the whistle on Brown, he told Brown that violence would only further enrage the South, and slaveholders might only retaliate further against slaves with devastating consequences. Instead of helping Brown, Douglass dissuaded freed blacks from joining Brown's group because he believed it was doomed to fail.

Despite that, in July 1859, Brown traveled to Harper's Ferry under an assumed name and waited for his recruits, but he struggled to get even 20 people to join him. Rather than call off the plan, however, Brown went ahead with it. That fall, Brown and his men used hundreds of rifles to seize the armory at Harper's Ferry, but the plan went haywire from the start, and word of his attack quickly spread. Local pro-slavery men formed a militia and pinned Brown and his men down while they were still at the armory.

Several of Hill's future comrades in the Army of Northern Virginia played a role in the Harpers Ferry raid. After being called to Harpers Ferry, Robert E. Lee took decisive command of a troop of marines stationed there, surrounded the arsenal, and gave Brown the opportunity to surrender peaceably. When Brown refused, Lee ordered the doors be broken down and Brown taken captive, an affair that reportedly lasted just three minutes. A few of Brown's men were killed, but Brown was taken alive. Lee earned acclaim for accomplishing this task so quickly and efficiently.

Young JEB Stuart played an active role in opposing the raid at Harpers Ferry. In October of 1859, while conducting business in Washington, D.C., Stuart volunteered to carry secret instructions to Lieutenant Colonel Robert E. Lee and then accompany him and a squad of U. S. Military Militia to Harpers Ferry, where Brown had staged a raid on the armory. While delivering Lee's written ultimatum to the leader of the raid, who was going by the pseudonym Isaac Smith, Stuart remembered "Old Ossawatomie Brown" from the events at Bleeding Kansas, and ultimately assisted in his arrest.

The fallout from John Brown's raid on Harpers Ferry was intense. Southerners had long suspected that abolitionists hoped to arm the slaves and use violence to abolish slavery, and Brown's raid seemed to confirm that. Meanwhile, much of the northern press praised Brown for his actions. In the South, conspiracy theories ran wild about who had supported the raid, and many believed prominent abolitionist Republicans had been behind the raid as well. On the day of his execution, Brown wrote, "I, John Brown, am now quite *certain* that the crimes of this *guilty land* will never be purged away but with *blood.* I had, as I now think vainly, flattered myself that without very much bloodshed it might be done."

The man in command of the troops present at Brown's hanging was none other than Thomas Jonathan Jackson, who was ordered to Charlestown in November 1859. After Brown's hanging, the future Stonewall Jackson began to believe war was inevitable, but he wrote his aunt, "I think we have great reason for alarm, but my trust is in God; and I cannot think that He will permit the madness of men to interfere so materially with the Christian labors of this country at home and abroad."

In his memoirs, General James Longstreet summed up the national mood in the 1850s, likening it to a "war-cloud". "Officers of the Northern and Southern States were anxious to see the portending storm pass by or disperse, and on many occasions we, too, were assured, by those who claimed to look into the future, that the statesman would yet show himself equal to the occasion, and restore confidence among the people."

Clearly men like Longstreet were hoping at the time for some sort of grand compromise that would avert war, but by the Fall of 1860, everyone could see the "war-cloud" on the horizon. With the election of Republican candidate Abraham Lincoln as president on November 6, 1860, many Southerners considered it the final straw. Someone they knew as a "Black Republican", leader of a party whose central platform was to stop the spread of slavery to new states, was now set to be inaugurated as President in March.

Throughout the fall and winter of 1860, Southern calls for secession became increasingly serious. In a last-ditched effort to save the Union, Kentucky's Senator John Crittenden tried to assume the stateliness of his predecessor Henry Clay. Crittenden, however, proved to be no Henry Clay: his proposal that a Constitutional Amendment reinstate the Missouri Compromise line and extend it to the Pacific failed. President Buchanan supported the measure, but President-Elect Lincoln said he refused to allow the further expansion of slavery under any conditions.

The Crittenden Compromise failed on December 18. Two days later, South Carolina seceded from the Union. President Buchanan sat on his hands, believing the Southern states had no right to secede, but that the Federal government had no effective power to prevent secession. In January, Mississippi, Florida, Alabama, Georgia, Louisiana and Kansas followed South Carolina's lead. The Confederacy was formed on February 4th, in Montgomery, Alabama, with former Secretary of War Jefferson Davis as its President. On February 23rd, Texas joined the Confederacy.

Lincoln's predecessor was among those who could see the potential conflict coming from a mile away. As the Confederacy continued to grow during his last months in office, President James Buchanan instructed the federal army to permit the Confederacy to take control of forts in its territory, hoping to avoid a war. Conveniently, this also allowed Southern forces to take control of important forts and land ahead of a potential war, which would make secession and/or a victory in a military conflict easier. Many Southern partisans within the federal government at the end of 1860 took advantage of these opportunities to help Southern states ahead of time.

One of the forts in the South was Fort Sumter, an important but undermanned and undersupplied fort in the harbor of Charleston, South Carolina. Buchanan attempted to resupply Fort Sumter in the first few months of 1860, but the attempt failed when Southern sympathizers in the harbor fired on the resupply ship.

In his Inauguration Speech, President Lincoln struck a moderate tone. Unlike most Inauguration Addresses, which are typically followed by balls and a "honeymoon" period, Lincoln's came amid a major political crisis. To reassure the South, he reiterated his belief in the legal status of slavery in the South, but that its expansion into the Western territories was to be restricted. He outlined the illegality of secession and refused to acknowledge the South's secession, and promised to continue to deliver U.S. mail in the seceded states. Most importantly, he pledged to not use force unless his obligation to protect Federal property was restricted: "In doing this there needs to be no bloodshed or violence, and there shall be none unless it be forced upon the national authority. The power confided to me will be used to hold, occupy, and posess the property and places belonging to the Government and to collect the duties and imposts; but beyond what may be necessary for these objects, there will be no invasion, no using of force against or among the people anywhere."

Lincoln had promised that it would not be the North that started a potential war, but he was also aware of the possibility of the South initiating conflict. Although he vowed not to fire the first shot, Lincoln was likely aware that his attempt to resupply Fort Sumter in Charleston Harbor would draw Southern fire; it had already happened under Buchanan's watch. After his inauguration, President Lincoln informed South Carolina governor Francis Pickens that he was sending supplies to the undermanned garrison at Fort Sumter. When Lincoln made clear that he would attempt to resupply the fort, Davis ordered Beauregard to demand its surrender and prevent the resupplying of the garrison.

In early April, the ship Lincoln sent to resupply the fort was fired upon and turned around. On April 9, Confederate President Davis sent word to General Beauregard to demand the fort's evacuation. At the time, the federal garrison consisted of Major Robert Anderson, Beauregard's artillery instructor from West Point, and 76 troops. Even before the bombardment, upon learning that he was opposed by Beauregard, Anderson remarked that the Southern forces in Charleston harbor would be exercised with "skill and sound judgment". Beauregard also remembered his former superior, and before the bombardment, he sent brandy, whiskey and cigars to Anderson and his garrison, gifts the Major refused.

At 4:30 a.m. on the morning of April 12, 1861, Beauregard ordered the first shots to be fired at Fort Sumter, effectively igniting the Civil War. After nearly 34 hours and thousands of rounds fired from 47 artillery guns and mortars ringing the harbor, on April 14, 1861, Major Anderson surrendered Fort Sumter, marking the first Confederate victory. No casualties were suffered on either side during the dueling bombardments across Charleston harbor, but, ironically, two Union soldiers were killed by an accidental explosion during the surrender ceremonies.

Beauregard

After the attack on Fort Sumter, support for both the northern and southern cause rose. Two days later, Lincoln issued a *call-to-arms* asking for 75,000 volunteers. That led to the secession of Virginia, Tennessee, North Carolina, and Arkansas, with the loyalty of border states like Kentucky, Maryland, and Missouri still somewhat up in the air. The large number of southern sympathizers in these states buoyed the Confederates' hopes that those too would soon join the South. Moreover, the loss of these border states, especially Virginia, all deeply depressed Lincoln. Just weeks before, prominent Virginians had reassured Lincoln that the state's historic place in American history made its citizens eager to save the Union. But as soon as Lincoln made any assertive moves to save the Union, Virginia seceded. This greatly concerned Lincoln, who worried Virginia's secession made it more likely other border states and/or Maryland would secede as well.

For his part, Hill had already seen the future, and in October 1860 he obtained a leave of absence from the U. S. Army. On March 1, 1861, he resigned his commission, even before his native Virginia seceded from the Union itself. After Virginia seceded from the Union on April 17, 1861, in the wake of the attack on Fort Sumter, Hill's devotion to the Southern cause compelled him to accept an appointment as a colonel of the Thirteenth Virginia Infantry Regiment.

Chapter 5: First Bull Run

After Fort Sumter, the Lincoln Administration pushed for a quick invasion of Virginia, with the intent of defeating Confederate forces and marching toward the Confederate capitol of Richmond. Lincoln pressed Irvin McDowell to push forward. Despite the fact that McDowell knew his troops were inexperienced and unready, pressure from the Washington politicians forced him to launch a premature offensive against Confederate forces in Northern Virginia. His strategy during the First Battle of Bull Run was grand, but it proved far too difficult for his inexperienced troops to carry out effectively.

McDowell's strategy during the First Battle of Bull Run was grand, and in many ways it was the forerunner of a tactic Lee and Jackson executed brilliantly on nearly the same field during the Second Battle of Bull Run in August 1862. McDowell's plan called for parts of his army to pin down Beauregard's Confederate soldiers in front while marching another wing of his army around the flank and into the enemy's rear, rolling up the line. McDowell assumed the Confederates would be forced to abandon Manassas Junction and fall back to the next defensible line, the Rappahannock River. In July 1861, however, this proved far too difficult for his inexperienced troops to carry out effectively.

On July 18, Union General Irwin McDowell set out with two divisions on a twelve-mile circuitous march west from Centreville, Virginia to cross Bull Run at Sudley Springs Ford, intending to strike Beauregard's troops at Manassas-Sudley Road in an effort to turn the Southern left flank. Meanwhile, another division was set to drive directly west along the turnpike and across Stone Bridge, while back at Centreville, another division stayed in reserve. The remaining division, scattered along the lines of communication all the way back to Washington but would ultimately take no part in the ensuing battle, made a total of 32,000 men at McDowell's disposal.

The First Battle of Bull Run made history in several ways. McDowell's army met Fort Sumter hero P.G.T. Beauregard's Confederate army near the railroad junction at Manassas on July 21, 1861. Located just 25 miles away from Washington D.C., many civilians from Washington came to watch what they expected to be a rout of Confederate forces. And for awhile, it appeared as though that might be the case.

McDowell's strategy fell apart though, thanks to railroads. Confederate reinforcements under General Joseph E. Johnston's Army, including Hill's regiment and a brigade led by his old classmate Jackson, arrived by train in the middle of the day, a first in the history of American warfare. With Johnston's army arriving midday on July 21, it evened up the numbers between Union and Confederate. Shoring up the Confederates' left flank, some of Johnston's troops, led by Jackson's brigade, helped reverse the Union's momentum and ultimately turn the tide. As the battle's momentum switched, the inexperienced Union troops were routed and retreated in disorder back toward Washington in an unorganized mass. With over 350 killed on each side, it was the deadliest battle in American history to date, and both the Confederacy and the Union were quickly served notice that the war would be much more costly than either side had believed.

Like in Mexico and Florida, however, Hill missed the brunt of the fighting. His men had been assigned to help guard the Confederates' right flank, so he missed the action that earned Stonewall Jackson his legendary nickname. Nevertheless, after participating in a series of minor skirmishes, on February 26, 1862, Hill was promoted to brigadier general and given command of a brigade in the ironically named Confederate Army of the Potomac.

Chapter 6: The Peninsula Campaign

After First Manassas, the victorious Confederate army under Joseph E. Johnston stayed camped near the outskirts of Washington D.C., while the North reorganized the Army of the Potomac under George B. McClellan. McClellan was widely considered a prodigy for his West Point years, his service in Mexico, his observation during the Crimean War, and his oft-forgotten campaign in Western Virginia against Robert E. Lee in 1861. Though he is best known for his shortcomings today, McClellan had nearly ended Lee's Civil War career before it started, as General Lee was blamed throughout the South for losing western Virginia after his defeat at the Battle of Cheat Mountain. Lee would eventually be reassigned to constructing coastal defenses on the East Coast, and when his men dug trenches in preparation for the defense of Richmond, he was derisively dubbed the "King of Spades". That Lee was even in position to assume command of the Army of Northern Virginia the following year during the Peninsula Campaign was due more to his friendship with Jefferson Davis than anything else. The fact Davis played favorites with his generals crippled the South throughout the war, but it certainly worked in the South's favor with Lee.

Lee may have been derided, but A.P. Hill was on the rise. During the winter and spring of 1862, Brigadier General Hill rose quickly in power, ultimately given command of what would later become the famed "Light Division." The largest division in the Army of Northern Virginia, it was originally comprised of about six brigades and 14,000-15,000 men. It would become Hill's trademark and claim-to-fame.

As he was reorganizing the Army of the Potomac, McClellan vastly overestimated the strength of Johnston's army, leading him to plan an amphibious assault on Richmond that avoided Johnston's army in his front. In response, Johnston moved his army toward Culpeper Court

House, which angered President Davis because it signified a retreat. For that reason, Davis brought Lee to Richmond as a military adviser, and he began to constrain Johnston's authority by issuing direct orders himself.

However, Johnston's movement had disrupted McClellan's anticipated landing spot. McClellan had already faced a number of issues in planning the campaign even before reaching the jumpoff point. The first option for the landing spot (Urbana) had been scrapped, and there was bickering over the amount of troops left around Washington without the Army of the Potomac fighting on the Overland line. Finally, in March of 1862, after nine months in command, General McClellan began his invasion of Virginia, initiating what would become known as the "Peninsula Campaign." Showing his proclivity for turning movement and grand strategy, McClellan completely shifted the theater of operations. Rather than march directly into Richmond and use his superior numbers to assert domination, he opted to exploit the Union sea dominance and move his army via an immense naval flotilla down the Potomac into Chesapeake Bay and land at Fort Monroe in Hampton, Virginia, at the southern tip of the Virginia Peninsula. In addition to his 130,000 thousand men, he moved 15,000 thousand horses and mules by boat as well. There he planned for an additional 80,000 men to join him, at which time he would advance westward to Richmond. One of the European observers likened the launch of the campaign to the "stride of a giant."

McClellan's Peninsula Campaign has been analyzed meticulously and is considered one of the grandest failures of the Union war effort, with McClellan made the scapegoat. In actuality, there was plenty of blame to go around, including Lincoln and his Administration, which was so concerned about Stonewall Jackson's army in the Shenandoah Valley that several Union armies were left in the Valley to defend Washington D.C., and even more were held back from McClellan for fear of the capital's safety. The Administration also micromanaged the deployment of certain divisions, and with Stanton's decision to shut down recruiting stations in early 1862, combined with the Confederacy concentrating all their troops in the area, the Army of the Potomac was eventually outnumbered in front of Richmond.

At the beginning of the campaign, however, McClellen had vastly superior numbers at his disposal, with only about 70,000 Confederate troops on the entirety of the peninsula and fewer than 17,000 between him and Richmond. McClellan was unaware of this decisive advantage, however, because of the intelligence reports he kept receiving from Allen Pinkerton, which vastly overstated the number of available Confederate soldiers.

As Johnston marched his army to oppose McClellan, he was fully aware that he was severely outnumbered, even if McClellan didn't know that. For that reason, he was in constant communication with the leadership in Richmond, and in April he continued trying to persuade Davis and Lee that the best course of action would be to dig in and fight defensively around

Richmond. President Davis would have none of it.

From the beginning, McClellan's caution and the narrow width of the Peninsula worked against his army. At Yorktown, which had been the site of a decisive siege during the Revolution, McClellan's initial hopes of surrounding and enveloping the Confederate lines through the use of the Navy was scuttled when the Navy couldn't promise that it'd be able to operate in the area. That allowed General John Magruder, whose Confederate forces were outmanned nearly 4-1, to hold Yorktown for the entire month of April. Magruder accomplished it by completely deceiving the federals, at times marching his men in circles to make McClellan think his army was many times larger. Other times, he spread his artillery batteries across the line and fired liberally and sporadically at the Union lines, just to give the impression that the Confederates had huge numbers. The ruse worked, leaving the Union command thinking there were 100,000 Confederates.

As a result of the misimpressions, McClellan chose not to attack Yorktown in force, instead opting to lay siege to it. In part, this was due to the decisive advantage the Union had in siege equipment, including massive mortars and artillery. The siege successfully captured Yorktown in early May with only about 500 casualties, but Magruder bought enough time for Johnston's army to confront McClellan on the Peninsula.

During the Civil War, one of the tales that was often told among Confederate soldiers was that Joseph E. Johnston was a crack shot who was a better bird hunter than just about everyone else in the South. However, as the story went, Johnston would never take the shot when asked to, complaining that something was wrong with the situation that prevented him from being able to shoot the bird when it was time. The story is almost certainly apocryphal, but it was aptly used to demonstrate the Confederates' frustration with a man who everyone regarded as a capable general who became known more for losing by not winning. Johnston was never badly beaten in battle, but he had a habit of strategically withdrawing until he had nowhere left to retreat.

After Yorktown, Johnston began his retreat toward Richmond, while McClellan's army pursued. In the process, a Union division under Brig. General Joseph Hooker encountered the Confederate rearguard near Williamsburg under Maj. General James Longstreet on May 5, 1862. While Hooker repeatedly attacked Confederate forces at Fort Magruder, Union Brig. General Winfield S. Hancock's First Brigade began bombarding Longstreet's left flank, which included Hill's brigade. Hill's brigade staved off a Union attack, and he was credited with performing well at the Battle of Williamsburg. A few weeks later, Hill was promoted to the rank of major general and granted division command, and Lee himself would later claim Hill was the best major general in his army at the time.

After Williamsburg, the Union army still had a nearly 2-1 advantage in manpower, so Johnston continued to gradually pull his troops back to a line of defense nearer Richmond as McClellan advanced. In conjunction, the U.S. Navy began moving its operations further up the James River, until it could get within 7 miles of the Confederate capital before being opposed by a Southern fort. McClellan continued to attempt to turn Johnston's flank, until the two armies were facing each other along the Chickahominy River. McClellan's Army of the Potomac got close enough to Richmond that they could see the city's church steeples.

By the end of May, Stonewall Jackson had startlingly defeated three separate Northern armies in the Valley, inducing Lincoln to hold back the I Corps from McClellan. When McClellan was forced to extend his line north to link up with troops that he expected to be sent overland to him, Johnston learned that McClellan was moving along the Chickahominy River. It was at this point that Johnston got uncharacteristically aggressive. Johnston had run out of breathing space for his army, and he believed McCellan was seeking to link up with McDowell's forces. Moreover, about a third of McClellan's army was south of the river, while the other parts of the army were still north of it, offering Johnston an enticing target. After a quick deluge turned the river into a rushing torrent that would make it impossible or the Union army to link back up or aid each other, Johnston drew up a very complex plan of attack for different wings of his army, and struck at the Army of the Potomac at the Battle of Seven Pines on May 31, 1862.

Like McDowell's plan for First Bull Run, the plan proved too complicated for Johnston's army to execute, and after a day of bloody fighting little was accomplished from a technical standpoint. At one point during the Battle of Seven Pines, Confederates under General James Longstreet marched in the wrong direction down the wrong road, causing congestion and confusion among other Confederate units and ultimately weakening the effectiveness of the massive Confederate counterattack launched against McClellan. Johnston wrote in his memoirs, "The operations of the Confederate troops in this battle were very much retarded by the dense woods and thickets that covered the ground, and by the deep mud and broad ponds of rain-water, in many places more than knee-deep, through which they had to struggle."

By the time the fighting was finished, nearly 40,000 had been engaged on both sides, and it was the biggest battle in the Eastern theater to date (second only to Shiloh at the time). However, McClellan was rattled by the attack, and near the end of the fighting that night Johnston had attempted to rally his men by riding up and down the battleline only to be nearly blown off his horse by artillery fire and having to be taken off the field. Johnston explained, "About seven o'clock I received a slight wound in the right shoulder from a musket-shot, and, a few moments after, was unhorsed by a heavy fragment of shell which struck my breast. Those around had me borne from the field in an ambulance; not, however, before the President, who was with General Lee, not far in the rear, had heard of the accident, and visited me, manifesting great concern, as he continued to do until I was out of danger." Having been seriously wounded, Johnston's command was given the following day to military advisor Robert E. Lee.

Lee

Hill and his men hadn't taken part in the battle, but the following day, on June 1, 1862, Major General Hill officially dubbed his division the "Light Division," immediately setting out to promote its reputation for speed and agility. After the War, one of the men serving in the famous division wrote, "The name was applicable, for we often marched without coats, blankets, knapsacks, or any other burdens except our arms and haversacks, which were never heavy and sometimes empty."

Although the Battle of Seven Pines was tactically inconclusive, McClellan's resolve to keep pushing forward vanished. He maneuvered his army so that it was all south of the Chickahominy, but as he settled in for an expected siege, Lee went about preparing Richmond's defenses and devising his own aggressive attacks.

With more Confederate troops swelling the ranks, Lee's army was McClellan's equal by late June, and on June 25, Lee commenced an all-out attempt to destroy McClellan's army in a series of fierce battles known as the Seven Days Battles. After a stalemate in the first fighting at Oak Grove, Lee's army kept pushing ahead, using Stonewall Jackson to attack McClellan's right. Although Stonewall Jackson was unusually lethargic during the week's fighting, the appearance of his "foot cavalry" spooked McClellan even more, and McClellan was now certain he was opposed by 200,000 men, more than double the actual size of Lee's army. It also made McClellan think that the Confederates were threatening his supply line, forcing him to shift his army toward the James River to draw supplies.

On June 26, the Union defenders sharply repulsed the Confederate attacks at Mechanicsville, in part due to the fact that Stonewall Jackson had his troops bivouac for the night despite the fact heavy gunfire indicating a large battle was popping off within earshot. Major General Hill showed "remarkable alacrity and remarkable drive", which was sorely lacking in many of Lee's commanders at that time, but at times he was also impetuous in command. At the Battle of Mechanicsville, Hill was directed to cross the Meadow Bridge and Mechanicsville roads and wait until Jackson could coordinate his attack against Union Brig. General Andrew Porter's Fifth Corp, north of the Chickahominy. Hill's Light Division was to advance when they heard Jackson's guns, then clear the Union pickets from Mechanicsville and then move to Beaver Dam Creek.

However, when Jackson was delayed and Hill thought he had waited long enough, even though General Lee's forces were only two miles away, Hill took it upon himself to launch an attack. It was an ill-conceived assault that would prove much more costly than Lee could ever have anticipated. General Lee's ordnance chief, Lieutenant Colonel Edward Porter Alexander, described Hill's miscalculation: "The full strength of the [Union] position, particularly the inaccessible feature of it, was not apparent to the eye until one had entirely crossed the plain swept by their fire and gotten actually up to the valley of the creek. A. P. Hill's men, advancing confidently, were at first allowed by the enemy to approach quite closely, when a sudden and tremendous fire of infantry and artillery at short range drove them back with some loss. We then brought up our artillery and a very severe duel between, perhaps, fifty guns [began]. . . ." Although Hill was not the only subordinate to blame for the ultimate failure of the plan, it resulted in a Union tactical victory, with the Confederates suffering heavy casualties while achieving none of their specific objectives.

While the Army of the Potomac kept retreating, McClellan managed to keep his forces in tact (mostly through the efforts of his field generals), ultimately retreating to Harrison's Landing on the James River and establishing a new base of operation. Feeling increasingly at odds with his superiors, in a letter sent from Gaines' Mills, Virginia dated June 28, 1862, a frustrated McClellan wrote to Secretary of War Stanton, "If I save the army now, I tell you plainly that I owe no thanks to any other person in the Washington. You have done your best to sacrifice this army." McClellan's argument, however, flies in the face of common knowledge that he had become so obsessed with having sufficient supplies that he'd actually moved to Gaines' Mill to accommodate the massive amount of provisions he'd accumulated. Ultimately unable to move his cache of supplies as quickly as his men were needed, McClellan eventually ran railroad cars full of food and supplies into the Pamunkey River rather than leave them behind for the

Confederates.

Despite the fact all of Lee's battle plans had been poorly executed by his generals, particularly Stonewall Jackson, he ordered one final assault against McClellan's army at Malvern Hill. Incredibly, McClellan was not even on the field for that battle, having left via steamboat back to Harrison's Landing. Biographer Ethan Rafuse notes McClellan's absence from the battlefield was inexcusable, literally leaving the Army of the Potomac leaderless during pitched battle, but McClellan often behaved coolly under fire, so it is likely not a question of McClellan's personal courage.

Ironically, Malvern Hill was one of the Union army's biggest successes during the Peninsula Campaign, and A.P. Hill was fortunate to be held in reserve with his men. Union artillery had silenced its Confederate counterparts, but Lee still ordered an infantry attack by D.H. Hill's division, which never got within 100 yards of the Union line. After the war, D.H. Hill famously referred to Malvern Hill, "It wasn't war. It was murder." Later that evening, as General Isaac Trimble (who is best known for leading a division during Pickett's Charge at Gettysburg) began moving his troops forward as if to attack, he was stopped by Stonewall Jackson, who asked "What are you going to do?" When Trimble replied that he was going to charge, Jackson countered, "General Hill has just tried with his entire division and been repulsed. I guess you'd better not try it."

After Malvern Hill, McClellan withdrew his army to Harrison's Landing, where it was protected by the U.S. Navy along the James River and had its flanks secured by the river itself. At this point, the bureaucratic bickering between McClellan and Washington D.C. started flaring up again, as McClellan refused to recommence an advance without reinforcements. After weeks of indecision, the Army of the Potomac was finally ordered to evacuate the Peninsula and link up with John Pope's army in northern Virginia, as the Administration was more comfortable having their forces fighting on one line instead of exterior lines. Upon his arrival in Washington, McClellan told reporters that his failure to defeat Lee in Virginia was due to Lincoln not sending sufficient reinforcements.

Following the Seven Days' Campaign, Major General Hill became embroiled in a dispute with Confederate general James Longstreet over a series of newspaper articles that appeared in the *Richmond Examiner,* with relations between Hill and Longstreet deteriorating to the point where Hill was placed under arrest. The two sides sent in their own portrayals in the papers, dueling back and forth.

"About four o'clock Monday afternoon, General James Longstreet having been called away, the command of his division was assumed by General A.P. Hill, who with both divisions --that of James Longstreet and his own-- engaged the enemy at a later hour in the evening.

The battle was thus fought under the immediate and sole command of General A.P. Hill, in charge of both divisions.

Never was a more glorious victory plucked from desperate and threatening circumstances.

One fact is very certain, and that is that the battle of Monday night was fought exclusively by General A.P. Hill and the forces under his command.

Hill's division has constantly been used on the enemy's front at every stage of the contest from Beaver Dam and Cold Harbor to the late field in the vicinity of Darbytown, to which no name has yet been given. It is a melancholy evidence of the achievements of this division, that out of a force of 14,000 men, with which it went into action on Friday evening last, it now cannot probably bring more than 6,000 efficient men into action."

Longstreet also responded in the papers:

"Since the commencement of the Chickahominy campaign some articles have appeared in the Richmond Examiner which are calculated to do injustice to some of the officers and to alarm our people. No one in the army has any objection to Major General A.P. Hill's being supplied with all the notoriety that the Examiner can furnish, provided no great injustice is done to others. His staff officer, through the columns of the Examiner, claims that he had command of the field on Monday for a short time, intimating an improper absence of some other officers. General Lee and Major General James Longstreet rode upon the field together, and some hours before Major General A.P. Hill. Both of these officers remained upon the field and slept there, neither having left it for an instant. Major General James Longstreet was absent from his usual position for an hour perhaps, for the purpose of putting one of Gen. Hill's brigades (Gregg's) into action.

The "eight thousand" claimed to have been lost by Gen. A.P. Hill's Division alone will cover the loss of the entire army during the week's campaign. Trifling wounds will swell the list above this figure, but the actual loss will fall short of it. Exaggerated statements of casualties, like those made by the Examiner, are calculated to be a great injury to the army, both at home and abroad."

After Hill reportedly challenged Longstreet to a duel, the dispute was resolved in July 1862 when Lee sent Hill and his division to reinforce Stonewall Jackson at Gordonsville, Virginia. By some accounts, when Hill reached Gordonsville he found there were five court martials against him, involving Jackson and other officers of his staff. Longstreet would later claim that Hill became a corps commander in 1863 based solely on the fact he was from Virginia, an incendiary and likely inaccurate charge.

Longstreet

Chapter 7: The Northern Virginia

Campaign

Even before McClellan had completely withdrawn his troops, Lee sent Jackson's forces northward to intercept the new army Abraham Lincoln had placed under Maj. General John Pope, formed out of the scattered troops in the Virginia area. Pope had found success in the Western theater, and he was uncommonly brash, instructing the previously defeated men now under his command that his soldiers in the West were accustomed to seeing the backs of the enemy. Pope's arrogance turned off his own men, and it also caught the notice of Lee.

On June 26, General Pope deployed his forces in an arc across Northern Virginia; its right flank under Maj. General Franz Sigel positioned at Sperryville on the Blue Ridge Mountains, its center columns under Maj. General Nathaniel P. Banks at Little Washington, and its left flank under Maj. General Irvin McDowell at Falmouth on the Rappahannock River. On July 13, Lee responded by sending Jackson with 14,000 men to Gordonsville, with Maj. General A. P. Hill's division of 10,000 men set to join him by July 27.

At the Battle of Cedar Mountain in Culpeper County, Virginia, on August 8 (or 9), Major General Hill is credited with coming to the aid of Jackson's men by launching a Light Division counterattack that stabilized the Confederate left flank, thus preventing it from being routed by Union Maj. General Nathaniel P. Banks. Jackson, who had not reconnoitered properly, was in danger of being beaten back by the vanguard of Banks' force when Hill came rushing in and changed the course of the battle, leading to a collapse of the Union right. Though outsiders thought Hill and Jackson worked like a "well oiled war machine," in reality, the two were maintaining an increasingly contentious relationship.

The fact the two generals were at each other's throats was somewhat ironic, given that both of them were stern men. One of the men in his regiment recalled Hill's actions during the battle:

"I saw A.P. Hill that day as he was putting his "Light Division" into battle, and was very much struck with his appearance. In his shirtsleeves and with drawn sword he sought to arrest the stragglers who were coming to the rear, and seeing a Lieutenant in the number, he rode at him and fiercely inquired: "Who are you, sir, and where are you going?" The trembling Lieutenant replied: "I am going back with my wounded friend." Hill reached down and tore the insignia of rank from his collar as he roughly said: "You are a pretty fellow to hold a commission -- deserting your colors in the presence of the enemy, and going to the rear with a man who is scarcely badly enough wounded to go himself. I reduce you to the ranks, sir, and if you do not go to the front and do your duty, I'll have you shot as soon as I can spare a file of men for the purpose." And then clearing the road, he hurried forward his men to the splendid service which was before them."

Following the Battle of Cedar Mountain, General Jackson amassed his corps and divisions, including Hill's Light Division, and marched (without opposition) to the Rappahannock River in eastern Virginia.

Once certain McClellan was in full retreat, Lee joined Jackson, planning to strike Pope before McClellan's troops could arrive as reinforcements. In late August 1862, in a "daring and unorthodox" move, Lee divided his forces and sent Jackson northward to flank them, ultimately bringing Jackson directly behind Pope's army and supply base. This forced Pope to fall back to Manassas to protect his flank and maintain his lines of communication. Recognizing Lee's genius for military strategy, General Jackson quickly became Lee's most trusted commander, and he would later say that he so trusted Lee's military instincts that he would even follow him into battle blindfolded.

When Pope's army fell back to Manassas to confront Jackson, his wing of Lee's army dug in along a railroad trench and took a defensive stance. The Second Battle of Manassas or Bull Run was fought August 28-30, beginning with the Union army throwing itself at Jackson the first two days. By daybreak on August 28, Major General Hill was positioned on the Confederate left along the "unfinished railroad," showing for the first time his ability to not only be a good offensive fighter but a good defensive fighter by holding the line against repeated Union attacks while three horses were shot out from under him. But regardless of his successes, his contentious relationship with Jackson proceeded to escalate, overshadowing his accomplishments.

When Longstreet's men finally arrived around noon on August 29, Lee informed Longstreet of his plan to attack the Union flank, which was at that time concentrating its efforts on General Jackson. Longstreet initially rejected Lee's suggestion to attack, recommending instead that a reconnaissance be conducted to survey the field. And although Longstreet's artillery was ultimately a major factor in helping Jackson resist the Union attack on August 29, his performance that day was described by some Lost Cause advocates as slow, and they considered his disobedience of General Lee insubordination. Lee's most famous biographer, Douglas Southall Freeman, later wrote: "The seeds of much of the disaster on July 2, 1863, at the Battle of Gettysburg were sown in that instant—when Lee yielded to Longstreet and Longstreet discovered that he would."

Nevertheless, the Second Battle of Bull Run or Manassas is considered one of Longstreet's most successful, While Jackson's men defended themselves the first two days, Lee used Longstreet's wing on August 30 to deliver a devastating flank attack before reinforcements from the retreating Army of the Potomac could reach the field. Longstreet's attack swept Pope's army off the field. Fought on the same ground as the First Battle of Manassas nearly a year earlier, the result was the same: a decisive Confederate victory that sent Union soldiers scrambling back to the safety of Washington.

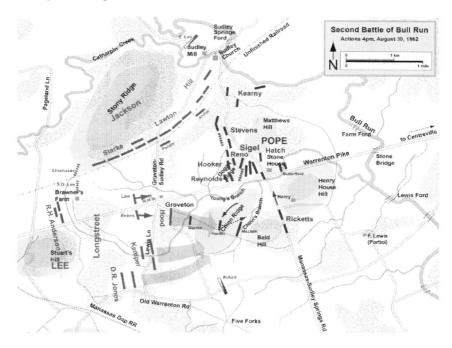

During the entirety of the Northern Virginia/Second Bull Run Campaign, Hill was involved in numerous disputes with Stonewall Jackson concerning Jackson's marching orders to Hill. Jackson had made several subordinates bristle because of his secrecy and his refusal to communicate objectives to them when on the march. By some accounts, Jackson sought to have Hill moved to another command, with most historians concurring that at a minimum, Jackson had Hill placed under arrest as his division entered Maryland in the fall of 1862, and subsequently had to be released by Lee's direct order so that he could participate in the capture of Harpers Ferry in September.

Chapter 8: The Maryland Campaign

After two days' fighting, Lee had achieved another major victory, and he now stood unopposed 12 miles away from Washington D.C. While Johnston and Beauregard had stayed in this position in the months after the first battle, Lee determined upon a more aggressive course: taking the fighting to the North.

In early September, convinced that the best way to defend Richmond was to divert attention to Washington, Lee had decided to invade Maryland after obtaining Jefferson Davis's permission. Today the decision is remembered through the prism of Lee hoping to win a major battle in the North that would bring about European recognition of the Confederacy, potential intervention, and possible capitulation by the North, whose anti-war Democrats were picking up political momentum. However, Lee also hoped that the fighting in Maryland would relieve Virginia's resources, especially the Shenandoah Valley, which served as the state's "breadbasket". And though largely forgotten today, Lee's move was controversial among his own men. Confederate soldiers, including Lee, took up arms to defend their homes, but now they were being asked to invade a Northern state. An untold number of Confederate soldiers refused to cross the Potomac River into Maryland.

In the summer of 1862, the Union suffered more than 20,000 casualties, and Northern Democrats, who had been split into pro-war and anti-war factions from the beginning, increasingly began to question the war. As of September 1862, no progress had been made on Richmond; in fact, a Confederate army was now in Maryland. And with the election of 1862 was approaching, Lincoln feared the Republicans might suffer losses in the congressional midterms that would harm the war effort. Thus, he restored General McClellan and removed General Pope after the second disaster at Bull Run. McClellan was still immensely popular among the Army of the Potomac, and with a mixture of men from his Army of the Potomac and Pope's Army of Virginia, he began a cautious pursuit of Lee into Maryland.

Historians believe that Lee's entire Army of Northern Virginia had perhaps 50,000 men at most and possibly closer to 30,000 during the Maryland campaign. However, Lee sized up George McClellan, figured he was a cautious general, and decided once again to divide his forces throughout Maryland. In early September, he ordered Jackson to capture Harpers Ferry while he and Longstreet maneuvered his troops toward Frederick. With McClellan now assuming command of the Northern forces, Lee expected to have plenty of time to assemble his troops and bring his battle plan to fruition.

As General Lee marched his Army of Northern Virginia down the Shenandoah Valley into Maryland, he planned to capture the garrison and arsenal at Harpers Ferry to secure his supply line back to Virginia. But even before they were far into Maryland, Jackson and Hill were getting on each other's nerves, and after one scolding from Jackson on September 3, witnesses noticed Hill responded to the reprimand "rather sullenly, his face flushing up."

During another march, Hill became furious after finding that Jackson had directly ordered his division to halt without informing Hill of the change in plans. When Hill asked his subordinates why they halted, and he was informed that it was Jackson's orders, he confronted Jackson and offered him his sword, telling him, "If you take command of my troops in my presence, take my sword also." Jackson responded, "Put up your sword and consider yourself in arrest." Another Confederate soldier remembered afterward that Hill "marched on foot with the rear guard all the day through Maryland, an old white hat slouched over his eyes, his coat off and wearing an old flannel shirt, looking mad as a bull."

Eventually, both of the generals cooled their tempers, and by September 10 Hill was asking to be restored to command ahead of battle, a request Jackson granted. A Confederate noted that after being restored to command, Hill " mounted his horse and dashed to the front of his troops, and looking like a young eagle in search of his prey, took command of his division to the delight of all his men."

To Jackson's advantage, Col. Dixon S. Miles, Union commander at Harpers Ferry, had insisted on keeping most of his troops near the town instead of taking up commanding positions on the most important position, Maryland Heights. After a day of minor skirmishes on September 12, concerted attacks by two Confederate brigades finally drove the Union troops from the surrounding heights on September 13. During the ensuing fighting that took place on Maryland Heights, additional Confederate columns under Stonewall Jackson arrived and discovered that critical positions to the west and south of town were not defended. By the morning of September 15, Jackson had positioned nearly 50 guns on Maryland Heights and at the base of Loudoun Heights. After a fierce artillery barrage and infantry assault, Union commanders realized the futility of resisting, opting then to surrender. Having played a significant role in capturing Harpers Ferry, Jackson's men began to march to link up with the rest of Lee's army, while Hill's Light Division was left behind to process Union prisoners.

Meanwhile, unbeknownst to the Confederates, the North received one of the greatest strokes of luck during the Civil War. For reasons that are still unclear, Union troops in camp at Frederick came across a copy of Special Order 191, wrapped up among three cigars. The order contained Lee's entire marching plans for Maryland, making it clear that the Army of Northern Virginia had been divided into multiple parts, which, if faced by overpowering strength, could be entirely defeated and bagged. The "Lost Order" quickly made its way to General McClellan, who took several hours to debate whether or not it was intentional misinformation or actually real. Once he decided it was accurate, McClellan is said to have famously boasted, "Here is a paper with which if I cannot whip *Bobby Lee*, I will be willing to go home."

The North's luck was helped by Confederate cavalry leader JEB Stuart, who had no clue orders had been lost and was busy handling public relations instead of reconnaissance. Now officially designated the "Eyes of the Army," in September of 1862, Stuart committed what many military historians deem his first tactical error when, for a five-day period at the beginning of the Maryland Campaign, he rested his men and entertained local civilians at a gala ball at Urbana, Maryland rather than keep the Union enemy under surveillance. With no incoming intelligence, Lee was unaware of Union General McClellan's location and the speed at which his forces approached.

Eventually, the Confederates figured out where McClellan was, and to Lee's great surprise, McClellan's army began moving at an uncharacteristically quick pace, pushing in on his Confederate forces at several mountain passes at South Mountain, including at Turner's Gap and Crampton's Gap. While Jackson's wing was forcing the Harpers Ferry garrison to surrender, Lee regathered his other scattered units around Sharpsburg near Antietam Creek. McClellan's army, which may have outnumbered Lee's forces by about 50,000 men, confronted the Confederates around the night of September 16.

Longstreet described the scene before the battle commenced: "The blue uniforms of the federals appeared among the trees that crowned the heights on the eastern bank of the Antietam. The number increased, and larger and larger grew the field of blue until is seemed to stretch as far as the eye could see, and from the tops of the mountains down to the edge of the stream gathered the great army of McClellan."

As fate would have it, the bloodiest day in the history of the United States took place on the 75th anniversary of the signing of the Constitution. On September 17, 1862, Lee's Army of Northern Virginia fought McClellan's Army of the Potomac outside Sharpsburg along Antietam Creek. That day, nearly 25,000 would become casualties, and Lee's army barely survived fighting the much bigger Northern army. The fighting that morning started with savage fighting on the Confederate left flank near Dunker church, in a corn field and forests. In one of the most legendary parts of the battle, John Bell Hood's division had come up to the field and had not eaten breakfast, so they were held in reserve and allowed to start preparing a meal. Just before they could eat, however, they were called into action, infuriating his men. Thankfully for the Confederates, it would be the Union who felt the brunt of their fury:

Hood's division helped the Confederates stave off the first major assault in the north, but Lee's army may have been saved by the Northern army's inability to cross the creek near "Burnside's Bridge". Ambrose Burnside had been given command of the "Right Wing" of the Army of the Potomac (the I Corps and IX Corps) at the start of the Maryland Campaign for the Battle of South Mountain, but McClellan separated the two corps at the Battle of Antietam, placing them on opposite ends of the Union battle line. However, Burnside continued to act as though he was a wing commander instead of a corps commander, so instead of ordering the IX corps, he funneled orders through General Jacob D. Cox. This poor organization contributed to the corps's hours-long delay in attacking and crossing what is now called "Burnside's Bridge" on the right flank of the Confederate line.

Making matters worse, Burnside did not perform adequate reconnaissance of the area, which afforded several easy fording sites of the creek out of range of the Army of Northern Virginia. Instead of unopposed crossings, his troops were forced into repeated assaults across the narrow bridge which was dominated by Confederate sharpshooters on high ground across the bridge. The delay allowed A.P. Hill to provide his most memorable Civil War service.

As Burnside's men pushed in on his right flank, Lee turned to see dust from a unit marching from the southwest. Had they been Union men, his entire army may have been bagged at Sharpsburg, and when Lee asked whose troops they were, one of his aides assured him, "They are flying the Virginia flags." Lee excitedly announced, "It is A.P. Hill from Harper's Ferry!"

One of Jackson's aides recalled Hill's arrival just in the nick of time:

"But then, just then, A.P. Hill, picturesque in his red battleshirt, with 3 of his brigades, 2500 men, who had marched 17 miles from Harpers Ferry and had waded the Potomac, appeared upon the scene. Tired and footsore, the men forgot their woes in that supreme moment, and with no breathing time braced themselves to meet the coming shock. They met it and stayed it. The blue line staggered and hesitated, and hesitating, was lost. At the critical moment A.P. Hill was always at his strongest. ... Again A.P. Hill, as at Manassas, Harper's Ferry, and elsewhere had struck with the right hand of Mars. No wonder both Lee and Jackson, when, in the delirium of their last moments on earth, they stood again to battle saw the form of A.P. Hill leading his columns on; but it is a wonder and a shame that the grave of this valiant Virginian has not a stone to mark it and keep it from oblivion."

Writer William Allan would note of Hill's performance:

"It was at this critical moment that A. P. Hill, who had marched seventeen miles from Harper's Ferry that morning, and had waded the Potomac, reached the field upon the flank of Burnside's victorious column. With a skill, vigor and promptness, which cannot be too highly praised, A. P. Hill formed his men in line, and threw them upon Burnside's flank. Toombs, and the other brigades of D. R, Jones's division, gave such aid as they were able. The Confederate artillery was used with the greatest courage and determination to check the enemy, but it was mainly A. P. Hill's attack which decided the day at this point, and drove Burnside in confusion and dismay back to the bridge. There is no part of General James Longstreet's article more unworthy than the single line in which he obscurely refers to the splendid achievement of a dead comrade, whose battles, like Ney's, were all for his country, and none against it, and who crowned a brilliant career by shedding his life's blood to avert the crowning disaster. A.P. Hill's march was a splendid one. He left Harper's Ferry sixteen hours after McLaws, but reached the battle-field only five hours behind him. McLaws had, however, the night to contend with. The vigor of Hill's attack, with hungry and march worn men, is shown by the fact that he completely overthrew forces twice as numerous as his own. Though his force of from two thousand to three thousand five hundred men was too small to permit of an extended aggressive, his arrival was not less opportune to Lee than was that of Blucher to Wellington at Waterloo, nor was his action when on the field in any way inferior to that of the Prussian field-marshal."

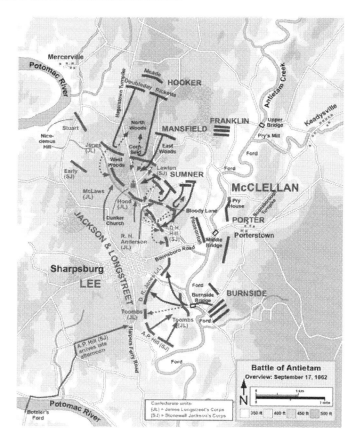

When told he had repulsed men under the command of Burnside, his West Point friend, Hill was reportedly asked if he knew his old classmate, to which he responded, ""Ought to! He owes me eight thousand dollars!" Hill had allegedly loaned the money to Burnside in their friendlier antebellum days.

In retrospect, Antietam was unquestionably the high point of Hill's career, and a success for which he should have received far more credit than he did. However, in order to fully understand the drama that unfolded there, historians suggest that the Battle of Antietam must be understood as a "feud erupting within a fight." In the month between Hill joining Jackson's command and Lee's defeat of Union general John Pope at Second Manassas (August 28–30, 1862), a series of events resulted in General Stonewall Jackson leveling charges against Hill regarding "neglect of duty." As a result, Jackson made little attempt to coordinate his battle strategy at Antietam with Hill. While many historians cite that Hill was often over-zealous and impatient on the battlefield, Jackson was notorious for playing his hand extremely "close to the vest," seldom sharing his over-all strategy even with his closest aides. Thus, the repercussions of the ongoing feud hindered any productive cooperation.

Although Hill's performance at Antietam was deemed particularly noteworthy—even by General Lee himself—it was sometimes credited to Jackson's command, even though Hill mostly acted independently. That made him guilty of acting without authority, but in this case his initiative to make command decisions may have saved his army.

After the battle, Hill congratulated his division: "You have done well and I am well pleased with you. You have fought in every battle from Mechanicsville to Shepherdstown, and no man can yet say that the Light Division was ever broken. You held the left at Manassas against overwhelming numbers and saved the army. You saved the day at Sharpsburg and at Shepherdstown. You were selected to face a storm of round shot, shell, and grape such as I have never before seen. I am proud to say to you that your services are appreciated by our general, and that you have a reputation in this army which it should be the object of every officer and private to sustain."

On the morning of September 18, Lee's army prepared to defend against a Union assault that ultimately never came. Finally, an improvised truce was declared to allow both sides to exchange their wounded. That evening, Lee's forces began withdrawing across the Potomac to return to Virginia, with McClellan, surprisingly, opting not to pursue, citing shortages of equipment and the fear of overextending his forces. Nevertheless, Antietam is now widely considered a turning point in the war. Although the battle was tactically a draw, it resulted in forcing Lee's army out of Maryland and back into Virginia, making it a strategic victory for the North and an opportune time for President Abraham Lincoln to issue the Emancipation Proclamation.

Chapter 9: Fredericksburg

In place of McClellan, Lincoln appointed Burnside, who had just failed at Antietam. Burnside didn't believe he was competent to command the entire army, a very honest (and accurate) judgment. However, Burnside also didn't want the command to fall upon Joe Hooker, who had been injured while aggressively fighting with his I Corps at Antietam in the morning. Thus, he accepted.

Meanwhile, Hill was engaged in disputes of his own, once again with Stonewall Jackson. With the feud now opened back up, Jackson wrote a sharp endorsement of Hill's request for a court of inquiry into his actions, denying flat out that he had kept a "black list" against the red headed Culpeper general. One wonders, however, if Hill's charge of a black list had merit. Richard Garnett, the commander of the Stonewall Brigade that Jackson made his scapegoat for the defeat in the March 1862 Valley battle of Kernstown, seems to have gotten into trouble mainly because Jackson -- who didn't want Garnett to command the brigade -- was looking specifically for any little thing to call on Garnett for messing up. After Jackson's death, it was noted by Kyd Douglas that "Hill did not forgive or forget," but apparently Jackson was of a similar unforgiving nature when it came to his commanders. That is not to say that Hill was not to some extent being petty, but it would be unfair to say all of the troubles were just a result of Powell Hill being a hot-head.

We can only imagine Lee's reaction to this argument --as seemingly petty as it was-- between two of his best chief lieutenants.

On October 3rd Jackson sent forward his charges against Hill. As the feud continued to boil over through an exchange of letters, Lee tried to get both men to drop it, but their wounded egos were too much even for their commanding general. As Jackson's mapmaker Jed Hotchkiss put it, "I hope all may blow by. Gen. Hill is a brave officer but perhaps too quick to resent seeming overstepping of authority. Gen. Jackson intends to do his whole duty. May good and not evil come out of this trouble."

Under pressure from Lincoln to be aggressive, Burnside laid out a difficult plan to cross the Rappahannock and attack the Confederates near Fredericksburg. The plan was doomed from the very beginning. On December 12, Burnside's army struggled to cross the river under fire from Confederate sharpshooters in the town.

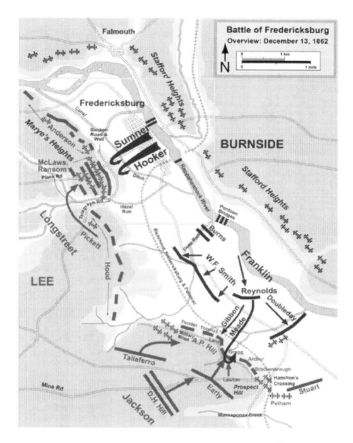

Major General Hill was positioned near the Confederate right along a ridge. However, due to swampy ground along his front, there was a 600-yard gap in Hill's front line, and the nearest brigade behind it was nearly a quarter mile away. Ultimately, dense vegetation prevented the brigade commander from seeing Union troops advancing on his position.

During the ensuing battle, Union Major General George Meade's division routed two of Hill's brigades and part of a third—with Hill requiring assistance from Major General Jubal Early's division to repulse the Union onslaught. In the final analysis, Hill's division had suffered over 2,000 casualties during the battle, which was nearly two-thirds of the casualties in Jackson's corps. The casualties included two of his brigade commanders, including the mortally wounded Maxcy Gregg.

After the battle, one of his Hill's brigade commanders, Brig. General James J. Archer, criticized Hill for leaving a gap in the division's front line, stating that Hill had been warned about it before the battle but did nothing to correct it. Additionally, many had noted that Hill had been absent from his division, with no record of where he was during the battle. However, these criticisms and allegations have detracted from a highly significant accomplishment, one described by Edward Porter Alexander, an artillery battalion commander under General Longstreet who stated: "As the Federals advanced [against Jackson's front lines] . . . Jackson's artillery along his whole line opened up on them very effectively. They developed a very heavy artillery fire in reply and their infantry pushed on a very handsome style and making a fine show. But as they came near enough to receive Jackson's artillery fire, their advance was checked. Several efforts were made to push them on but all failed except at one point upon the line of A. P. Hill's division." Thus, although history records that Hill played only a minor role in this Confederate victory (and by some reports, was missing in action), even his minimal involvement proved highly significant to the outcome.

However, the battle is mostly remembered for the piecemeal attacks the Union army made on heavily fortified positions Longstreet's men took up on Marye's Heights. With the massacre at Antietam still fresh in his mind (partially caused by the Confederates having not constructed defensive works), Longstreet ordered trenches, abatis (obstacles formed by felled trees with sharpened branches), and fieldworks to be constructed - which to Longstreet's credit, set a precedent for all future defensive battles of the Army of Northern Virginia. To his thinking, if the artillery didn't keep Union forces at bay, the twenty-five hundred Confederates lined up four-deep behind a quarter-mile long four-foot stone wall would deter even the most foolhardy. Thus when it was learned that General Burnside was planning a direct assault on "the Heights," even the other Union generals couldn't believe it.

As they threw themselves at Longstreet's heavily fortified position along the high ground, the Northern soldiers were mowed down again and again. General Longstreet compared the near continuous fall of soldiers on the battlefield to "the stead dripping of rain from the eaves of a house." Still, Burnside sent wave after wave up the hill, with the Union injured (or those just cowering in the field) trying to stop the advancing men by grabbing at their legs and feet-- begging them to turn back. In the end, a recorded 14 assaults were made on Marye's Heights, all of which failed, with over 12,650 Union soldiers killed, wounded, or gone missing. Despite all their efforts, not one Union soldier got within 100 feet of the wall at Marye's Heights before being shot or forced to withdraw.

As men lay dying on the field that night, the Northern Lights made a rare appearance. Southern soldiers took it as a divine omen and wrote about it frequently in their diaries. The Union soldiers saw less divine inspiration in the Northern Lights and mentioned it less in their own. The Battle of Fredericksburg also spawned one of Lee's most memorable quotes. During the battle, Lee turned to Longstreet and commented, "It is well that war is so terrible, otherwise we would grow too fond of it."

That night, both Hill and Jackson visited the mortally wounded Maxcy Gregg, and one of Jackson's men recalled:

"When night came over the battlefield of Fredericksburg, December 13, 1862, we were in our saddles on the hill near Hamilton's Crossing. General Jackson, with his staff and some couriers, turned to leave the field and find our headquarters wagons, and he directed me to go to Mr. Yerby's house and present his regards and sympathy to General Maxcy Gregg, who was there seriously wounded. I found General Gregg on a bed in the center of a large room, surrounded by surgeons and other officers. I conveyed my message to him personally. He was much affected and desired me to thank General Jackson for his thoughtful remembrance.

It was nearly daybreak when I returned to the headquarters camp, and wrapped myself again in my blankets. But I was not yet asleep, when again an orderly at my tent door said, "Captain, the general wants you." Struggling into my boots once more, I found the general making his toilet, with a tin basin of water and a rough towel.

He said, "I have just had a message from General Gregg, who is nearing his end at the Yerby house, asking that I call to see him as I go to the front this morning. I wish you to ride with me, captain!"

Dressing hurriedly, I got into the saddle and rode with General Jackson to the Yerby house.

There was an affecting interview between Jackson and Gregg, a large man, who was suffering greatly and failing rapidly. Gregg wished to explain and express regret for an endorsement he had written on some paper which he feared was offensive to General Jackson. Jackson did not know to what Gregg referred, and soon interrupted the sufferer to say that it had given him no offense whatever, and then, with Gregg's hand in his, he added, "The doctors tell me that you have not long to live. Let me ask you to dismiss this matter from your mind and turn your thoughts to God and to the world to which you go." Both were much moved. General Gregg with tears said: "I thank you; I thank you very much." Silently we rode away, and as the sun rose, General Jackson was again on the hill near Hamilton's Crossing. And that day Burnside began his retreat to the north of the Rappahannock."

During a break in campaigning following the Battle of Fredericksburg, Hill repeatedly requested that Lee call a court of inquiry to address charges leveled by Brig. General James J. Archer and others, including Stonewall Jackson, but Lee did not wish to disrupt the cooperation of his two most experienced field commanders, thus denying Hill's request.

Chapter 10: Chancellorsville

After Fredericksburg, both armies pulled back for winter, but the feud between Jackson and Hill was as hot as ever. Hill confided his frustration in a letter to cavalry leader JEB Stuart:

"Many thanks in sending me the letter. It found me with only one arm useful -- the other swollen as big as old Sacketts leg. I suppose I am to vegetate here all winter under that crazy old Presbyterian fool -- I am like the porcupine all bristles, and all sticking out too, so I know we will have a smash up before long. I don't like the complexion here. I think a fatal sin has been committed, provided the Yanks have the sense to take advantage of it, which they don't often do, for they sometimes won't {take} the peach when held to their lips. How do you like PAXTON Brig. Gen.! The Almighty will get tired, helping Jackson after a while, and then he'll get the damnedest thrashing-- and the shoe pinches, for I should get my share and probably all the blame, for the people will never blame Stonewall for any disaster."

With matters coming to a head once again between Hill and Jackson, the frustrated Lee finally had enough, saying, "Then let him who thinks he has been injured most prove himself most magnanimous by forgiving most." With that stern but delicate scolding, both men backed down once again.

Lee had concluded an incredibly successful year for the Confederates in the East, but the South was still struggling. The Confederate forces in the West had failed to win a major battle, suffering defeat at places like Shiloh in Tennessee and across the Mississippi River. As the war continued into 1863, the southern economy continued to deteriorate. Southern armies were suffering serious deficiencies of nearly all supplies as the Union blockade continued to be effective as stopping most international commerce with the Confederacy. Moreover, the prospect of Great Britain or France recognizing the Confederacy had been all but eliminated by the Emancipation Proclamation.

Given the unlikelihood of forcing the North's capitulation, the Confederacy's main hope for victory was to win some decisive victory or hope that Abraham Lincoln would lose his reelection bid in 1864, and that the new president would want to negotiate peace with the Confederacy. Understandably, this colored Confederate war strategy, and unquestionably Lee's.

After the Fredericksburg debacle and the "Mud March" fiasco that left a Union advance literally dead in its tracks, Lincoln fired Burnside and replaced him with "Fighting Joe" Hooker. Hooker had gotten his nickname from a clerical error in a newspaper's description of fighting, but the nickname stuck, and Lee would later playfully refer to him as F.J. Hooker. Hooker had stood out for his zealous fighting at Antietam, and the battle may very well have turned out differently if he hadn't been injured at the head of the I Corps. Now he was in command of a 100,000 man Army of the Potomac, and he devised a complex plan to cross the Rappahannock River with part of his force near Fredericksburg to pin down Lee while using the other bulk to turn Lee's left, which would allow his forces to reach the Confederate rear.

From April 27–28, 1863, the three corps constituting the vanguard of the Army of the Potomac began their march towards Chancellorsville under the leadership of Union Major General Henry W. Slocum. By dawn on April 29, pontoon bridges had been constructed to span the Rappahannock River south of Fredericksburg, and Union Major General John Sedgwick's forces began to cross. Arriving on the scene on the afternoon on April 30, General Hooker established his headquarters while Major General George Stoneman's cavalry attempted to reach Lee's rear guard. Realizing that the Confederates were not opposing the river crossings, Hooker ordered Major General Daniel E. Sickles to move the Third Corps from Falmouthon during the night of April 30–May 1; by morning, Hooker had approximately 70,000 men concentrated in and around Chancellorsville.

Before dawn on May 1, Jackson had sent his men marching west to join forces with Confederate Major General Richard H. Anderson, and at 11:20 am, the Confederate and Union armies collided--the first shots fired. Despite holding a favorable position, General Hooker had decided before beginning the campaign that he would fight the battle defensively, forcing Lee and his small army to attack his larger one. General Jackson believed Hooker would ultimately retreat across the Rappahannock River if met with sufficient opposition, but Lee assumed the Union general had invested too much to withdraw, so he decided that if the Union troops were still in position on May 2, he would launch a full-out attack.

Hooker's plan initially worked perfectly, with the division of his army surprising Lee. Lee was outnumbered two to one and now had to worry about threats on two fronts. Incredibly, Lee once again decided to divide his forces in the face of the enemy, sending Stonewall Jackson to turn the Union army's right flank while the rest of the army maintained positions near Fredericksburg. The Battle of Chancellorsville is one of the most famous of the Civil War, and the most famous part of the battle was Stonewall Jackson's daring march across the Army of the Potomac's flank, surprising the XI Corps with an attack on May 2, 1863.

After putting his men in place, Jackson ordered the Twenty-Third Georgia Infantry to guard the rear of the column--but they were ultimately driven south, forced to make a stand at the "unfinished railroad bed." By 5:00 p.m. the Georgians were overwhelmed by Union troops-- with most subsequently captured. Moving in two brigades from his "Light Division," Major General Hill managed to turn back from the flanking march, preventing any further damage to Jackson's column.

The surprise was a costly success however. Jackson scouted out ahead of his lines later that night and was mistakenly fired upon by his own men, badly wounding him. After personally dressing Jackson's wounds, Hill briefly took command of the Second Corps, until he was himself wounded in the legs, leaving him unable to walk or ride a horse. Hill relinquished command to Brig. General Robert E. Rodes, who realized he was over his head and directed JEB Stuart himself to take temporary command of the Second Infantry Corps, a decision Lee seconded when news reached him.

Although this change in command effectively ended the flanking attack underway, Stuart proved to be a remarkably adaptive leader and very effective infantry commander, launching a successful, well-coordinated assault against the Union right flank at Chancellorsville the following day. Hooker began to lose his nerve, and he was injured during the battle when a cannonball nearly killed him. Historians now believe that Hooker may have commanded part of the battle while suffering from a concussion.

On May 4, as Hooker abandoned the high ground at Hazel Grove in favor of Fairview, Stuart showed particular acumen by immediately taking control of the position and ordering thirty pieces of artillery to bombard the Union positions, not only forcing General Hooker's troops from Fairview (which Stuart then captured for the Confederacy), but essentially decimating the Union lines while destroying Hooker's headquarters at Chancellor House. Of this well-played turn of events, Stuart wrote: "As the sun lifted the mist that shrouded the field, it was discovered that the ridge on the extreme right was a fine position for concentrating artillery. I immediately ordered thirty pieces to that point, and, under the happy effects of the battalion system, it was done quickly. The effect of this fire upon the enemy's batteries was superb."

Stuart's effective utilization of a mere 20,000 men to snatch victory from a Union force numbering over 80,000 prompted Confederate General Porter Alexander to comment, "Altogether, I do not think there was a more brilliant thing done in the war than Stuart's extricating that command from the extremely critical position in which he found it." Some historians have speculated that Stuart's success at Hazel Grove was what induced Dan Sickles to disobey George Meade's orders on Day 2 at Gettysburg and advance his III Corps a mile out in front of the rest of the Union line to occupy high ground. Perhaps fearful of a replay like Chancellorsville, that fateful decision would dominate the fighting on the second day of the war's greatest battle.

By the end of the battle, the Army of the Potomac had once again been defeated, retreating across the river. But Lee would also lose his "right hand". Jackson had been shot multiple times, twice in the left arm. After being painfully carried back behind the Confederate lines, Jackson had his left arm amputated. When Lee heard of Jackson's injuries, he sent his religious leader Chaplain Lacy to Stonewall with the message, "Give him my affectionate regards, and tell him to make haste and get well, and come back to me as soon as he can. He has lost his left arm, but I have lost my right arm."

After the amputation, Stonewall was transported to Thomas C. Chandler's plantation, well behind the battle lines, to convalesce. He seemed to be recovering, and his wife and newborn daughter joined him at the plantation, but his doctors were unaware Jackson was exhibiting common symptoms that indicated oncoming pneumonia. Jackson lay dying in the Chandler plantation outbuilding on Sunday, May 10, 1863 with his wife Anna at his side. He comforted his wife, telling her, "It is the Lord's Day...my wish is fulfilled. I always wanted to die on Sunday." Ironically enough, despite their differences, a delirious Jackson mentioned Hill in his last words, the war still clearly on his mind: "Tell A. P. Hill to prepare for actions! Pass the infantry to the front! Tell Major Hawks..." His final words were "Let us cross over the river, and rest under the shade of the trees."

Chapter 11: The Pennsylvania Campaign

In the spring of 1863, General Lee discovered that McClellan had known of his plans and was able to force a battle at Antietam before all of General Lee's forces had arrived. General Lee now believed that he could successfully invade the North again, and that his defeat before was due in great measure to a stroke of bad luck. In addition, General Lee hoped to supply his army on the unscathed fields and towns of the North, while giving war ravaged northern Virginia a rest. After Chancellorsville, Longstreet and Lee met to discuss options for the Confederate Army's summer campaign. Longstreet advocated detachment of all or part of his corps to be sent to Tennessee, citing Union Maj. General Ulysses S. Grant's advance on Vicksburg, the critical Confederate stronghold on the Mississippi River. Longstreet argued that a reinforced army under Bragg could defeat Rosecrans and drive toward the Ohio River, compelling Grant to release his hold on Vicksburg. Lee, however, was opposed to a division of his army and instead advocated a large-scale offensive (and raid) into Pennsylvania. In addition, General Lee hoped to supply his army on the unscathed fields and towns of the North, while giving war ravaged northern Virginia a rest.

Knowing that victories on Virginia soil meant little to an enemy that could simply retreat, regroup, and then return with more men and more advanced equipment, Lee set his sights on a Northern invasion, aiming to turn Northern opinion against the war and against President Lincoln. With his men already half-starved from dwindling provisions, Lee intended to confiscate food, horses, and equipment as they pushed north--and hopefully influence Northern politicians into giving up their support of the war by penetrating into Harrisburg or even Philadelphia. Given the right circumstances, Lee's army might even be able to capture either Baltimore or Philadelphia and use the city as leverage in peace negotiations.

In the wake of Jackson's death, Lee reorganized his army, creating three Corps out of the previous two, with A.P. Hill and Richard S. Ewell "replacing" Stonewall. Lee said of Hill, "A.P. Hill is the best soldier of the grade with me. He fights his troops well and takes care of them." Ewell had distinguished himself during the Peninsula Campaign, suffering a serious injury that historians often credit as making him more cautious in command upon his return. Hill's promotion was controversial among some of the other officers, particularly Longstreet, who would later write in his memoirs, "As the senior major-general of the army, and by reason of distinguished services and ability, General Ewell was entitled to the command of the Second Corps, but there were other major-generals of rank next below Ewell whose services were such as to give them claims next after Ewell's, so that when they found themselves neglected there was no little discontent, and the fact that both the new lieutenant-generals were Virginians made the trouble more grievous."

During the first weeks of summer of 1863, as JEB Stuart screened the army and completed several well-executed offenses against Union cavalry, many historians think it likely that he had already planned to remove the negative effect of Brandy Station by duplicating one of his now famous circumnavigating rides around the enemy army. But as Lee began his march north through the Shenandoah Valley in western Virginia, it is highly unlikely that is what he wanted or expected.

Before setting out on June 22, the methodical Lee gave Stuart specific instructions as to the role he was to play in the Pennsylvania offensive: as the "Eyes of the Army" he was to guard the mountain passes with part of his force while the Army of Northern Virginia was still south of the Potomac River, and then cross the river with the remainder of his army and screen the right flank of Confederate general Richard Stoddert Ewell's Second Corps as it moved down the Shenandoah Valley, maintaining contact with Ewell's army as it advanced towards Harrisburg.

But instead of taking the most direct route north near the Blue Ridge Mountains, Stuart chose a much more ambitious course of action. Stuart decided to march his three best brigades (under Generals Hampton and Fitzhugh Lee, and Col. John R. Chambliss) between the Union army and Washington, north through Rockville to Westminster, and then into Pennsylvania--a route that would allow them to capture supplies along the way and wreak havoc as they skirted Washington. In the aftermath, the *Washington Star* would write: "The cavalry chief [Stuart] interpreted his marching orders in a way that best suited his nature, and detached his 9000 troopers from their task of screening the main army and keeping tabs on the Federals. When Lee was in Pennsylvania anxiously looking for him, Stuart crossed the Potomac above Washington and captured a fine prize of Federal supply wagons . . . ."

But to complicate matters even more, as Stuart set out on June 25 on what was probably a glory-seeking mission, he was unaware that his intended path was blocked by columns of Union infantry that would invariably force him to veer farther east than he or Lee had anticipated. Ultimately, his decision would prevent him from linking up with Ewell as ordered and deprive Lee of his primary cavalry force as he advanced deeper and deeper into unfamiliar enemy territory. According to Halsey Wigfall (son of Confederate States Senator Louis Wigfall) who was in Stuart's infantry, "Stuart and his cavalry left [Lee's] army on June 24 and did not contact [his] army again until the afternoon of July 2, the second day of the [Gettysburg] battle."

According to Stuart's own account, on June 29 his men clashed briefly with two companies of Union cavalry in Westminster, Maryland, overwhelming and chasing them "a long distance on the Baltimore road," causing a "great panic" in the city of Baltimore. On June 30, the head of Stuart's column then encountered Union Brig. General Judson Kilpatrick's cavalry as it passed through Hanover--reportedly capturing a wagon train and scattering the Union army--after which Kilpatrick's men were able to regroup and drive Stuart and his men out of town. Then after a twenty-mile trek in the dark, Stuart's exhausted men reached Dover, Pennsylvania, on the morning of July 1 (which they briefly occupied).

Late on the second day of the battle, Stuart finally arrived, bringing with him the caravan of captured Union supply wagons, and he was immediately reprimanded by Lee. One account describes Lee as "visibly angry" raising his hand "as if to strike the tardy cavalry commander." While that does not sound like Lee's style, Stuart has been heavily criticized ever since, and it has been speculated Lee took him to task harshly enough that Stuart offered his resignation. Lee didn't accept it, but he would later note in his after battle report that the cavalry had not updated him as to the Army of the Potomac's movements.

Given great discretion in his cavalry operations before the battle, Stuart's cavalry was too far removed from the Army of Northern Virginia to warn Lee of the Army of the Potomac's movements. As it would turn out, Lee's army inadvertently stumbled into Union cavalry and then the Union army at Gettysburg on the morning of July 1, 1863, walking blindly into what became the largest battle of the war.

On June 25, 1863, Confederate General Richard Ewell, positioned at Chambersburg in South-Central Pennsylvania, divided his corps, assigning Major General Early to lead one division to York *via* Gettysburg. Ransacking York on June 28 (as well as destroying a ten-mile section of the Northern Central railroad), Early intended to proceed to Harrisburg but when he reached the bridge spanning the Susquehanna River, he discovered that it had been burned by a Union detachment. The following day, Ewell received word from General Lee to converge on Cashtown, Pennsylvania and await the remainder of the Army of Northern Virginia.

It is believed that one of the first notices Lee got about the Army of the Potomac's movements actually came from a spy named "Harrison", a man who apparently worked undercover for Longstreet but of whom little is known. Harrison reported that General George G. Meade was now in command of the Union Army and was at that very moment marching north to meet Lee's army. According to Longstreet, he and Lee were supposedly on the same page at the beginning of the campaign. "His plan or wishes announced, it became useless and improper to offer suggestions leading to a different course. All that I could ask was that the policy of the campaign should be one of defensive tactics; that we should work so as to force the enemy to attack us, in such good position as we might find in our own country, so well adapted to that purpose—which might assure us of a grand triumph. To this he readily assented as an important and material adjunct to his general plan." Lee later claimed he "had never made any such promise, and had never thought of doing any such thing," but in his official report after the battle, Lee also noted, "It had not been intended to fight a general battle at such a distance from our base, unless attacked by the enemy.

Without question, the most famous battle of the Civil War took place outside of the small town of Gettysburg, Pennsylvania, which happened to be a transportation hub, serving as the center of a wheel with several roads leading out to other Pennsylvanian towns. Lee was unaware of Meade's position when an advanced division of Hill's Corps marched toward Gettysburg on the morning of July 1. It has often been claimed that Hill's men moved toward Gettysburg that morning due to a report that a Gettysburg factory might provide much needed shoes for the Confederate Army infantrymen.

While that is unclear, what is known is that the battle began with John Buford's Union cavalry forces skirmishing against the advancing division of Hill's classmate Henry Heth just outside of town. Buford intentionally fought a delaying action that was meant to allow John Reynolds' I Corps to reach Gettysburg and engage the Confederates, which eventually set the stage for a general battle. Hill was still at Cashtown sick with an unknown illness and was not even aware that his corps had started a battle.

Heth

The I Corps was led by Pennsylvanian General John F. Reynolds, an effective general that had been considered for command of the entire army in place of Hooker and was considered by many the best general in the army. Since Lee had invaded Pennsylvania, many believe that Reynolds was even more active and aggressive than he might have otherwise been. In any event, Reynolds was personally at the front positioning two brigades, exhorting his men, "Forward men! Forward for God's sake, and drive those fellows out of the woods."

As he was at the front positioning his men, Reynolds fell from his horse, having been hit by a bullet behind the ear that killed him almost instantly. With his death, command of the I Corps fell upon Maj. Gen. Abner Doubleday, the Civil War veteran wrongly credited for inventing baseball. Despite the death of the corps commander, the I Corps successfully managed to drive the Confederates in their sector back, highlighted by sharp fighting from the Iron Brigade, a brigade comprised of Wisconsin, Indiana, and Michigan soldiers from the "West". In an unfinished railroad cut, the 6th Wisconsin captured the 2nd Mississippi, and regimental commander Rufus Dawes reported, "The officer replied not a word, but promptly handed me his sword, and his men, who still held them, threw down their muskets. The coolness, self possession, and discipline which held back our men from pouring a general volley saved a hundred lives of the enemy, and as my mind goes back to the fearful excitement of the moment, I marvel at it."

Around noon, the battle hit a lull, in part because Confederate division commander Henry Heth was under orders to avoid a general battle in the absence of the rest of the Army of Northern Virginia. At that point, however, the Union had gotten the better of the fighting, and the Confederate army was concentrating on the area, with more soldiers in Hill's corps in the immediate vicinity and Ewell's corps marching from the north toward the town.

As the Union's I Corps held the line, General Oliver O. Howard and his XI Corps came up on the right of the I Corps, eager to replace the stain the XI Corps had suffered at Chancellorsville thanks to Stonewall Jackson. As a general battle began to form northwest of town, news was making its way back to Meade several miles away that Reynolds had been killed, and that a battle was developing.

Meade had been drawing up a proposed defensive line several miles away from Gettysburg near Emmitsburg, Maryland, but when news of the morning's fighting reached him, Meade sent II Corps commander Winfield Scott Hancock ahead to take command in the field, putting him in temporary command of the "left wing" of the army consisting of the I, II, III and XI Corps. Meade also charged Hancock with determining whether to fight the general battle near Gettysburg or to pull back to the line Meade had been drawing up. Hancock would not be the senior officer on the field (Oliver Howard outranked him), so the fact that he was ordered to take command of the field demonstrates how much Meade trusted him.

As Hancock headed toward the fighting, and while the Army of the Potomac's I and XI Corps engaged in heavy fighting, they were eventually flanked from the north by Early's division, which was returning toward Gettysburg from its previous objective. For the XI Corps, it was certainly reminiscent of their retreat at Chancellorsville, and they began a disorderly retreat through the streets of the small town. Fighting broke out in various places throughout the town, while some Union soldiers hid in and around houses for the duration of the battle. Gettysburg's citizens also fled in the chaos and fighting.

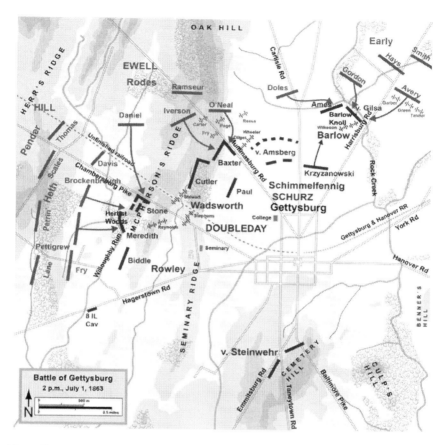

Battle of Gettysburg
2 p.m., July 1, 1863

After a disorderly retreat through the town itself, the Union men began to dig in on high ground to the southeast of the town. When Hancock met up with Howard, the two briefly argued over the leadership arrangement, until Howard finally acquiesced. Hancock told the XI Corps commander, "I think this the strongest position by nature upon which to fight a battle that I ever saw." When Howard agreed, Hancock replied, "Very well, sir, I select this as the battle-field."

As the Confederates sent the Union corps retreating, Lee arrived on the field and saw the importance of the defensive positions the Union men were taking up along Cemetery Hill and Culp's Hill. Late in the afternoon, Lee sent discretionary orders to Ewell that Cemetery Hill be taken "if practicable", but ultimately Ewell chose not to attempt the assault. Lee's order has been criticized because it left too much discretion to Ewell, leaving historians to speculate on how the more aggressive Stonewall Jackson would have acted on this order if he had lived to command this wing of Lee's army, and how differently the second day of battle would have proceeded with Confederate possession of Culp's Hill or Cemetery Hill. Discretionary orders were customary for General Lee because Jackson and Longstreet, his other principal subordinate, usually reacted to them aggressively and used their initiative to act quickly and forcefully. Ewell's decision not to attack, whether justified or not, may have ultimately cost the Confederates the battle. Edwin Coddington, widely considered the historian who wrote the greatest history of the battle, concluded, "Responsibility for the failure of the Confederates to make an all-out assault on Cemetery Hill on July 1 must rest with Lee. If Ewell had been a Jackson he might have been able to regroup his forces quickly enough to attack within an hour after the Yankees had started to retreat through the town. The likelihood of success decreased rapidly after that time unless Lee were willing to risk everything."

With so many men engaged and now taking refuge on the high ground, Meade, who was an engineer like Lee, abandoned his previous plan to draw up a defensive line around Emmittsburg a few miles to the south. After a council of war, the Army of the Potomac decided to defend at Gettysburg.

Day 1 by itself would have been one of the 25 biggest battles of the Civil War, and it was a tactical Confederate victory. Union casualties were almost 9,000, and the Confederates suffered slightly more than 6,000. But the battle had just started, and thanks to the actions of Meade and Hancock, the largest battle on the North American continent would take place on the ground of their choosing.

Hill was circumspect in his description of Day 1, writing in his post-battle account:

On the morning of June 29, the Third Corps, composed of the divisions of Major-Generals Anderson, Heth, and Pender, and five battalions of artillery, under command of Col. R. L. Walker, was encamped on the road from Chambersburg to Gettysburg, near the village of Fayetteville. I was directed to move on this road in the direction of York, and to cross the Susquehanna, menacing the communications of Harrisburg with Philadelphia, and to co-operate with General Ewell, acting as circumstances might require.

Accordingly, on the 29th I moved General Heth's division to Cash-town, some 8 miles from Gettysburg, following on the morning of the 30th with the division of General Pender, and directing General Anderson to move in the same direction on the morning of July 1. On arriving at Cashtown, General Heth, who had sent forward Pettigrew's brigade to Gettysburg, reported that Pettigrew had encountered the enemy at Gettysburg (principally cavalry), but in what force he could not determine. A courier was then dispatched with this information to the general commanding, and with orders to start Anderson early; also to General Ewell, informing him, and that I intended to advance the next morning and discover what was in my front.

On July 1, at 5 a.m., Heth took up the line of march, with Pegram's battalion of artillery, followed by Pender, with McIntosh's battalion of artillery, Colonel Walker with the remainder of the artillery being with General Anderson. About 3 miles from Gettysburg, Heth's advance brigade (Archer's) encountered the advance of the enemy. Archer and Davis were thrown into line, and, with some pieces of artillery from Pegram, the enemy were steadily driven back to the wooded hills this side of Gettysburg, where their principal force (since ascertained to be the First and Eleventh Corps) were disposed to dispute our farther advance.

Heth's whole division was now thrown into line; Davis on the left of the road, Archer, Pettigrew, and Brockenbrough on the right, and Pender's formed in his rear; Thomas on the left, and Lane, Scales, and Perrin on the right. Pegram's and McIntosh's battalions of artillery were put in position on the crest of a hill overlooking the town of Gettysburg. Heth's division drove the enemy, encountering a determined resistance.

About 2.30 o'clock, the right wing of Ewell's corps made its appearance on my left, and thus formed a right angle with my line. Pender's division was then ordered forward, Thomas' brigade being retained in reserve, and the rout of the enemy was complete, Perrin's brigade taking position after position of the enemy, and driving him through the town of Gettysburg. The want of cavalry had been and was again seriously felt.

Under the impression that the enemy were entirely routed, my own two divisions exhausted by some six hours' hard fighting, prudence led me to be content with what had been gained, and not push forward troops exhausted and necessarily disordered, probably to encounter fresh troops of the enemy. These two divisions were bivouacked in the positions won, and Anderson, who had just come up, was also bivouacked some 2 miles in rear of the battle-ground.

The results of this fight were, for the Third Corps, 2 pieces of artillery and 2,300 prisoners, and the almost total annihilation of the First Corps of the enemy. Major-General Heth was slightly wounded; Brigadier-General Archer was taken prisoner by the enemy; Brigadier-General Scales also wounded. Pettigrew's brigade, under its gallant leader, fought most admirably, and sustained heavy loss.

By the morning of July 2, Major General Meade had put in place what he thought to be the optimal battle strategy. Positioning his now massive Army of the Potomac in what would become known as the "fish hook", he'd established a line configuration that was much more compact and maneuverable than Lee's, which allowed Meade to shift his troops quickly from inactive parts of the line to those under attack without creating new points of vulnerability.

Moreover, Meade's army was taking a defensive stance on the high ground anchored by Culp's Hill, Cemetery Hill, and Cemetery Ridge. Meade also personally moved the III Corps under Maj. General Daniel Sickles into position on the left of the line.

On the morning of July 2, Meade was determined to make a stand at Gettysburg, and Lee was determined to strike at him. That morning, Lee decided to make strong attacks on both Union flanks while feinting in the middle, ordering Ewell's corps to attack Culp's Hill on the Union right while Longstreet's corps would attack on the Union left. Lee hoped to seize Cemetery Hill, which would give the Confederates the high ground to harass the Union supply lines and command the road to Washington, D.C. Lee also believed that the best way to do so would be to use Longstreet's corps to launch an attack up the Emmitsburg Road, which he figured would roll up the Union's left flank, presumed to be on Cemetery Hill. Lee was mistaken, due in part to the fact Stuart and his cavalry couldn't perform reconnaissance. In fact, the Union line extended farther south than Cemetery Hill, with the II Corps positioned on Cemetery Ridge and the III Corps nearly as far south as the base of Little Round Top and Round Top. Moreover, Ewell protested that this battle plan would demoralize his men, since they'd be forced to give up the ground they had captured the day before.

As it turned out, both attacks ordered by Lee would come too late. Though there was a controversy over when Lee ordered Longstreet's attack, Longstreet's march got tangled up and caused several hours of delay. Lost Cause advocates attacking Longstreet would later claim his attack was supposed to take place as early as possible, although no official Confederate orders gave a time for the attack. Lee gave the order for the attack around 11:00 a.m., and it is known that Longstreet was reluctant about making it; he still wanted to slide around the Union flank, interpose the Confederate army between Washington D.C. and the Army of the Potomac, and force Meade to attack them. Between Longstreet's delays and the mixup in the march that forced parts of his corps to double back and make a winding march, Longstreet's men weren't ready to attack until about 4:00 p.m.

Though Hill wasn't ordered to be part of these attacks, his men ended up taking part in fighting along the center of the line during Longstreet's attack on the Union left. As Longstreet's men began their circuitous march, Union III Corps commander Dan Sickles took it upon himself to advance his entire corps one half mile forward to a peach orchard, poising himself to take control of higher ground. Some historians assert that Sickles had held a grudge against Meade for taking command from his friend Joseph Hooker and intentionally disregarded orders. It has also been speculated by some historians that Sickles moved forward to occupy high ground in his front due to the devastation unleashed against the III Corps at Chancellorsville once Confederates took high ground and operated their artillery on Hazel Grove. Sickles and Meade would feud over the actions on Day 2 in the years after the war, after Sickles (who lost a leg that day) took credit for the victory by disrupting Lee's attack plans. Historians have almost universally sided with

Meade, pointing out that Sickles nearly had his III Corps annihilated during Longstreet's attack.

Whatever the reasoning for Sickles' move, this unauthorized action completely undermined Meade's overall strategy by effectively isolating Sickles' corps from the rest of the Union line and exposing the Union left flank in the process. By the early afternoon of July 2, nothing but the fog of war was preventing the Confederates from turning and crushing Sickles' forces, then moving to outflank the entire Union Army.

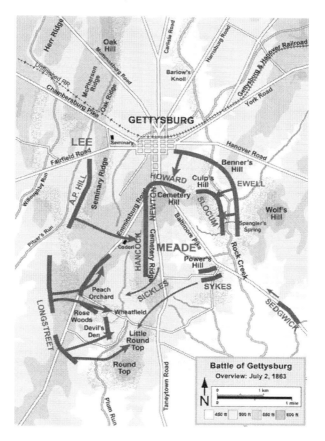

With General George Meade once again in command, General Hancock and the II Corps was positioned on Cemetery Ridge, roughly in the center of the Union line. Since Lee intended to strike at both Union flanks, theoretically Hancock's men should very well not have been engaged at all on the second day of the battle. But as a result of the fact Sickles had moved his men so far out of position, it created a major gap in the Union line and brought the III Corps directly into Longstreet's path. It was 4:00 p.m. by the time Longstreet's two divisions were in position for the attack, and they were taken completely by surprise when they found the III Corps in front of them on the Emmitsburg Road.

Thus, in the late afternoon, the fighting on Day 2 began in earnest, and Longstreet's assault commenced by smashing into Sickles III Corps, engaging them in a peach orchard, wheat field, and Devil's Den, an outcropping of boulders that provided the Confederates prime cover. When it became obvious that Sickles' III Corps was in dire straits, the chaos in that sector acted like a vacuum that induced both sides to pour more men into the vicinity. Moreover, when Sickles was injured by a cannonball that nearly blew off his leg, command of the III Corps fell upon II Corps commander Hancock as well. As Meade tried to shuffle reinforcements to his left, Hancock sent in his II Corps' First Division (under Brig. General John C. Caldwell) to reinforce the III Corps in the wheat field. The fighting in the wheat field was so intense that Caldwell's division would be all but annihilated during the afternoon.

At the same time, men from Confederate General A. P. Hill's corps made their advance toward the Union center, forcing the Army of the Potomac to rally defenses and rushed unit to critical spots to patch the holes. With Hill in his front and Longstreet's attack to his left, Hancock was in the unenviable position of having to attempt to resist Confederate advances spread out over a few miles, at least until more and more reserves could be rushed over from the other side of the Union line to the army's left flank. At one point, Hancock ordered a regiment to make what was essentially a suicidal bayonet charge into the face of Hill's Confederates on Cemetery Ridge. Hancock sent the First Minnesota to charge a Confederate brigade four times its size. One of the Minnesota volunteers, one William Lochren later said, "Every man realized in an instant what the order meant -- death or wounds to us all; the sacrifice of the regiment to gain a few minutes time and save the position, and probably the battlefield -- and every man saw and accepted the necessity of the sacrifice." While extremely costly to the regiment (the Minnesotans suffered 87% casualties, the worst of any regiment at Gettysburg), this heroic sacrifice bought time to organize the defensive line and kept the battle from turning in favor of the Confederates. Hancock would write of them, "I cannot speak too highly of this regiment and its commander in its attack, as well as in its subsequent advance against the enemy, in which it lost three-fourths of the officers and men engaged."

Hill would write of the action:

"On the morning of July 2, Anderson was ordered to the front, and relieved Heth's division, extending to our right and along a crest of hills which faced the Cemetery Hill at Gettysburg, and, continuing to the right, ran nearly parallel to the Emmitsburg road.

On the 2d, then, my position was this: Pender's division occupying the crest from the theological seminary, extending to the right and joined by Anderson's, who carried on the line, almost entirely covering the whole front occupied by the enemy; Heth's division (now commanded by General Pettigrew) in reserve. Colonel Walker had distributed his artillery along this line in the most eligible positions. The corps of General Longstreet (McLaws' and Hood's divisions) was on my right, and in a line very nearly at right angles to mine. General Longstreet was to attack the left flank of the enemy, and sweep down his line, and I was ordered to co-operate with him with such of my brigades from the right as could join in with his troops in the attack. On the extreme right, Hood commenced the attack about 2 o'clock; McLaws about 5.30 o'clock.

Soon after McLaws moved forward, General Anderson moved forward the brigades of Wilcox, Perry, and Wright, en échelon. The charge of these three brigades was very gallantly made, and pressed on until Wilcox's right had become separated from McLaws' left. Wilcox and Wright drove the enemy from their intrenchments, inflicting very heavy loss upon them. Wilcox's brigade succeeded in capturing eight pieces of artillery and Wright's brigade about twenty. The enemy threw forward heavy re-enforcements, and no supports coming to these brigades, the ground so hardly won had to be given up, and the brigades occupied their former positions in line of battle. The three brigades lost heavily in this attack. On this day, also, the Confederacy lost the invaluable services of Maj. Gen. W. D. Pender, wounded by a shell, and since dead. No man fell during this bloody battle of Gettysburg more regretted than he, nor around whose youthful brow were clustered brighter rays of glory."

As Longstreet's assault on the Union left continued, his line naturally got more and more entangled as well. As Longstreet's men kept moving to their right, they reached the base of Little Round Top and Round Top, two rocky hills south of Gettysburg proper, at the far left. When Meade's chief engineer, Brig. General Gouverneur Warren, spotted the sun shining off the bayonets of Longstreet's men as they moved toward the Union left, it alerted the Army of the Potomac of the need to occupy Little Round Top, high ground that commanded much of the field.

With Warren having alerted his superiors to the importance of Little Round Top, Strong Vincent's brigade moved into position, under orders from Warren to "hold this ground at any costs," As part of Strong Vincent's brigade, Chamberlain's 20th Maine was on the left of the line, and thus Chamberlain's unit represented the extreme left of the Army of the Potomac's line.

In front of Vincent's brigade was General Evander Law's advancing Alabama Brigade (of Hood's Division). Law ordered 5 regiments to take Little Round Top, the 4th, 15th, and 47th Alabama, and the 4th and 5th Texas, but they had already marched more than 20 miles just to reach that point. They were now being asked to charge up high ground on a muggy, hot day.

Nevertheless, the Confederates made desperate assaults against Little Round Top, even after being repulsed by the Union defenders several times. In the middle of the fighting, after he saw Confederates trying to push around his flank, Chamberlain stretched his line until his regiment was merely a single-file line, and he then had to order his left (southernmost) half to swing back, thus forming an angle in their line in an effort to prevent a flank attack. Despite suffering heavy losses, the 20th Maine held through two subsequent charges by the 15th Alabama and other Confederate regiments for nearly 2 hours.

Chamberlain

Even after repulsing the Confederates several times, Chamberlain and his regiment faced a serious dilemma. With casualties mounting and ammunition running low, in desperation, Chamberlain *claimed* to have ordered his left wing to initiate an all-out, pivoting bayonet charge. With the 20th Maine charging ahead, the left wing wheeling continually to make the charging line swing like a hinge, thus creating a simultaneous frontal assault and flanking maneuver, they ultimately succeeded in not only taking the hill, but capturing 100 Confederate soldiers in the process. Chamberlain suffered two slight wounds in the battle, one when a shot ricocheted off his sword scabbard and bruised his thigh, another when his right foot was struck by a piece of shrapnel. With this success, Chamberlain was credited with preventing the Union flank from being penetrated and keeping the Confederates from pouring in behind Union lines.

Ultimately, it was the occupation and defense of Little Round Top that saved the rest of the Union line at Gettysburg. Had the Confederates commanded that high ground, it would have been able to position artillery that could have swept the Union lines along Cemetery Ridge and Cemetery Hill, which would have certainly forced the Army of the Potomac to withdraw from their lines. Chamberlain would be awarded the coveted Congressional Medal of Honor for "daring heroism and great tenacity in holding his position on the Little Round Top against repeated assaults, and carrying the advance position on the Great Round Top", and the 20th Maine's actions that day became one of the most famous attacks of the Battle of Gettysburg and the Civil War as a whole.

The fighting on the Union left finally ended as night fell. George Sykes, the commander of the V Corps, later described Day 2 in his official report, "Night closed the fight. The key of the battle-field was in our possession intact. Vincent, Weed, and Hazlett, chiefs lamented throughout the corps and army, sealed with their lives the spot intrusted to their keeping, and on which so much depended.... General Weed and Colonel Vincent, officers of rare promise, gave their lives to their country."

Ewell's orders from Lee had been to launch a demonstration on the Union right flank during Longstreet's attack, which started at about 4:00 p.m. as well, and in support of the demonstration by Hill's corps in the center. For that reason, Ewell would not launch his general assault on Culp's Hill and Cemetery Hill until 7:00 p.m.

While the Army of the Potomac managed to desperately hold on the left, Ewell's attack against Culp's Hill on the other end of the field met with some success in pushing the Army of the Potomac back. However, the attack started so late in the day that nightfall made it impossible for the Confederates to capitalize on their success. Due to darkness, a Confederate brigade led by George H. Steuart was unaware that they were firmly beside the Army of the Potomac's right flank, which would have given them almost unlimited access to the Union army's rear and its supply lines and line of communication, just 600 yards away. the main line of communication for the Union army, the Baltimore Pike, only 600 yards to their front. Col. David Ireland and the 137th New York desperately fought to preserve the Union army's flank, much the same way Chamberlain and the 20th Maine had on the other side, and in the process the 137th lost a third of their men.

Ewell's men would spend the night at the base of Culp's Hill and partially up the hill, in positions that had been evacuated by Union soldiers after Meade moved some of them to the left to deal with Longstreet's attack. It would fall upon the Confederates to pick up the attack the next morning.

That night, Meade held another council of war. Having been attacked on both flanks, Meade and his top officers correctly surmised that Lee would attempt an attack on the center of the line the next day. Moreover, captured Confederates and the fighting and intelligence of Day 2 let it be known that the only Confederate unit that had not yet seen action during the fighting was George Pickett's division of Longstreet's corps.

If July 2 was Longstreet's worst day of the Civil War, July 3 was almost certainly Robert E. Lee's. After the attack on July 2, Longstreet spent the night continuing to plot potential movements around Little Round Top and Big Round Top, thinking that would again get the Confederate army around the Union's flank. Longstreet himself did not realize that a reserve corps of the Union army was poised to block that maneuver.

Longstreet did not meet with Lee on the night of July 2, so when Lee met with him the following morning he found Longstreet's men were not ready to conduct an early morning attack, which Lee had wanted to attempt just as he was on the other side of the lines against Culp's Hill. With Pickett's men not up, however, Longstreet's corps couldn't make such an attack. Lee later wrote that Longstreet's "dispositions were not completed as early as was expected."

When Lee learned Longstreet couldn't commence an attack in the early morning, he attempted to stop Ewell from launching one, but by then it was too late. Ewell's men engaged in fighting along Culp's Hill, until the fighting fizzled out around noon. By then, Lee had already planned a massive attack on the Union center, combined with having Stuart's cavalry attack the Union army's lines in the rear. A successful attack would split the Army of the Potomac at the same time its communication and supply lines were severed by Stuart, which would make it possible to capture the entire army in detail.

There was just one problem with the plan, as Longstreet told Lee that morning: no 15,000 men who ever existed could successfully execute the attack. The charge required marching across an open field for about a mile, with the Union artillery holding high ground on all sides of the incoming Confederates. Longstreet ardently opposed the attack, but, already two days into the battle, Lee explained that because the Army of the Potomac was here on the field, he must strike at it. Longstreet later wrote that he said, "General, I have been a soldier all my life. I have been with soldiers engaged in fights by couples, by squads, companies, regiments, divisions, and armies, and should know, as well as any one, what soldiers can do. It is my opinion that no fifteen thousand men ever arrayed for battle can take that position." Longstreet proposed instead that their men should slip around the Union forces and occupy the high ground, forcing Northern commanders to attack them, rather than *vice versa.*

Realizing the insanity of sending 15,000 men hurtling into all the Union artillery, Lee planned to use the Confederate artillery to try to knock out the Union artillery ahead of time. Although old friend William Pendleton was the artillery chief, the artillery cannonade would be supervised by Edward Porter Alexander, Longstreet's chief artillerist, who would have to give the go-ahead to the charging infantry because they were falling under Longstreet's command. Alexander later noted that Longstreet was so disturbed and dejected about ordering the attack that at one point he tried to make Alexander order the infantry forward, essentially doing Longstreet's dirty work for him.

As Stuart was in the process of being repulsed, just after 1:00 p.m. 150 Confederate guns began to fire from Seminary Ridge, hoping to incapacitate the Union center before launching an infantry attack. Confederate brigadier Evander Law said of the artillery bombardment, "The cannonade in the center ... presented one of the most magnificent battle-scenes witnessed during the war. Looking up the valley towards Gettysburg, the hills on either side were capped with crowns of flame and smoke, as 300 guns, about equally divided between the two ridges, vomited their iron hail upon each other."

However, the Confederate artillery they mostly overshot their mark. The artillery duel could be heard from dozens of miles away, and all the smoke led to Confederate artillery constantly overshooting their targets. Eventually, Union artillery chief Henry Hunt cleverly figured that if the Union cannons stopped firing back, the Confederates might think they successfully knocked out the Union batteries. On top of that, the Union would be preserving its ammunition for the impending charge that everyone now knew was coming. When they stopped, Lee, Alexander, and others mistakenly concluded that they'd knocked out the Union artillery.

A short time later, Confederate General George Pickett, commander of one of the three divisions under General Longstreet, prepared for the charge that would forever bear his name, even though he commanded only about a third of the force and was officially under Longstreet's direction. Today historians typically refer to the charge as the Pickett-Pettigrew-Trimble Assault or Longstreet's Assault to be more technically correct. Since A.P. Hill was sidelined with illness, Pettigrew's and Trimble's divisions were delegated to Longstreet's authority as well. To make matters worse, Hill's sickness resulted in organizational snafus. Without Hill to assign or lead troops, some of his battle-weary soldiers of the previous two days were tapped to make the charge while fresh soldiers in his corps stayed behind.

The charge was to begin with Pickett's division of Virginians, and shortly after the Union guns fell silent, with his men in position, Pickett asked Longstreet to give the order to advance. Longstreet could only nod, fearing that "to verbalize the order may reveal his utter lack of confidence in the plan." With that, around 2:00 p.m. about 12,500-15,000 Confederates stepped out in sight and began their charge with an orderly march starting about a mile away, no doubt an inspiring sight to Hancock and the Union men directly across from the oncoming assault.

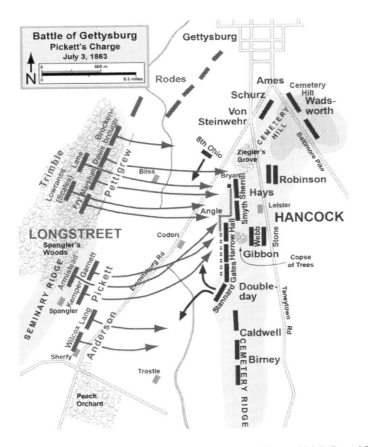

As the Confederate line advanced, Union cannon on Cemetery Ridge and Little Round Top began blasting away, with Confederate soldiers continuing to march forward. One Union soldier later wrote, "We could not help hitting them with every shot . . . a dozen men might be felled by one single bursting shell." By the time Longstreet's men reached Emmitsburg Road, Union artillery switched to firing grapeshot (tin cans filled with iron and lead balls), and as the Confederate troops continued to approach the Union center, Union troops positioned behind the wall cut down the oncoming Confederates, easily decimating both flanks. Lt. Col. Franklin Sawyer of the 8th Ohio reported, "They were at once enveloped in a dense cloud of smoke and dust. Arms, heads, blankets, guns and knapsacks were thrown and tossed in to the clear air. ... A moan went up from the field, distinctly to be heard amid the storm of battle."

While some of the men did manage to advance to the Union line and engage in hand-to-hand combat, it was of little consequence. In the midst of the fighting, as he was conferring with one of his brigadier generals, General Stannard, Hancock suddenly felt a searing pain in his thigh. He had just been severely wounded when a bullet struck the pommel of his saddle and entered his inner right thigh, along with wood splinters and a large bent nail. Helped from his horse by his aides, he removed the saddle nail himself and applied a tourniquet, colorfully swearing at his own men while demanding that they not let him bleed to death. Nevertheless, he refused to remove himself to the rear until the offensive had concluded.

After about an hour, nearly 6,500 Confederates were dead or wounded, five times that of the Union, with all 13 regimental commanders in Pickett's division killed or wounded. In the aftermath of the defeat, General Longstreet stated, "General Lee came up as our troops were falling back and encouraged them as well as he could; begged them to reform their ranks and reorganize their forces . . . and it was then he used the expression . . . 'It was all my fault; get together, and let us do the best we can toward saving which is left to us.'"

Today Pickett's Charge is remembered as the American version of the Charge of the Light Brigade, a heroic but completely futile march that had no chance of success. In fact, it's remembered as Pickett's Charge because Pickett's Virginians wanted to claim the glory of getting the furthest during the attack in the years after the war. The charge consisted of about 15,000 men under the command of James Longstreet, with three divisions spearheaded by Pickett, Trimble, and Pettigrew. Trimble and Pettigrew were leading men from A.P. Hill's corps, and Hill was too disabled by illness that day to choose the men from his corps to make the charge. As a result, some of the men who charged that day had already engaged in heavy fighting.

The charge suffered about a 50% casualty rate, as the Confederates marched into hell. The men barely made a dent in the Union line before retreating in disorder back across the field, where Lee met them in an effort to regroup them in case the Union counterattacked. At one point, Lee ordered Pickett to reform his division, to which Pickett reportedly cried, "I have no division!" Pickett's post-battle report was apparently so bitter that Lee ordered it destroyed. Though the charge was named Pickett's Charge by newspapers for the purpose of praising Pickett's Virginians for making the furthest progress, Pickett felt the charge had tarnished his career, and he remained upset that his name remained associated with the sharply repulsed attack.

Pickett

One of the Virginians who marched straight into Hancock's II Corps was his old friend Lewis A. Armistead, who was leading one of Pickett's brigades. Armistead famously led his brigade with his hat atop his sword, serving as a visual cue for his men, and they actually breached the II Corps' line, making it about as far as any Confederate got. In the fighting, Armistead was mortally wounded and captured, dying days later. Armistead's dying wishes were to deliver his Bible and other personal valuables to Hancock's wife Almira, which Longstreet had done.

Trimble and Pettigrew, the other two leaders of the charge, were both wounded in the fighting, with Trimble losing a leg and Pettigrew suffering a minor wound to the hand. All of Pickett's brigadiers were injured. In addition to Armistead's mortal wounding, Kemper was seriously wounded and captured. Meanwhile Richard Garnett, whose courage had been impugned and challenged by Stonewall Jackson unfairly in 1862, had suffered a previous leg injury and insisted on riding his horse during the charge, despite the obvious fact that riding a horse clearly indicated he was an officer. Garnett was killed during the charge, and it's unknown where he fell or where he was buried.

Of all three infantry corps of the Army of Northern Virginia who fought at Gettysburg, Hill's suffered the most casualties, prompting Lee to order them to lead the swift retreat back into Virginia. By this point, Hill had began to complain incessantly of health problems of unknown origin, and would continue to do so throughout the remainder of his command. No matter the source of the complaints, real or imagined, it clearly began to diminish his ability to lead. Lee's famous biographer Douglas Southall Freeman believed Hill's nerves got the better of him after he was given command of a corps, writing, "Chance or a psychosomatic malady left Powell Hill unable, after the first day's fighting [at the Wilderness], to exercise field command. He did not recover until the most serious fighting was over at Spotsylvania, but he did his utmost to keep in touch with his troops." Conversely, modern biographer William Hassler argued, " Evidence strongly suggests that Hill suffered from chronic malaria. Bouts of this disease in an individual chronically infected with the parasite are induced by undue fatigue, exposure, climatic changes, dampness, and lower body resistance -- all factors that were present in Hill's case. Interestingly, the pattern of his illness which shows evidence of symptoms that might border on psycho-neurosis or psycho-somatic disease is also rather true with chronic clinical malaria. In fact, the added responsibilities of corps command conceivably could stimulate the trigger mechanism for these malarial attacks."

Regardless, Hill recounted the climactic day and the end of the campaign in his post-battle account:

"On the morning of the 3d, the divisions of my corps occupied the same positions as on the 2d. The reserve batteries were all brought up, and put in position along the crest of the ridge facing the enemy's line. In addition, the battalion of Colonel Alexander, of Longstreet's corps, was put in position in front of the right wing of Anderson's division, and on the ground won by Wilcox and Wright. I was directed to hold my line with Anderson's division and the half of Pender s (now commanded by General Lane), and to order Heth's division (commanded by Pettigrew), and Lane's and Scales' brigades, of Pender's division, to report to Lieutenant-General Longstreet as a support to his corps in the assault on the enemy's lines. As the troops were filing off to their positions, Major-General Trimble reported to me for the command of Pender's division, and took command of the two brigades destined to take part in the assault.

At 1 o'clock our artillery opened, and for two hours rained an incessant storm of missiles upon the enemy's lines. The effect was marked along my front, driving the enemy entirely from his guns.

The assault was then gallantly made, Heth's division and Trimble's two brigades on the left of Pickett. Anderson had been directed to hold his division ready to take advantage of any success which might be gained by the assaulting column, or to support it, if necessary. To that end, Wilcox and Perry were moved forward to eligible positions. The assault failed, and, after almost gaining the enemy's works, our troops fell back in disorder. The enemy made no attempt to pursue. Major-General Trimble, Brigadier-General Pettigrew, and Colonel Fry, commanding Archer's brigade, were wounded while most gallantly leading their troops. General Trimble and Colonel Fry were both taken prisoners.

The troops resumed their former positions, and remained thus until the night of the 4th, when the march was taken up toward Hagerstown, by Fairfield and Waynesborough.

At Hagerstown, we lay in line of battle from the 7th to the night of the 13th, when I moved my corps in the direction of the pontoon bridge at Falling Waters. Being the rear guard of the army, such dispositions as were necessary were made to repel any advance of the enemy. Anderson's division crossed without molestation, and Pender's was in the act of crossing when the enemy made their appearance. A small body of cavalry charged Pettigrew's and Archer's brigades, and were annihilated. Only 2 of ours killed; but, unfortunately for the service, one of them was the gallant and accomplished Pettigrew.

Subsequently the enemy pressed on vigorously, and I directed General Heth to retire his troops and cross the river. In doing this, some loss was sustained, principally in stragglers, and not exceeding 500, composed of men from the various brigades of the army. Two pieces of artillery were broken down on this night march, and abandoned. Colonel Walker brought off three guns captured on the field of Gettysburg.

On the 21st, the march was resumed toward Culpeper Court-House. On the 23d, Wright's brigade, under Colonel Walker, was left to guard Manassas Gap until relieved by General Ewell. This brigade was attacked while there by an overwhelming force of the enemy, but held its ground stubbornly until relieved by Ewell's corps, when it marched with him to Culpeper. General Ewell speaks in high terms of the admirable conduct of this brigade.

Continuing the march on the morning of the 24th, at Newby's Cross-Roads a brigade of the enemy's cavalry attempted to arrest our march. Heth's' division (his own and Pender's) was leading. General Benning's brigade, of Longstreet's corps was also along, and rendered prompt and valuable assistance. The enemy were soon put to flight in confusion, and no more annoyance occurred on the march to Culpeper Court-House.

On August 1, Anderson's division was sent out on the road to Brandy [Station], to repel some of the enemy's cavalry, which had driven back our cavalry and were quite near the court-house. This was handsomely done by Mahone's brigade and Perry's, and with but trifling loss.

The total loss of the Third Corps in this campaign was 849 killed, 4,289 wounded, and 3,844 missing. The larger portion of those reported missing were killed or wounded in the fight of July 3, but the possession of the field by the enemy prevented a true count."

Chapter 12: The Fall of 1863

During the Confederate "Autumn Campaign" of 1863, Lieutenant General Hill was highly criticized for launching his corps "too hastily" at the Battle of Bristoe Station, fought on October 14, 1863. His corps was easily repulsed by Union Maj. General Gouverneur K. Warren's Second Corps, resulting in heavy Confederate losses. Although General Lee did not openly criticize Hill for his costly misstep, he assigned him to detail the dead and wounded after hearing his account of the bloody incident.

Hill went out of his way to deflect blame being placed on his division commander and friend, Henry Heth, writing to him, "Having been informed that it was probable some misapprehension existed in regard to your management of your division at Gettysburg, Falling Waters, and Bristoe, it is but simple justice to you that I say your conduct on all those occasions met with my approbation. At Gettysburg the first day's fight, mainly fought by your division, was a brilliant victory. You were wounded that day, and not again in command of your division until the retreat commenced. At Falling Waters the enemy were kept at bay until the army had crossed the Potomac, and the prisoners taken by the enemy were stragglers, and not due to any fault of yours. At Bristoe the attack was ordered by me, and most gallantly made by your division; another corps of the enemy coming up on your right was unforeseen, as I had supposed that other troops were taking care of them. I write you this letter that you may make such use of it as may be deemed advisable by you."

Aside from serving in a minor, supportive capacity at the Battle of Mine Run (November 27-- December 2, 1863) and a brief visit to Richmond in January 1864, Hill remained with his corps in its winter encampments near Orange Court House, until the spring of 1864. In one memorable episode, he graciously received a pair of spurs from a group of women from Columbia, South Carolina, writing to their spokeswoman:

"My Dear Miss Mary:

The very handsome pair of spurs so kindly presented to me by yourself and young friends have been received, and I thank you most heartily for the token of good will and of the esteem in which you hold services incident to my position. If I have done aught to win these spurs, the gallant soldiers of your own native State are entitled partly to the credit. They have never faltered when the charge was sounded. The noble, steadfast devotion of the few in the field should cull a blush of shame to the cheeks of those fattening at home upon the distress of their country. At all events, mete out to them the punishment you threaten and never let them know the cheer of the domestic fireside, or be smiled upon by "Heaven's last, best gift" -- women.

When these cruel wars are over, Miss Mary, I shall be reminded of Columbia, and I hope spurred to visit in that direction to meet my kind friends. Please remember me affectionately to your young friends, and give to each a kiss for me, which I will repay to you with interest when we meet.

Very affectionately, your friend, A.P. Hill."

That winter, Hill also had the benefit of having his family in camp. Dolly joined the general that winter, along with his two daughters, but even their presence was not enough to keep him healthy. Hill continued to suffer sporadic illnesses during the months between campaigns.

Chapter 13: The Overland Campaign

With Lee continuing to hold off the Army of the Potomac in a stalemate along the same battle lines at the end of 1863, Lincoln shook things up. In March 1864, Grant was promoted to lieutenant general and given command of all the armies of the United States. His first acts of command were to keep General Halleck in position to serve as a liaison between Lincoln and Secretary of War Edwin Stanton. And though it's mostly forgotten today, Grant technically kept General Meade in command of the Army of the Potomac, even though Grant attached himself to that army before the Overland Campaign in 1864 and thus served as its commander for all intents and purposes.

Grant

In May 1864, with Grant now attached to the Army of the Potomac, the Civil War's two most famous generals met each other on the battlefield for the first time. Lee had won stunning victories at battles like Chancellorsville and Second Bull Run by going on the offensive and taking the strategic initiative, but Grant and Lincoln had no intention of letting him do so anymore. Grant ordered General Meade, "Lee's army is your objective point. Wherever Lee goes, there you will go also."

By 1864, things were looking so bleak for the South that the Confederate war strategy was simply to ensure Lincoln lost reelection that November, with the hope that a new Democratic president would end the war and recognize the South's independence. With that, and given the shortage in manpower, Lee's strategic objective was to continue defending Richmond, while hoping that Grant would commit some blunder that would allow him a chance to seize an opportunity.

On May 4, 1864, Grant launched the Overland Campaign, crossing the Rapidan River near Fredericksburg with the 100,000 strong Army of the Potomac, which almost doubled Lee's hardened but battered Army of Northern Virginia. It was a similar position to the one George McClellan had in 1862 and Joe Hooker had in 1863, and Grant's first attack, at the Battle of the Wilderness, followed a similar pattern. Nevertheless, Lee proved more than capable on the defensive.

From May 5-6, Lee's men won a tactical victory at the Battle of the Wilderness, which was fought so close to where the Battle of Chancellorsville took place a year earlier that soldiers encountered skeletons that had been buried in (too) shallow graves in 1863. Moreover, the woods were so thick that neither side could actually see who they were shooting at, and whole brigades at times got lost in the forest. Still, both armies sustained heavy casualties while Grant kept attempting to move the fighting to a setting more to his advantage, but the heavy forest made coordinated movements almost impossible.

Hill's corps held back multiple Union attacks during the first day of the Battle of the Wilderness (near Richmond, Virginia, May 5–7, 1864), but became extremely disorganized in the process. According to surviving testimony, despite requests from several division commanders to straighten and fortify his line after the first day of fighting, Hill is said to have flatly refused—resulting in his corps being driven back by Union forces on the second day of the battle, requiring the First Corps under General Longstreet to come to his rescue.

The Confederates had won a tactical victory at a staggering cost, inflicting 17,000 casualties on

Grant and suffering 11,000 of their own. Grant disengaged from the battle in the same position as Hooker before him at Chancellorsville, McClellan on the Virginian Peninsula, and Burnside after Fredericksburg. His men got the familiar dreadful feeling that they would retreat back across the Rapidan toward Washington, as they had too many times before. This time, however, Grant made the fateful decision to keep moving south, inspiring his men by telling them that he was prepared to "fight it out on this line if it takes all Summer."

Using the Union V Corps under Major General Gouverneur K. Warren, Grant moved forward in a series of flanking maneuvers that continued to move the army steadily closer to Richmond. But Lee continued to parry each thrust. The next major battle took place at Spotsylvania Court House from May 8-21, with the heaviest fighting on May 12 when a salient in the Confederate line nearly spelled disaster for Lee's army.

Though Hill has been mostly praised for his role during the Battle of the Wilderness, the strain once again left him debilitated by illness. As Lee's army moved to counter Grant near Spotsylvania, Lee wrote General Ewell, "General Hill has reported to me that he is so much indisposed that he fears he must relinquish the command of his corps. In that case, I shall be obliged to put General Early in command of it." Indeed, Hill traveled with the army in an ambulance.

That did not mean Hill was not completely invested in the fighting, however. From his ambulance, Hill watched Ambrose Wright's brigade get repulsed by the Union army in a small engagement and went so far as to demand court of inquiry to look at Wright's actions. Lee chided Hill, diplomatically telling him, "These men are not an army; they are citizens defending their country. General Wright is not a soldier; he's a lawyer. I cannot do many things that I could do with a trained army. The soldiers know their duties better than the general officers do, and they have fought magnificently. We must make do with what we have. You understand all of this, but if you humiliated General Wright, the people of Georgia would not understand. Besides, whom would you put in his place? You'll have to do what I do. When a man makes a mistake, I call him to my tent, talk to him, and use the authority of my position to make him do the right thing the next time."

Under General Grant's direct orders, at 4:30 a.m. on May 12, 1864, Hancock's II Corps burst out through the rain and fog, leading a large-scale assault at Spotsylvania Court House that caught the Confederates completely by surprise. Breaking through Lee's front line at "the mule shoe" with relative ease, Hancock's corps effectively split the Confederate Army in half--capturing approximately twenty guns and 2,800 prisoners in the process, the majority of General Jackson's legendary "Stonewall Brigade".

In their zeal, however, the Union forces lost their cohesion, allowing the Confederates to launch an exuberant counterattack that resulted in savage, unrelenting fighting in the rain lasting hours, while bodies piled up on both sides. (Men were literally trampled under the mud as soldiers advanced to take the place of their fallen comrades.) Fighting raged around the "Bloody Angle" for hours, with soldiers fighting hand to hand before the Confederates finally dislodged the Union soldiers. At midnight, the Confederates finally abandoned "Mule Shoe," but Grant had failed to break Lee's defenses as planned.

For the next two weeks, Grant pursued Lee, sending a number of his commanders to outmaneuver Lee's army; attempting to disrupt Lee's supply lines and threaten his rear, thus forcing him out of the trenches to fight, or further retreat.

Lee's army continued to stoutly defend against several attacks by the Army of the Potomac, but massive casualties were inflicted on both sides. After Spotsylvania, Grant had already incurred about 35,000 casualties while inflicting nearly 25,000 casualties on Lee's army. Grant, of course, had the advantage of a steady supply of manpower, so he could afford to fight the war of attrition. It was a fact greatly lost on the people of the North, however, who knew Grant's track record from Shiloh and saw massive casualty numbers during the Overland Campaign. Grant was routinely criticized as a butcher.

As fate would have it, the only time during the Overland Campaign Lee had a chance to take the initiative was after Spotsylvania. During the fighting that came to be known as the Battle of North Anna, Lee was heavily debilitated with illness. Grant nearly fell into Lee's trap by splitting his army in two along the North Anna before avoiding it. The sick Lee would pin the blame on Hill, issuing one of his sharpest criticisms of the war: "General Hill, why did you let those people cross here? Why didn't you throw your whole force on them and drive them back as Jackson would have done?" Though Hill was not truly at fault, and the scolding was a byproduct of Lee's illness, Hill took the criticism in stride and held his tongue.

By the time the two armies reached Cold Harbor near the end of May 1864, Grant incorrectly thought that Lee's army was on the verge of collapse. Though his frontal assaults had failed spectacularly at places like Vicksburg, Grant believed that Lee's army was on the ropes and could be knocked out with a strong attack. The problem was that Lee's men were now masterful at quickly constructing defensive fortifications, including earthworks and trenches that made their positions impregnable. While Civil War generals kept employing Napoleonic tactics, Civil War soldiers were building the types of defensive works that would be the harbinger of World War I's trench warfare.

On June 3, 1864, sensing he could break Lee's army, Grant ordered a full out assault at dawn in the hopes of catching the rebels before they could fully entrench. As fate had it, Hancock's men became part of the vanguard of an attack that would go down in history as one of the bloodiest and costliest failures of the War. Although the story of Union soldiers pinning their names on the back of their uniforms in anticipation of death at Cold Harbor is apocryphal, the frontal assault on June 3 inflicted thousands of Union casualties in about half an hour. In just minutes, 7,000 Union soldiers were killed or wounded as 30,000 Confederate soldiers successfully held the line against 50,000 Union troops, losing just 1,500 men in the process. Though credited with a valiant attempt, Hancock's efforts were overshadowed by Grant's horrendous failure and costly bad judgment.

With another 12,000 casualties at Cold Harbor, Grant had suffered about as many casualties in a month as Lee had in his entire army at the start of the campaign. Grant later admitted, "I have always regretted that the last assault at Cold Harbor was ever made...No advantage whatever was gained to compensate for the heavy loss we sustained."

Although Grant's results were widely condemned, he continued to push toward Richmond. After Cold Harbor, Grant managed to successfully steal an entire day's march on Lee and crossed the James River, attacking the Confederacy's primary railroad hub at Petersburg, which was only a few miles from Richmond. By the time Lee's army reached Petersburg, it had been defended by P.G.T. Beauregard, but now the Army of Northern Virginia had been pinned down at Petersburg. Grant knew that once Lee got wind that Union forces were on the move, he would send his best units to strengthen Petersburg lines. But as had happened several times before, Grant's generals hesitated to act, allowing Confederate general P. G. T. Beauregard to build new interior defenses by June 16. And even though Union forces were able to crack through Confederate lines by June 17, darkness fell before they could make on real inroads. The two armies dug in, and Grant prepared for a long term siege of the vital city.

The situation was exactly what Lee had hoped to avoid, as he wrote to Hill. "I am glad that you are able to make the disposition of the troops you propose, as it meets my views, as expressed in a former note to you. Now that you have your troops in a line, I hope you will strengthen it as much as possible and hold it. I have little fear of your ability to maintain your position if our men do as they generally do. The time has arrived, in my opinion, when something more is necessary than adhering to lines and defensive positions. We shall be obliged to go out and prevent the enemy from selecting such positions as he chooses. If he is allowed to continue that course we shall at last be obliged to take refuge behind the works of Richmond and stand a siege, which would be but a work of time. You must be prepared to fight him in the field, to prevent him taking positions such as he desires, and I expect the co-operation of all the corps commanders in the course which necessity now will oblige us to pursue. It is for this purpose that I desire the corps to be kept together and as strong as possible, and that our absentees will be brought forward and every attention given to refreshing and preparing the men for battle. Their arms and ammunition should be looked to and cooked provisions provided ahead. R. E. LEE, General. P. S.--I am anxious to get recommendations to fill the vacancies in the different commands in your corps. R. E. L."

Making it apparent that he clearly understood that defending Richmond was imperative to the survival of the Confederacy, Hill is quoted as stating resolutely, "[I] did not want to survive the surrender of the Confederate Capital."

Chapter 14: The Siege of Petersburg

During the Siege of Petersburg (June 9, 1864--March 25, 1865), Lieutenant General Hill and his men participated in several battles during various Union offensives, most notably the Battle of the Crater.

The most famous battle took place when Union engineers burrowed underneath the Confederate siege lines and lit the fuse on a massive amount of ammunition, creating a "crater" in the field. But even then, the Battle of the Crater ended with a Union debacle, as Union forces swarmed into the crater instead of around it, giving the Confederates the ability to practically shoot fish in a barrel. Hill heard the explosion from his headquarters 4 miles away, and by the time he reached the chaos, his subordinate William Mahone had taken charge, sending his men into the breach to fight. Lee would later write to the Confederate Secretary of War, "General A. P. Hill reports that General Mahone in retaking the salient possessed by the enemy this morning recovered the four guns with which it was armed, captured 12 stand of colors, 74 officers, including Brigadier-General Bartlett and staff, and 855 enlisted men. Upward of 500 of the enemy's dead are lying unburied in the trenches. His loss slight."

Hill was also victorious in skirmishing at Reams' Station later in the siege, fighting both illness and the Union enemy with vigor. Lee reported, "General A. P. Hill attacked the enemy in his intrenchments at Reams' Station yesterday evening, and at the second assault carried his entire line. Cooke's and MacRae's North Carolina brigades, under General Heth, and Lane's North Carolina brigade, of Wilcox's division, under General Conner, with Pegram's artillery, composed the assaulting column. One line of breast-works was carried by the cavalry under General Hampton with great gallantry, who contributed largely to the success of the day. Seven stand of colors, 2,000 prisoners, and 9 pieces of artillery are in our possession. The loss of the enemy in killed and wounded is reported to be heavy, ours relatively small.' Our profound gratitude is due to the Giver of all victory and our thanks to the brave men and officers engaged."

However, during the winter of 1864–1865, Hill reported himself too ill to execute his duties on several occasions. His comrades noted he looked worn down, and at one point Hill said he hoped McClellan won the election in 1864 because "if it becomes necessary to surrender, I would prefer to do so to McClellan." One Confederate noted, ""Much he suffered during the last campaign from a grevious malady, yet the vigor of his soul disdained to consider the weakness of his body and accepting without murmur the privations of that terrible winter, he remained steadfastly to his duty."

Still, Hill struck an impressive sight, with one aide commenting, "He was constantly on the lines, riding with a firm, graceful seat, looking every inch a soldier. Like General Lee, he was rarely much attended. One staff officer and a single courier formed his usual escort, and often he made the rounds alone. Of ordinary height, his figure was slight but athletic, his carriage erect, and his dress plainly neat. His expression was grave but gentle, his manner so courteous as almost to lack decision, but was contradicted by rigidity about the mouth and chin, and bright flashing eyes that even in repose told another tale. In moments of excitement he never lost self-control nor composure of demeanor, but his glance was as sharp as an eagle's, and his voice could take a metallic ring."

By March 1865, his health had deteriorated to the point where he had to ask for a leave of absence to recuperate in Richmond. Meanwhile, his family joined him in camp once again, and Hill's mood improved even if his well-being did not. He wrote to his sister Lucy:

"Dolly and the children are with me, and we are just as comfortable as people can expect to be in these times. The children are growing so rapidly, doing so well. Russy is as fat as a butterball and the greatest talker you ever saw. And your little namesake, Lucy Lee, is certainly the sweetest little cherub ever born, gentle and genial as a May morning, and easily managed.

I have just returned from the hardest trip I have ever had, down the rail road after Warren. I could not succeed in bringing him to fight, though I marched 40 miles one day and night. We succeeded however in turning him back from Weldon.

Our army here, as always, is ready to do its duty, and men and officers in good spirits. I suppose now we shall, in addition to Grant, have Sherman on our hands. Well the Army of Northern Virginia is equal to it, and however much you task its powers, will always respond, and I hope successfully.

By the beginning of 1865, the Confederacy was in utter disarray. The main Confederate army in the West under John Bell Hood had been nearly destroyed by General George H. Thomas's men at the Battle of Franklin in late 1864, and Sherman's army faced little resistance as it marched through the Carolinas. Although Confederate leaders remained optimistic, by the summer of 1864 they had begun to consider desperate measures in an effort to turn around the war. From 1863-1865, Confederate leaders had even debated whether to conscript black slaves and enlist them as soldiers. Even as their fortunes looked bleak, the Confederates refused to issue an official policy to enlist blacks. It was likely too late to save the Confederacy anyway.

By the time Lincoln delivered his Second Inaugural Address in March 1865, the end of the war was in sight. That month, Lincoln famously met with Grant, Sherman, and Admiral David Porter at City Point, Grant's headquarters during the siege, to discuss how to handle the end of the war.

In late March of 1865, Union cavalryman General Phil Sheridan destroyed what was left of Confederate general Jubal Early's cavalry near Waynesborough, Virginia, and then moved 12,000 men into position at General Lee's right flank near the crossroads known as Five Forks, effectively threatening Lee's supply line. Knowing that without unfettered access to men and supplies both he and Richmond could not withstand the battle that was imminent, Lee sent what infantry and cavalrymen he could muster to hold Five Forks, including Pickett's troops.

On March 31, Pickett's men engaged Union general Phil Sheridan's forces, leading to an ultimate showdown the following day at Five Forks. When the Battle of Five Forks finally commenced, however, Pickett was two miles away, said to have been enjoying a shad bake with Generals Fitzhugh Lee and Thomas L. Rosser. Thus by the time he reached the battlefield, it was too late; Union troops had already overrun Pickett's defense lines. Historians have attributed it to unusual environmental acoustics that prevented Pickett and his staff from hearing the battle despite their close proximity, not that it mattered to the Confederates at the time.

The following day, battles raged across the siege lines of Petersburg, eventually spelling doom for Lee's defenses, and A.P. Hill himself. In the early morning of April 2, Lee, Hill and Longstreet were all conferring when news reached that their lines were breaking. Hill immediately mounted a horse and rode toward his lines, moving so quickly that Lee actually sent his own aide after him to warn him to be careful.

Hill and the aide, Colonel Venable, came upon two Union soldiers and convinced them to surrender. After securing their surrender, Hill kept riding until he reached Lt. Col. William Poague's artillery, which he personally ordered to fire. Leaving Venable there, Hill now rode with just one aide as he headed southwest in an attempt to reach General Heth. During the ride, hill turned to him and said, "Sergeant, should anything happen to me, you must go back to General Lee and report it."

Along the Boydton Plank Road, the two Confederates came upon a couple of Union soldiers from the 138th Pennsylvania Infantry, Daniel Wolford and William Mauk. Seeing the two riders approaching, the two Union soldiers ducked behind a tree and took aim at their targets, now a mere 20 yards away. Hill's aide yelled at them to surrender, shouting, "If you fire you will be swept to hell... our men are here --surrender!" Hill echoed the demand, shouting at them, "Surrender!" In response, Mauk turned to Wolford and said, "Let us shoot them."

Wolford's shot at Hill's aide missed, but Mauk's shot struck Hill directly, passing through his gauntlet and into his chest, clean through his heart and out his back. As Hill fell to the ground mortally wounded, his aide grabbed his horse's bridle and raced away. As news of Hill's demise began to spread, men like Lee and Hill's chief of staff, Colonel Palmer, openly wept. Upon hearing the news, Lee moaned, "He is at rest now, and we who are left are the ones to suffer." Palmer was given the unenviable task of informing Hill's widow, who was seven months pregnant. When Palmer arrived, Dolly broke down, crying, "The General is dead! You would not be here if he had not been killed!"

Hill's body was recovered by the Confederates shortly after the battle ended, and his family had hoped to take Hill to Richmond for burial, but because the city was occupied by Union forces the funeral had to take place in Chesterfield County without the usual military honors. In February of 1867, the body of General Hill was transferred to Hollywood Cemetery in Richmond, Virginia. Then in the late 1880s, several former Confederates raised funds for a proper monument to be built in Hill's honor in Richmond, where his remains were interred in the base of the monument when it was dedicated on May 30, 1892.

One of Lee's aides wrote of Hill's death:

"Thus terminated the career of one of the most brilliant and successful leaders in the Southern Army. From the day he crossed the Chickahominy at Mechanicsville, in June, 1862, and opened the attack on the army under General McClellan, to the day of his death, he was a constant and reliable support to General Lee in the operations of his army.

Every chapter in the history of the Army of Northern Virginia is illumined with the story of the gallant and successful conduct of the troops under his command and the record of the series of brilliant operations on our right in the siege of the city of Petersburg in the spring of 1865, in resisting the extension of the lines of the army under General Grant, may be said to be a diary of the command of A.P. Hill.

It is a singular fact, worthy of record, that in the last moments of both General Jackson and General Lee, when the mind wandered, in the very shadow of death, each should have uttered a command to A.P. Hill, the beloved and trusted lieutenant -- ever ready, ever sure and reliable, always prompt to obey and give the desired support. When the strife was fiercest they were wont to call on Hill."

Chapter 15: Hill's Legacy

In the late 1880s, several former Confederates raised funds for a monument to be built in

Richmond to honor Hill, the spot where his remains were transferred upon its dedication on May 30, 1892. Today part of the Hermitage Road Historic District of Richmond, the A. P. Hill Monument is located in the center of the intersection of Laburnum Avenue and Hermitage Road. This monument is the only one of its type in Richmond, under which the individual of honor is actually interred.

The United States military honored Hill by naming Fort A. P. Hill in his honor. The fort is located in Caroline County, Virginia, about halfway between Richmond and Washington, D.C.

During World War II, the United States Navy named a Liberty Ship the SS *A. P. Hill* in his honor.

Hill's sword is on display at the Chesterfield County Museum in Chesterfield, Virginia.

Immediately following the death of Stonewall Jackson at Guinea Station on the Chandler Plantation on May 10, 1863, a rumor began to spread throughout the Confederacy that Jackson's dying words were "A. P. Hill." Subsequently, seven years later when Robert E. Lee died on October 12, 1870 of a stroke, Lee too was reported to have uttered "Tell Hill he must come up." That Hill was mentioned in the final words of the two Confederate legends became something of an urban legend that has survived into modern times.

However, accounts presented by those present at Jackson's final moments contend that the renowned general's dying words were actually, "Tell A. P. Hill to prepare for actions! Pass the infantry to the front! Tell Major Hawks . . . Let us cross over the river and rest under the shade of the trees." Furthermore, historians discount any such utterance as coming from Lee as current medical opinions believe Lee would have been unable to speak following a stroke capable of consequently ending his life.

In the final analysis, many historians today describe Hill as the logical product of two very different parents: one an outgoing and gregarious, highly respected merchant, farmer, and local politician; one a small, frail, and introverted brooding woman believed to have suffered chronic hypochondria. Thus, historians attribute "Powell's" inherent bravery and gentlemanly manners as traits from his father; his dark, brooding tendencies from his mother.

Known for his red "battle shirt" and hard-hitting attacks at the head of his famed "Light Division," Lieutenant General Ambrose Powell Hill, Jr. has ultimately gone down in American history as an unsurpassed combat officer and an aggressive, fast-moving division commander. Even so, Hill did not escape considerable controversy and criticism during the War, and that has continued into the present day.

Described by many as having a "frail physique", with some historians believing his repeated bouts with various illnesses were related to the venereal disease he contracted as a West Point cadet, it is generally agreed that he most likely suffered a psychological disorder (perhaps inherited from his mother) that reduced his effectiveness beginning at the Battle of Gettysburg—then more apparent at the Wilderness and Spotsylvania Court House. It angered several of his fellow officers that he frequently reported himself ill during times of crisis, leaving them to assume that he was doing so to avoid responsibility and the pressure of command.

Today, some historical analysts apply the so-called "Peter Principle" to Hill; an example of the popular contention that in an organization where promotion is based on achievement, success, and merit, that organization's members will eventually be promoted beyond their level of ability. Thus, although Hill was extremely successful commanding his famed "Light Division," he was less effective as a corps commander, but he was compelled to accept promotion and its accompanying responsibility.

Historian Larry Tagg describes Hill as "always emotional . . . so high strung before battle that he had an increasing tendency to become unwell when the fighting was about to commence." It was perhaps a condition he compensated for by adopting a "cocky" swagger and combative attitude. Often donning what his men referred to as his "battle shirt" (a red calico hunting shirt) when about to enter battle, the men under his command are said to have passed the word: "Little Powell's got on his battle shirt!" That was the signal to get the weapons ready and brace for battle.

A paradox of personality traits, Hill was said to have sometimes been quite affectionate with the rank-and-file soldiers under his command, with one officer calling him "the most lovable of all Lee's generals." But his manners were sometimes so courteous as to lack decisiveness, and other times his actions were impetuous. Hill was notoriously short-tempered and moody: an argument with Longstreet almost led to a duel, while a dispute with Jackson resulted in Hill being placed under arrest as his division entered Maryland in 1862.

Hill's generalship and administrative skills were sometimes lackluster, at other times inspired, and he ultimately missed significant periods of the campaigns due to unspecified illness. Nevertheless, despite his idiosyncrasies, by War's end, Hill was one of the Civil War's most highly regarded generals on either side of the Mason-Dixon Line. Next to Stonewall Jackson and James Longstreet, Robert E. Lee called "Little Powell" his most trusted lieutenant.

In 1988, Professor Emeritus of American History at Penn State Warren W. Hassler, author of numerous books and treatises on the Civil War, addressed a meeting of the Cincinnati Civil War Round Table to discuss A. P. Hill and his place in American history. Hassler had this insight to provide:

"Most of you, myself included I think, in general have a very limited knowledge of A.P. Hill. I think that Clifford Dowdy (author of numerous works on the Civil War including *The Land They Fought For: the Story of the South as the Confederacy, 1832 - 1865*) was voicing the same feeling I had after delving into the various materials available on A.P. Hill. Namely, that he has been neglected despite the fact that he was ranked next to Longstreet and Jackson by Lee as the third ablest general in the Army of Northern Virginia right around the time of Chancellorsville.

The problem is that Hill was not deliberately trying to create an aura of mystery about him, he was a very outgoing person, very extroverted. Apparently the diary that he kept was lost, as were his personal records and papers. Some were destroyed in a fire and others were given to autograph seekers and scattered to the winds. I've uncovered one or two A.P. Hill autographed items, but they are extremely scarce. This makes presenting a biography of A.P. Hill a difficult challenge. In contrast to most of the speakers you hear . . . I make no pretense or profess that [mine] is the definitive biography. I don't think it will ever be written, unless by happenstance there is a trunk full of memorabilia in somebody's attic that may contain some materials of A.P. Hill.

During the summer following Seven Days [Seven Days' Battles, June 25--July 1, 1862] Hill was transferred [due to a] fault that he had. That fault was that he was supremely proud, which can be a good characteristic, and it had its advantages as far as Hill was concerned. It also had terrible detrimental affects as well. Hill was so hypersensitive to criticism or imagined insults that during the period following the Seven Days' battles considerable friction developed. The press reports, which sided one way or the other with either Longstreet or Hill, gave them the credit for the success of the Seven Days' Campaign. Well, the thing got way out of hand and it escalated to the point where reports reached Lee that a dual between Longstreet and Hill was impending. Lee couldn't, of course, afford to lose either one of them. His solution, and it was the only one he had unless he wanted to lose Hill to another theater of the war, was to assign Hill to Jackson. . . . What I'm getting at is; this was the atmosphere in which Hill went. As a matter of fact when Hill reached Gordonsville he found there were five court marshals against him involving Jackson and other officers of his staff.

[Another] of Hill's flaws was that he had a tendency . . . to leave gaps in his [battle] line. At Second Manassas [August 28–30, 1862] he left a gap between [Generals] Craig and Thomas and the Federals poured through. He had to get Pender to restore the line and repair the one hundred and fifty-yard breach that was there. At Fredericksburg there was a six hundred-yard gap that he had left between Archer and Lane in the front line facing a bog. This brings out another factor about Hill at Fredericksburg. The same thing happened in the Wilderness.

I would say, and it is my opinion, that A.P. Hill would deserve at least an A- rating as a divisional commander. As a corp commander I'd probably give him not much more than a C or a C+. His ranking as a corp commander has to be tempered because, in the first place, everyone expected a Jackson. To paraphrase Senator Bentsen, 'A.P. Hill was no Jackson.' He was able and competent but not the genius that Jackson was. You also have to remember that after Gettysburg few southern generals really sparkled? It was a period that signaled the decline of the Confederate fortunes. Their resources were dwindling both in manpower and material. That would be my assessment of Hill. As much as I love him, in fairness, that's what I would say."

Given Hill's mixed record, and his arguments with Jackson and Longstreet, why was he so revered among his Confederate comrades? In a sense, Hill spent so much time in the legendary Army of Northern Virginia that he became closely associated with it regardless of his own individual efforts. As his brother-in-law put it upon hearing of his death, "We learned that a man had been killed, whose name had so long been associated with the army of Northern Virginia and its victories, that it almost seemed as if his life must be identified with its existence. The officer who was the very incarnation of the chivalry, the high-souled constancy, the glorious vigor of that army—General A. P. Hill—was dead. He was a hero, and he died like one. When the lines around Richmond were forced— his gallant corps overpowered, he was slain in the front still facing the enemy. His record had been completed, and he gave his life away, as if it were worthless after the cause to which he had pledged it was lost."

Bibliography

Alexander, Bevin. *How the South Could Have Won the Civil War*. New York: Crown Publishers, 2007.

Aphillcsa.goellnitz.org website: "And Then A.P. Hill Came Up, the Life and Career of General Ambrose Powell Hill." Accessed 11.02.2012.

Cincinnati Civil War Round Table website, "The Haunting Mystery of A. P. Hill," by Warren W. Hassler: http://www.cincinnaticwrt.org/data/ccwrt_history/talks_text/hassler_ap_hill.html Accessed 11.06.2012.

EncyclopediaVirginia.org website, "A. P. Hill": http://encyclopediavirginia.org/Hill_A_P_18251865#start_entry Accessed 11.03.2012.

Garrison, Webb. *Civil War Trivia*. Nashville, TN: Rutledge Hill Press, 1992.

Lanning, Michael Lee. *The Civil War 100*. Illinois: Sourcebooks, Inc., 2006.

Pollard, Edward Alfred. *The Lost Cause; a New Southern History of the War of the Confederates*. Accessed via: http://www.perseus.tufts.edu/hopper/text?doc=Perseus%3Atext%3A2001.05.0183 11.05.2012.

Robertson, James I., Jr. *General A.P. Hill: The Story of a Confederate Warrior*. New York: Vintage Publishing, 1992.

Sears, Stephen, W. (ed.). *The Civil War: The Second Year Told by Those Who Lived it*. New York: Penguin Books, 2012.

Tagg, Larry. *The Generals of Gettysburg*. Campbell, CA: Savas Publishing, 1998.

Albert Sidney Johnston and P.G.T. Beauregard
Chapter 1: Johnston's Early Years

Albert Sidney Johnston was destined to be one of the Civil War's most important generals, if only because of the coincidental timing and location of his birth. Born on February 2, 1803, Albert was the youngest son of Dr. John Johnston, a pioneering physician who was among the earliest settlers of the village of Washington in Mason County, Kentucky. John Johnston's family had originally hailed from Connecticut, where his family was a prominent, well-to-do Scotch family settled in Salisbury. But shortly after marrying Mary Stoddard in 1783, John headed west to Kentucky, which was still largely unsettled at the turn of the 19th century. Despite being a physician whose skills could have been put to use better near bigger cities, John was content to live in a more isolated village, even as it drove him into poverty. He eventually racked up so much debt that he had to give up all his property to discharge his debts, only to have the property bought by his oldest son and given back to him.

John's first wife died after bearing him 3 sons, so he married Albert's mother, Abigail Harris, in 1793. Abigail came from a religious background, with her father being described by one acquaintance as "the old John Knox Presbyterian of the place…anecdotes are still told of the spirit and courage with which he defended his Church." One man who knew Albert and the family, J.S. Chambers, would later note, "I always thought General Johnston inherited his frank, manly nature from his father. His mother was a gentle, quiet woman; while the old doctor was bold and blunt to a remarkable degree. He had no concealments, and was physically energetic, and mentally bold and independent. He had a large practice, and was often called into consultation in difficult, or rather in desperate, cases."

Given his origins, it's perhaps not surprising that Albert grew up in fairly stern surroundings. His son and biographer, William Preston Johnston, would later note that Albert's schooling was "Spartan", but that it conformed to the manner in which he grew up. Still, as a youngster Albert couldn't help but be lively and energetic, traits that made him a natural leader among friends and soldiers. At the same time, his oldest sister described him as polite, not just fearless, which was seconded by Chambers, who added, "He was six or seven years my senior, yet I remember him with great distinctness. He was my beau-ideal of a manly, handsome boy. He went to school for several years to James Grant, about one mile and a half west of Washington. Hie was active and energetic in the athletic games of the period, and fond of hunting on Saturdays, and always stood well in his classes, having a special talent for mathematics. He was grave and thoughtful in his deportment, but, when drawn out, talked well, and was considered by his associates and teachers as a boy of fine capacity."

Albert's son William would later recount one story that Albert told him when he was young:

"General Johnston sometimes told an anecdote of his early boyhood, from which he was wont to draw many a valuable moral. Playing marbles 'for keeps' --a species of boyish gaming — was a favorite sport of his schoolboy days; and he was so skillful and successful a marble-player that at one time he had won a whole jar full of white alleys, taws, potters, etc. It was then that the design entered his breast of winning all the marbles in the town, in the State, and eventually in the world. Filled with enthusiasm at the vastness of his project, he cast about for the means; and finally concluded, as the first step, to secure his acquisitions by burying them. He buried his jar very secretly, reserving only marbles enough 'to begin life on.' Purpose lent steadiness to his aim, so that again he beat all his rivals 'in the ring,' and added daily to his store. Only one competitor stood against him, whose resources seemed to consist not so much in skill as in an exhaustless supply of marbles, that were sacrificed with a recklessness arguing unlimited pocket-money. At last he, too, succumbed, and the victor went with a jar larger than the first, to add it to his spoils. To his dismay, however, he found his hoard plundered and his treasure gone. The inferior, but desperate, marble-player had furtively watched him, robbed him, and then staked and lost his ill-gotten gains. The second jar contained the same marbles as the first, and larceny had contended for empire with ambition. General Johnston said that he felt the lesson as a distinct rebuke to his avarice and rapacity; the plans he had built upon success vanished; and he learned that world-wide renown as a marble-player was merely 'vanity and vexation of spirit.'"

When Albert was a teenager, he desired a change of scenery and began lobbying his father John to let him go to school in Virginia. But after he was allowed to go there, he found it so disappointing that he left after just one session, after which he worked in a drug-store, something that probably pleased his physician father. Eventually, Albert was sent to school at Transylvania University in Lexington, Kentucky, where he struck up a friendship with another young man by the name of Jefferson Davis.

Jefferson Davis

Albert wouldn't spend much more time at Transylvania, or the rest of Kentucky for that matter. Whatever he had been thinking about for a profession went out the window during the War of 1812. As his son would later note:

"He studied hard, but at the end of the term became restless, from a desire to enter the navy. The gallant achievements of the American Navy in the war against Great Britain, and the subsequent daring exploits of Decatur at Algiers, had doubtless inspired him with the desire to emulate these high examples. His friends Duke and Smith, under the same impulse, sought and obtained warrants as midshipmen. But this project received no favor at home. His father and family opposed it; and, in order to divert his mind from brooding over a plan on which he had set his heart, it was proposed that he should accompany his sister, Mrs. Byers, and her husband, who were going to Louisiana. In the autumn of 1819 he went with them to the parish of Rapides, whither all his brothers had preceded him, and made a visit to his eldest brother, Josiah Stoddard Johnston. This visit was attended with important consequences to the adventurous youth, changing the theatre of his ambition from sea to land. Indeed, as the youngest son, the Benjamin of the household, sent to this new land of plenty by the old man, his father, he was received with a double portion of kindness by the elder brother, who, now in middle life, had already achieved a conspicuous position."

Despite his family's attempts to discourage him from a military career, Albert Sidney Johnston was deadset on this new path, and it would take him east to West Point in 1822.

Chapter 2: Johnston at West Point

Before he was 20 years old, Albert Sidney Johnston found himself at the West Point Military Academy. Today West Point is considered the country's elite military academy, but when Johnston was appointed to West Point, it was a highly unimpressive school consisting of a few ugly buildings facing a desolate, barren parade ground. Established with just five officers and ten cadets of the Corps of Engineers on March 16, 1802, the Academy was built on a spot just 50 miles north of New York City that had been a key Hudson River military fortress during the Revolutionary War. Cadets attending during the "Point's" first several decades were obliged to maintain their daily regimen despite knowing the school might shut down at any moment, as the federal government frequently questioned why it should provide free education.

One thing that was not unimpressive, however, was Johnston himself. In fact, Albert was one of the most respected and admired members of his class. Classmate N.C. Macrae noted that Johnston "commanded the respect of all who knew him", and William H.C. Bartlett claimed "none had a larger share of affectionate regards of his classmates. Albert also excelled at the school, as noted by classmate Edward B. White: "During our few years at West Point, he was esteemed by us all as a high-minded, honorable gentleman and soldier, for whom we entertained much affection, and whose death was unaffectedly mourned by the few of us who survive. He was, as a mark of his good conduct and soldierly bearing, a non-commissioned and commissioned officer of the corps of cadets, I think, during his whole term; a distinction much valued and desired by all of us."

Johnston's most famous classmate also happened to be one he had already met. As fate would have it, Jefferson Davis was at West Point, and the two became closer. Davis would later note, "He was sergeant-major, and afterward was selected by the commandant for the adjutancy, then the most esteemed office in the corps…He was not a hard student, though a fair one. His quickness supplied this defect. He did not have an enemy in the corps, or an unkind feeling to any one, though he was select in his associates."

The future Confederate president's point about Johnston's scholarly bearing was borne out by one anecdote of Albert's West Point days:

"He devoted himself earnestly to the preparation for the examination, and was satisfied with his mastery of the whole course except two problems; but, when he was called upon to come forward, the subject presented to him for discussion was one of these very problems. He was compelled to decline, hoping for better fortune next time; but, to his dismay, by a coincidence not included in his doctrine of chances, the professor gave him the other neglected problem. He was again obliged to say that he was unprepared. He was ordered to take his seat; but, feeling that his reputation and future standing were at stake, he briefly yet forcibly stated the fact that these were the only two exceptions to his knowledge of the course. The superintendent sternly ordered him to take his seat, which he did. If the matter had ended here, he would probably have lost his commission as well as his grade; but, as soon as the class was dismissed, he sent a written communication to the examiners, stating the facts, and challenging the most rigorous examination. There was some indisposition to grant the reexamination; but it was finally accorded to him, through the friendly intervention of General Worth, then commandant of the Corps of Cadets, who had been greatly pleased with his bearing under such difficult circumstances, as well as with his previous conduct as a cadet. It was a most trying ordeal. The board took him at his word, and gave him a long and most searching examination; after which, however, in spite of a reduction on account of his misadventure, and of a want of skill in drawing, he was graded eighth in his class. He was not only grateful to Worth for this good turn, but always retained an admiration for him as a dashing soldier. Worth had a large measure of knowledge and experience, and was full of martial spirit and generosity, which, with his handsome person and gallant bearing, made him a model for these young soldiers. He always treated Johnston with marked consideration; and, after the Mexican War, recommended him as leader for a difficult enterprise."

Albert Sidney Johnston would wind up graduating 8th in his class out of 41 cadets, an impressive enough ranking that Johnston would be allowed to choose which service branch he preferred upon being commissioned into the Army. Though Johnston liked cavalry, no cavalry corps existed yet, and most top-ranking cadets preferred artillery, having been thoroughly trained in engineering. But Johnston chose the infantry, due to his experience on the frontier and the fact that an infantry assignment would probably ensure he would head west. As a result, he was brevetted Second-Lieutenant Albert Sidney Johnston and assigned to the Second Infantry.

Though Johnston and his classmates never could have known it at the time, West Point would become the foremost military academy in the nation, and it would churn out the cadets who became the most important generals in the Civil War. With that, the future generals' years at West Point became a source of both camaraderie and colorful stories A clerical error by West Point administrators ensured that Hiram Ulysses Grant forever became known as Ulysses S. Grant, and years after Robert E. Lee met Johnston and Jefferson Davis at West Point, George H. Thomas and William Tecumseh Sherman met each other and Richard S. Ewell. During the 1850s, classes included men like John Bell Hood, Union general Phil Sheridan and James

Birdseye McPherson, who would become the only commanding general of a Union army to die in a Civil War battle when he fell in 1864 during Sherman's Atlanta Campaign.

The most famous West Point class in history was the Class of 1846, which boasted more than a dozen future Civil War generals. The Class of 1846 included a shy kid named Thomas Jonathan Jackson who made few friends and struggled with his studies, finishing 17th in his class 15 years before becoming Stonewall. Also in that class was A.P. Hill, who was already in love with the future wife of George McClellan, a young prodigy who finished second in the class of 1846. A popular and mischievous George Pickett would play hooky at the local bar and struggle just to finish last in the class, and the Class of 1846 also churned out critical Union generals like Jesse Reno, Darius Couch, and George Stoneman.

Lee

Chapter 3: Beauregard's Early Years

Creole by birth, Pierre Gustave-Toutant Beauregard (also Pierre Gustave Toutant Beauregard, P. G. T. Beauregard, and G. T. Beauregard) was born on May 28, 1818 at the "Contreras," his family's sugar-cane plantation in St. Bernard Parish, Louisiana, about 20 miles outside New Orleans. Pierre was the third of seven children born to Jacques Toutant-Beauregard (of French and Welsh lineage), and Hélène Judith de Reggio (a descendant of an Italian noble family that had migrated to France and then America).

The wealthy Jacque Toutant-Beauregard traced his French-Welch lineage back to the 13th century, with his family tree including the prestigious names Cartier and Ducro. His grandfather, the first of the family to settle in Louisiana, came to Louisiana Colony during the time of the illustrious French King Louis the XIV (1638--1715), his wife a descendant of the distinguished de Reggio family--an Italian family of dukes--who migrated to America to establish their royal line in the New World. It is said that Jacque gave his son Pierre a "rich and ringing" name befitting of his ancient heritage should it appear in the future annals of fame.

Throughout his life, Beauregard identified with French heroes like Napoleon Bonaparte, and Southerners were struck by the "foreign" otherness of him. To understand why, it's essential to remember that in 1818, when Pierre was born, it had only been 15 years since French-settled Louisiana had ceded from France, and the Parish of St. Bernard near New Orleans was still fiercely *French*. The Contreras Plantation owned by the wealthy Toutant-Beauregard family stood in the parish as a monument to French aristocracy, the Toutant-Beauregard name ranking high among the French elite.

While a great deal of public attention was conferred upon Pierre Gustave-Toutant Beauregard after his stint in the Mexican-American War (and more so by the time of the Civil War), it appears that as a child he lived a relatively cloistered life, growing up within Louisiana high society and having little contact with the English-speaking world. Beauregard wouldn't learn to speak English until he was a teenager, and almost nothing was written (or perhaps survived translation) about his early years.

Growing up in an environment that was partly of the "plantation South" and partly foreign to anything the South had ever experienced before, the home in which Pierre was born was a large, one-story structure, not in the tradition of later *grand* plantation mansions, but reflective of European aristocracy of late 18th century America. Pierre grew up surrounded by slaves who tended the sugar plantation, saw to his family's every need, and as babies, were suckled by black wet-nurses from places like West Africa, Antigua, or perhaps Trinidad. With black children as his earliest companions and playmates, Pierre sometimes allowed them to accompany him when he rode in the fields, hunted in the woods, or took his boat into the bayous.

Spiritually, Pierre was raised to consider himself and his surroundings part of France, not the American "South". Given his family background, it was instilled in him at birth that he was *Creole* -- a Frenchman of Old World substance who had come to America to become a feudal aristocrat. Accordingly, their geographic and topographic location, and privileged societal position, made owning slaves to operate their sugarcane fields only appropriate. And as aristocrats and "Toutant-Beauregards," their rewards were lusty eating and drinking, grandiose merrymaking, and luxurious living. They prized fine manners, breeding, tradition and honor, even to the point that many outsiders found it to be *pompous absurdity*. Given that gentlemanly behavior, dignity, chivalry, and aristocratic demeanor were the ideal qualities glorified in the antebellum South, being considered pompous was no easy feat.

Like other aristocratic families that settled in America, and particularly in their area, Beauregard's family was in constant fear of being absorbed; their bloodline diluted (or *polluted*). So they remained largely to themselves, strutting and striking boastful poses when among the "Yankees." Pierre and his family looked to New Orleans as "civilization" and the only source of spiritual inspiration in the States, and to Paris as "home."

Although little was written about Pierre's early years, it is known that he attended a private school from the ages of eight to eleven, and he was then sent to a French boarding school in New York City, which was fast growing into the heart of Yankee country. In New York, he grew into a quiet, studious, and reserved young man, in stark contrast to how he acted and would be remembered in adulthood. Toutant-Beauregard oral tradition does, however, relate particular incidents which provide glimpses of Pierre's later personality.

For example, when he was about 9 years old, a man teased Pierre in front of friends and relatives about his failure during a hunting outing. Seizing a stick, Pierre chased the man into an outhouse and refused to allow him to leave until he apologized. Another incident, which took place at about age 10 during his first Communion at the Church of St. Louis, describes Pierre as becoming distracted by the sound of drums outside just as he was approaching the church altar. A moment later, he dashed outside to witness the activity. This anecdote seems to illustrate that even as a boy, Pierre had already developed the heart of a soldier.

After attending New Orleans' French-speaking private schools from about the age of eight to age eleven, at 12 Pierre was sent to a French boarding school in New York City, where he learned to read, speak, and write English for the first time. Although this decision broke with Creole custom - proper aristocracy only attended schools in New Orleans or France - the school, widely known as the "French School," was operated by two brothers named Peugnet who had served under Napoleon Bonaparte. Thus the school came with a French pedigree, and even among contemporary Americans, Napoleon was a legend. With a curriculum that emphasized mathematics and commercial subjects, Pierre quickly became a driven student who worked hard and consistently made good grades. Pierre remained there for the next four years, returning home only at Christmas and during the summer.

However, attendance at the 'French School' also had an unforeseen effect on Pierre. In addition to providing excellent instruction in mathematics, accounting, and other business-related subjects, the Peugnet brothers often regaled students with their military exploits while serving under Napoleon. These tales inspired the wide-eyed, 12 year old Pierre to read all the books and written accounts available on Napoleon and his famous battles, and soon began to aspire to live the life of his hero. Even before completing his studies at the 'French School,' Pierre announced that he intended to become a soldier, asking his father to secure him an appointment at the Military Academy at West Point.

Far from agreeing with Pierre's decision, his father flatly objected to a military education in the States. Although he favored collaborating with Americans as necessary, he thought that to actually become *one* of them was carrying the integration much too far. Nevertheless, Pierre refused to be deterred, a trait that would come to distinguish him throughout his life, and he stood his ground, insisting that it was his decision to make. Eventually, his family yielded.

In 1834, 16 year old Pierre was admitted to the United States Military Academy at West Point, New York. Upon enrolling, he dropped the hyphen from his surname (Gustave-Toutant), and began treating Toutant as a middle name to fit in with his classmates' Anglo names. From that point on, he rarely used his first name at all, preferring "G. T. Beauregard."

Due to his diminutive size, haughty demeanor, and prevalent French accent, not to mention his obsession with Napoleon Bonaparte, Beauregard's classmates often referred to him as "Little Napoleon," as well as "Little Creole," "Bory," "Little Frenchman," and "Felix" -- nicknames that would follow him throughout his life.

As fate would have it, Beauregard's artillery instructor at the Academy was Robert Anderson, the man who would later become the Union Major in charge of the federal garrison at Fort Sumter in 1861, and the one who would ultimately surrender the fort to Beauregard in the first fighting of the Civil War. While at the Academy, Anderson was so impressed with Beauregard's military aptitude that he got him a temporary post as an assistant instructor.

Robert Anderson

Beauregard graduated second in his class in 1838, out of a total of 45 cadets, having excelled as both an artilleryman and military engineer. Upon graduation, Pierre was commissioned Lieutenant G. T. Beauregard, lieutenant of engineers.

Chapter 4: Johnston's Early Army Assignments

Albert Sidney Johnston would later come to claim Texas as his native state, but after West Point he was initially given assignments on the East Coast, and the first notable incident in his early military career was his decision to turn down an offer. Johnston's older brother was by now a Senator and an acquaintance with men like Henry Clay, offering his younger brother access to important men like the President and General Winfield Scott. During one encounter with Scott, Johnston apparently made enough of an impression to receive an offer that would have been an immediate promotion. But much to the chagrin of his brother, Albert turned it down, as his brother would later recount, "I well remember my disappointment when, as a very young and handsome man, he was offered the position of aide to General Scott, and, from his own judgment, refused it, saying that, 'although much gratified to have been mentioned by General Scott, he felt that the life of inactivity in a large city did not accord with his views, and that he preferred to go off to the far West, and enter at once upon the duties of his profession.' His brother did not think it right to oppose his inclination, although General Scott was our particular friend. As for myself, I fairly scolded and wept at this determination."

As a result, Johnston's assignment took him north to an assignment in New York at Sackett's Harbor on Lake Ontario, where he would spend a winter. Far removed from anything approaching hostilities, Johnston's closest call was during some horsing around that almost turned fatal:

"But a single incident is preserved of General Johnston's winter at Sackett's Harbor. This he sometimes cited as an illustration of the recklessness of youth. He was engaged with some fellow-officers in artillery-practice on the ice of Lake Ontario, when a wild party of sleighers kept dashing across the line of fire, near the target. Meaning to rebuke this bravado with a good scare, he waited for the rush of their Canadian ponies near his target, and then fired. He succeeded so well that, for an instant, the whole party was enveloped in snow and splintered ice, and seemed to be blotted out. A moment after they emerged from the frosty spray with wild yells and affrighted gestures, and returned no more. He felt during the instant of suspense that murder had been done, and the relief of the revelers at their escape was not greater than his own. He accepted the adventure, however, as a lesson in something more than artillery-practice."

In 1827, Johnston finally headed west, where he was stationed near St. Louis, Missouri. At the time, Missouri was strategically situated as the nation's crossroads between the frontier, the Midwest, and the East, and the assignment meant Johnston and his regiment might be sent in any direction as necessary. As it turned out, that direction would be north, to deal with Native American tribes. In the Summer and Fall, the U.S. Army had to deal with several hostile tribes located in present-day Wisconsin, and it was here that Johnston had his first important encounters with the Indians. Johnston described his impressions in a letter:

"The detachment of the Sixth Regiment which left this place was accompanied by two companies of the Fifth Regiment from St. Peter's, up the Wisconsin River as far as the portage, where it was met by a detachment of the Second Regiment from Green Bay, under the command of Major Whistler. The Winnebagoes, in council, agreed to deliver up the leading men in the several outrages committed against the whites. Accordingly, Red Bird, Le Soleil, and two others, the son and brother-in-law of Red

Bird, were given up, there; and two more, afterward, at Prairie du Ohien, belonging to the Prairie La Crosse band. They bound themselves to hold a council in the spring for the determination of the boundary-line; and to permit the miners of Fever River to proceed peaceably in their "diggings," till the true boundary was determined.

Although, after seeing the Sacs and Foxes, Menomonees, Sioux, etc., my romantic ideas of the Indian character had vanished, I must confess that I consider Red Bird one of the noblest and most dignified men I ever saw. When he gave himself up, he was dressed, after the manner of the Sioux of the Missouri, in a perfectly white hunting-shirt of deer-skin, and leggins and moccasins of the same, with an elegant head-dress of birds' feathers; he held a white flag in his right hand, and a beautifully-ornamented pipe in the other. He said: "I have offended. I sacrifice myself to save my country," etc. He displayed that stoic indifference which is wrongfully attributed to the Indian character alone. I'll stop. I am not going to write a whole letter about a rascally Indian."

While stationed in Missouri for the next few years, Johnston met a woman who his contemporaries considered a nearly perfect match for him:

"In the customary interchange of hospitalities, Miss Henrietta Preston was on a visit to these relations when she met Lieutenant Johnston, and the interest that she at once inspired was reciprocated. This mutual attachment was thorough and unbroken; and Lieutenant Johnston, being sent for a great part of the year 1828 on recruiting service to Louisville, Kentucky, Miss Preston's home, became engaged to her. They were married January 20, 1829. There were many points of resemblance between Albert Sidney Johnston and his wife; and a friend, who knew them both well, has told me that he never knew two people more alike in character. Another, a relation, says they were often mistaken for brother and sister. But this was true rather as to the outcome of character in similar sentiments, and the same philosophy of life, than in their original traits or acquired habits of mind. The affinity was one of sympathy in feelings and aspiration; and the usual law of attraction, based upon contrast of character and community of tastes, was reversed. As they were both persons of most loyal natures, these coincidences increased. Mrs. Johnston was above middle size-five feet six inches in height-and of agreeable person, with a full form, a brilliant color, hazel eyes, dark hair, and somewhat irregular but pleasing features. Her voice had wonderful harmony in its modulations. Her manner was full of dignity and ease, but vivacious and engaging, and her conversation has been variously characterized as piquant, graceful, and eloquent. Mrs. Johnston was a woman of firm yet gentle temper, and, as the eldest daughter of a struggling family, the confidante and counselor of her mother, had been trained to a severe self-discipline. She was eminently benevolent and forbearing. Gifted with a poetic temperament, and very fond of verse, she wrote it with facility and feeling; while her husband, rigorously schooled in a training almost exclusively mathematical, and loving unrefracted truth, jocularly called it good prose spoiled. With these traits, with high literary culture, and with strong religious impulses, she had formed a lofty ideal of the aims and duties of life; and this ideal, she thoroughly believed, was realized by her husband."

Johnston's first son was born in 1831, but he didn't have much time to celebrate before he was called to service in the war against the Native chief Black Hawk. In early 1832, Chief Black Hawk was leading a group of Native Americans comprised of Sauks, Meskwakis, and Kickapoos into Illinois, ostensibly to avoid coming into conflict with white settlers pushing west. However, Black Hawk's reputation as fighting on the side of the British during the War of 1812 was well established, which led to the labeling of his group as the "British Band". Unsure of Black Hawk's intentions, settlers mobilized on the frontier to combat them. In response to Black Hawk's movements, militias were called out, and Johnston's Army regiment headed to the wilds of Wisconsin, the heart of "Indian country."

Johnston kept a journal during his service in the short war, describing the Indians as fierce: "No time was to be lost. An active and cruel enemy was now busy in the work of death and devastation, since the last levy was disbanded. Their mode of warfare is such that, while you keep a sufficient force in motion against them to contend with their main body, you must necessarily keep troops at every assailable point on the frontier to hold in check small parties, which it is their custom to detach to a great distance. Thus military men, acquainted only with the warfare of civilized nations, are surprised that so many troops are called into the field to subdue a comparatively small body of savages. Great allowance, in estimating for a militia force, must be made for the probable daily diminution, or actual loss of strength, from a variety of causes, which do not affect a regular force in the least; this, in addition to what is said of the enemy, will explain the reason why so large a militia force is usually called out."

Plaster bust of Black Hawk

After the Black Hawk War, Johnston continued to spend his time stationed in Missouri, until he received an offer that he didn't want to pass up. While in Louisville, Johnston heard about a call to arms from Stephen F. Austin, who was there appealing to Americans to come fight for Texan Independence. After materially helping the Texans who would show up and ask for help, Johnston eventually decided to actually join the fight.

In 1836, Johnston became the aide-de-camp for Sam Houston, and later that year he was given the rank of colonel in the Republic of Texas Army on August 5, 1836. A few months later, he became a brigadier-general in the Texas Army, and he later became Secretary of War. His son William would explain Albert's motivations in the biography of his father, while implicitly analogizing the War for Texan Independence to the Civil War:

"Albert Sidney Johnston shared in the general sympathy with the Texan cause, but there were personal reasons which increased the intensity of his own feelings. In early youth, as has been mentioned, he had spent some time in Alexandria, Louisiana, then a border village, and consequently had familiar recollections of many from that region who were now earnest actors in the events of the revolution. His brothers, too, had taken part in Magee's expedition in 1812, and the remembrance of their extraordinary sufferings may have further influenced him. It is now difficult to estimate how far mental disquietude and the spirit of adventure may have entered into his motives. He was unhappy, he was unemployed, and here was a field open alike to his energies, his patriotism, and his philanthropy.

It was the cause of a community struggling for self-government against a central despotism, for the maintenance of guaranteed and vested rights against a military usurpation, for constitutional freedom against chronic anarchy. It was a contest between 20,000 Americans, kindred in race and sentiment, who had been invited by Mexico to take possession of the soil, and 8,000,000 alien Mexicans, incapable of stable government. It was the weak against the strong, order against political confusion, Americans against a foreign enemy. The men of that day had been bred in republican ideas and nurtured with visions of the greatness and the expansive force of our people, and they were willing to lay down fortune and life to forward these mighty ends.

Albert Sidney Johnston was a republican from the bottom of his heart, and, though not a propagandist in either temper or sentiment, he was a sincere believer in the blessings of regulated liberty and the supremacy of law. With these ideas of public right, and with the conviction of his call to render public service, he thought his talents could not be put to better use than in aiding to secure their liberties to men of his own race, who were ready to sacrifice all else to achieve them. Originally, however, the most potent motive that urged him to enlist in this enterprise was the hope that, Texas having been freed, he might promote its annexation to the United States; and, since readmission into the army was impossible, that he might employ the sword, for which his country deemed she had no need, in laying an empire at her feet. Of course, after he had devoted himself to the cause of Texas, her interests became paramount; but he frequently admitted that, in the first instance, he was in large measure animated by the desire of assisting to add another star to the American constellation. Indeed, strong as were his feelings in behalf of the infant nation, he did not consummate his resolution to enter its service until the Government of the United States had recognized its independence. With this sanction he felt no further hesitation, and threw himself into the cause with all the ardor of his nature."

Chapter 5: Beauregard's Early Assignments

Though initially assigned to the artillery unit, Lieutenant G. T. Beauregard was quickly reassigned to the engineering corps, and from 1838 to 1839 he assisted in the construction of Fort Adams on Brenton's Point at Newport, Rhode Island. From 1840 to 1844, he was stationed near his home in Louisiana, where he was instrumental in two major engineering projects at the passes of the Mississippi River and in the construction of Fort Livingston on Grand Terre Island at Barataria Bay. Later in 1844, he was assigned to a post in Pensacola, Florida for a short time, and then Fort McHenry in Baltimore, Maryland.

By all accounts, he was a highly proficient and thorough worker. Moreover, being an engineer was one of the foremost professions for demonstrating military competence, and envisioning and drawing lines during this time would help Beauregard immensely in future combat.

In 1841, Lieutenant G. T. Beauregard married Marie Antoinette Laure Villeré (March 22, 1823 – March 21, 1850), the daughter of Jules Villeré, a wealthy sugarcane planter in Plaquemines Parish, Louisiana, and member of one of the most prominent French Creole families in the country. Marie's paternal grandfather, Jacques Villeré, was the second governor of Louisiana.

Described as having blue eyes and fair skin, Marie and G. T. had three children together: René (1843–1910), Henri (1845–1915), and Laure (1850–1884). Marie died in March 1850 while giving birth to Laure.

One year after the passing of Marie Antoinette, in 1851 G. T. married Caroline Deslonde, daughter of André Deslonde, a wealthy sugarcane planter from St. James Parish, Louisiana. Caroline was a sister-in-law of John Slidell, a U. S. Senator from Louisiana who later became famous as one of the Confederate diplomats seized by the U.S. Navy on the British ship RMS Trent, igniting an international incident that nearly brought Great Britain into the war.

Caroline and G. T. had no children together. In March of 1864, Caroline died in New Orleans while Louisiana was under Union occupation.

Chapter 6: Mexican-American War

"Few comprehend the ravages and perils of war. They are not to be found in the reports of the battle-field, which account for but a small portion of the waste of life or the dangers encountered. The unaccustomed life of a soldier, privations without number, and hard marches under a vertical sun, or in the chilly hours of the night, make up a bill of mortality treble that of the fiercest warfare. This was the case with the British army in the Peninsular War. It has been peculiarly so with ours in this war; and, I have no doubt, if any one would take the trouble to examine, it would be found the history of all warfare." – Albert Sidney Johnston during the Mexican-American War

The Mexican-American War was one of the crucial forging grounds for the country's future Civil War generals, and so it was with Johnston and Beauregard.

During the Mexican-American War, G. T. Beauregard served as an engineer under Lt. General Winfield Scott, field promoted to brevet captain for the Battles of Contreras and Churubusco (August 20, 1847), and then major for the siege of Chapultepec Castle (September 13, 1847), where he was wounded in the shoulder and thigh. Becoming noted for his eloquent oratory skills, he was able to persuade his commanding officers (including General Scott) to change their planned tactics for attacking the fortress of Chapultepec, a change that helped assure a successful campaign.

Winfield Scott

In September of 1847, Major G. T. Beauregard was one of the first officers to enter Mexico City, distinguishing himself in the assault against the western gates of the city. After the battle, Beauregard stated that he considered his contributions in reconnaissance and devising of strategy to be more significant than other engineer colleagues, one of which was a captain named Robert E. Lee. When Beauregard did not receive as many field commissions as Lee, he made his displeasure known. Beauregard, the "Little Napoleon", also worked with young George McClellan, the "Young Napoleon", and together they fought at Churubusco and Chapultepec, even conducting joint missions for General Scott.

McClellan

After several years in the service of the Republic of Texas, Albert Sidney Johnston was on the verge of retirement. He had suffered a wound to his pelvis during a duel in 1837, and the frontier had exposed him to malaria and other illnesses. Moreover, he had grown tired of civil service in government, which he found was no substitute for a military career.

Johnston remarried while down in Texas and took up the more simple life of a farmer, but when the Mexican-American War started, Johnston quickly rejoined the U.S. Army, this time as a member of the 1st Texas Rifle Volunteers. Johnston even stayed on after his enlistment expired, and he worked to convince others to stay as well. In addition to being an Inspector General of Volunteers, Johnston fought at Monterrey, describing the action in a letter home to his son:

"My regiment was disbanded at Camargo on the 24th of August, under the construction of the law given by the War Department in reference to six months volunteers. Soon after, General Taylor offered me the appointment of inspector-general of the field division of volunteers under Major-General Butler, which I accepted, as I was desirous of participating in the campaign which was about to commence. The army moved from Camargo, and was concentrated at Ceralvo on the 12th; and marched thence to Monterey, successively in divisions, on the 13th, 14th, and 15th, as follows: Twiggs's division on the 13th, Worth's on the 14th, and Butler's on the 15th. They were again united at Marin on the 17th, and arrived together at the forest of St. Domingo, three miles from Monterey, on the 19th. The 19th and 20th were passed in reconnoitring the position of the enemy's defenses and making the necessary disposition for the attack. These arrangements having been made, and General Worth's division having occupied the gorge of the mountain above the city on the Saltillo road, the attack was commenced by General Worth, who had by his position taken all their defenses in reverse, and pressed by him on the 21st until he had captured two of their batteries. At daylight, on the 22d, he took the height which commanded a strong work on the slope of the hill in the direction of the city, at the bishop's palace, and on Wednesday entered the city, fighting from house to house with his infantry (regulars and dismounted Texans), and along the streets with his light artillery. In cooperation with the attack of General Worth, General Taylor ordered Twiggs's division to attack their admirably arranged and powerful system of defense at the lower end of the city; here was the means of greatest resistance. This attack was supported by Butler's division, with the exception of the Louisville Legion, which was ordered to take a position near the mortar which was throwing shells into the main fort near the upper end of the city. These divisions approached the city under a tremendous shower of artillery and musketry from the fort and numerous batteries, suffering great loss. Twiggs's division attacked the batteries, and afterward filed off by the right flank toward a tete-de-pont (a species of fort), across a branch of the St. Juan, which runs through the city. The Tennesseans and Mississippians of Butler's division and a few regulars under Captain Backus, moving rapidly in support, attacked the first battery or redoubt, a strong work armed with artillery and escopetas or muskets, and bravely carried the work (Alexander McClung, at the head of the Mississippians of his wing of the regiment, being the first to enter), driving the enemy from it with considerable loss. The Ohio regiment, under Colonel Mitchell, entered the town more to the right, and attacked the works with great courage and spirit; but here was concentrated the fire of all their works. From this point, or a little in the rear, the regulars had been forced back with great loss of officers and men, after keeping up the attack for more than an hour, and after having lost in killed and wounded a great number. Having been ordered to retire, the Ohio regiment did so in tolerably good order. As it debouched from the streets of the city, believing that it was routed, the lancers of the enemy charged the Ohio regiment; but it had none of the vim of an American charge, and was easily repulsed with some loss to them. On the night of the 22d the enemy abandoned their strong line of defense at the lower end of the city, and retired to the plazas and barricades.

During these operations the light artillery and howitzers kept up a terrible fire of shot and shells against the enemy. On Wednesday, the 23d, the Texans and Mississippians were ordered to attack in the streets, and fight and work their way through the houses to the plaza. These orders were faithfully executed, so that at night they had arrived as near the public square (plaza) at the lower part as Worth had at the upper part of the city.2 On Thursday the Mexicans sent in, early in the morning, a white flag; and during the day articles of capitulation were agreed to, by which the city, its defenses, public property, munitions of war, etc., were surrendered to the United States army, except their army, which is allowed to march beyond designated limits, viz.: Rinconada (the main pass of the mountains), Linares, and St. Fernando — a line passing through these points being the boundary. Within these limits the armies will remain for eight weeks, or until their respective governments can be heard from. Thus, after a series of brilliant and sanguinary actions, we have possession of this beautiful and strongly-fortified place. Butler's division sustained about half the loss of the army, say 250 killed and wounded, not less and perhaps many more. General Butler was wounded in the leg, while I, finely mounted throughout, escaped with my huge frame without a scratch. I endeavored to do my duty well, and I presume my conduct will be spoken of approvingly. Send a copy of this to Henry, and my love to your uncles George and Will, and to Aunt Mary and Margaret."

General "Fighting Joe" Hooker, who would also become a noted Civil War general, described Johnston's presence at Monterrey to his son as well, telling him, "It was all the work of a few moments, but was long enough to satisfy me of the character of your father. It was through his agency, mainly, that our division was saved from a cruel slaughter; and the effect on the part of the army, serving on that side of the town, would have been almost, if not quite, irreparable. The coolness and magnificent presence your father displayed on this field, brief as it was, left an impression on my mind that I have never forgotten. They prepared me for the stirring accounts related to me by his companions on the Utah campaign, and for his almost godlike deeds on the field on which he fell, at Shiloh."

Chapter 7: Beauregard Before the Civil War

In 1848, G. T. Beauregard returned from Mexico and for the next 12 years was put in charge of what the U. S. Engineer Department called the "Mississippi and Lake Defenses in Louisiana." Despite this title, however, much of his engineering work was done elsewhere, on the Florida coast and in Alabama, repairing old forts and building new ones. He also beefed-up the defenses of Forts St. Philip and Jackson on the Mississippi River below New Orleans and supervised construction of Fort Proctor, located east of New Orleans on the banks of Lake Borgne.

In 1852 while still in the Army, Beauregard actively campaigned for Franklin Pierce, the Democratic presidential candidate and former general of the Mexican-American War, a man who had been greatly impressed with Beauregard's performance at Mexico City. When elected the 14th President of the United States in 1853, Pierce appointed Beauregard Superintending Engineer of the New Orleans Federal Customs House, a huge granite building built in 1848 that was sinking unevenly into the moist Louisiana soil. Developing a highly inventive renovation program, Beauregard was able to stabilize the structure successfully, and continued to serve in this position until 1860.

On March 3, 1853, after 14 years of continuous service at the rank of lieutenant, G. T. Beauregard was promoted to captain. Once again seeing duty in Louisiana, he improved the navigability of the shipping channels at the mouth of the Mississippi River (basically seeing to it that trees were ripped from the river bed), supervised the repair of the fortifications in Mobile Bay and along the lower Mississippi River, and upgraded the levee system. Also, while working on a board of Army and Navy engineers, Beauregard created and patented an invention he called a "self-acting bar excavator" to be used by ships in crossing bars of sand and clay.

Bored with life as a peacetime military officer, late in 1856 during his service in New Orleans, Beauregard informed the U.S. Army Engineer Department that he intended to join the filibuster William Walker, who had seized control of Nicaragua and had offered Beauregard the rank of second-in-command of his private army. Filibustering was the term given to organizing private military expeditions into Latin America with the intention of establishing English-speaking colonies under individual control (essentially dictatorships). Beauregard's superior officers, however, convinced him to change his mind, which ultimately proved the wise move. Although Walker was able to get himself elected in 1856 and serve until 1857, he was defeated by a coalition of Central American armies in 1860 and executed by the government of Honduras.

William Walker

In 1858, G. T. Beauregard briefly entered the political arena as a reform candidate for mayor of New Orleans, where he was supported by both the Whig and Democratic parties to challenge the Know Nothing Party candidate, Gerard Stith. On June 7, he was just narrowly defeated.

Taking advantage of his brother-in-law's political influence, on January 23, 1861, Representative and Louisiana State Senator John Slidell obtained an appointment for Beauregard as superintendent of the U.S. Military Academy at West Point, New York. Five days later, however, his appointment was revoked after Louisiana seceded from the Union and he openly stated that he would join the Confederacy as a matter of course. Subsequently, Beauregard protested his dismissal to the War Department, citing that they had cast "improper reflection upon [his] reputation or position in the Corps of Engineers" by forcing him out as a Southern officer even before any hostilities began. Effectuating the shortest tenure in the Academy's history, his dismissal essentially ended his career as a United States military officer.

Chapter 8: Johnston Before the Civil War

After the Mexican-American War, Johnston spent a little more time farming on a plantation, writing to one of his acquaintances, "My crops are small, but since I have become a farmer I have the gratification of success in everything I have attempted; and in gardening I have succeeded as well. We have had a great abundance of strawberries; and at this time we have a good variety of excellent vegetables-artichokes, pie-plant, fine heads of early York cabbage, squash, tomatoes, Irish potatoes, and your favorite yams of last year's crop, which we have never been without since we came here. Our cantelupes will soon be ripe, and in a short time we will have plenty of figs and watermelons." He also acutely felt the great distance that separated him from his family, writing to his daughter, "It is a great disappointment to me; but we have learned to repine at nothing, believing that there is a Power that orders all things for the best-that even those things that are seemingly to our finite mental vision a chastisement are ultimately for some good beyond our ken."

In due time, however, Johnston was named a major in the U.S. Army by his former superior, Zachary Taylor, and he became Paymaster in December 1849, a post he served in for over 5 years. Johnston was later made colonel of the 2nd U.S. Cavalry in 1855 by President Franklin Pierce. Johnston went about organizing the regiment from scratch, and one of his subordinates was George H. Thomas, who would later become recognized as the Rock of Chickamauga during the Civil War. In fact, Thomas would become colonel of the 2nd U.S. after Johnston resigned his Army commission to fight for the Confederates.

Given their location, Johnston would soon be called upon to take part in a campaign against the Mormons being led by Brigham Young in Utah. The unforgiving environment would make it extremely difficult for the U.S. Army to attempt to remove Young from power in the territory, as

Johnston made clear in letters on the campaign:

"The country over the distance to be traversed, and, in fact, to this place-125 miles-presents the appearance of a great desert, including the whole space between the Rocky Mountains and the range in front of us. There is neither tree nor bush anywhere, except in the water-courses. They are sparsely fringed with stunted willows, cottonwood, and aspen. The upland is everywhere covered with wild-sage and its varieties and with grass in bunches in season. Grass is found on all the water-courses in abundance in summer. The bad condition of our animals, and the country before us almost destitute of subsistence, offered but little encouragement to the hope of reaching our destination this winter, and I had already had under consideration the most suitable position to pass the winter. On our march from the South Pass we had fine roads and fine weather, and effected the march in eight days, uniting the troops and supplies on the 3d of November, with the exception of Cooke's command. Two days were occupied in distributing clothing and making arrangements to resume our march.

On the 6th of November it was resumed, and then commenced the storm and wintry cold, racking the bones of our men and starving our oxen, and mules, and horses, already half starved. They died on the road and at our camps by hundreds, and so diminished were their numbers that from camp to camp, only four or five miles, as many days were required to bring them all up, as it was necessary to give time to rest the animals, now incapable of protracted efforts, and to hunt for food. In this way fifteen days were consumed in making thirty-five miles to this place, the nearest and best place for shelter and fuel for the troops, and for shelter and grass for the animals. The struggle then amid snow and arctic cold (the thermometer 16° below zero) was for a place of safety. If any doubt existed before this storm of the propriety of risking the troops on the mountains before us before spring, or of the ability to accomplish the march, the destruction among our draught-animals, the necessity of saving all the oxen left for food, even if capable of further exertion, now dispelled that doubt and solved the question.

Colonel Cooke's command arrived here with the rear of the main body on the 19th of November. The storm which he encountered on the Sweetwater, and on through the South Pass, destroyed more than half of his horses and a large number of his mules, although he had corn for them. In that high region, much higher than where we were, the cold must have been much more intense than experienced by us, and his animals, I presume, perished mainly from cold. I have the satisfaction to say that the privations of the march were endured by officers and men without complaint, or, perhaps, I might more justly say, with cheerfulness. The troops are in fine health and condition. The winter, thus far, has not been so rigorous as to prevent often the daily instruction of the troops. They have proved themselves to be hardy enough for any service; a few only — as many as thirty or less — have been frost-bitten, but now our scouts bivouac, when necessary, in the passes without suffering.

The horses and mules, and the cattle left, after slaughtering as many as would serve until April, have been distributed on Smith's and Henry's Forks, and most of them will get through the winter. We have, of course, a large number yet, and hope many of them will be fit for service after they have the spring grass a while. I have not, however, trusted to that, but, soon after I established my camp here, I dispatched Captain Marcy to New Mexico for draught-mules, and a remount for dragoons and batteries, and expect him to return before the 1st of May. If I get the spring supplies from Laramie in time I will be able to advance as soon as the route is practicable, in May, with an effective force, much improved by drilling the recruits.

The Mormons have declared, as fully as words and actions can manifest intentions, that they will no longer submit to the Government, or to any government but their own. The people of the Union must now submit to a usurpation of their territory — to have a government erected in their midst, not loyal to, or rather not acknowledging any dependence upon, or allegiance to the Federal Government-and what is not less impolitic and entirely incompatible with our institutions, must allow them to ingraft their social organization upon ours and make it a part of our system, or they must act with the vigor and force to compel them to submit. This is due to the dignity and honor of the Government."

Chapter 9: 1850s Politics and the Election of 1860

Throughout the 1850s, American politicians tried to sort out the nation's intractable issues. In an attempt to organize the center of North America – Kansas and Nebraska – without offsetting the slave-free balance, Senator Stephen Douglas of Illinois proposed the Kansas-Nebraska Act. The Kansas-Nebraska Act eliminated the Missouri Compromise line of 1820, which the Compromise of 1850 had maintained. The Missouri Compromise had stipulated that states north of the boundary line determined in that bill would be free, and that states south of it *could* have slavery. This was essential to maintaining the balance of slave and free states in the Union. The Kansas-Nebraska Act, however, ignored the line completely and proposed that all new territories be organized by popular sovereignty. Settlers could vote whether they wanted their state to be slave or free.

Stephen Douglas, "The Little Giant"

When popular sovereignty became the standard in Kansas and Nebraska, the primary result was that thousands of zealous pro-slavery and anti-slavery advocates both moved to Kansas to influence the vote, creating a dangerous (and ultimately deadly) mix. Numerous attacks took place between the two sides, and many pro-slavery Missourians organized attacks on Kansas towns just across the border.

The best known abolitionist in Bleeding Kansas was a middle aged man named John Brown. A radical abolitionist, Brown organized a small band of like-minded followers and fought with the armed groups of pro-slavery men in Kansas for several months, including a notorious incident known as the Pottawatomie Massacre, in which Brown's supporters murdered five men. Over 50 people died before John Brown left the territory, which ultimately entered the Union as a free state in 1859.

John Brown

After his activities in Kansas, John Brown spent the next few years raising money in New England, which would bring him into direct contact with important abolitionist leaders, including Frederick Douglass. Brown had previously organized a small raiding party that succeeded in raiding a Missouri farm and freeing 11 slaves, but he set his sights on far larger objectives. In 1859, Brown began to set a new plan in motion that he hoped would create a full scale slave uprising in the South. Brown's plan relied on raiding Harpers Ferry, a strategically located armory in western Virginia that had been the main federal arms depot after the Revolution. Given its proximity to the South, Brown hoped to seize thousands of rifles and move them south, gathering slaves and swelling his numbers as he went. The slaves would then be armed and ready to help free more slaves, inevitably fighting Southern militias along the way.

In recognition of how important escaped slave Frederick Douglass had become among abolitionists, Brown attempted to enlist the support of Douglass by informing him of the plans. While Douglass didn't blow the whistle on Brown, he told Brown that violence would only further enrage the South, and slaveholders might only retaliate further against slaves with devastating consequences. Instead of helping Brown, Douglass dissuaded freed blacks from joining Brown's group because he believed it was doomed to fail.

Despite that, in July 1859, Brown traveled to Harper's Ferry under an assumed name and waited for his recruits, but he struggled to get even 20 people to join him. Rather than call off the plan, however, Brown went ahead with it. That fall, Brown and his men used hundreds of rifles to seize the armory at Harper's Ferry, but the plan went haywire from the start, and word of his attack quickly spread. Local pro-slavery men formed a militia and pinned Brown and his men down while they were still at the armory.

After being called to Harpers Ferry, Robert E. Lee took decisive command of a troop of marines stationed there, surrounded the arsenal, and gave Brown the opportunity to surrender peaceably. When Brown refused, Lee ordered the doors be broken down and Brown taken captive, an affair that reportedly lasted just three minutes. A few of Brown's men were killed, but Brown was taken alive. Lee earned acclaim for accomplishing this task so quickly and efficiently.

The fallout from John Brown's raid on Harpers Ferry was intense. Southerners had long suspected that abolitionists hoped to arm the slaves and use violence to abolish slavery, and Brown's raid seemed to confirm that. Meanwhile, much of the northern press praised Brown for his actions. In the South, conspiracy theories ran wild about who had supported the raid, and many believed prominent abolitionist Republicans had been behind the raid as well. On the day of his execution, Brown wrote, "I, John Brown, am now quite *certain* that the crimes of this *guilty land* will never be purged away but with *blood.* I had, as I now think vainly, flattered myself that without very much bloodshed it might be done."

The man in command of the troops present at Brown's hanging was none other than Thomas Jonathan Jackson, who was ordered to Charlestown in November 1859. After Brown's hanging, the future Stonewall Jackson began to believe war was inevitable, but he wrote his aunt, "I think we have great reason for alarm, but my trust is in God; and I cannot think that He will permit the madness of men to interfere so materially with the Christian labors of this country at home and abroad."

By the Fall of 1860, everyone could see the "war-cloud" on the horizon. With the election of Republican candidate Abraham Lincoln as president on November 6, 1860, many Southerners considered it the final straw. Someone they knew as a "Black Republican", leader of a party whose central platform was to stop the spread of slavery to new states, was now set to be inaugurated as President in March.

Throughout the fall and winter of 1860, Southern calls for secession became increasingly serious. In a last-ditched effort to save the Union, Kentucky's Senator John Crittenden tried to assume the stateliness of his predecessor Henry Clay. Crittenden, however, proved to be no Henry Clay: his proposal that a Constitutional Amendment reinstate the Missouri Compromise line and extend it to the Pacific failed. President Buchanan supported the measure, but President-Elect Lincoln said he refused to allow the further expansion of slavery under any conditions.

The Crittenden Compromise failed on December 18. Two days later, South Carolina seceded from the Union. President Buchanan sat on his hands, believing the Southern states had no right to secede, but that the Federal government had no effective power to prevent secession. In January, Mississippi, Florida, Alabama, Georgia, Louisiana and Kansas followed South

Carolina's lead. The Confederacy was formed on February 4th, in Montgomery, Alabama, with former Secretary of War Jefferson Davis as its President. On February 23rd, Texas joined the Confederacy.

Chapter 10: The Start of the Civil War

Lincoln's predecessor was among those who could see the potential conflict coming from a mile away. As the Confederacy continued to grow during his last months in office, President James Buchanan instructed the federal army to permit the Confederacy to take control of forts in its territory, hoping to avoid a war. Conveniently, this also allowed Southern forces to take control of important forts and land ahead of a potential war, which would make secession and/or a victory in a military conflict easier. Many Southern partisans within the federal government at the end of 1860 took advantage of these opportunities to help Southern states ahead of time.

One of the forts in the South was Fort Sumter, an important but undermanned and undersupplied fort in the harbor of Charleston, South Carolina. Buchanan attempted to resupply Fort Sumter in the first few months of 1860, but the attempt failed when Southern sympathizers in the harbor fired on the resupply ship.

Lincoln had promised that it would not be the North that started a potential war, but he was also aware of the possibility of the South initiating conflict. After he was sworn in, Lincoln sent word to the Governor of South Carolina that he was sending ships to resupply Fort Sumter, to which the governor replied demanding that federal forces evacuate it.

Although G. T. Beauregard had hoped to be named commander of the New Orleans volunteers, on February 20 the state legislature appointed native North Carolinian Braxton Bragg with the rank of major general. Aware that Beauregard might resent him (and make for bad blood), Bragg offered him the rank of colonel, which Beauregard rejected, enrolling instead as a private in the "Orleans Guards," an elite battalion of French Creole aristocrats. Bragg would command the New Orleans forces until April 16 and then on March 7 be promoted to brigadier general of the Confederate States Army, becoming one of the most important Confederate generals in the West.

Meanwhile, Beauregard made his case with former Senator John Slidell, now serving as advisor for the newly-chosen Confederate President Jefferson Davis, lobbying Slidell for a senior position in the Confederate States Army. Jefferson Davis, however, was less concerned with appointing field commanders than with the political tension building at Fort Sumter in Charleston Harbor, so he appointed Beauregard commander of Charleston's defenses. With his experience as both a military engineer and persuasive Southern spokesman, Beauregard was the perfect person to put in change of the potentially volatile circumstances if war was to be avoided, which Davis hoped was still a possibility.

On March 1, 1861, Beauregard was appointed Brigadier General of the Provisional Army of the Confederate States. Arriving in Charleston, South Carolina on March 3, 1861, he met with Governor Andrew Pickens to inspect the defenses of the harbor, which he ultimately deemed unsatisfactory. For the next month, Beauregard went about strengthening the harbor's defenses as the political tensions continued to mount.

Although he vowed not to fire the first shot, Lincoln was likely aware that his attempt to resupply Fort Sumter in Charleston Harbor would draw Southern fire; it had already happened under Buchanan's watch. After his inauguration, President Lincoln informed South Carolina governor Francis Pickens that he was sending supplies to the undermanned garrison at Fort Sumter. When Lincoln made clear that he would attempt to resupply the fort, Davis ordered Beauregard to demand its surrender and prevent the resupplying of the garrison.

In early April, the ship Lincoln sent to resupply the fort was fired upon and turned around. On April 9, Confederate President Davis sent word to General Beauregard to demand the fort's evacuation. At the time, the federal garrison consisted of Major Robert Anderson, Beauregard's artillery instructor from West Point, and 76 troops. Even before the bombardment, upon learning that he was opposed by Beauregard, Anderson remarked that the Southern forces in Charleston harbor would be exercised with "skill and sound judgment". Beauregard also remembered his former superior, and before the bombardment, he sent brandy, whiskey and cigars to Anderson and his garrison, gifts the Major refused.

Despite the mutual admiration and pleasantries, both men had serious work ahead of them. Davis ordered Beauregard that if Anderson wouldn't evacuate the fort, "proceed in such a manner as you may determine to reduce it." As ordered, Beauregard demanded that Anderson surrender the fort before a scheduled Union expedition to re-provision the fort with bread could arrive. In the early morning of April 12, negotiations with Anderson broke down, prompting Beauregard to order a bombardment of Sumter from nearby Fort Johnson. At 4:30 am that morning, April 12, 1861, Beauregard ordered the first shots to be fired at Fort Sumter, effectively igniting the Civil War. After nearly 34 hours and thousands of rounds fired from 47 artillery guns and mortars ringing the harbor, on April 14, 1861, Major Anderson surrendered Fort Sumter, marking the first Confederate victory. No casualties were suffered on either side during the dueling bombardments across Charleston harbor, but, ironically, two Union soldiers were killed by an accidental explosion during the surrender ceremonies.

Biographer T. Harry Williams described Beauregard, the "Hero of Fort Sumter," as "the South's first paladin." The New York *World* wrote: "One result of the Charleston fight will be to restore Beauregard to favor of the southern people. Truly he is boastful, egotistical, untruthful, and wanting in tact, but he is certainly the most marvelous engineer of modern times. By his genius and professional skill he has erected batteries in Charleston Harbor that would sink all the wooden fleets of the world did they come under fire."

George Peter Alexander Healy's portrait of Beauregard, 1861

Of course, the fact that Beauregard was both the Confederates' first hero and was a creole caught the eyes of the South. As one writer described him, "On first meeting, most people were struck by [Beauregard's] 'foreign' appearance. His skin was smooth and olive-complexioned. His eyes, half-lidded, were dark, with a trace of Gallic melancholy about them. His hair was black (though by 1860 he maintained this hue with dye). He was strikingly handsome and enjoyed the attentions of women, but probably not excessively or illicitly. He sported a dark mustache and goatee, and he rather resembled Napoleon III, then ruler of France—although he often saw himself in the mold of the more celebrated Napoleon Bonaparte."

Immediately following the Fort Sumter engagement, General G. T. Beauregard was elevated to hero status among Southerners; a walking, talking living legend. But upon his return to the Confederate Capital of Richmond, not all Southerners saw him as representative of the Southern gentleman--nor of the Confederate Army. Many, in fact, took umbrage with Beauregard's haughty posturing and "undignified" arrogance--his impeccably tailored uniform--referring to him as "Little Napoleon," a little man, more show than substance. Many even labeled him 'nothing more than an ambitious despot.' And once he began openly criticizing President Davis, he not only made enemies of Davis himself, but Davis' many supporters. When Beauregard's portrait appeared on the June, 1863 cover of *Southern Illustrated News*, long after his initial luster had faded, many Southerners who couldn't see the attraction in the first place were puzzled and annoyed by his continuing popularity.

After the attack on Fort Sumter, support for both the northern and southern cause rose. Two days later, Lincoln issued a *call-to-arms* asking for 75,000 volunteers. That led to the secession of Virginia, Tennessee, North Carolina, and Arkansas, with the loyalty of border states like Kentucky, Maryland, and Missouri still somewhat up in the air. The large number of southern sympathizers in these states buoyed the Confederates' hopes that those too would soon join the South. Moreover, the loss of these border states, especially Virginia, all deeply depressed Lincoln. Just weeks before, prominent Virginians had reassured Lincoln that the state's historic place in American history made its citizens eager to save the Union. But as soon as Lincoln made any assertive moves to save the Union, Virginia seceded. This greatly concerned Lincoln, who worried Virginia's secession made it more likely other border states and/or Maryland would secede as well.

Despite the loss of Fort Sumter, the North expected a relatively quick victory. Their expectations weren't unrealistic, due to the Union's overwhelming economic advantages over the South. At the start of the war, the Union had a population of over 22 million. The South had a population of 9 million, nearly 4 million of whom were slaves. Union states contained 90% of the manufacturing capacity of the country and 97% of the weapon manufacturing capacity. Union states also possessed over 70% of the total railroads in the pre-war United States at the start of the war, and the Union also controlled 80% of the shipbuilding capacity of the pre-war United States.

After the attack on Fort Sumter, support for both the northern and southern cause rose. President Lincoln requested that each loyal state raise regiments for the defense of the Union, with the intent of raising an enormous army that would subdue the rebellion.

In late Spring 1861, Davis ordered Beauregard to northern Virginia as second-in-command to General Joseph E. Johnston, where he was to oppose the federal forces building up under McDowell. Though Johnston was the superior in rank, he ceded authority to Beauregard near Manassas Junction, leaving Beauregard in command there. At Manassas, Beauregard took charge of the Confederate forces assembling near the rail junction at Manassas and had his men construct defenses along a 14 mile front along Bull Run Creek. Meanwhile, Johnston was gathering and training additional troops in the Shenandoah Valley.

On June 1, 1861, Beauregard issued a proclamation to the people of Virginia that elucidated in no uncertain terms his attitude about the justification for the War: "A reckless and unprincipled tyrant has invaded your soil. Abraham Lincoln, regardless of all the moral, legal, and constitutional restraints, has thrown abolitionist hosts among you who are murdering and imprisoning your citizens, confiscating and destroying your property, and committing other acts of violence and outrage too shocking and revolting to humanity to be enumerated."

On July 18, Union General Irwin McDowell set out with two divisions on a twelve-mile circuitous march west from Centreville, Virginia to cross Bull Run at Sudley Springs Ford, intending to strike Beauregard's troops at Manassas-Sudley Road in an effort to turn the Southern left flank. Meanwhile, another division was set to drive directly west along the turnpike and across Stone Bridge, while back at Centreville, another division stayed in reserve. The remaining division, scattered along the lines of communication all the way back to Washington but would ultimately take no part in the ensuing battle, made a total of 32,000 men at McDowell's disposal.

Unbeknownst to McDowell, however, several days earlier, General Beauregard had received advance warning of troop movement from a civilian and had forwarded a coded message to Jefferson Davis along with a request to move General Joseph E. Johnston and his 12,000 men from the Shenandoah Valley to Manassas, via rail. Beauregard's intelligence placed the Union Army within attack position by July 17.

The First Battle of Bull Run made history in several ways. McDowell's army met Fort Sumter hero P.G.T. Beauregard's Confederate army near the railroad junction at Manassas on July 21, 1861. Located just 25 miles away from Washington D.C., many civilians from Washington came to watch what they expected to be a rout of Confederate forces. And for awhile, it appeared as though that might be the case.

McDowell's strategy fell apart though, thanks to railroads. Confederate reinforcements under General Joseph E. Johnston's Army, including JEB Stuart's cavalrymen and a brigade led by Thomas Jonathan Jackson, arrived by train in the middle of the day, a first in the history of American warfare. With Johnston's army arriving midday on July 21, it evened up the numbers between Union and Confederate. Shoring up the Confederates' left flank, some of Johnston's troops, led by Jackson's brigade, helped reverse the Union's momentum and ultimately turn the tide. As the battle's momentum switched, the inexperienced Union troops were routed and retreated in disorder back toward Washington in an unorganized mass. With over 350 killed on each side, it was the deadliest battle in American history to date, and both the Confederacy and the Union were quickly served notice that the war would be much more costly than either side had believed.

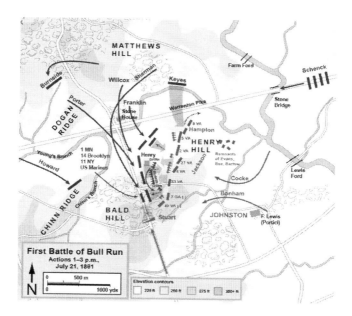

First Battle of Bull Run
Actions 1–3 p.m.,
July 21, 1861

Ironically, McDowell commanded the Army of Northeastern Virginia and Joseph E. Johnston commanded the Army of the Potomac at First Bull Run. A little over a year later it would be Lee's Army of Northern Virginia fighting elements of the Union Army of the Potomac at Second Bull Run, on nearly the same ground.

It was also during First Manassas or Bull Run that Jackson earned the famous nickname "Stonewall", but there is an enduring mystery over the origin of his nickname. What is known is that during the battle, Jackson's brigade arrived as reinforcements at a crucial part of the battlefield on the Confederate left. Confederate Brigadier General Barnard Bee, commanding a nearby brigade, commanded his men to reestablish their battle line next to Jackson's brigade, shouting, "There is Jackson standing like a stone wall. Rally behind the Virginians." General Bee was mortally wounded shortly after that command and died the following day. Thus, it remains unclear whether Bee was complimenting Jackson's brigade for standing firm or whether he was criticizing Jackson's brigade for inaction. Without Bee around to explain his command, nobody will ever know for certain. However, that has not stopped people from debating Bee's comment.

Regardless, the nickname Stonewall stuck, and Jackson was henceforth known as Stonewall Jackson. His brigade also inherited the title, known throughout the war as the Stonewall brigade. hough credit for the victory would ultimately go to General "Stonewall" Jackson and his

"Stonewall Brigade," it was Beauregard (now identified in the field by the French Army kepi cap he wore) who had called for the countermeasure that allowed Jackson to turn the tide of the battle. Beauregard himself had four horses shot out from under him during the fighting and at one point was left without a horse to pursue the retreating Union troops. Still, Beauregard has not been without critics. Renowned historian William C. Davis noted that during the battle, "Beauregard acted chiefly as a dime novel general, leading the charge of an individual regiment, riding along the line to cheer the troops, accepting the huzzas of the soldiers and complementing them in turn." Nevertheless, as the hero of Fort Sumter, Beauregard's participation eclipsed all but Jackson's.

Stonewall Jackson

After the battle ended and the Union Army was in rapid retreat, Beauregard stated sardonically that had Richmond dispatched adequate supplies to their army, he would have been able to pursue the Union Army all the way to Washington, implying that Davis had short-changed his troops and cost the Confederates an even greater victory. In his Official Report, which made its way into the newspapers, Beauregard suggested that Davis had prevented the pursuit and destruction of McDowell's army, as well as the potential capture of Washington D.C. itself.

This, of course, only added to the animosity Davis already felt toward the celebrity-seeking general, and it would eventually lead to Beauregard being sidelined during the middle of the war. Of course, having won at Fort Sumter and First Bull Run, Beauregard was indispensable in the summer of 1861, and it should be noted, that General Johnston also complained that lack of supplies had prevented his army from advancing against Washington. Furthermore, many cite Davis' "taking the field" at the Bull Run battlefield on July 21, 1861 as nothing more than a publicity stunt perpetuated by the headline-seeking Davis to insinuate a military role for himself.

On July 21, Beauregard was promoted to full general, one of only eight in the Confederate Army, his date of rank making him the fifth most senior general behind Samuel Cooper, Albert Sidney Johnston, Robert E. Lee, and Joseph E. Johnston. With the Confederates remaining massed outside Washington D.C., Beauregard remained busy with everything from discussing grand strategy to working on a new Confederate battle flag. Beauregard had been confused during the battle by the Confederates' first national flag, the "Stars and Bars", at one point nearly making a critical mistake because he thought Johnston's reinforcements were advancing Union troops. Beauregard had a big hand in working to have the eventual Confederate battle flag formalized, and it has remained the most popular symbol of the Confederates ever since.

However, Beauregard continued to bristle under the leadership of Jefferson Davis, making him the first prominent general to do so, but hardly the last. Beauregard's suggestion of invading Maryland and threatening the rear of Washington D.C. was met with a deaf ear, though Davis accepted it in 1862 when Lee suggested an invasion that culminated with the Battle of Antietam. Fed up, Beauregard asked to be reassigned to New Orleans, where he (correctly) anticipated the Union would attack.

Johnston had been in the service of the U.S. Army for decades, but like so many other Southerners, he ultimately decided to side with a State over the Union:

"But, devoted as General Johnston was to the Union, he could not forget that he was also the citizen of a State. To Texas he had sworn allegiance; his estate and his best years had been spent in shielding her; he had aided to merge her autonomy and to limit her independent sovereignty by annexation, and he knew that when she entered the Union it was by treaty, as an equal, and that the Constitution was the bond to which she had consented. She had performed her covenant faithfully; it was the North by which it had been trampled into the dust. She had, therefore, the right to renounce the broken contract, or to try to enforce it, as she deemed most expedient. If she elected to secure her liberties by withdrawing from a Union in which they were assailed, her action would be justified by either the letter of the bond, or by the "inalienable right," as the Declaration of Independence has it, of a people to choose their own form of government. It was an act of sovereignty, for which the State was responsible to whatever other community should choose to dispute it; but not to its own citizens, who were bound to adhere to it the more closely the more it was endangered.

Now, though General Johnston was satisfied that Texas and the other Southern States had ample grounds for resistance or withdrawal, and the right to take the extremest measures to secure themselves, he did not believe the means adopted were wise or expedient. His mind was too sternly practical to allow him to suppose, when the clearest guarantees of the Constitution had failed to restrain partisan zeal and the lust of dominion, that these passions would be arrested now by the assertion of a disputed right. He was sure that peaceable secession was impossible, and therefore thought that it was a remedy to be tried only when all others had been exhausted, and not until every effort at conciliation had failed, and every sacrifice had been made to preserve the Union. Nor was he without hopes that, if an interval were left for returning reason to resume its sway, fanaticism might be dethroned, and the people would demand equity and peace. But, if resistance was to be made, he thought it should be attempted on no doubtful issue, but only after radical tactics had fully laid bare the purposes of that party. Such delay would unite the South, justify its action, and give the opportunity for cooperation, organization, and the accumulation of adequate means of defense. Delusive as were these hopes, they were those of a patriot, and had much to do in shaping General Johnstones conduct in the opening of the war."

Thus, in early May 1861, Johnston resigned his commission, which at the time had him stationed far west as the commander of the U.S. Army Department of the Pacific in California. But given his position, and the fact he had to cross through Union held territory, it was a journey just to make it to Confederate soil. Johnston actually had to evade arrest just to reach Arizona that July, allowing him to enter the service of the South.

Chapter 11: Johnston Gains A Command

After the long trek, Johnston made his way to Richmond and arrived on September 5, 1861, just two days after the Confederates in the West had committed their first grievous mistake. After Virginia seceded, both the North and South hoped to have the border slave states on their side, particularly Kentucky and Missouri. Moreover, President Jefferson Davis decided early on upon a strategy that would have the Confederates defend as much Southern territory as they could, despite the fact that stretched their outnumbered forces thinner than they otherwise would have been had they concentrated.

As a result, Davis had forces stretched from the Mississippi River as far east as the Allegheny Mountains, with Tennessee being a crucial Confederate defensive location. However, Confederates under the command of Maj. Gen. Leonidas Polk and Brig. Gen. Gideon J. Pillow were moved into the capital of Kentucky on September 3, prompting Kentucky's governor to request Union assistance to drive the occupiers out of Columbus. With that, Kentucky was destined to remain in the Union fold, no doubt gratifying President Abraham Lincoln, who famously stated, "I hope to have God on my side, but I must have Kentucky."

As a remarkably experienced career Army officer, and a personal favorite of Jefferson Davis, it's no surprise that Johnston received an important post after arriving at Richmond. In fact, he was given command of almost the entire Western theater: "General Albert Sidney Johnston, Confederate States Army, is assigned to the command of Department No. 2, which will hereafter embrace the States of Tennessee and Arkansas, and that part of the State of Mississippi west of the New Orleans, Jackson & Great Northern and Central Railroad; also, the military operations in Kentucky, Missouri, Kansas, and the Indian country immediately west of Missouri and Arkansas. He will repair to Memphis, Tennessee, and assume command, fixing his headquarters at such point as, in his judgment, will best secure the purposes of the command." Along with that, Johnston was made the second most senior general in the Confederate Army, behind only Adjutant-General Cooper, ahead of Robert E. Lee, Joseph Johnston and P.G.T. Beauregard.

Due to the rash actions of more inexperienced officers, Johnston took command in the West at a tenuous time, as noted by his son: "General Johnston had hardly assumed command when he found the Federal armies in possession of nearly the whole of Missouri, and continually menacing Columbus, the left flank of his line in Kentucky, with heavy forces massed at Cairo." Johnston also quickly learned about the difficulties of trying to raise and organize an army in his department; the governors of the Confederate states were hesitant to marshal soldiers for purposes other than the defense of their native state.

Thus, when Johnston entered Kentucky with an army, it was a meager 4,000 strong army, and he still felt compelled to delicately address the state of Kentucky in the wake of Polk's and Pillow's mistakes:

"Proclamation. whereas, the armed occupation of a part of Kentucky by the United States, and the preparations which manifest the intention of their Government to invade the Confederate States through that territory, has imposed it on-these last as a necessity of self-defense to enter that State and meet the invasion upon the best line for military operations; and whereas, it is proper that the motives of the Government of the Confederate States in taking this step should be fully known to the world: now, therefore, I, Albert Sidney Johnston, General and commander of the Western Department of the army of the Confederate States of America, do proclaim that these States have thus marched their troops into Kentucky with no hostile intention toward its people, nor do they desire or seek to control their choice in regard to their Union with either of the Confederacies, or to subjugate their State, or hold its soil against their wishes. On the contrary, they deem it to be the right of the people of Kentucky to determine their own position [in regard to the belligerents. It is for them to say whether they will join either Confederacy, or maintain a separate existence as an independent and sovereign State. The armed occupation of their soil, both as to its extent and duration, will, therefore, be strictly limited by the exigencies of self-defense on the part of the Confederate States. These States intend to conform to all the requirements of public law, and international amity as between themselves and Kentucky, and accordingly I hereby command all who are subject to my orders to pay entire respect to the rights of property and the legal authorities within that State, so far as the same may be compatible with the necessities of self-defense. If it be the desire of the people of Kentucky to maintain a strict and impartial neutrality, then the effort to drive out the lawless intruders who seek to make their State the theatre of War will aid them in the attainment of their wishes. If, as it may not be unreasonable to suppose, those people desire to unite their fortunes with the Confederate States, to whom they are already bound by so many ties of interest, then the appearance and aid of Confederate troops will assist them to make an opportunity for the free and unbiased expression of their will upon the subject. But if it be true, which is not to be presumed, that a majority of those people desire to adhere to the United States and become parties to the War, then none can doubt the right of the other belligerent to meet that War whenever and wherever it may be waged. But harboring no such suspicion, I now declare, in the name of the Government which I serve, that its army shall be withdrawn from Kentucky so soon as there shall be satisfactory evidence of the existence and execution of a like intention on the part of the United States."

Meanwhile, Johnston realized it was imperative to build and organize an army. When he had taken command of his large department, he only had about 40,000 total soldiers at his disposal, and they were stretched across a vast amount of territory. Furthermore, there was a general shortage of ammunition and resources. As his son would put it in his biography, "[I]t is thus apparent that the real question to be determined was not as between an offensive and a defensive campaign; this had already been settled by the physical and political considerations mentioned, and by the preponderance in the Federal strength, organization, and resources. The real questions were, how and where to maintain the semblance of a force sufficient for defense until an army could be created." In addition to taking up defensive positions, Johnston had to content himself to executing raids here and there, all in an attempt to mask his department's weakness.

At the beginning of 1862, Johnston had to deal with yet another setback, after inexperienced brigadier generals Felix Zollicoffer and Maj. Gen. George B. Crittenden rashly attacked Union troops along the Cumberland river at the Battle of Mill Springs. Soldiers under the command of Johnston's former subordinate George H. Thomas sharply repulsed them, inflicting casualties upon about 13% of the Confederate army. After that, Davis ordered P.G.T. Beauregard to the department, in the hopes that his fame from Fort Sumter and First Bull Run would help with recruiting. Around the same time, Johnston took the brigade Davis sent him, which was commanded by General John B. Floyd, and sent him to take command at Fort Donelson with orders to escape if the fort could not be held.

Chapter 12: Fort Henry and Fort

Donelson

While the Lincoln Administration and most Northerners were preoccupied with trying to capture Richmond in the summer of 1861, it would be the little known Ulysses S. Grant who delivered the Union's first major victories, over a thousand miles away from Washington. Grant's new commission led to his command of the District of Southeast Missouri, headquartered at Cairo, after he was appointed by "The Pathfinder", John C. Fremont, a national celebrity who had run for President in 1856. Fremont was one of many political generals that Lincoln was saddled with, and his political prominence ensured he was given a prominent command as commander of the Department of the West early in the war before running so afoul of the Lincoln Administration that he was court-martialed.

Grant

Regardless of how Grant got to the position he did, he immediately began to reveal his strategic military competence. On September 6, 1861, Grant quickly seized a strategic position at Paducah, Kentucky at the mouth of the Tennessee River. Grant's men first fought at Belmont, Missouri on November 7, a diversionary attack that proved inconclusive after the Union forces were initially successful but the Confederates were able to quickly rally and hold the field. But had it not been for Grant's decisiveness, his men may not have gotten out alive. He was credited with demonstrating exceptional independent initiative, quick decision-making, and fought aggressively to protect his men.

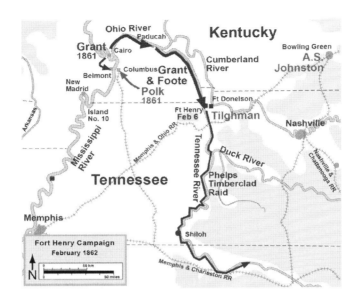

Map of the Fort Henry and Fort Donelson Campaign

Unhappy that his regiment was being used only for defensive and diversionary purposes, in January of 1862, Grant persuaded General Halleck to allow his men to launch a campaign on the Tennessee River. As soon as Halleck acquiesced, Grant moved against Fort Henry, in close coordination with the naval command of Flag Officer Andrew Hull Foote. The tag team of infantry and naval bombardment helped force the capitulation of Fort Henry on February 6, 1862.

The surrender of Fort Henry was followed immediately by an attack on Fort Donelson on the Cumberland River, which earned Grant his famous nickname "Unconditional Surrender". Grant's forces enveloped the Confederate garrison at Fort Donelson, which included Confederate generals Simon Buckner, John Floyd, and Gideon Pillow. In one of the most bungled operations of the war, the Confederate generals tried and failed to open an escape route by attacking Grant's forces on February 15. Although the initial assault was successful, General Pillow inexplicably chose to have his men pull back into their trenches, ostensibly so they could take more supplies before their escape. Instead, they simply lost all the ground they had taken, and the garrison was cut off yet again.

During the early morning hours of February 16, the garrison's generals held one of the Civil War's most famous councils of war. Over the protestations of cavalry officer Nathan Bedford

Forrest, who insisted the garrison could escape, the three generals agreed to surrender their army, but none of them wanted to be the fall guy. General Floyd was worried that the Union might try him for treason if he was taken captive, so he turned command of the garrison over to General Pillow and escaped with two of his regiments. Pillow had the same concern and turned command over to General Buckner before escaping alone by boat. Meanwhile, Forrest successfully rallied about 700 troops and fought through the siege across the river.

Despite all of these successful escapes, General Buckner decided to surrender to Grant. As a long-standing legend describes, when asked for terms of surrender, Grant sent a letter stating, "No terms except an unconditional and immediate surrender."

Forrest

Floyd

Buckner

Pillow

Grant's campaign was the first major success for the Union, which had already lost the disastrous First Battle of Bull Run in July 1861 and was reorganizing the Army of the Potomac in anticipation of the Peninsula Campaign, which would fail in the summer of 1862. It also exposed the weakness of the outmanned Confederates, who were stretched too thin, but rather than admit weakness in public, Johnston instead personally took the blame. After he had to withdraw from Nashville in late February and let it fall to Don Carlos Buell's Union Army on February 25, 1862, there were public calls for Johnston's removal. Naturally, his friend Jefferson Davis had his back, stating, "If Sidney Johnston is not a general, we had better give up the war, for we have no general."

In early 1862, General Beauregard once again demonstrated his oratory skills, making a formal plea to Mississippi Valley plantation owners to "send your plantation-bells to the nearest railroad depot, subject to my order, to be melted into cannon for defense of your plantations." And while many Southerners romanticized the gesture (with artist Adalbert J. Volck even depicting the act in the now-famous print, *Offering of Church Bells to Be Cast into Cannon*), the scornful Confederate General Braxton Bragg was quick to point out the public relations motivation for the call, stating that the Confederacy already had plenty of metal in New Orleans and more cannon than men who knew how to fire them. As Beauregard's fame grew, even his fellow officers began to resent his style.

Regardless of Beauregard's grandstanding, he continued to find himself in the thick of the war's most important battles. The losses of Fort Henry and Fort Donelson had dismayed the Confederates, who were determined to take the offensive in an attempt to wrest control of Tennessee from the Union. With that, Beauregard was sent to Tennessee to become second-in-command to Albert Sidney Johnston in March 1862.

Privately, Johnston wrote a memorandum detailing some of the problems that were plaguing his command in late 1861 and early 1862:

"I took command at Bowling Green on the 28th day of October, 1861, the force being nearly 12,000 men. From the best information we could get, the forces of the enemy were estimated at nearly twice the number of our own when I assumed command. There were many reasons why Bowling Green was held and fortified. It was a good base of military operations; was a proper depot for supplies; was capable, if fortified, of being held against largely superior numbers. If the army should be such that a forward movement was practicable, it could be held by a garrison, and our effective force be left free to operate against an enemy in the field. It was in supporting distance of Tennessee, from and through which reinforcements and munitions must come, if the people of Kentucky should be either hostile or neutral. My force was too weak and too illy appointed to advance against greatly superior numbers, perfectly equipped and provided, and being much more rapidly reinforced than my own. Our advance into Kentucky had not been met by the enthusiastic uprising of friends, which we, and many in and out of that State, had believed would take place. Arms were scarce, and we had none to give them. No prudent commander would thus hazard the fate of an entire army, so much weaker than the enemy, and dependent upon support not certain to come, and wanting in arms and discipline if it should.

Muldrough's Hill possessed no strategic importance, was worthless as a base of operations, and I had ordered General Buckner, in the first place, not to advance to that position, because the Green River, flowing directly across the line between Bowling Green and Muldrough's Hill, and being navigable, gave the enemy every desirable facility to cut the line in two in the rear of any force at Muldrough's Hill. Buckner's force was small, was illy armed, had no transportation except by rail, was deficient in many necessary appointments for making a campaign, and many of his men were fresh from home and wholly undisciplined. The enemy's forces increased much more rapidly than Buckner's; and the ratio of increase was fully preserved after I took command."

Chapter 13: The Armies Catch Their Breath

Grant had just secured Union command of precious control over much of the Mississippi River and much of Kentucky and Tennessee, but that would prove to be merely a prelude to the Battle of Shiloh, which at the time would be the biggest battle ever fought on the continent. After the victories at Fort Henry and Fort Donelson, Grant was now at the head of the Army of the

Tennessee, which was about 45,000 strong and firmly encamped at Pittsburg Landing on the western side of the Tennessee River. Meanwhile, his department head, Henry "Old Brains" Halleck, ordered Don Carlos Buell's army to join Grant's, thereby concentrating their armies before launching an offensive.

Before they could launch their offensive, however, the Confederates, under the command of Johnston, launched their own. The losses of the two forts had dismayed the Confederates, making President Davis too eager to try to regain momentum by quickly launching an offensive in an attempt to wrest control of Tennessee from the Union.

Near the end of February, Johnston reported his dispositions to the Confederate government:

"Headquarters, Western Department, Murfreesboro, Tennessee, February 27, 1862.

Sir: The fall of Fort Donelson compelled me to withdraw the forces under my command from the north bank of the Cumberland, and to abandon the defense of Nashville, which, but for that disaster, it was my intention to protect to the utmost. Not more than 11,000 effective men were left under my command to oppose a column of General Buell's of not less than 40,000 troops moving by Bowling Green, while another superior force under General Thomas outflanked me to the east, and the armies from Fort Donelson, with the gunboats and transports, had it in their power to ascend the Cumberland, now swollen by recent floods, so as to interrupt all communications with the south.

The situation left me no alternative but to evacuate Nashville or sacrifice the army. By remaining, the place would have been unnecessarily subjected to destruction, as it is very indefensible, and no adequate force would have been left to keep the enemy in check in Tennessee.

Under the circumstances I moved the main body of my command to this place on the 17th and 18th instant, and left a brigade under General Floyd to bring on such stores and property as were at Nashville, with instructions to remain until the approach of the enemy, and then to rejoin me. This has been in a great measure effected, and nearly all the stores would have been saved, but for the heavy and unusual rains which have washed away the bridges, swept away portions of the railroad, and rendered transportation almost impossible. General Floyd has arrived here. The rear-guard left Nashville on the night of the 23d. Edgefield, on the north bank of the Cumberland, opposite the city, was occupied yesterday by the advanced pickets of the enemy. I have remained here for the purpose of augmenting my forces and securing the transportation of the public stores. By the junction of the command of General Crittenden and the fugitives from Fort Donelson, which have been reorganized as far as practicable, the force now under my command will amount to about 17,000 men. General Floyd, with a force of some 2,500 men, has been ordered to Chattanooga to defend the approaches toward North Alabama and Georgia, and the communications between the Mississippi and the Atlantic, and with the view to increase his forces by such troops as may be sent forward from the neighboring States. The quartermaster's, commissary's, and ordnance stores which are not required for immediate use have been ordered to Chattanooga, and those which will be necessary on the march have been forwarded to Huntsville and Decatur. I have ordered a depot to be established at Atlanta for the manufacture of supplies for the quartermaster's department, and also a laboratory for the manufacture of percussion-caps and ordnance-stores, and, at Chattanooga, depots for distribution of these supplies. The machinery will be immediately sent forward.

Considering the peculiar topography of this State, and the great power which the enemy's means afford them upon the Tennessee and Cumberland, it will be seen that the force under my command cannot successfully cover the whole line against the advance of the enemy. I am compelled to elect whether he shall be permitted to occupy Middle Tennessee, or turn Columbus, take Memphis, and open the valley of the Mississippi. To me the defense of the valley seems of paramount importance, and consequently I will move this corps of the army, of which I have assumed the immediate command, toward the left bank of the Tennessee, crossing the river near Decatur, in order to enable me to cooperate or unite with General Beauregard for the defense of Memphis and the Mississippi. The department has sent eight regiments to Knoxville for the defense of East Tennessee, and the protection of that region will be confided to them and such additional forces as may be hereafter sent from the adjacent States. General Buckner was ordered by the department to take command of the troops at Knoxville, but, as at that time he was in presence of the enemy, the order was not fulfilled.

As it would be almost impossible for me under present circumstances to superintend the operations at Knoxville and Chattanooga, I would respectfully suggest that the local commanders at those points should receive orders from the department directly, or be allowed to exercise their discretion.

I have the honor to remain, very respectfully, your obedient servant,

A. S. Johnston, General C. S. A.

In the middle of March, Johnston was in the process of linking up the armies in his department and consolidating them into one fighting force that would approach about 55,000 soldiers, making his army nearly the equal of Grant's. The Confederate forces were linking up at Corinth, Georgia, only about 20 miles away from Grant's army. Thus, it would not take much time for Johnston to launch his offensive north against Grant, hopefully before Buell could link up with his army. On March 18, Johnston wrote to Davis:

"The enemy are now at Nashville, about 50,000 strong, advancing in this direction by Columbia. He has also forces, according to the report of General Bragg, landing at Pittsburg, from 25,000 to 50,000, and moving in the direction of Purdy.

This army corps, moving to join Bragg, is about 20,000 strong. Two brigades, Hindman's and Wood's, are, I suppose, at Corinth. One regiment of Hardee's division (Lieutenant-Colonel Patton commanding) is moving by cars to-day (20th March), and Statham's brigade (Crittenden's division). The brigade will halt at Iuka, the regiment at Burnsville; Cleburne's brigade, Hardee's division, except regiment, at Burnsville; and Carroll's brigade, Crittenden's division, and Helm's cavalry, at Tuscumbia; Bowen's brigade at Cortland; Breckinridge's brigade, here; the regiments of cavalry of Adams and Wharton, on the opposite bank of the river; Scott's Louisiana regiment at Pulaski, sending forward supplies; Morgan's cavalry at Shelbyville, ordered on.

To-morrow, Breckinridge's brigade will go to Corinth; then Bowen's. When these pass Tuscumbia and Iuka, transportation will be ready there for the other troops to follow immediately from those points, and, if necessary, from Burnsville. The cavalry will cross and move forward as soon as their trains can be passed over the railroad-bridge.

I have troubled you with these details, as I cannot properly communicate them by telegram.

The test of merit in my profession with the people is success. It is a hard rule, but I think it right. If I join this corps to the forces of Beauregard (I confess a hazardous experiment), then those who are now declaiming against me will be without an argument. Your friend,

A. S. Johnston."

Davis responded to that letter:

My dear General: Yours of the 18th inst. was this day delivered to me by your aide, Mr. Jack. I have read it with much satisfaction. So far as the past is concerned, it but confirms the conclusions at which I had already arrived. My confidence in you has never wavered, and I hope the public will soon give me credit for judgment, rather than continue to arraign me for obstinacy.

You have done wonderfully well, and now I breathe easier in the assurance that you will be able to make a junction of your two armies. If you can meet the division of the enemy moving from the Tennessee before it can make a junction with that advancing from Nashville, the future will be brighter. If this cannot be done, our only hope is that the people of the Southwest will rally en masse with their private arms, and thus enable you to oppose the vast army which will threaten the destruction of our country.

I have hoped to be able to leave here for a short time, and would be much gratified to confer with you, and share your responsibilities. I might aid you in obtaining troops; no one could hope to do more unless he underrated your military capacity. I write in great haste, and feel that it would be worse than useless to point out to you how much depends upon you.

Johnston's son William summed up the situation at the beginning of April, just before the climactic Battle of Shiloh: "Grant felt safe at Shiloh, because he knew he was numerically stronger than his adversary. His numbers and his equipment were superior to those of his antagonist, and the discipline and morale of his army ought to have been so. The only infantry of the Confederate army which had ever seen a combat were some of Polk's men, who were at Belmont; Hindman's brigade, which was in the skirmish at Woodsonville; and the fugitives of Mill Spring. In the Federal army were the soldiers who had fought at Belmont, Fort Henry, and Donelson- 30,000 of the last. There were many raw troops on both sides. Some of the Confederates received their arms for the first time that week."

As he began to move his army north, Johnston issued general orders to be read to his army:

"I have put you in motion to offer battle to the invaders of your country. With the resolution and discipline and valor becoming men fighting, as you are, for all worth living or dying for, you can but march to a decisive victory over the agrarian mercenaries sent to subjugate you and to despoil you of your liberties, your property, and your honor. Remember the precious stake involved; remember the dependence of your mothers, your wives, your sisters, and your children, on the result; remember the fair, broad, abounding land, and the happy homes that would be desolated by your defeat.

The eyes and hopes of eight millions of people rest upon you; you are expected to show yourselves worthy of your lineage, worthy of the women of the South, whose noble devotion in this war has never been exceeded in any time. With such incentives to brave deeds, and with the trust that God is with us, your generals will lead you confidently to the combat-assured of success."

When Johnston began moving his army of about 45,000 north towards Grant's position, he hoped to catch Grant by surprise, a plan that Beauregard thought had no chance of success. The element of surprise seemed even more unlikely when their initial plan of attacking on April 5 was ruined by stormy weather. Adding to Beauregard's consternation, the Confederates' weapons were so poor and their recruits so raw that many of them had to test-fire their weapons for the sake of practicing, something Beauregard figured would cost them the element of surprise anyway. Others yelled loudly at the sight of a deer.

There were other serious problems that forced the Confederate officers to debate whether or not to make an attack at all. Johnston's son explained:

"It was now learned that many of the troops had improvidently thrown away or consumed their provisions, and at the end of three days were out of subsistence. General Bragg promised, however, to remedy this from his alleged well-stocked commissariat. But General Beauregard earnestly advised the idea of attacking the enemy should be abandoned, and that the whole force should return to Corinth, inasmuch as it was scarcely possible they would be able to take the Federals unawares, after such delay and the noisy demonstrations which had been made meanwhile. He urged the enemy would be now found formidably intrenched and ready for the attack; that success had depended on the power to assail them unexpectedly, for they were superior in number, and in large part had been under fire. On the other hand, few comparatively of the Confederates had that advantage, while a large part were too raw and recently enrolled to make it proper to venture them in an assault upon breastworks which would now be thrown up. And this unquestionably was the view of almost all present.

General Johnston, having listened with grave attention to the views and opinions advanced, then remarked, in substance, that he recognized the weight of the objections to an attack under the circumstances involved by the unfortunate loss of time on the road. But, nevertheless, he still hoped the enemy was not looking for offensive operations, and that he would yet be able to surprise them; and that, having put his army in motion for a battle, he would venture the hazard."

Despite Beauregard's suggestion not to attack Grant, Johnston rejected his principal subordinate's advice, telling him he would "attack them if they were a million." Beauregard predicted, "In the struggle tomorrow we shall be fighting men of our own blood, Western men, who understand the use of firearms. The struggle will be a desperate one."

As it turned out, Union forces somehow did not hear any of the sounds coming from the firing or marching of Johnston's army, even as it camped just 3 miles away from them on April 5, the night before the Battle of Shiloh. That same night, Grant telegraphed his department head, Henry Halleck, "I have scarcely the faintest idea of an attack (general one) being made upon us, but will be prepared should such a thing take place." In actuality, Grant was considerably overstating the preparedness of his army, and he had discounted such a possibility so much that he would be 10 miles away from the battlefield when the Battle of Shiloh started at dawn the next morning. He had been injured days earlier when his horse fell on him, and he could not move without crutches, so he was down river convalescing when Johnston's army threatened to overrun his on

Chapter 14: The Beginning of the Battle

A replica of Shiloh Church. The original was ruined during the battle.

"Men of Arkansas! They say you boast of your prowess with the bowie-knife. Today you wield a nobler weapon — the bayonet. Employ it well." – Albert Sidney Johnston

The men who became Civil War generals had been taught the art of war employed by Napoleon over 50 years earlier during their West Point days, so naturally they used Napoleonic tactics. In the early 19th century, those tactics saw Napoleon dominate the European continent and win crushing victories against large armies. However, the weapons available in 1861 were far more accurate than they had been 50 years earlier. In particular, new rifled barrels created common infantry weapons with deadly accuracy of up to 100 yards, at a time when generals were still leading massed infantry charges with fixed bayonets and attempting to march their men close enough to engage in hand-to-hand combat.

By the end of the Civil War, the generals and the soldiers had learned so many bloody lessons that the warfare at places like Petersburg resembled the trench warfare of World War I more than Waterloo. In fact, the first thing armies would do after establishing their defensive line was to begin digging, fortifying their positions with earthworks, abates, trenches, and anything that could protect them. Positions became unassailable if an army was allowed to work on their defensive line for more than 24 hours.

Unfortunately, Grant's army had yet to learn that lesson in April 1862. Despite having been camped out along the western bank of the Tennessee River for a considerable period of time, his army did not dig in and established no defensive fortifications to prepare for a potential Confederate attack. That failure to prepare was all the more ironic because the position was so strong defensively, with water guarding both flanks of Grant's army and making it extremely difficult to attack.

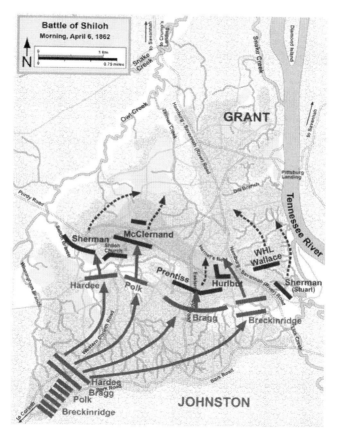

Early on the morning of April 6, Johnston deployed his army for battle along the Corinth Road with the intent of striking Grant's army and confidently told his men, "Tonight we will water our horses in the Tennessee River." In his report to the Confederate government after the battle, Beauregard explained how the lines were drawn up for the attack:

"It was then decided that the attack should be made on the next morning, at the earliest hour practicable, in accordance with the orders of movement; that is, in three lines of battle, the first and second extending from Owl Creek, on the left, to Lick Creek, on the right, a distance of about 3 miles, supported by the third and the reserve. The first line, under Major-General Hardee, was constituted of his corps, augmented on his right by Gladdens brigade, of Major-General Bragg's corps, deployed in line of battle, with their respective artillery following immediately by the main road to Pittsburg and the cavalry in rear of the wings. The second line, composed of the other troops of Bragg's corps, followed the first at a distance of 500 yards in the same order as the first. The army corps under General Polka followed the second line, at a distance of about 800 yards, in lines of brigades deployed, with their batteries in rear of each brigade, moving by the Pittsburg road, the left wing supported by cavalry. The reserve, under Brigadier-General Breckinridge, followed closely the third line in the same order, its right wing supported by cavalry.

These two corps constituted the reserve, and were to support the front lines of battle, by being deployed, when required, on the right and left of the Pittsburg road, or otherwise act according to the exigencies of the battle."

At about 5:00 a.m., a Union reconnaissance party comprised of the 25th Missouri made contact with Johnston's army and engaged in a brief skirmish around 5:15 a.m., which could have destroyed the element of surprise right then and there. While that certainly woke up nearby Union soldiers, the senior officers around Pittsburg Landing discredited the notion that the Confederate army was nearby. William Tecumseh Sherman, who was the senior Union officer on the field that morning, reacted dismissively when told the Confederates were preparing to attack, telling the messenger, "There is no enemy nearer than Corinth."

Sherman

Meanwhile, miscommunication between Beauregard and Johnston hampered the Confederate attack before it even started. Johnston had telegraphed President Davis his plan, "Polk the left, Bragg the center, Hardee the right, Breckinridge in reserve." But Johnston's main focus was the attack on the Union left, which he hoped would interpose his army between Grant's army and the Tennessee River, which would cut off its supply line and its path to retreat. Johnston instructed Beauregard to direct the logistics from the rear while he was at the front, but Beauregard thought the battle plan should be to attack in three waves and try to drive Grant's army eastward into the Tennessee River, a plan wildly at odds with Johnston's. On top of that, Beauregard had fallen so ill that he was all but confined to a hospital bed in an ambulance in the rear the entire first day of the battle, even when command would fall upon him.

The Battle of Shiloh began in earnest around 6:00 a.m. with an attack on the Union right by the William Hardee's division and an attack on the Union left by Braxton Bragg's divisions. Their divisions were formed in one line about 3 miles long, but the length of their line and its lack of depth would quickly lead to their men getting intermingled, and officers would gradually lose command over their soldiers. That wasn't the only difficulty confronting the Confederate troops, as explained by Hardee's post-battle report:

"By the order of battle our troops were arranged in two parallel lines, the first, under my command, being composed of my corps, consisting of the brigades of Brigadier-

Generals Hindman, Wood, and Cleburne, numbering 6,789 effective men, and the brigade of Brigadier-General Gladden, which was attached to my command to till the interval between my right and Lick Creek. The second was composed of five brigades, under Major-General Bragg, 1,000 yards in rear of mine, while four brigades, under Major-General Polk, supported the left, and three under Brigadier-General Breckinridge supported the right of the lines.

The order was given to advance at daylight on Sunday, April 6. The morning was bright and bracing. At early dawn the enemy attacked the skirmishers in front of my line, commanded by Major (now Colonel) Hardcastle, which was handsomely resisted by that promising young officer. My command advanced, and in half an hour the battle became fierce.

Hindman's brigade engaged the enemy with great vigor in the edge of a wood and drove him rapidly back over the field toward Pittsburg, while Gladden's brigade, on the right, about 8 o'clock, dashed upon the encampments of a division under the command of General Prentiss. At the same time Cleburne's brigade, with the Fifteenth Arkansas, deployed as skirmishers, and the Second Tennessee, en échelon on the left, moved quickly through the fields, and though far outflanked by the enemy on our left, rushed forward under a terrific fire from the serried ranks drawn up in front of the camp. A morass covered his front, and being difficult to pass, caused a break in the brigade. Deadly volleys were poured upon the men as they advanced from behind bales of hay, logs, and other defenses, and after a series of desperate charges the brigade was compelled to fall back."

Bragg's division encountered similar difficulties, as Bragg would note in his official report after the battle:

"The night was occupied by myself and a portion of my staff in efforts to bring forward provisions for a portion of the troops then suffering from their improvidence. Having been ordered to march with five days' rations, they were found hungry and destitute at the end of three days. This is one of the evils of raw troops, imperfectly organized and badly commanded; a tribute, it seems, we must continue to pay to universal suffrage, the bane of our military organization. In this condition we passed the night, and at dawn of day prepared to move.

The enemy did not give us time to discuss the question of attack, for soon after dawn he commenced a rapid musketry fire on our pickets. The order was immediately given by the commanding general and our lines advanced. Such was the ardor of our troops that it was with great difficulty they could be restrained from closing up and mingling with the first line. Within less than a mile the enemy was encountered in force at the encampments of his advanced positions, but our first line brushed him away, leaving the rear nothing to do but to press on in pursuit. In about one mile more we encountered him in strong force among almost the entire line. His batteries were posted on eminences, with strong infantry supports.

Finding the first line was now unequal to the work before it, being weakened by extension and necessarily broken by the nature of the ground, I ordered my whole force to move up steadily and promptly to its support. The order was hardly necessary, for subordinate commanders, far beyond the reach of my voice and eye in the broken country occupied by us, had promptly acted on the necessity as it arose, and by the time the order could be conveyed the whole line was developed and actively engaged.

From this time, about 7.30 o'clock, until night the battle raged with little intermission. All parts of our line were not constantly engaged, but there was no time without heavy firing in some portion of it. My position for several hours was opposite my left center Ruggles' division), immediately in rear of Hindman's brigade, Hardee's corps.
In moving over the difficult and broken ground the right brigade of Ruggles' division, Colonel Gibson commanding, bearing to the right, became separated from the two left brigades, leaving a broad interval."

Bragg

Despite the Confederates' difficulties, however, the element of surprise was so strong that the initial assault couldn't help but be successful. Like Johnston's army, Grant's army was full of raw recruits, and when they were caught by surprise without adequate defensive works, many of them broke and ran toward Pittsburg Landing. Those that fought had to do so without the benefit of any semblance of orders from their officers, leading to a complete breakdown on the Union left. Grant took pains to describe his army's inexperience, writing in his memoirs, "Three of the five divisions engaged on Sunday were entirely raw, and many of the men had only received their arms on the way from their States to the field. Many of them had arrived but a day or two before and were hardly able to load their muskets according to the manual. Their officers were equally ignorant of their duties. Under these circumstances it is not astonishing that many of the regiments broke at the first fire. In two cases, as I now remember, colonels led their regiments from the field on first hearing the whistle of the enemy's bullets. In these cases the colonels were constitutional cowards, unfit for any military position; but not so the officers and men led out of danger by them. Better troops never went upon a battle-field than many of these, officers and men, afterwards proved themselves to be, who fled panic stricken at the first whistle of bullets and shell at Shiloh."

Grant and Sherman would play down how badly they were caught offguard by simply referencing the Confederates driving in their pickets and advanced guard that morning, but the truth was that the Confederate attack came bearing down upon the Union's defensive line almost immediately. Bragg would later note, "Contrary to the views of such as urged an abandonment of the attack, the enemy was found utterly unprepared, many being surprised and captured in their tents, and others, though on the outside, in costumes better fitted to the bed-chamber than to the battle-field."

Even still, Sherman would later claim in his official report that he was unsure of the Confederates' designs until about 2 hours into the battle:

"Shortly after 7 a.m., with my entire staff, I rode along a portion of our front, and when in the open field before Appler's regiment the enemy's pickets opened a brisk fire on my party, killing my orderly, Thomas D. Holliday, of Company H, Second Illinois Cavalry. The fire came from the bushes which line a small stream that rises in the field in front of Appler's camp and flows to the north along my whole front. This valley afforded the enemy a partial cover, but our men were so posted as to have a good fire at him as he crossed the valley and ascended the rising ground on our side.

About 8 a.m. I saw the glistening bayonets of heavy masses of infantry to our left front in the woods beyond the small stream alluded to, and became satisfied for the first time that the enemy designed a determined attack on our whole camp."

As Bragg and Hardee moved forward with a disorganized but successful attack on both flanks of the Union army, Johnston was exposing himself at so many points along the front that his men began to grow nervous that he might get himself killed. One Confederate officer recalled: "Colonel Preston then carried the order to Hindman's brigade, who made a splendid and victorious charge. . . It was while under this fire that Captain Brewster expostulated with General Johnston against his exposing his person. I was not near enough to hear his reply, but it had no effect, for he smilingly rode to the brow of the hill where we could distinctly see the enemy retreating." In addition to putting himself in harm's way, Johnston's position at the front meant that Beauregard had to make important command decisions from the rear. About an hour and a half into the battle, at about 7:30 a.m., Beauregard plugged the holes in the Confederates' line by sending Polk's corps in on the left and Breckinridge's corps in on the right. While the timing was fortuitous in plugging gaps, especially in Bragg's line, it meant the attack continued to move forward in one line, with no secondary lines truly in reserve that could sustain an advance if one part of the line started to falter.

At the time, though, it wasn't clear whether strategic depth would even be necessary as the Confederates continued pushing a general rout of the Union forces in their front. Union General Jesse Hildebrand would note that whole regiments in his brigade got separated in the general confusion and retreat, and Sherman verified it, noting, "Hildebrand's brigade had substantially disappeared from the field, though he himself bravely remained." Sherman, who would suffer two wounds during the day and have a third bullet pass through his cap, later noted of the initial retreat:

"Although our left was thus turned, and the enemy was pressing our whole line, I deemed Shiloh so important, that I remained by it and renewed my orders to Colonels McDowell and Buckland to hold their ground; and we did hold these positions until about 10 a.m., when the enemy had got his artillery to the rear of our left flank and some change became absolutely necessary. Two regiments of Hildebrand's brigade—Appler's and Mungen's—had already disappeared to the rear, and Hildebrand's own regiment was in disorder. I therefore gave orders for Taylor's battery—still at Shiloh—to fall back as far as the Purdy and Hamburg road, and for McDowell and Buckland to adopt that road as their new line. I rode across the angle and met Behr's battery at the cross-roads, and ordered it immediately to come into battery, action right. Captain Behr gave the order, but he was almost immediately shot from his horse, when drivers and gunners fled in disorder, carrying off the caissons, and abandoning five out of six guns, without firing a shot. The enemy pressed on, gaining this battery, and we were again forced to choose a new line of defense. Hildebrand's brigade had substantially disappeared from the field, though he himself bravely remained. McDowell's and Buckland's brigades maintained their organizations, and were conducted by my aides, so as to join on General McClernand's right, thus abandoning my original camps and line. This was about 10 1/2 a.m., at which time the enemy had made a furious attack on General McClernand's whole front. He straggled most determinedly, but, finding him pressed, I moved McDowell's brigade directly against the left flank of the enemy, forced him back some distance, and then directed the men to avail themselves of every cover-trees, fallen timber, and a wooded valley to our right. We held this position for four long hours, sometimes gaining and at others losing ground; General McClernand and myself acting in perfect concert, and struggling to maintain this line."

Meanwhile, when Grant heard the sounds of artillery that morning, he headed toward Pittsburg Landing via boat, and he reached the battlefield around 8:30 a.m. to find his army in a precarious position. Once he arrived he immediately went about trying to order reinforcements to bolster his retreating line, including Bull Nelson's division (several miles away at Savannah) and Lew Wallace's division, which had been held in reserve at Crump's Landing.

Lew Wallace was considered a rising star in the Union Army, but his career was ruined by the events of April 6. After being ordered into battle by Grant, confusion in the battle plans and the rapid retreat of the Union army resulted in Wallace taking a different route than the one Grant ordered, and when Wallace arrived he found himself in the rear of the advancing Confederate army. Before Wallace could take advantage of that position in the Confederate rear, however, he was ordered to countermarch back toward Pittsburg Landing. Wallace's division would arrive there at about 7:00 p.m., around the end of the first day's fighting. Grant would later blame Wallace in his memoirs, writing, "I never could see and do not now see why any order was necessary further than to direct him to come to Pittsburg landing, without specifying by what route. His was one of three veteran divisions that had been in battle, and its absence was severely felt. Later in the war General Wallace would not have made the mistake that he committed on the 6th of April, 1862. I presume his idea was that by taking the route he did he would be able to come around on the flank or rear of the enemy, and thus perform an act of heroism that would redound to the credit of his command, as well as to the benefit of his country."

Lew Wallace

Grant was circumspect in discussing the effectiveness of the Confederates' initial assault:

"The Confederate assaults were made with such a disregard of losses on their own side that our line of tents soon fell into their hands. The ground on which the battle was fought was undulating, heavily timbered with scattered clearings, the woods giving some protection to the troops on both sides. There was also considerable underbrush. A number of attempts were made by the enemy to turn our right flank, where Sherman was posted, but every effort was repulsed with heavy loss. But the front attack was kept up so vigorously that, to prevent the success of these attempts to get on our flanks, the National troops were compelled, several times, to take positions to the rear nearer Pittsburg landing."

Chapter 15: The Hornet's Nest

"There was no hour during the day when there was not heavy firing and generally hard fighting at some point on the line, but seldom at all points at the same time. It was a case of Southern dash against Northern pluck and endurance." – Ulysses S. Grant

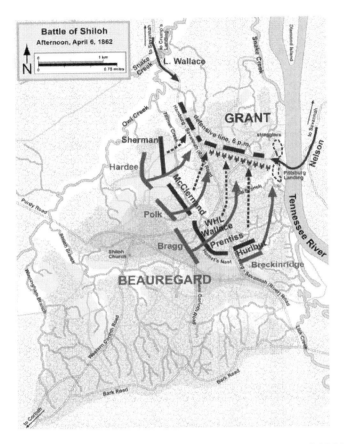

As the Union soldiers fell back, their center took up a defensive position in a field full of natural features ideal for maintaining a defensive posture. The Hornet's Nest was a field that ran along an open road, but trying to advance up the road exposed attackers to an enfilading fire from the side, so Confederate soldiers would end up throwing themselves against Union defenders from the divisions led by Benjamin M. Prentiss and W. H. L. Wallace over the course of several hours. In the biography of his father, William Preston Johnston described the Hornet's Nest: "Here, behind a dense thicket on the crest of a hill, was posted a strong force of as hardy troops as ever fought, almost perfectly protected by the conformation of the ground, and by logs and other rude and hastily prepared defenses. To assail it an open field had to be passed, enfiladed by the fire of its batteries. It was nicknamed by the Confederates, by a very mild metaphor, 'The Hornets' nest.'"

The road on the left and Hornet's Nest to the right of it.

Further evidence of the inexperience on both sides would be found in the action around the Hornet's Nest. Historians estimate that the Confederates made somewhere between 8-14 separate assaults against the Union line in the Hornet's Nest, even though the position could be turned if the Confederates on their left or right pushed back one or both of the Union army's flanks, which was eventually what happened.

Wallace

Once again, officers struggled to maintain any sense of control over their men in the Hornet's Nest, with units making their own arbitrary decisions down to the regimental and battalion levels. For the Union this was further complicated by the fact that division commander Wallace was mortally wounded in the struggle. Ultimately, Confederates led by Brig. Gen. Daniel Ruggles brought nearly 50 cannons to bear on the Hornet's Nest and were able to provide withering fire, compelling Union defenders, some of whom had been in the Hornet's Nest for 7 hours, to fall back.

However, as the Union line generally began to crumble and retreat, not everyone got the message. In the center of the line was Prentiss's division, and his men became a salient in the Union line when the units on their flanks fell back. Grant explained in his memoirs:

"In one of the backward moves, on the 6th, the division commanded by General Prentiss did not fall back with the others. This left his flanks exposed and enabled the enemy to capture him with about 2,200 of his officers and men. General Badeau gives four o'clock of the 6th as about the time this capture took place. He may be right as to the time, but my recollection is that the hour was later. General Prentiss himself gave the hour as half-past five. I was with him, as I was with each of the division commanders that day, several times, and my recollection is that the last time I was with him was about half-past four, when his division was standing up firmly and the General was as cool as if expecting victory. But no matter whether it was four or later, the story that he and his command were surprised and captured in their camps is without any foundation whatever. If it had been true, as currently reported at the time and yet believed by thousands of people, that Prentiss and his division had been captured in their beds, there would not have been an all-day struggle, with the loss of thousands killed and wounded on the Confederate side."

Prentiss

It was also during the fighting around the Hornet's Nest that the Confederates suffered their worst casualty of all. As the Union army kept retreating, Johnston began planning for his army to wheel on its left, thereby advancing his left flank toward Pittsburg Landing and the Tennessee River. Riding near Colonel Munford while watching the advancing Confederates attacking the retreating Federals. Munford later recalled their exchange: "We sat on our horses, side by side, watching that brigade as it swept over the ridge; and, as the colors dipped out of sight, the general said to me, 'That checkmates them.' I told him I was glad to hear him announce 'checkmate,' but that 'he must excuse so poor a player for saying he could not see it.' He laughed, and said, 'Yes, sir, that mates them.' The completion of this movement faced the troops at an angle of about 45° toward the left, when the forward movement became uniform."

At this point, Johnston again exposed himself to danger by riding to an advanced spot near the front of the line. Munford recounted, "Their bodies were almost entirely protected, but their position enabled them to see the entire persons of our troops, who, when they came in sight, were within easy musket-range and wholly unprotected. They opened upon us a murderous fire. General Johnston moved forward with his staff to a depression about thirty yards behind our front line, where the bullets passed over our heads; but he could see more than half of his line, and, if an emergency arose, could meet it promptly."

After being told by one of his officers that one of the man's brigades wouldn't charge forward, Johnston personally inspired them and prepared to lead a charge: "General Johnston rode out in front, and slowly down the line. His hat was off. His sword rested in its scabbard. In his right hand he held a little tin cup, the memorial of an incident that had occurred earlier in the day. As they were passing through a captured camp, an officer had brought from a tent a number of valuable articles, calling General Johnston's attention to them. He answered, with some sternness: 'None of that, sir; we are not here for plunder!' And then, as if regretting the sharpness of the rebuke, for the anger of the just cuts deep, he added, taking this little tin cup, 'Let this be my share of the spoils to-day.'"

Johnston then began directing an advance against the Union left in a cotton field along a peach orchard, riding in the center of his men's front. While ordering them to prepare to use bayonets during the charge, the two sides exchanged a fierce volley of gunfire and artillery. The Union defenders began to fall back, but Johnston's horse had been shot in 4 places, and one of the bullets had cut a hole in the sole of his boot, a seemingly insignificant wound. But as it turned out, the minie ball, which historians now believe was friendly fire, had clipped an artery, and unbeknownst to Johnston, he was bleeding heavily in his boot.

Governor Harris, who was with Johnston at the time, recalled the general's final moments:

"As I approached him, he said 'Governor, they came very near putting me hors de combat in that charge,' holding out and pointing to his foot. Looking at it, I discovered that a musket-ball had struck the edge of the sole of his boot, cutting the sole clear across, and ripping it off to the toe. I asked eagerly: 'Are you wounded? Did the ball touch your foot?' He said, 'No;' and was proceeding to make other remarks, when a Federal battery opened fire from a position which enfiladed our line just established. He paused in the middle of. a sentence to say, 'Order Colonel Statham to wheel his regiment to the left, charge, and take that battery.' I galloped to Colonel Statham, only about two hundred yards distant, gave the order, galloped back to the general where a moment before I had left him, rode up to his right side, and said, 'General, your order is delivered, and Colonel Statham is in motion;' but, as I was uttering this sentence, the general reeled from me in a manner that indicated he was falling from his horse. I put my left arm around his neck, grasping the collar of his coat, and righted him up in the saddle, bending forward as I did so, and, looking him in the face, said, 'General, are you wounded?' In a very deliberate and emphatic tone he answered, 'Yes, and I fear seriously.' At that moment I requested Captain Wickham to go with all possible speed for a surgeon, to send the first one he could find, but to proceed until he could find Dr. Yandell, the medical director, and bring him. The general's hold upon his rein relaxed, and it dropped from his hand. Supporting him with my left hand, I gathered his rein with my right, in which I held my own, and guided both horses to a valley about 150 yards in rear of our line, where I halted, dropped myself between the two horses, pulling the general over upon me, and eased him to the ground as gently as I could. When laid upon the ground, with eager anxiety I asked many questions about his wounds, to which he gave no answer, not even a look of intelligence.

Supporting his head with one hand, I untied his cravat, unbuttoned his collar and vest, and tore his shirts open with the other, for the purpose of finding the wound, feeling confident from his condition that he had a more serious wound than the one which I knew was bleeding profusely in the right leg; but I found no other, and, as I afterward ascertained, he had no other. Raising his head, I poured a little brandy into his mouth, which he swallowed, and in a few moments I repeated the brandy, but he made no effort to swallow; it gurgled in his throat in his effort to breathe, and I turned his head so as to relieve him.

In a few moments he ceased to breathe. I did not consult my watch, but my impression is that lie did not live more than thirty or forty minutes from the time he received the wound."

As Johnston's son would note in his biography, the wound "was not necessarily fatal. General Johnston's own knowledge of military surgery was adequate for its control by an extemporized tourniquet, had he been aware or regardful of its nature." Unfortunately for the Confederates, the severity of the wound was only discovered upon their commander's death. Johnston's body was wrapped up so that his fate was hidden from his troops as the officers on the scene raced back toward the rear to inform Beauregard. At a critical juncture in the fighting, with the Union army still on the ropes and the Confederates seeking to deal it a death blow, the Confederates had lost their commander.

The monument to Johnston on the Shiloh battlefield

Chapter 16: Holding the Line

As the Confederate commander fell dead, the Union line had fallen back to a more condensed line around Pittsburg Landing itself, with a three mile front from the Tennessee River on their left to the River Road on their right, intentionally keeping the road open for Lew Wallace's lost division. By this time, Don Carlos Buell's army was getting near enough that an advanced brigade of his under Col. Jacob Ammen was ferried across the Tennessee River and took up a spot on the left of the Union's defensive line. The new position, so close to the river, allowed for the use of Union gunboats in the defense as well.

Braxton Bragg summed up the situation in the late afternoon in his report:

"It was now probably past 4 o'clock, the descending sun warning us to press our advantage and finish the work before night should compel us to desist. Fairly in motion, these commands again, with a common head and a common purpose, swept all before them. Neither battery nor battalion could withstand their onslaught. Passing through camp after camp, rich in military spoils of every kind, the enemy was driven headlong from every position and thrown in confused masses upon the river bank, behind his heavy artillery and under cover of his gunboats at the Landing. He had left nearly the whole of his light artillery in our hands and some 3,000 or more prisoners, who were cut off from their retreat by the closing in of our troops on the left under Major-General Polk, with a portion of his reserve corps, and Brigadier-General Ruggles, with Anderson's and Pond's brigades of his division.

The prisoners were dispatched to the rear under a proper guard, all else being left upon the field that we might press our advantage. The enemy had fallen back in much confusion and was crowded in unorganized masses on the river bank, vainly striving to cross. They were covered by a battery of heavy guns, well served, and their two gunboats, which now poured a heavy fire upon our supposed positions, for we were entirely hid by the forest. Their fire, though terrific in sound and producing some consternation at first, did us no damage, as the shells all passed over and exploded far beyond our positions."

Despite the strength of the Union's defensive position, two Confederate brigades made a desperate charge only to be repulsed. Around 6:00 p.m., Beauregard made one of the war's most controversial decisions by calling off the Confederate advance against the tightly huddled Union army, which was in the position of being forced to either defend successfully or be driven into the river and destroyed. At the time, Beauregard figured that he had the battle won anyway, having surrounded Grant's men along the river, and he didn't want to risk a confusing night attack against Grant's line, which was concentrated with artillery as a result of being so tightly encircled. That night, the overconfident Beauregard wired Richmond to inform authorities that the Confederates had won a "complete victory":

"The battle commenced on the 6th of April. We attacked the enemy in a strong position in front of Pittsburg; and, after a severe battle of ten hours, duration, thanks be to the Almighty, we gained a complete victory, driving the enemy from every position. The loss on both sides is heavy, including the commander-in-chief, General A. S. Johnston, who fell gallantly leading his troops into the thickest of the fight.

The chief command then devolved upon me, though at the time I was greatly prostrated and suffering from the prolonged sickness with which I had been afflicted since early in February. The responsibility was one which, in my physical condition, I would have gladly avoided, though cast upon me when our forces were successfully pushing the enemy back upon the Tennessee River, and though supported on the immediate field by such corps commanders as Major-Generals Polk, Bragg, and Hardee, and Brigadier-General Breckinridge commanding the reserve.

It was after six o'clock, P. M., as before said, when the enemy's last position was carried, and his force finally broke and sought refuge behind a commanding eminence, covering the Pittsburg Landing, not more than half a mile distant, and under the guns of the gunboats, which opened on our eager columns a fierce and annoying fire with shot and shell of the heaviest description. Darkness was close at hand. Officers and men were exhausted by a combat of over twelve hours, without food, and jaded by the march of the preceding day through mud and water; it was, therefore, impossible to collect the rich and opportune spoils of war scattered broadcast on the field left in our possession, and impracticable to make any effective dispositions for their removal to the rear."

Beauregard would later be forced to explain, "I thought I had General Grant just where I wanted him and could finish him up in the morning." Beauregard was terribly wrong because he was unaware that Don Carlos Buell's Army of the Ohio was within marching distance of Grant's men. That night, 18,000 more soldiers slipped into Pittsburg Landing, heavily bolstering Grant's forces and leaving Beauregard's men well outnumbered. At the same time, Grant's army was so disorganized that he didn't even attempt to reestablish his soldiers in their proper regiments, noting in his memoirs, "The nature of this battle was such that cavalry could not be used in front; I therefore formed ours into line in rear, to stop stragglers—of whom there were many. When there would be enough of them to make a show, and after they had recovered from their fright, they would be sent to reinforce some part of the line which needed support, without regard to their companies, regiments or brigades."

Buell

Grant also recalled his first meeting with Buell that night:

On one occasion during the day I rode back as far as the river and met General Buell, who had just arrived; I do not remember the hour, but at that time there probably were as many as four or five thousand stragglers lying under cover of the river bluff, panic-stricken, most of whom would have been shot where they lay, without resistance, before they would have taken muskets and marched to the front to protect themselves. This meeting between General Buell and myself was on the dispatch-boat used to run between the landing and Savannah. It was brief, and related specially to his getting his troops over the river. As we left the boat together, Buell's attention was attracted by the men lying under cover of the river bank. I saw him berating them and trying to shame them into joining their regiments. He even threatened them with shells from the gunboats near by. But it was all to no effect. Most of these men afterward proved themselves as gallant as any of those who saved the battle from which they had deserted. I have no doubt that this sight impressed General Buell with the idea that a line of retreat would be a good thing just then. If he had come in by the front instead of through the stragglers in the rear, he would have thought and felt differently. Could he have come through the Confederate rear, he would have witnessed there a scene similar to that at our own. The distant rear of an army engaged in battle is not the best place from which to judge correctly what is going on in front. Later in the war, while occupying the country between the Tennessee and the Mississippi, I learned that the panic in the Confederate lines had not differed much from that within our own. Some of the country people estimated the stragglers from Johnston's army as high as 20,000. Of course this was an exaggeration."

Buell wasn't the only one to express serious concern about the state of Grant's army. A news correspondent with the *Cincinnatti Gazette* reported about the scene he saw that night:

"Our whole army is crowded in the region of Wallace's camps, and to a circuit of one-half to two-thirds of a mile around the landing. We have been falling back all day. We can do it no more. The next repulse puts us into the river; and there are not transports enough to cross a single division till the enemy would be upon us. .... We have lost nearly all our camps and camp-equipage. We have lost nearly half our field-artillery. We have lost a division general, and two or three regiments of our soldiers as prisoners. We have lost --how dreadfully we are afraid to think — in killed and wounded. The hospitals are full to overflowing. A long ridge-bluff is set apart for surgical uses. It is covered with the maimed, the dead, and the dying. And our men are discouraged by prolonged defeat. . . . Meanwhile, there is a lull in the firing. For the first time since sunrise you fail to catch the angry rattle of musketry or the heavy booming of the field-guns. . . . On the bluffs above the river is a sight that may well make our cheeks tingle. There are not less than 5,000 skulkers lining the banks... Remember the situation. It was half-past 4 o'clock-perhaps a quarter later still. Every division of our army on the field had been repulsed. The enemy were in the camps of four out of five of them. We were driven to within little over half a mile of the landing. Behind us was a deep, rapid river. Before us was a victorious enemy. And still there was an hour for fighting. 'Oh, that night or Blucher would come!' 'Oh, that night or Lew Wallace would come!' Nelson's division of General Buell's army evidently couldn't cross in time to do us much good. We didn't yet know why Lew Wallace wasn't on the ground. In the justice of our cause, and in that semicircle of twenty-two guns in position, lay all the hope we could see."

However, those who were aware of Buell's location were a lot more confident about the Union's chances, including some of the Confederates. As Buell's army began to cross the Tennessee River, Confederate cavalry under the legendary cavalier Nathan Bedford Forrest detected the presence of Buell's reinforcements and reported the intelligence to Beauregard, but that contradicted other intelligence Beauregard had received that claimed Buell's army was not marching toward Pittsburg Landing. While Beauregard remained confident about his chances the next day, Forrest confided to brigadier Patrick Cleburne, "If the enemy comes on us in the morning, we'll be whipped like hell."

Grant famously shared Forrest's confidence as well, later writing in his memoirs, "So confident was I before firing had ceased on the 6th that the next day would bring victory to our arms if we could only take the initiative, that I visited each division commander in person before any reinforcements had reached the field. I directed them to throw out heavy lines of skirmishers in the morning as soon as they could see, and push them forward until they found the enemy, following with their entire divisions in supporting distance, and to engage the enemy as soon as found. To Sherman I told the story of the assault at Fort Donelson, and said that the same tactics would win at Shiloh. Victory was assured when Wallace arrived, even if there had been no other support. I was glad, however, to see the reinforcements of Buell and credit them with doing all there was for them to do."

Grant's confidence wasn't simply a matter of hindsight. That evening, as the cries of the wounded pierced the air and kept soldiers on both sides awake, and as a thunderstorm passed through and brought a downpour, Sherman found Grant sitting under a tree. Sherman turned to the commander and said, "Well, Grant, we've had the devil's own day, haven't we?" Grant looked up at Sherman and replied, "Yes. Lick 'em tomorrow though."

Chapter 17: April 7

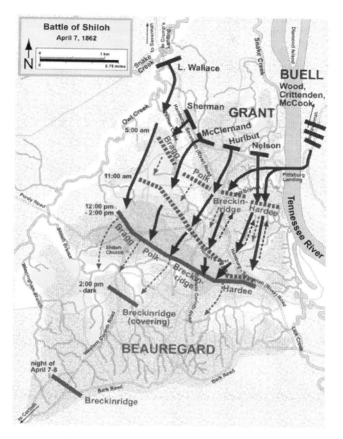

The Confederates had suffered over 8,000 casualties on April 6, including their commanding general, and the disorder and number of stragglers left Beauregard with an estimated 20,000 soldiers fit for combat the following morning. Meanwhile, Buell's army had added nearly 20,000 men to Grant's army, bringing its effective fighting numbers up to about 45,000. On top of that, many Confederates had retired to their rear for lack of supplies, with some of Polk's men reportedly retiring as far back as their bivouac site on the night before the battle.

Beauregard was still unaware that he was badly outnumbered and planned to advance in the morning, only to be surprised that Grant's army began a general advance along their entire line at dawn. Indicative of the back-and-forth sniping that would take place after the battle, Buell and Grant were operating their men independently, with Buell insisting on controlling his own army. Of course, the Confederates had suffered a similar state of disorganization, with little command control above the brigade level, and there was even a delay bringing Polk's division back to the battlefield, where he was supposed to represent the center of the line. It wasn't until 10:00 a.m. that Beauregard had a stable defensive line.

Ironically, it was Lew Wallace's lost division, which had found its way to the right of the Union line, that saw the first major fighting as it began driving back a Confederate brigade led by Col. Preston Pond around 7:00 a.m. Sherman later noted of the fighting around there that it was "the severest musketry fire I ever heard." On the other side of the line, Bull Nelson's division advanced as far as the Hornet's Nest by the late morning, along with Crittenden's and McCook's divisions, where they first met serious resistance from Beauregard's army.

By noon, Beauregard was aware of his precarious predicament. In addition to being heavily outnumbered, he was running critically low on supplies and ammunition. Realizing that he could no longer take the offensive, Beauregard launched diversionary counterattacks near Shiloh Church, which gave the Union officers pause and made them more cautious, and he then began an orderly retreat of his army, using Breckinridge's 5,000 men as a rearguard. As the Confederates began heading back toward Corinth, the exhausted Union soldiers were only too happy not to give serious chase, except for Lew Wallace's relatively fresh division, which kept up an unsupported chase until nightfall.

With the fighting of April 7 over, Grant and Buell began arguing over whether or not to continue the pursuit of the Confederates, given that there was about an hour of daylight still to use. But Grant had made his decision, arguing that his men were too exhausted. With that, the Battle of Shiloh was over.

Chapter 18: The Aftermath of Shiloh

On April 8, Grant had Sherman conduct a cautious pursuit of the Confederates, which led to a brief skirmish at Fallen Timbers that nearly changed the course of the Civil War. Sherman sent forth skirmishers from the 77th Ohio, which was approaching a Confederate field hospital until it got tangled up among fallen trees. The Confederate rearguard consisted of cavalry led by Forrest, who surprised the 77th Ohio and Sherman with a daring charge led personally by Forrest himself. Sherman explained:

"As we approached the ridge, down came, with a yell, Forrest's cavalry firing left and right with pistols, over the skirmish line, over the supports, and right among me and my staff. Fortunately, I had sent my adjutant, Hammond, back to the brigade to come forward into line quickly. My Aide-de-Camp, McCoy, was knocked down, horse and rider, into the mud, but I and the rest of my staff ingloriously fled, pell mell, throught he mud, closely followed by Forrest and his men, with pistols already emptied. We sought safety behind the brigade in the act of forming 'forward into line,' and Forrest and his followers were in turn 'surprised' by a fire of the brigade which emptied many a saddle, and gave Forrest himself a painful wound, but he escaped to the woods on the south of the road."

As it turned out, Forrest had charged out far in advance of his own men and only became aware of it when Sherman's soldiers started yelling out, "Kill him! Kill him and his horse!" From point blank range, a Union soldier on the ground pushed his musket right up to Forrest's side and fired a shot that struck him above the hip and nearly into his spine. Somehow Forrest managed to lift up the soldier and shield his own body with the man as he began riding toward the Confederate line. Forrest would later be credited with killing 30 Union soldiers and losing 29 horses, and Fallen Timbers gave him one of the many wounds he would suffer during the war. Sherman later noted that had Forrest's pistols not been empty, "my career would have ended right there."

Once Beauregard's army had safely made it back to Corinth, the post-battle analysis and accusations began in earnest. Grant's army had just won the biggest battle in the history of North America, with nearly 24,000 combined casualties among the Union and Confederate forces. Usually the winner of a major battle is hailed as a hero, but Grant was hardly a winner at Shiloh. The Battle of Shiloh took place before costlier battles at places like Antietam and Gettysburg, so the extent of the casualties at Shiloh shocked the nation. Moreover, at Shiloh the casualties were viewed as needless; Grant was pilloried for allowing the Confederates to take his forces by surprise, as well as the failure to build defensive earthworks and fortifications, which nearly resulted in a rout of his army. Speculation again arose that Grant had a drinking problem, and some even assumed he was drunk during the battle. Though the Union won, it was largely viewed that their success owed to the heroics of General Sherman in rallying the men and Don Carlos Buell arriving with his army, and General Buell was happy to receive the credit at Grant's expense.

Grant himself was not above playing the blame game. Miscommunication between Grant and division commander Lew Wallace resulted in Wallace failing to properly march his men into the fight while the Confederates were advancing on the first day. For the rest of his life, Grant blamed Wallace for the failure, but historians do not believe the miscommunication was actually his fault. Nevertheless, with Grant and Halleck heaping the blame Wallace for the near loss at Shiloh, it permanently tarnished Wallace's military career, and he was removed from his command in June 1862. Still, it's likely that any military accomplishments Lew Wallace may have lost out on during the Civil War would have been eclipsed by his authorship in 1880 of the classic *Ben-Hur* anyway.

Although Halleck agreed with Grant that Lew Wallace deserved the blame Grant was giving him, Grant was ultimately the fall guy. As a result of the Battle of Shiloh, General Halleck demoted Grant to second-in-command of all armies in his department, an utterly powerless position. And when word of what many considered a "colossal blunder" reached Washington, several congressmen insisted that Lincoln replace Grant in the field. Lincoln famously defended Grant, telling critics, "I can't spare this man. He fights."

Lincoln may have defended Grant, but he found precious few supporters, and the negative attention bothered Grant so much that it is widely believed he turned to alcohol again. While historians still debate that, what is known is that he considered resigning his commission, only to be dissuaded from doing so by General Sherman. Sherman had experienced the same career path as Grant, with failed business ventures, a stint in the Mexican-American War, early success in the Civil War and then a failure that nearly cost him his career (in Sherman's case, a nervous breakdown). As Sherman would later note, he supported Grant when Grant was drunk, and Grant supported him when he was crazy. Although Grant stayed in the army, it's unclear what position he would have held if Lincoln had not called Halleck to Washington to serve as general-in-chief in July 1862. At the same time, Halleck was given that position in large measure due to Grant's successes in the department under Halleck's command. Thankfully for the Union, Halleck's departure meant that Grant was reinstated as commander.

Sherman captured the essence of it all in his memoirs:

"Probably no single battle of the war gave rise to such wild and damaging reports. It was publicly asserted at the North that our army was taken completely by surprise; that the rebels caught us in our tents; bayoneted the men in their beds; that General Grant was drunk; that Buell's opportune arrival saved the Army of the Tennessee from utter annihilation, etc. These reports were in a measure sustained by the published opinions of Generals Buell, Nelson, and others, who had reached the steamboat-landing from the east, just before nightfall of the 6th, when there was a large crowd of frightened, stampeded men, who clamored and declared that our army was all destroyed and beaten. Personally I saw General Grant, who with his staff visited me about 10 a.m. of the 6th, when we were desperately engaged. But we had checked the headlong assault of our enemy, and then held our ground. This gave him great satisfaction, and he told me that things did not look as well over on the left. He also told me that on his way up from Savannah that morning he had stopped at Crump's Landing, and had ordered Lew Wallace's division to cross over Snake Creek, so as to come up on my right, telling me to look out for him. He came again just before dark, and described the last assault made by the rebels at the ravine, near the steamboat-landing, which he had repelled by a heavy battery collected under Colonel J. D. Webster and other officers, and he was convinced that the battle was over for that day. He ordered me to be ready to assume the offensive in the morning, saying that, as he had observed at Fort Donelson at the crisis of the battle, both sides seemed defeated, and whoever assumed the offensive was sure to win. General Grant also explained to me that General Buell had reached the bank of the Tennessee River opposite Pittsburg Landing, and was in the act of ferrying his troops across at the time he was speaking to me."

Naturally, Grant wasn't the only one to come under fire. In the aftermath of the battle, Beauregard's judgment came under heavy scrutiny from President Davis and his commanders for choosing not to exploit the tactical advantage presented the first day, which ultimately resulted in major losses. To outside observers and many Confederates, Johnston's men had been gloriously and successfully advancing until his mortal wounding, only for Grant's forces to turn the tide the following day with Beauregard in command. Jefferson Davis would bemoan that Johnston's loss was a turning point not just in the battle but the entire war itself.

Naturally, Johnston was revered in his death as a national hero. Beauregard issued a general order to the army after Shiloh mourning his death and praising Johnston:

"Soldiers: Your late commander-in-chief, General A. S. Johnston, is dead; a fearless soldier, a sagacious captain, a reproachless man, has fallen-one who, in his devotion to our cause, shrank from no sacrifice; one who, animated by a sense of duty, and sustained by a sublime courage, challenged danger, and perished gallantly for his country while leading forward his brave columns to victory. His signal example of heroism and patriotism, if imitated, would make his army invincible.

A grateful country will mourn his loss, revere his name, and cherish his many virtues."

Before learning of the disastrous second day of the Battle of Shiloh, Davis announced the victory and the death of Johnston to the Confederate Congress:

"The great importance of the news just received from Tennessee induces me to depart from the established usages, and to make to you this communication in advance of official reports. From official telegraphic dispatches, received from official sources, I am able to announce to you, with entire confidence, that it has pleased Almighty God to crown the Confederate arms with a glorious and decisive victory over our invaders.

On the morning of the 6th, the converging columns of our army were combined by its commander-in-chief, General Albert Sidney Johnston, in an assault on the Federal army, then encamped near Pittsburg, on the Tennessee River.

After a hard-fought battle of ten hours, the enemy was driven in disorder from his position, and pursued to the Tennessee River, where, under the cover of the gunboats, he was at the last accounts endeavoring to effect his retreat by aid of his transports. The details of this great battle are yet too few and incomplete to enable me to distinguish with merited praise all of those who may have conspicuously earned the right to such distinction, and I prefer to delay our own gratification in recommending them to your special notice, rather than incur the risk of wounding the feelings of any by failing to include them in the list. When such a victory has been won over troops as numerous, well disciplined, armed, and appointed, as those which have been so signally routed, we may well conclude that one common spirit of unflinching bravery and devotion to our country's cause must have animated every breast, from that of the commanding general to that of the humblest patriot who served in the ranks. There is enough in the continued presence of invaders on our soil to chasten our exultation over this brilliant success, and to remind us of the grave duty of continued exertion until we shall extort from a proud and vainglorious enemy the reluctant acknowledgment of our right to self-government.

But an All-wise Creator has been pleased, while vouchsafing to us his countenance in battle, to afflict us with a severe dispensation, to which we must bow in humble submission. The last, long, lingering hope has disappeared, and it is but too true that General Albert Sidney Johnston is no more! The tale of his death is simply narrated in a dispatch from Colonel William Preston, in the following words:

General Johnston fell yesterday, at half-past 2 o'clock, while leading a successful charge, turning the enemy's right, and gaining a brilliant victory. A Min16-ball cut the artery of his leg, but he rode on until, from loss of blood, he fell exhausted, and died without pain in a few moments. His body has been intrusted to me by General Beauregard, to be taken to New Orleans, and remain until instructions are received from his family.

My long and close friendship with this departed chieftain and patriot forbid me to trust myself in giving vent to the feelings which this intelligence has evoked. Without doing injustice to the living, it may safely be said that our loss is irreparable. Among the shining hosts of the great and good who now cluster around the banner of our country, there exists no purer spirit, no more heroic soul, than that of the illustrious man whose death I join you in lamenting.

In his death he has illustrated the character for which through life he was conspicuous — that of singleness of purpose and devotion to duty with his whole energies. Bent on obtaining the victory, which he deemed essential to his country's cause, he rode on to the accomplishment of his object, forgetful of self, while his very life-blood was ebbing away fast. His last breath cheered his comrades on to victory. The last sound he heard was their shout of victory. His last thought was his country, and long and deeply will his country mourn his loss."

Albert Sidney Johnston was one of the most experienced leaders the Confederates had, but historians judging his decisions in the Western department have found plenty to criticize. Grant's memoirs continue to be celebrated and critically acclaimed for their candor, and he gave a rather candid opinion of Albert Sidney Johnston's generalship:

"I had known Johnston slightly in the Mexican war and later as an officer in the regular army. He was a man of high character and ability. His contemporaries at West Point, and officers generally who came to know him personally later and who remained on our side, expected him to prove the most formidable man to meet that the Confederacy would produce.

I once wrote that nothing occurred in his brief command of an army to prove or disprove the high estimate that had been placed upon his military ability; but after studying the orders and dispatches of Johnston I am compelled to materially modify my views of that officer's qualifications as a soldier. My judgment now is that he was vacillating and undecided in his actions.

All the disasters in Kentucky and Tennessee were so discouraging to the authorities in Richmond that Jefferson Davis wrote an unofficial letter to Johnston expressing his own anxiety and that of the public, and saying that he had made such defence as was dictated by long friendship, but that in the absence of a report he needed facts. The letter was not a reprimand in direct terms, but it was evidently as much felt as though it had been one. General Johnston raised another army as rapidly as he could, and fortified or strongly intrenched at Corinth. He knew the National troops were preparing to attack him in his chosen position. But he had evidently become so disturbed at the results of his operations that he resolved to strike out in an offensive campaign which would restore all that was lost, and if successful accomplish still more. We have the authority of his son and biographer for saying that his plan was to attack the forces at Shiloh and crush them; then to cross the Tennessee and destroy the army of Buell, and push the war across the Ohio River. The design was a bold one; but we have the same authority for saying that in the execution Johnston showed vacillation and indecision. He left Corinth on the 2d of April and was not ready to attack until the 6th. The distance his army had to march was less than twenty miles. Beauregard, his second in command, was opposed to the attack for two reasons: first, he thought, if let alone the National troops would attack the Confederates in their intrenchments; second, we were in ground of our own choosing and would necessarily be intrenched. Johnston not only listened to the objection of Beauregard to an attack, but held a council of war on the subject on the morning of the 5th. On the evening of the same day he was in consultation with some of his generals on the same subject, and still again on the morning of the 6th. During this last consultation, and before a decision had been reached, the battle began by the National troops opening fire on the enemy. This seemed to settle the question as to whether there was to be any battle of Shiloh. It also seems to me to settle the question as to whether there was a surprise.

I do not question the personal courage of General Johnston, or his ability. But he did not win the distinction predicted for him by many of his friends. He did prove that as a general he was over-estimated."

Despite Grant's estimation, there's no question that Johnston's deaths was one of the great what-ifs of the Civil War, if only because the Confederate commanding generals in the West that followed would prove to be wildly inept. Pemberton would surrender tens of thousands of soldiers to Grant the following year at Vicksburg, Bragg would prove himself not up to the challenge of commanding an army at Chickamauga and Chattanooga, Joseph Johnston would be relieved of command during Sherman's 1864 Atlanta Campaign, and John Bell Hood would all but destroy his own army against George H. Thomas in the Franklin-Nashville Campaign. Albert Sidney Johnston may not have been as great a general as his friend Jefferson Davis thought he was, but it's likely that he would have provided far more competent leadership in the critical Western theater than the Confederates otherwise had received. And with Robert E. Lee's Army of Northern Virginia constantly frustrating the Army of the Potomac in the East, the results of the Civil War may have been far different had Grant and Sherman not been so successful throughout the West.

At the same time, Johnston's death early in the war has also had the effect of obscuring his name and legacy among those who read about and study the Civil War. Despite being the most senior officer to die in battle and one of only two commanding generals to be killed in action during the Civil War, Americans are far less familiar with the Confederacy's highest ranking field officer than they are with men who were his junior in rank and ability.

Johnston's tomb in Austin, Texas

Chapter 19: The Rest of Beauregard's Civil War Career

In the weeks following the Battle of Shiloh, a stream of intelligence reports began rolling in to Union General Halleck's headquarters that the Confederates were amassing troops at Corinth, Mississippi. Assistant Secretary of War Thomas A. Scott, who was traveling with Halleck as a War Department observer, wired Washington in mid-May, stating, "The enemy are concentrating a powerful army [at Corinth]." According to their intelligence, General Beauregard had 60,000 "fresh troops" (by one report), with another saying that 100,000 troops were waiting at Corinth--with more arriving daily. A captured army surgeon assured Grant that reinforcements would soon raise the number of Confederates to 200,000. With a Beauregard-led attack considered imminent, the Union Army was kept poised to take the defensive at a moment's notice.

Little did they know they were victims of a ruse initiated in part by the deceptive Beauregard. Although Union troops had moved slowly and cautiously toward Corinth (averaging less than one mile a day), a month after Shiloh, Halleck--who had taken to the field for the first time to personally take command of his troops--and his 100,000 found themselves approaching the rebel lines. But despite what they'd been led to believe, Beauregard had just over 50,000 men. Recognizing that he didn't have the manpower to stand up to Halleck's much larger and better rested army, as Union troops moved into position, Beauregard abruptly moved his forces under the cover of darkness, but not before arranging one final deception: he had steam engines come puffing and whistling into town at regular intervals, accompanied by the sound of loud cheers, thus giving the impression of arriving troops.

Finally, on May 30, 1862, as the last few Confederate troops blew up the remaining supplies to keep them from Union hands, General Pope led his regiments slowly into town, only to find it abandoned. Leaving Halleck and Pope feeling like fools, Beauregard kept his troops on the move until they were well out of danger, some 50 miles south at Tupelo, Mississippi. Beauregard had earned himself a reputation for crafty and unpredictable field command.
Immediately following the Siege of Corinth, Beauregard turned over command of his forces to General Braxton Bragg and took himself off active duty; placing himself on sick leave. Citing that Beauregard had gone on sick leave without authorization, President Davis relieved him of his command and gave it to General Bragg. Historians believe Davis had been waiting for justification to give the command to Bragg due to his dislike for Beauregard and friendship with Bragg dating back to the Mexican-American War.

As it turned out, Bragg ultimately proved to be one of the Confederacy's biggest goats. Bragg's slowness prevented the Confederates from winning a greater victory at the Battle of Chickamauga, and his siege of Chattanooga was lifted shortly thereafter by Grant, paving the way for Sherman's Atlanta campaign in 1864.
At Beauregard's request, the Confederate Congress petitioned President Davis to restore Beauregard to his command in the West, but in August of 1862, Davis instead placed him in command of the Department of South Carolina-Georgia-Florida coasts, replacing Maj. General John C. Pemberton. Aware that he was being systematically kept from the important battles of the War, he nonetheless performed admirably, successfully preventing the capture of Charleston by Union naval and land attacks.

On April 7, 1863, Rear Admiral Samuel Francis Du Pont, commander of the South Atlantic

Blockading Squadron, led an "ironclad" attack against Fort Sumter that was effectively repulsed by highly accurate artillery fire under Beauregard's direction. Then from July through September of that year, land forces under Brig. General Quincy A. Gillmore launched a series of attacks on Fort Wagner on Morris Island (and other fortifications at the mouth of Charleston harbor) while Rear Admiral John A. Dahlgren attempted to destroy Fort Sumter, all of which were effectively resisted by troops under Beauregard's command. Because the assault on Fort Sumter had failed and the attempted seizure of Morris Island thwarted, any further threat to Charleston had ended.

Beauregard's engineering past also greatly assisted him in devising some innovations during his time on the coast. During his command, Beauregard toyed with experimental submarines and the first "torpedoes", which were water mines. Other experimental craft included affixing a battering ram armed with an explosive to a small boat that could then move quickly up alongside a big U.S. Navy boat and hit it with the torpedo.

In fact, Beauregard was prominently involved in the construction of the most famous submarine of the Civil War. In April of 1862 shortly after the Battle of Shiloh, General G. T. Beauregard became involved in the construction of the *Hunley*, a four feet high, cigar-shaped submarine built to house an eight-man crew. The *Hunley* was equipped to fire one of the explosives into the hull of a U.S. Navy ship before turning around to evade capture. During a practice run in August of 1863, however, and another in October of that year, a total of thirteen men had been killed, including the ship's namesake, Horace Hunley.

The project was nearly scrapped, but one of the remaining crew members thought the underwater craft deserved a third try. On February 17, 1864, Beauregard approved a midnight mission that resulted in the crew of the *Hunley* delivering a spar torpedo into the hull of the Union steam sloop the *Housatonic*, creating a massive hole and making it the first ship ever sunk by a submarine.

In addition to that first, the *Hunley* also created one of the most enduring mysteries of the war. Despite their successful mission, the *Hunley* never returned to port that night. In 1995 the remains of the *Hunley* were found four miles from shore, buried in mud, with its crew members still at their stations. When, why, and how the *Hunley* sunk continue to be fiercely debated by historians and scholars.

While visiting his troops in Florida in March of 1864 after they had just repelled a Union advance at Jacksonville, Beauregard received a telegram that his second wife, Caroline Deslonde, had died on March 2. Union Maj. General Nathaniel P. Banks provided a steamer to carry her body upriver for burial in her native Louisiana parish. Beauregard wrote that he would like to rescue "her hallowed grave" at the head of an army, but his days of independent command were long behind him.

The Hunley suspended in the air by a crane

By April of 1864, G. T. Beauregard had resigned himself to the reality that there would be little opportunity for military glory, as it was highly unlikely that there would be any more significant assaults against Charleston. Clearly, the prospects for a major field command were unlikely as well, so he requested a leave of absence to recover from fatigue and a chronic throat ailment. Instead, he received orders to report to Weldon, North Carolina near the Virginia border. Lincoln had brought General Grant to the east, where he attached himself to the Army of the Potomac, and the Confederates were preparing for Grant's advance and were concerned that attacks south of Richmond could interrupt critical supply lines to Richmond and the Army of Northern Virginia under General Lee.

Once again, Beauregard had been inadvertently placed in a pivotal role. On May 4, 1864, Grant launched the Overland Campaign, crossing the Rapidan River near Fredericksburg with the 100,000 strong Army of the Potomac, which almost doubled Lee's hardened but battered Army of Northern Virginia. It was a similar position to the one George McClellan had in 1862 and Joe Hooker had in 1863, and Grant's first attack, at the Battle of the Wilderness, followed a similar pattern. Nevertheless, Lee proved more than capable on the defensive. From May 5-6, Lee's men won a tactical victory at the Battle of the Wilderness, which was fought so close to where the Battle of Chancellorsville took place a year earlier that soldiers encountered skeletons that had been buried in (too) shallow graves in 1863. Both armies sustained heavy casualties while Grant kept attempting to move the fighting to a setting more to his advantage, but the heavy forest made coordinated movements almost impossible. On the second day, the aggressive Lee used General Longstreet's corps to counterattack on the second day, but the battle ended in a stalemate.

Grant disengaged from the battle in the same position was Hooker before him at Chancellorsville, McClellan on the Virginian Peninsula, and Burnside after Fredericksburg. His men got the familiar dreadful feeling that they would retreat back across the Rapidan toward Washington, as they had too many times before. This time, however, Grant made the fateful decision to keep moving south, inspiring his men by telling them that he was prepared to "fight it out on this line if it takes all Summer."

As Grant moved south against Lee, Union Maj. General Benjamin Butler launched the surprise "Bermuda Hundred Campaign," with landings up the James River. Having convinced General Braxton Bragg (who after the disastrous defeat at Chattanooga in 1863 had been removed from command and became Jefferson Davis' military adviser) not to transfer units of his small force north of Richmond, coupled with Butler's own relative incompetence, Beauregard was successful in bottling-up that Union army, effectively nullifying its threat to Petersburg and Lee's supply line. In the aftermath of this highly-effective strategy, Lee offered Beauregard command of the right wing of the Army of Northern Virginia, due to Longstreet's near fatal injury at the Battle of the Wilderness, but Beauregard refused to leave his department without orders from the War Department.

Meanwhile, using the Union V Corps under Major General Gouverneur K. Warren, Grant moved forward in a series of flanking maneuvers that continued to move the army steadily closer to Richmond. With each move by Grant, Lee continued to parry each thrust. The next major battle took place at Spotsylvania Court House from May 8-21, with the heaviest fighting on May 12 when a salient in the Confederate line nearly spelled disaster. Fighting raged around the "Bloody Angle" for hours, with soldiers fighting hand to hand before the Confederates finally dislodged the Union soldiers."

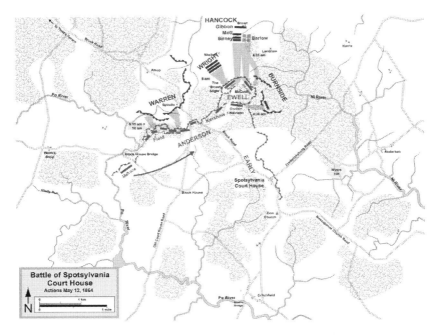

Lee's army continued to stoutly defend against several attacks by the Army of the Potomac, but massive casualties were inflicted on both sides. After Spotsylvania, Grant had already incurred about 35,000 casualties while inflicting nearly 25,000 casualties on Lee's army. Grant, of course, had the advantage of a steady supply of manpower, so he could afford to fight the war of attrition. It was a fact greatly lost on the people of the North, however, who knew Grant's track record from Shiloh and saw massive casualty numbers during the Overland Campaign. Grant was routinely criticized as a butcher.

As fate would have it, the only time during the Overland Campaign Lee had a chance to take the initiative was after Spotsylvania. During the fighting that came to be known as the Battle of North Anna, Lee was heavily debilitated with illness. Grant nearly fell into Lee's trap by splitting his army in two along the North Anna before avoiding it. By the time the two armies reached Cold Harbor near the end of May 1864, Grant incorrectly thought that Lee's army was on the verge of collapse. Though his frontal assaults had failed spectacularly at places like Vicksburg, Grant believed that Lee's army was on the ropes and could be knocked out with a strong attack. The problem was that Lee's men were now masterful at quickly constructing defensive fortifications, including earthworks and trenches, that made their positions impregnable. While Civil War generals kept employing Napoleonic tactics, Civil War soldiers were building the types of defensive works that would be the harbinger of World War I's trench warfare.

At Cold Harbor, Grant decided to order a massive frontal assault against Lee's well fortified and entrenched lines. His decision was dead wrong, literally. Although the story of Union soldiers pinning their names on the back of their uniforms in anticipation of death at Cold Harbor is apocryphal, the frontal assault on June 3 inflicted thousands of Union casualties in about half an hour. With another 12,000 casualties at Cold Harbor, Grant had suffered about as many casualties in a month as Lee had in his entire army at the start of the campaign. Grant later admitted, "I have always regretted that the last assault at Cold Harbor was ever made...No advantage whatever was gained to compensate for the heavy loss we sustained."

After the Confederate victory at Cold Harbor on June 12, 1864, Beauregard attempted in vain to convince his superiors that Grant's next move would be to cross the James River and attempt to seize Petersburg, the main railroad hub of the Confederacy situated just miles away from Richmond. Beauregard proved prophetic; after Cold Harbor, Grant managed to successfully steal an entire day's march on Lee and crossed the James River, moving on the Confederacy's primary railroad hub at Petersburg with two Union Army corps totaling 16,000 men on June 15.

Incredibly, the war was saved right then and there by the quick and skillful defense of Petersburg organized by Beauregard and his 5,400 men, outnumbered 3 to 1 by the Union attackers. With Union forces breathing down their necks, Beauregard sent urgent messages to both Lee and the War Department asking for immediate reinforcements, despite serious doubts they could reach him in time. After the war, when the back and forth messages were publicly published, one historian noted, "Nothing illustrates better the fundamental weakness of the Confederate command system than the weary series of telegrams exchanged in May and early June between Davis, Bragg, Beauregard, and Lee. Beauregard evaded his responsibility for determining what help he could give Lee; Davis and Bragg shirked their responsibility to decide, when he refused. The strangest feature of the whole affair was that, in the face of Lee's repeated requests, nobody in the high command thought to order Beauregard to join Lee."

Meanwhile, for three days Union General William "Baldy" Smith seized Confederate artillery and occupied Confederate trenches, winning key positions that gave him and his troops unobstructed entrance into Petersburg. With each passing day, Beauregard assumed retreat was inevitable. But then just as events reached the critical point, Smith lost his nerve and decided to wait for reinforcements before launching his main attack, giving Confederate troops ample time to arrive and successfully fend off a series of assaults characterized as "poorly coordinated" and "driven home without vigor." Ultimately, Lee managed to get his Army of Northern Virginia to Beauregard before the Union could muster a proper attack.

By June 20, Grant had called off all attacks and opted to make a siege of Petersburg. And while Beauregard was credited with preventing a Union occupation -- the saving of Petersburg deemed his greatest military achievement -- Grant had nonetheless succeeded in occupying a fixed position that would greatly limit Lee's movement and give Grant the upper hand. Although Beauregard's actions had saved Petersburg from occupation -- and probable destruction -- they resulted in a ten-month siege of the city that ultimately proved successful for the North anyway.

In October of 1864, Jefferson Davis called G. T. Beauregard to Augusta, Georgia and offered him command of the newly created Department of the West, responsible for the five Southern states from Georgia west to the Mississippi River, with the armies of Generals John Hood and Richard Taylor under his *ostensible* command. Though it was an unrewarding administrative job limited to logistical and advisory responsibilities, with no actual operational control of the armies, Beauregard was anxious to return to the field after nearly four months, so he accepted the assignment.

The primary field operation of the Department of the West was General Hood's Franklin-Nashville Campaign, a planned invasion of Tennessee which he undertook despite Beauregard's counsel that it made little operational or logistical sense. Hood showed little regard for Beauregard's input, communicated his plans only begrudgingly, and subsequently made numerous reckless moves with no forethought to the consequences or his supply line, which Beauregard attempted to maintain nonetheless.

While Hood traveled through Alabama and into Tennessee to try to draw Sherman away from the South, Sherman instead left some men under the command of George H. Thomas and began his famous "March to the Sea" from Atlanta to Savannah, which brought Beauregard's attention back to Georgia. But with inadequate local forces -- and reluctant to strip defenses from other locations to concentrate them against Sherman -- he was unable to stop or even delay Sherman's advance. Additionally, Sherman had done such an excellent job of deceiving the Confederates as to the intermediate and final targets of his march, that by December 21 when Savannah fell and Sherman headed north toward South Carolina, Hood had lost so many men at the Battle of Nashville that Beauregard had very few to send against Sherman regardless.

Even so, Beauregard attempted to concentrate his small forces before Sherman could reach Columbia, South Carolina, sending a series of urgent dispatches to Richmond to warn President Davis and General Lee (who was now commander of all the Confederate armies). But Davis and Lee refused to believe that Sherman was advancing as quickly as Beauregard had communicated, believing the attention-seeking General was overreacting. Ostensibly concerned about Beauregard's "feeble health," Lee recommended to Davis that General Joseph E. Johnston assume command of Beauregard's troops, which came about on February 22, 1865. Though outwardly cooperative and courteous to Johnston, Beauregard was bitterly disappointed by this unwarranted and mortifying treatment. For the remainder of the war, Beauregard would be Johnston's subordinate, assigned to routine matters without combat responsibilities.

by the beginning of 1865, the Confederacy was in utter disarray. The main Confederate army in the West under John Bell Hood had been nearly destroyed by General Thomas's men at the Battle of Franklin in late 1864, and Sherman's army faced little resistance as it marched through the Carolinas. Although Confederate leaders remained optimistic, by the summer of 1864 they had begun to consider desperate measures in an effort to turn around the war. From 1863-1865, Confederate leaders had even debated whether to conscript black slaves and enlist them as soldiers. Even as their fortunes looked bleak, the Confederates refused to issue an official policy to enlist blacks. It was likely too late to save the Confederacy anyway.

By the time Lincoln delivered his Second Inaugural Address in March 1865, the end of the war was in sight. That month, Lincoln famously met with Grant, Sherman, and Admiral David Porter at City Point, Grant's headquarters during the siege, to discuss how to handle the end of the war.

George P.A. Healy's famous 1868 painting, "The Peacemakers", depicts the meeting at

City Point

Lee's siege lines at Petersburg were finally broken on April 1 at the Battle of Five Forks, which is best remembered for General George Pickett (best remembered for Pickett's Charge) enjoying a cod bake lunch while his men were being defeated. Historians have attributed it to unusual environmental acoustics that prevented Pickett and his staff from hearing the battle despite their close proximity, not that it mattered to the Confederates at the time. Between that and Gettysburg, Pickett and Lee were alleged to have held very poor opinions of each other by the end of the war, and there is still debate as to whether Lee had ordered Pickett out of the army during the Appomattox campaign. The following day, battles raged across the siege lines of Petersburg, eventually spelling the doom for Lee's defenses. On April 2, 1865, Lee abandoned Petersburg, and thus Richmond with it.

Lee's battered army began stumbling toward a rail depot in the hopes of avoiding being surrounded by Union forces and picking up much needed food rations. While Grant's army continued to chase Lee's retreating army westward, the Confederate government sought to escape across the Deep South. On April 4, President Lincoln entered Richmond and toured the home of Confederate President Jefferson Davis.

Fittingly, the food rations did not arrive as anticipated. On April 7, 1865, Grant sent Lee the first official letter demanding Lee's surrender. In it Grant wrote, "The results of the last week must convince you of the hopelessness of further resistance on the part of the Army of Northern Virginia in this struggle. I feel it is so, and regret it as my duty to shift myself from the responsibility of any further effusion of blood by asking of you the surrender of that portion of the Confederate States army known as the Army of Northern Virginia."

When Lee proposed to hear the terms, the communications continued until April 9, when the two met at Appomattox Court House. When Lee and Grant met, the styles in dress captured the personality differences perfectly. Lee was in full military attire, while Grant showed up casually in a muddy uniform. The Civil War's two most celebrated generals were meeting for the first time since the Mexican-American War.

The Confederate soldiers had continued fighting while Lee worked out the terms of surrender, and they were understandably devastated to learn that they had surrendered. Some of his men had famously suggested to Lee that they continue to fight on. Porter Alexander would later rue the fact that he suggested to Lee that they engage in guerrilla warfare, which earned him a stern rebuke from Lee. As a choked-up Lee rode down the troop line on his famous horse Traveller that day, he addressed his defeated army, saying, "Men, we have fought through the war together. I have done my best for you; my heart is too full to say more."

Appomattox is frequently cited as the end of the Civil War, but there still remained several Confederate armies across the country, mostly under the command of General Joseph E. Johnston, who Lee had replaced nearly 3 years earlier. On April 26, Johnston and Beauregard surrendered all of the forces in their department to General Sherman. Over the next month, the remaining Confederate forces would surrender or quit. The last skirmish between the two sides took place May 12-13, ending ironically with a Confederate victory at the Battle of Palmito Ranch in Texas. Two days earlier, Jefferson Davis had been captured in Georgia.

Upon his release, Beauregard traveled to Mobile, Alabama and then took a U. S. naval transport home.

Chapter 20: Beauregard's Final Years

Immediately following the War, Beauregard considered leaving the United States to accept a foreign command before ultimately deciding against it. However, he did serve as adjutant general for the Louisiana state militia from 1879 to 1888.

After the Civil War, G. T. Beauregard was initially opposed to seeking amnesty as a former Confederate officer, the public swearing of an oath of loyalty to the United States, but both Lee and Johnston counseled him to do so. On September 16, 1865, he swore allegiance before the mayor of New Orleans.

In the wake of the Confederate surrender, Beauregard spoke out about the inadequacies of Southern leadership that by his description had resulted in the Southern defeat, saying, "We needed for president either a military man of high order, or a politician of the first-class without military pretensions. The South did not fall crushed by the mere weight of the North; but it was nibbled away at all sides and ends because its executive head never gathered and wielded its great strength under the ready advantages that greatly reduced or neutralized its adversary's physical superiority."

With his fame and heroic reputation now extending far beyond U. S. borders, both Egypt and Romania approached him with offers to lead their armies; positions he turned down. In 1865, however, he momentarily considered a position in the Brazilian Army, but ultimately declined it, citing that President Johnson's positive attitude toward the South had swayed his decision. "I prefer to live here, poor and forgotten, than to be endowed with honor and riches in a foreign country."

Beauregard's first employment following the War was in October 1865 as chief engineer and general superintendent of the New Orleans, Jackson & Great Northern Railroad. In 1866 he was promoted to president of the railroad, a position he retained until 1870 when he was ousted in a hostile takeover. This job overlapped with that of president of the New Orleans & Carrollton Street Railway [New Orleans, Jackson, & Mississippi Railroad] (1866–1876), where he invented a system of cable-powered street railway cars. Here again, although Beauregard made a financial success of the company, he was ultimately fired by stockholders who wished to take direct management of the company.

On July 4, 1868, Beauregard was one of several Confederate officers issued a mass pardon by President Andrew Johnson. His final privilege as an American citizen, the right to run for public office, was restored when his petition to Congress resulted in a bill signed by President Grant on July 24, 1876 on his behalf.

As a life-long Democrat, Beauregard worked to end Republican rule during the Reconstruction, from 1865 to 1877. His resentment over the excesses of Reconstruction was the principal motivation for leaving the United States and his flirtation with joining foreign armies (which continued until 1875). Becoming an active and outspoken member in the Reform Party (an association of conservative New Orleans businessmen who spoke in favor of civil rights for the recently freed slaves), like the other members, Beauregard hoped to form alliances between African-Americans and Democrats to vote out the Radical Republicans in the state legislature.

After losing two executive railway positions, Beauregard invested his time in a variety of companies and civil engineering pursuits, but his personal wealth was finally assured in 1877, when he was recruited as a supervisor of the Louisiana Lottery. Along with former Confederate general Jubal Early, the two presided over lottery drawings and made numerous public appearances, lending respectability to the endeavor for the next 15 years. Around 1892, however, the public grew opposed to government-sponsored gambling, so the lottery was closed down by the legislature.

In 1888, Beauregard was elected Commissioner of Public Works in New Orleans, and then appointed by the governor of Virginia to be the grand marshal of the festivities associated with the laying of the cornerstone of Robert E. Lee's statue in Richmond. When Jefferson Davis died in 1889, however, Beauregard refused the honor of heading the funeral procession, saying "We have always been enemies. I cannot pretend I am sorry he is gone. I am no hypocrite."

Despite his later accomplishments, Beauregard's final years were, unfortunately, marked by bitter verbal quarrels with Generals Joseph E. Johnston, Jefferson Davis, and Colonel William Preston Johnston (son of Albert Sidney Johnston and *aide-to-camp* to Davis) over their published accounts of the War and their description of Beauregard's role in it. Their critical and unflattering analysis of his contributions would irk him to his final days.

Even before the end of the Civil War, G. T. Beauregard had begun conveying his military experiences via the written word, penning *Principles and Maxims of the Art of War* in 1863. He was then the un-credited co-author of Alfred Roman's *The Military Operations of General Beauregard in the War Between the States* published in 1884, and author of *Report on the Defense of Charleston* and *A Commentary on the Campaign and Battle of Manassas,* published in 1891. He also contributed "The Battle of Bull Run" to *Century Illustrated Monthly Magazine* in November 1884. During these years, Beauregard and Davis both published a series of bitter accusations and counter-accusations blaming each other for the Confederate defeat.

When John Bell Hood and his wife died in 1879 leaving ten destitute orphans, Beauregard used his influence to get Hood's memoirs published, with all proceeds going to the children.

On February 20, 1893, Pierre Gustave-Toutant (G. T. Beauregard) died in his sleep in New Orleans, with the official cause of death deemed heart disease, aortic insufficiency, and [probably] myocarditis. Edmund Kirby Smith, the last surviving full general of the Confederacy, served as the "chief mourner" as Beauregard was interred in the vault of the Army of Tennessee in historic Metairie Cemetery in New Orleans, Louisiana.

Beauregard Parish in western Louisiana is named for General Beauregard, as is Camp Beauregard, a National Guard camp near Pineville in central Louisiana.

The unincorporated community of Beauregard, Alabama is named for Beauregard.

An equestrian monument by Alexander Doyle depicts Beauregard at Beauregard Circle, the intersection where Esplanade Avenue enters City Park, in New Orleans.

Beauregard's residence in New Orleans is now called the "Beauregard-Keyes House," and is operated as an historic house museum.

Chapter 21: Beauregard's Legacy

According to several modern scholars, although G. T. Beauregard proved to be a capable and effective combat commander during the Civil War, his penchant for questioning orders from his superiors frequently bordered on blatant insubordination, and although he often displayed sound (even clever) strategic judgment, more often than not his plans were unworkable due to over-complexity, over-reliance on details, and general lack of practicality, leading his superiors to find him lacking in common sense. In short, he had serious deficiencies as a general officer.

Nonetheless, military historians place Beauregard on the list of the South's more *able* commanders and far superior to the North's inept John Pope and Ambrose Burnside. But while garnering respect for his successes on the battlefield, Beauregard was often accused of gross over-reaction to circumstances--or gross over-confidence—with his judgment repeatedly called into question. Today, even his reasoning to fire the first shots at Fort Sumter has been reexamined.

Although Beauregard's orders were to "demand the evacuation" of Fort Sumter and "if refused to proceed to reduce it," as his own aides reported, upon receipt of the ultimatum, Fort Sumter commander Major Robert Anderson's response was, "If you do not batter the fort to pieces about us, we shall be starved out in a few days." With the resupply ship having been fired upon and turning around without bringing provisions to the fort, Anderson would have eventually been starved out indeed. Thus, while Anderson was compelled to await orders from his superiors regarding surrender of the pivotal fort, he provided Beauregard an *out*; a way to prevent bloodshed.

But as post-War documents now illuminate, Beauregard was needlessly alarmed by the report of four steamers bringing bread to Anderson, and six Men-o-War ships said to be anchored off the coast. In reality, only one war-ship was present, a second didn't arrive until one and a half hours after the bombardment commenced, and a third arrived at 7:00 a.m. the next morning. Thus it seems probable that the order to bombard the fort--the very order which ignited the Civil War—may have been unnecessary.

Similarly, a reexamination of the events surrounding the Battle of Shiloh makes it apparent that the covert arrival of eighteen thousand Union soldiers under General Don Buell into Pittsburg Landing should have been an impossibility had Beauregard followed simple protocol, posting sentries and sending out scouts, rather than instituting a more complex plan that circumvented fundamental tactics. Beauregard's overconfidence needlessly cost the Confederates a victory at Shiloh, as well as the lives of hundreds of men and untold Confederate resources.

While Beauregard's retractors readily cite his technical weaknesses as illustrative of his many "shortcomings," there can be no denying that his contributions to technological and psychological warfare not only affected the outcome of several key battles of the Civil War but changed the face of warfare forever.

As the first to utilize an underwater missile delivery system, there is little doubt that his use of a submarine to incapacitate the Union steam sloop the *Housatonic* changed not just the course of the War at Charleston Bay but all future naval warfare. Likewise, his urging to use trains to transport troops to battle sites added a dimension to land warfare that has helped decide the outcome of battles here and throughout the world to this day. And while many thought Beauregard's field strategies too complex to be practical, his use of "misinformation"--the issuing of false reports or organizing deceptive measures to give the pretense of greater troop strength--added a psychological dimension to warfare that proved quite effective.

As the South's first *bona fide* hero, the momentum of Beauregard's early surge of popularity proved nearly enough to overcome later issues with his reputation: his penchant for grandiose and impractical battle plans, his bitter -- often petty -- feud with President Davis, and his inability to sustain the highest commands in the Confederate Army for any length of time. His early rise to fame even served to obscure the fact that only by a great stretch of the imagination was he the "model" of the South--or North, for that matter--with his Gallic name, dark skin, French-laced accent, and devotion to the Roman Catholic Church.

Yet in the wake of the Confederacy taking an official "stance" against the Federals, not only did Beauregard's exotic bearing seem somehow appropriate to represent Southern audacity and fierce individualism, it even seemed to fit the ideal of supreme Southern leadership; at one point he was urged to challenge Davis for the Presidency. Thus, despite all his apparent (and suspected) flaws, after the War, General G. T. Beauregard was one of four generals whose portraits routinely hung prominently in Southern homes, along with Robert E. Lee, JEB Stuart, and "Stonewall" Jackson, all recognized heroes of the "Lost Cause."

In 1867, a gray-haired and tired-looking Beauregard was depicted in a decidedly heroic battlefield in a French lithograph titled, *Général G. T. Beauregard*, a scene recalling the early glories of his career. But then as if to counteract Beauregard's potential legacy, group portraits taken between 1861 and 1862--which had initially depicted Beauregard sitting prominently next to Jefferson Davis were revisited, with Lee replacing Beauregard in front and Beauregard relegated to a seat in the back row. Historians are uncertain whether this adjustment was made at the behest of Davis or Lee.

Even though General G. T. Beauregard led the Confederacy at many important battles and defeated many Union rivals, polls today place him somewhere in the middle of the list of Civil War commanders, in terms of importance and accomplishments.

Bibliography

Catton, Bruce. *This Hallowed Ground*. New York: Doubleday & Company, Inc., 1956.

Civil War Home. "Pierre Gustave Toutant Beauregard." Retrieved via: http://www.civilwarhome.com/beaubio.htm 05.26.2012.

Eicher, John H., and Eicher, David J. *Civil War High Commands*. Stanford University Press, 2001.

Gaffney, P., and D. Gaffney. *The Civil War: Exploring History One Week at a Time*. New York: Hyperion, 2011.

Garrison, Webb. *Civil War Curiosities*. Nashville: Rutledge Hill Press, 1994.

Lanning, Michael Lee. *The Civil War 100*. Illinois: Sourcebooks, Inc., 2006.

National Park Service Department of the Interior, "The Battle of Shiloh." Accessed via http://www.nps.gov/history/history/online_books/civil_war_series/22/sec13.htm 05.28.2012.

Neely, Mark E., Holzer, Harold & Boritt, Gabor S. *The Confederate Image*. Chapel Hill: The University of North Carolina Press, 1987.

Ojeda, Auriana (editor). *The Civil War: 1850--1895, Volume 5*. Farmington Hills: Greenhaven, 2003.

Stepp, John. W. and Hill, William I. (editors). *Mirror of War, The Washington Star Reports the Civil War*. The Evening Star Newspaper Co., 1961.

Williams, Harry, T. *P. G. T. Beauregard, Napoleon in Grey*. Louisiana State University Press, 1995.

Chris Emmett. The General and the Poet: Albert Sidney Johnston and Sidney Lanier: A Luminary Follows a Star. San Antonio, TX: Naylor. 1937.

William Preston Johnston. The Life of Gen. Albert Sidney Johnston, Embracing his Services in the Armies of the United States, the Republic of Texas, and the Confederate States. New York: D. Appleton. 1878.

Avery C. Moore. Destiny's Soldier: General Albert Sidney Johnston. San Francisco, CA: Fearon. 1958.

Charles P. Roland. Albert Sidney Johnston: Soldier of Three Republics. Austin, TX: University of Texas Press. 1964.

Joseph E. Johnston
Chapter 1: Johnston's Early Years

Joseph Eggleston Johnston was born on February 3, 1807 at Longwood House in Cherry Grove, near Farmville, Prince Edward County, Virginia, the seventh son to Peter and Mary Valentine Wood Johnston. Mary was a niece of the famed American patriot and Virginian Governor, Patrick Henry. Joseph's grandfather, Peter Johnston, immigrated to Virginia from Scotland in 1726.

Joseph was named for Joseph Eggleston, a major under whom his father Peter served in the American Revolutionary War. Together the two fought under the command of Harry "Light-Horse" Lee, Robert E. Lee's father. Joseph's father was a well-known and respected district judge; his brother Charles Clement Johnston served as a congressman; and his nephew John Warfield Johnston was a senator, all representing Virginia.

While little information pertaining to Joseph's early years has survived, it is known that sometime in the very first years of life, the family home, "Longwood House," burned down. Subsequently rebuilt, in 1827 it became the birthplace of Charles S. Venable, one of Robert E. Lee's staff officers, and is now the home of the president of Longwood University.

In 1811, the Johnston family moved to Abingdon, Virginia, a town near the Tennessee border, where Joseph's father Peter built a home he dubbed "Panecillo." Sometime after moving to Abingdon, Virginia in 1811, Joseph attended Abingdon Academy, a local all-male military institute (which is now defunct).

Shortly before his inauguration as U. S. Vice President in 1825, Secretary of War John C. Calhoun nominated Joseph for admission to the United States Military Academy at West Point, New York.

Little is known about Johnston's time at West Point, largely due to the fact that Johnston's memoirs focus entirely on his Civil War service and literally start in 1861. Johnston seems to have been successful at academics and received relatively few disciplinary demerits, as evidenced by his class standing. When he graduated in July 1829, he was 13th out of the 46 cadets in his class. Joseph was appointed Second Lieutenant Joseph Eggleston Johnston of the Fourth U. S. Artillery.

Though they didn't know it at the time, the West Point classes of those days would later become known for the prominent Civil War generals who went to school together and graduated. In 1846, a shy kid named Thomas Jonathan Jackson made few friends and struggled with his studies, finishing 17th in his class 15 years before becoming Stonewall, while George Pickett was more preoccupied with playing hooky at a local bar before finishing last in the same class as Jackson. The Class of 1846 also included A.P. Hill, who was already in love with the future wife of George McClellan, a young prodigy who finished second in the class of 1846. Years earlier, a clerical error by West Point administrators ensured that Hiram Ulysses Grant forever became known as Ulysses S. Grant. William Tecumseh Sherman was roommates with George H. Thomas, who later became one of his principal subordinates and the "Rock of Chickamauga".

Johnston's class was no exception. Among the other graduates of the 1828-29 classes were 11 who would go on to become top Confederate leaders, including Robert E. Lee, Joseph E. Johnston, Jefferson Davis, and Albert Sidney Johnston (no relation to Joseph). Second Lieutenant Joseph Johnston would subsequently become the first West Point graduate to be promoted to a general officer in the U. S. Regular Army, reaching a higher rank than even classmate Robert E. Lee, who famously never received a demerit during his time at West Point.

Jefferson Davis

Nearly 40 years after Johnston graduated, the time spent at West Point among these men was even more closely scrutinized. By then, the animosity between Johnston and Jefferson Davis was legendary, and it certainly had an adverse impact upon the Confederate war effort during the War. It was claimed that the origins of the animosity between the two went all the way back to their days as West Point cadets. Rumored to have begun when the two vied for the affection of the same young woman, a daughter of a tavern owner by some accounts, Davis apparently challenged Johnston to a fistfight. It was said that Johnston walked away victor, and by some accounts, Davis carried a grudge for the remainder of his life. Those who believed this legend pointed to it as the reason Davis was hyper-critical of Johnston's field decisions during the Civil War.

Chapter 2: Early Military Career

In 1831, two years after Joseph graduated from West Point Military Academy and posted at Fort Columbus, New York, his father Peter died. From 1830 to 1837, Joseph Eggleston Johnston served in the U. S. artillery. Posted first at Fort Columbus, New York from 1830 to 1831, he was promoted to first lieutenant before being transferred to Fort Monroe, Virginia where he attended artillery school until 1832.

Though he did not actively participate in the fighting during the Black Hawk War (a conflict fought in 1832 between the United States Army and Native Americans led by Sauk leader Black Hawk), he was part of the "Blackhawk Expedition" on the frontier along the Mississippi River.

From 1832 to 1833, First Lieutenant Johnston was part of a garrison stationed at Charleston Harbor during South Carolina's threatened "nullification". In 1832, the issue of tariffs on the importation of foreign goods nearly ripped the nation apart and ignited a civil war three decades before one actually occurred. Four years earlier, a tariff had been passed that taxed the importation of manufactured goods, many of which came from the industries of Great Britain. This tax was passed with the intention of protecting industry in the Northern states from competition from foreign industrial countries. The South, however, was less industrial and relied on the export of cotton; by reducing the competitiveness of British industry, the economy there was less able to afford to import cotton from the United States. To the South, the protective tariffs were one-sided and supported the North at the expense of the South, and the region loudly opposed them.

In 1832, a new tariff was passed that was less harsh than the one from 1828, but the South still opposed the bill. In response, South Carolina began to consider passing an ordinance of nullification, prohibiting the tariff within its borders. Vice President Calhoun encouraged the act, and supported its Constitutionality. On November 19th, South Carolina adopted the Ordinance of Nullification, overturning the tariffs of 1828 and 1832 within its borders. It also vowed that any attempts to enforce the law within its borders would lead to the state's secession from the Union.

Modern American jurisprudence has ensured that federal laws are supreme to state laws when they are in conflict, but South Carolina's assertion that it had the ability to nullify a federal law dated all the way back to the "Kentucky and Virginia Resolutions", which were drafted by Jefferson and Madison. Together, the two drafted the first major political documents advocating the rights of the states to nullify federal law that the states believed was unconstitutional. Citing this doctrine of "nullification," various states in both the North and South asserted the states' rights to consider federal laws invalid. The Resolutions sought to nullify the Alien and Sedition Acts within those states back in the late 18th century, Northern states debated nullification during the War of 1812, and in 1860, Southern states would take nullification one step further to outright secession, leading to the Civil War.

Amid the crisis, President Andrew Jackson was reelected by a wide margin. He did not, however, win the state of South Carolina, which nominated its own candidate, John Floyd of the Nullifier Party. Within less than a week of his reelection, Jackson stated his position on the Nullification Crisis. He said that John Calhoun's doctrine of Nullification was an "impractical absurdity," defied Constitutional law, and was tantamount to treason. President Jackson absolutely denied that a state had the right to overturn federal law, and he committed the U.S. military to quelling any attempts to do that in South Carolina. Ten days later, Vice President Calhoun resigned, having won a seat in the U.S. Senate, and he continued to support Nullification throughout the crisis.

Jackson

To give added support to his demands, the President asked Congress for an authorization to use force in January of 1833. On February 20th, Congress passed the Force Bill, known as the "Bloody Bill," which authorized Jackson to use military force in South Carolina. Jackson went beyond this, vowing to personally murder John C. Calhoun and "hang him high as Hamen." Such belligerent militance was typical of President Jackson. Eventually Congress managed a compromise in March, authored by the "Great Compromiser" Henry Clay himself. The new bill reduced all tariffs for a ten year period and was signed into law on March 15th. South Carolina revoked its Ordinance of Nullification, though it nullified the Force Bill in the same act.

Regardless, the Nullification Crisis was over.

Johnston also served at Fort Macon, North Carolina in 1834, and Fort Monroe, Virginia in 1834, where he served until the outbreak of the Seminole War

Though he was still in the Army during the beginning of the Seminole War and was said to have served with distinction, Johnston resigned his commission in the U. S. Army in March of 1837 and subsequently studied civil engineering, the kind of field that would serve commanders well in the 1860s. During the Second Seminole War (1835-1842), Johnston mostly worked as a civilian topographic engineer aboard a ship led by American naval officer and hydrologist William Pope McArthur, who was involved in the first surveys of the Pacific Coast for the U. S. Coast and Geodetic Survey.

McArthur

On January 12, 1838 at Jupiter, Florida, Johnston was part of a team of sailors who went ashore only to be attacked by a band of hostile Native Americans. In the fighting, Johnston later claimed that there were "no less than thirty bullet holes in my clothing", and one bullet grazed his scalp, leaving a permanent scar.

Having encountered more combat activity in Florida as a civilian than he had as an active artillery officer, Joseph decided he might as well rejoin the Army. It's unclear whether he returned to active combat duty or served as a topographical engineer.

On July 10, 1845 in Baltimore, Maryland, Joseph married Lydia Mulligan Sims McLane

(1822–1887). Lydia was the daughter of Louis McLane, who was president of the Baltimore and Ohio Railroad and a prominent former politician (congressman and senator from Delaware, minister to London, England, and a member of President Andrew Jackson's cabinet). Joseph and his wife would have no children.

Like Robert E. Lee and other West Point graduates who had found themselves mostly relegated to peacetime duty in the 1830s and 1840s, Johnston was enthusiastic about the outbreak of the Mexican-American War and the oportunity to actively participate in war. Chosen to serve on Lt. General Winfield Scott's staff during the Siege of Veracruz, a 20-day siege lasting from March 9 through 29, 1847 that ended with the surrender and occupation of the city, First Lieutenant Johnston was selected to carry the surrender demand to the Veracruz provincial governor. He was then in the vanguard of the advance inland under Brig. General David E. Twiggs and was severely wounded while performing reconnaissance prior to the Battle of Cerro Gordo (April 18, 1847). For that, Johnston was appointed brevet lieutenant colonel for "meritorious conduct."

Winfield Scott

After a few weeks recouperating in a military field hospital, in May of 1847 Brevet Lieutenant Colonel Johnston rejoined his unit at Puebla, east of Mexico City. During the advance against Mexico City and a siege that culminated on August 7, he was placed second in command of a regiment of U. S. "Voltigeurs" (light infantry or "skirmishers"). Distinguishing himself at the Battles of Contreras and Churubusco on August 19-20, 1847, where he was wounded again at Chapultepec, Johnston received two additional brevet promotions and ultimately finished the war as a brevet colonel of volunteers. After the end of that war, however, he reverted to his peacetime rank of captain in the topographical engineers.

In the aftermath of the Mexican-American War, General Winfield Scott is said to have remarked humorously, "Johnston is a great soldier, but he had an unfortunate knack of getting himself shot in nearly every engagement!" Indeed, Johnston sustained five separate wounds during his short stint in Mexico. Still, the worst injury Johnston suffered in Mexico wasn't a battle wound; it was the death of his nephew, Preston Johnston. When Robert E. Lee informed Johnston that Preston had been killed by Mexican artillery at Contreras, both officers wept. It was a loss Johnston would grieve for the remainder of his life.

Robert E. Lee circa 1850

Johnston met several other junior officers who became future Civil War generals in Mexico, including Ulysses S. Grant, Thomas Jonathan "Stonewall" Jackson, George McClellan, P.G.T. Beauregard, James Longstreet, Braxton Bragg, George Meade, Joseph Hooker, George Thomas, and Jefferson Davis.

Chapter 3: Antebellum Years

In the wake of the Mexican-American War, Captain Johnston served as chief topographical engineer for the Department of Texas, involved in the Texas-United States boundary survey, from 1848 to 1853.

During the 1850s, Johnston displayed what historians term "an early indication of his sensitivity for rank and prestige," demonstrated by sending letters to the War Department suggesting that he should be returned to a combat regiment with his wartime rank of colonel reinstated. However, Secretary of War Jefferson Davis rejected the idea, possibly due to the already existent animosity between the two men, and with that he established a precedent that would continue throughout the Civil War, much to Johnston's continual irritation.

Despite that rejection, Davis apparently thought well enough of Johnston's abilities to appoint him lieutenant colonel in one of the newly-formed regiments, the First U.S. Cavalry, which was established at Fort Leavenworth, Kansas under Col. Edwin V. "Bull" Sumner on March 1, 1855. At this same time, Robert E. Lee was appointed lieutenant colonel of the Second U. S. Cavalry unit under Colonel Albert Sidney Johnston.

In this position, Captain Johnston participated in actions against the Sioux in Wyoming Territory, and in the violence known as "Bleeding Kansas". During this time, Johnston developed a close friendship with one of his junior officers, Captain George B. McClellan, a man who would subsequently become one of his principal opponents during the Civil War.

In the fall of 1856, Captain Johnston was transferred to a depot for new recruits at Jefferson Barracks, Missouri. In 1857 he led surveying expeditions to determine the official Kansas border. Later that same year, Secretary of War Jefferson Davis was replaced with former Governor of Virginia (and future Confederate general) John B. Floyd--a cousin to Johnston by marriage—who immediately overturned Davis' decision concerning Johnston's highest brevet rank (that of brevet colonel for Cerro Gordo), an action that caused grumbling within the U. S. Army about nepotism.

In 1859, President James Buchanan named Johnston's brother-in-law, Robert McLane, minister to Mexico and assigned Johnston to accompany him to visit Mexican Constitutional President Benito Juárez's government in Veracruz. Johnston was ordered to inspect possible military routes across the country in the event of further hostilities, since Juárez was involved with resisting the French occupation of Mexico, which the U. S. supported.

On June 10, 1860, Brig. General Thomas S. Jesup, Quartermaster General of the U. S. Army, died, and General Winfield Scott submitted four names as a replacement: Robert E. Lee, Charles F. Smith, Albert Sidney Johnston, and Joseph E. Johnston. Although Jefferson Davis, now a member of the Senate Military Affairs Committee, favored his friend Albert Sidney Johnston, Secretary of War Floyd chose Joseph E. Johnston, his cousin-by-marriage. Naturally, this sparked another rash of favoritism charges.

On June 28, 1860, Captain Johnston was promoted to brigadier general; incurring a position he did not especially enjoy, a desk job in Washington, D. C. Quite unlike the field command he would have preferred, he was forced to deal with the pressures of the imminent sectional crisis on the near horizon, and the ethical dilemma of administering war documents that might soon prove useful to his native South should secession result. Nevertheless, it was a temptation he is said to have resisted.

Chapter 4: Heading Toward Civil War

In the 1850s, the United States was still trying to sort out its intractable issues. In an attempt to organize the center of North America – Kansas and Nebraska – without offsetting the slave-free balance, Senator Stephen Douglas of Illinois proposed the Kansas-Nebraska Act. The Kansas-Nebraska Act eliminated the Missouri Compromise line of 1820, which the Compromise of 1850 had maintained. The Missouri Compromise had stipulated that states north of the boundary line determined in that bill would be free, and that states south of it *could* have slavery. This was essential to maintaining the balance of slave and free states in the Union. The Kansas-Nebraska Act, however, ignored the line completely and proposed that all new territories be organized by popular sovereignty. Settlers could vote whether they wanted their state to be slave or free.

Stephen Douglas, "The Little Giant"

When popular sovereignty became the standard in Kansas and Nebraska, the primary result was that thousands of zealous pro-slavery and anti-slavery advocates both moved to Kansas to influence the vote, creating a dangerous (and ultimately deadly) mix. Numerous attacks took place between the two sides, and many pro-slavery Missourians organized attacks on Kansas towns just across the border.

The best known abolitionist in Bleeding Kansas was a middle aged man named John Brown. A radical abolitionist, Brown organized a small band of like-minded followers and fought with the armed groups of pro-slavery men in Kansas for several months, including a notorious incident known as the Pottawatomie Massacre, in which Brown's supporters murdered five men. Over 50 people died before John Brown left the territory, which ultimately entered the Union as a free state in 1859.

John Brown

After his activities in Kansas, John Brown spent the next few years raising money in New England, which would bring him into direct contact with important abolitionist leaders, including Frederick Douglass. Brown had previously organized a small raiding party that succeeded in raiding a Missouri farm and freeing 11 slaves, but he set his sights on far larger objectives. In 1859, Brown began to set a new plan in motion that he hoped would create a full scale slave uprising in the South. Brown's plan relied on raiding Harpers Ferry, a strategically located armory in western Virginia that had been the main federal arms depot after the Revolution. Given its proximity to the South, Brown hoped to seize thousands of rifles and move them south, gathering slaves and swelling his numbers as he went. The slaves would then be armed and ready to help free more slaves, inevitably fighting Southern militias along the way.

In recognition of how important escaped slave Frederick Douglass had become among abolitionists, Brown attempted to enlist the support of Douglass by informing him of the plans. While Douglass didn't blow the whistle on Brown, he told Brown that violence would only further enrage the South, and slaveholders might only retaliate further against slaves with devastating consequences. Instead of helping Brown, Douglass dissuaded freed blacks from joining Brown's group because he believed it was doomed to fail.

Despite that, in July 1859, Brown traveled to Harper's Ferry under an assumed name and waited for his recruits, but he struggled to get even 20 people to join him. Rather than call off the plan, however, Brown went ahead with it. That fall, Brown and his men used hundreds of rifles to seize the armory at Harper's Ferry, but the plan went haywire from the start, and word of his attack quickly spread. Local pro-slavery men formed a militia and pinned Brown and his men down while they were still at the armory.

After being called to Harpers Ferry, Robert E. Lee took decisive command of a troop of marines stationed there, surrounded the arsenal, and gave Brown the opportunity to surrender peaceably. When Brown refused, Lee ordered the doors be broken down and Brown taken captive, an affair that reportedly lasted just three minutes. A few of Brown's men were killed, but Brown was taken alive. Lee earned acclaim for accomplishing this task so quickly and efficiently.

Young JEB Stuart played an active role in opposing the raid at Harpers Ferry. In October of 1859, while conducting business in Washington, D.C., Stuart volunteered to carry secret instructions to Lieutenant Colonel Robert E. Lee and then accompany him and a squad of U. S. Military Militia to Harpers Ferry, where Brown had staged a raid on the armory. While delivering Lee's written ultimatum to the leader of the raid, who was going by the pseudonym Isaac Smith, Stuart remembered "Old Ossawatomie Brown" from the events at Bleeding Kansas, and ultimately assisted in his arrest.

The fallout from John Brown's raid on Harpers Ferry was intense. Southerners had long suspected that abolitionists hoped to arm the slaves and use violence to abolish slavery, and Brown's raid seemed to confirm that. Meanwhile, much of the northern press praised Brown for his actions. In the South, conspiracy theories ran wild about who had supported the raid, and many believed prominent abolitionist Republicans had been behind the raid as well. On the day of his execution, Brown wrote, "I, John Brown, am now quite *certain* that the crimes of this *guilty land* will never be purged away but with *blood.* I had, as I now think vainly, flattered myself that without very much bloodshed it might be done."

The man in command of the troops present at Brown's hanging was none other than Thomas Jonathan Jackson, who was ordered to Charlestown in November 1859. After Brown's hanging, the future Stonewall Jackson began to believe war was inevitable, but he wrote his aunt, "I think we have great reason for alarm, but my trust is in God; and I cannot think that He will permit the madness of men to interfere so materially with the Christian labors of this country at home and abroad."

While men like the future Stonewall Jackson were hoping at the time for some sort of grand compromise that would avert war, by the Fall of 1860 everyone could see war on the horizon. With the election of Republican candidate Abraham Lincoln as president on November 6, 1860, many Southerners considered it the final straw. Someone they knew as a "Black Republican", leader of a party whose central platform was to stop the spread of slavery to new states, was now set to be inaugurated as President in March.

Throughout the fall and winter of 1860, Southern calls for secession became increasingly serious. In a last-ditched effort to save the Union, Kentucky's Senator John Crittenden tried to assume the stateliness of his predecessor Henry Clay. Crittenden, however, proved to be no Henry Clay: his proposal that a Constitutional Amendment reinstate the Missouri Compromise line and extend it to the Pacific failed. President Buchanan supported the measure, but President-Elect Lincoln said he refused to allow the further expansion of slavery under any conditions.

The Crittenden Compromise failed on December 18. Two days later, South Carolina seceded from the Union. President Buchanan sat on his hands, believing the Southern states had no right to secede, but that the Federal government had no effective power to prevent secession. In January, Mississippi, Florida, Alabama, Georgia, Louisiana and Kansas followed South Carolina's lead. The Confederacy was formed on February 4th, in Montgomery, Alabama, with former Secretary of War Jefferson Davis as its President. On February 23rd, Texas joined the Confederacy.

Lincoln's predecessor was among those who could see the potential conflict coming from a mile away. As the Confederacy continued to grow during his last months in office, President James Buchanan instructed the federal army to permit the Confederacy to take control of forts in its territory, hoping to avoid a war. Conveniently, this also allowed Southern forces to take control of important forts and land ahead of a potential war, which would make secession and/or a victory in a military conflict easier. Many Southern partisans within the federal government at the end of 1860 took advantage of these opportunities to help Southern states ahead of time.

One of the forts in the South was Fort Sumter, an important but undermanned and undersupplied fort in the harbor of Charleston, South Carolina. Buchanan attempted to resupply Fort Sumter in the first few months of 1860, but the attempt failed when Southern sympathizers in the harbor fired on the resupply ship.

In his Inauguration Speech, President Lincoln struck a moderate tone. Unlike most Inauguration Addresses, which are typically followed by balls and a "honeymoon" period, Lincoln's came amid a major political crisis. To reassure the South, he reiterated his belief in the legal status of slavery in the South, but that its expansion into the Western territories was to be restricted. He outlined the illegality of secession and refused to acknowledge the South's secession, and promised to continue to deliver U.S. mail in the seceded states. Most importantly, he pledged to not use force unless his obligation to protect Federal property was restricted: "In doing this there needs to be no bloodshed or violence, and there shall be none unless it be forced upon the national authority. The power confided to me will be used to hold, occupy, and posess the property and places belonging to the Government and to collect the duties and imposts; but beyond what may be necessary for these objects, there will be no invasion, no using of force against or among the people anywhere."

Chapter 5: The Start of the Civil War

Lincoln had promised that it would not be the North that started a potential war, but he was also aware of the possibility of the South initiating conflict. Although he vowed not to fire the first shot, Lincoln was likely aware that his attempt to resupply Fort Sumter in Charleston Harbor would draw Southern fire; it had already happened under Buchanan's watch. After his inauguration, President Lincoln informed South Carolina governor Francis Pickens that he was sending supplies to the undermanned garrison at Fort Sumter. When Lincoln made clear that he would attempt to resupply the fort, Davis ordered Beauregard to demand its surrender and prevent the resupplying of the garrison.

In early April, the ship Lincoln sent to resupply the fort was fired upon and turned around. On April 9, Confederate President Davis sent word to General Beauregard to demand the fort's evacuation. At the time, the federal garrison consisted of Major Robert Anderson, Beauregard's artillery instructor from West Point, and 76 troops. Even before the bombardment, upon learning that he was opposed by Beauregard, Anderson remarked that the Southern forces in Charleston harbor would be exercised with "skill and sound judgment". Beauregard also remembered his former superior, and before the bombardment, he sent brandy, whiskey and cigars to Anderson and his garrison, gifts the Major refused.

At 4:30 a.m. on the morning of April 12, 1861, Beauregard ordered the first shots to be fired at Fort Sumter, effectively igniting the Civil War. After nearly 34 hours and thousands of rounds fired from 47 artillery guns and mortars ringing the harbor, on April 14, 1861, Major Anderson surrendered Fort Sumter, marking the first Confederate victory. No casualties were suffered on either side during the dueling bombardments across Charleston harbor, but, ironically, two Union soldiers were killed by an accidental explosion during the surrender ceremonies.

Beauregard

After the attack on Fort Sumter, support for both the northern and southern cause rose. Two days later, Lincoln issued a *call-to-arms* asking for 75,000 volunteers. That led to the secession of Virginia, Tennessee, North Carolina, and Arkansas, with the loyalty of border states like Kentucky, Maryland, and Missouri still somewhat up in the air. The large number of southern sympathizers in these states buoyed the Confederates' hopes that those too would soon join the South. Moreover, the loss of these border states, especially Virginia, all deeply depressed Lincoln. Just weeks before, prominent Virginians had reassured Lincoln that the state's historic place in American history made its citizens eager to save the Union. But as soon as Lincoln made any assertive moves to save the Union, Virginia seceded. This greatly concerned Lincoln, who worried Virginia's secession made it more likely other border states and/or Maryland would secede as well.

Despite the loss of Fort Sumter, the North expected a relatively quick victory. Their expectations weren't unrealistic, due to the Union's overwhelming economic advantages over the South. At the start of the war, the Union had a population of over 22 million. The South had a population of 9 million, nearly 4 million of whom were slaves. Union states contained 90% of the manufacturing capacity of the country and 97% of the weapon manufacturing capacity. Union states also possessed over 70% of the total railroads in the pre-war United States at the start of the war, and the Union also controlled 80% of the shipbuilding capacity of the pre-war United States.

As Johnston makes it clear at the beginning of his Civil War memoirs, his choice of sides was always dependent on whether the state of Virginia stayed in the Union or joined the Confederacy. Johnston discusses the decision in the wake of Fort Sumter:

"The composition of the convention assembled in Richmond in the spring of 1861, to consider the question of secession, proved that the people of Virginia did not regard Mr. Lincoln's election as a sufficient cause for that measure, for at least two-thirds of its members were elected as "Union men." And they and their constituents continued to be so, until the determination to "coerce" the seceded States was proclaimed by the President of the United States, and Virginia required to furnish her quota of the troops to be organized for the purpose. War being then inevitable, and the convention compelled to decide whether the State should aid in the subjugation of the other Southern States, or join them in the defense of principles it had professed since 1789 -- belong to the invading party, or to that standing on the defensive — it chose the latter, and passed its ordinance of secession. The people confirmed that choice by an overwhelming vote.

The passage of that ordinance, in secret session on the 17th of April, was not known in Washington, where, as Quartermaster-General of the United States Army, I was then stationed, until the 19th. I believed, like most others, that the division of the country would be permanent; and that, apart from any right of secession, the revolution begun was justified by the maxims so often repeated by Americans, that free government is founded on the consent of the governed, and that every community strong enough to establish and maintain its independence has a right to assert it. Having been educated in such opinions, I naturally determined to return to the State of which I was a native, join the people among whom I was born, and live with my kindred, and, if necessary, fight in their defense.

Accordingly, the resignation of my commission, written on Saturday, was offered to the Secretary of War Monday morning. That gentleman was requested, at the same time, to instruct the Adjutant-General, who had kindly accompanied me, to write the order announcing its acceptance, immediately.

No other officer of the United States Army of equal rank, that of brigadier-general, relinquished his position in it to join the Southern Confederacy."

Thus, when his native state of Virginia seceded from the Union in 1861, Brigadier General Johnston resigned his commission in the Regular Army, writing on April 22, "I must go with the South, though the action is in the last degree ungrateful. I owe all that I am to the government of the United States. It has educated me and clothed me with honor. To leave the service is a hard necessity, but I must go. Though I am resigning my position, I trust I may never draw my sword against my flag." Now at the age of 54, Joseph Johnston had served more than 30 years in the service of the United States government, and as he was quick to note, he was the highest-ranking U. S. Army officer to resign his commission to join the South.

On May 4, 1861, Johnston was commissioned a major general in the Virginia militia, but just two weeks later he lost that position to Robert E. Lee after the Virginia Convention decided that only one major general was required in the state army, and that Lee was the better candidate. Johnston was humiliated, and when he was subsequently offered a brigadier general commission from the state, he declined it. Instead, on May 14 he accepted instead a brigadier general commission in the Confederate Army.

Johnston relieved Colonel Thomas Jonathan "Stonewall" Jackson of command at Harpers Ferry that month, and his first official command decision was ordering the evacuation of the pivotal armory. Johnston insisted that he simply didn't have the manpower to hold it, immediately causing consternation among his superiors. By July, Johnston had organized the Army of the Shenandoah.

Although the North blockaded the South throughout the Civil War and eventually controlled the entire Mississippi River by 1863, the war could not be won without land battles, which doomed hundreds of thousands of soldiers on each side. This is because the Civil War generals began the war employing tactics from the Napoleonic Era, which saw Napoleon dominate the European continent and win crushing victories against large armies. However, the weapons available in 1861 were far more accurate than they had been 50 years earlier. In particular, new rifled barrels created common infantry weapons with deadly accuracy of up to 100 yards, at a time when generals were still leading massed infantry charges with fixed bayonets and attempting to march their men close enough to engage in hand-to-hand combat.

On May 14, 1861, Brig. General Irvin McDowell was appointed by President Abraham Lincoln to command the Army of Northeastern Virginia. After Fort Sumter, the Lincoln Administration pushed for a quick invasion of Virginia, with the intent of defeating Confederate forces and marching toward the Confederate capitol of Richmond. Lincoln pressed Irvin McDowell to push forward. Despite the fact that McDowell knew his troops were inexperienced and unready, pressure from the Washington politicians forced him to launch a premature offensive against Confederate forces in Northern Virginia. His strategy during the First Battle of Bull Run was grand, but it proved far too difficult for his inexperienced troops to carry out effectively.

McDowell

In late Spring 1861, Davis ordered Beauregard to northern Virginia as second-in-command to General Johnston, where he was to oppose the federal forces building up under McDowell. Though Johnston was the superior in rank, he ceded authority to Beauregard near Manassas Junction, leaving Beauregard in command there. At Manassas, Beauregard took charge of the Confederate forces assembling near the rail junction at Manassas and had his men construct defenses along a 14 mile front along Bull Run Creek. Meanwhile, Johnston continued gathering and training additional troops in the Shenandoah Valley.

McDowell's strategy during the First Battle of Bull Run was grand, and in many ways it was the forerunner of a tactic Lee and Jackson executed brilliantly on nearly the same field during the Second Battle of Bull Run or Manassas in August 1862. McDowell's plan called for parts of his army to pin down Beauregard's Confederate soldiers in front while marching another wing of his army around the flank and into the enemy's rear, rolling up the line. McDowell assumed the Confederates would be forced to abandon Manassas Junction and fall back to the next defensible line, the Rappahannock River. In July 1861, however, this proved far too difficult for his inexperienced troops to carry out effectively.

On July 18, Union General Irwin McDowell set out with two divisions on a twelve-mile circuitous march west from Centreville, Virginia to cross Bull Run at Sudley Springs Ford, intending to strike Beauregard's troops at Manassas-Sudley Road in an effort to turn the Southern left flank. Meanwhile, another division was set to drive directly west along the turnpike and across Stone Bridge, while back at Centreville, another division stayed in reserve. The remaining division, scattered along the lines of communication all the way back to

Washington but would ultimately take no part in the ensuing battle, made a total of 32,000 men at McDowell's disposal.

The First Battle of Bull Run made history in several ways. McDowell's army met Fort Sumter hero P.G.T. Beauregard's Confederate army near the railroad junction at Manassas on July 21, 1861. Located just 25 miles away from Washington D.C., many civilians from Washington came to watch what they expected to be a rout of Confederate forces. A Confederate observer of the time described the scenario as "a procession including gay women and strumpets who carried picnic baskets, opera glasses, and champagne."

For awhile, it appeared as though it would be a Union victory, but McDowell's strategy fell apart thanks to railroads. Confederate reinforcements under General Johnston arrived by train in the middle of the day, a first in the history of American warfare. With Johnston's army arriving midday on July 21, it evened up the numbers between Union and Confederate. Although he was the senior officer when he arrived, Johnston realized he lacked familiarity with the terrain, so he continued to defer tactical planning of the battle to his junior, Brig. General Beauregard.

By midday on July 21, Beauregard was still unclear as to the tack General Irvin McDowell was planning, so Johnston decided to reconnoiter—deciding that the critical point was to the north of his headquarters (the Lewis house, "Portici") at a place called Henry House Hill, announcing, "The battle is there . . . I am going!" Following Johnston's lead, Beauregard advanced to discover that Johnston had encountered what remained of the Confederate Fourth Alabama--all of whose field officers had been killed. Rallying the disoriented men to reinforce the newly-forming Confederate line, Johnston is said to have consoled humiliated Brig. General Barnard Bee, urging him to lead his men back into the fight.

Convinced that Johnston's talents would be best applied to organizing newly-arriving reinforcements rather than providing *at-the-front* tactical leadership, Beauregard relegated Johnston to an organizational role for the remainder of the battle--allowing Beauregard to initiate an advance of the entire Confederate front line, which resulted in crumbling the Union line and forcing a hasty Union withdrawal.

Upon shoring up the Confederates' left flank, it was Johnston's troops, led by Jackson's brigade, that helped reverse the Union's momentum and ultimately turn the tide. As the battle's momentum switched, the inexperienced Union troops were routed and retreated in disorder back toward Washington in an unorganized mass. With over 350 killed on each side, it was the deadliest battle in American history to date, and both the Confederacy and the Union were quickly served notice that the war would be much more costly than either side had believed.

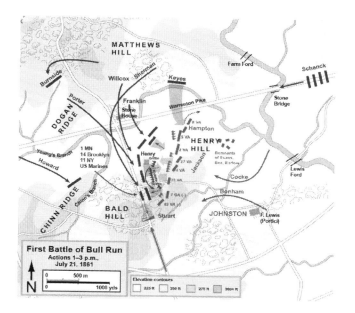

Ironically, McDowell commanded the Army of Northeastern Virginia and Joseph E. Johnston commanded the Army of the Potomac at First Bull Run. A little over a year later it would be Lee's Army of Northern Virginia fighting elements of the Union Army of the Potomac at Second Bull Run, on nearly the same ground.

Ironically, McDowell commanded the Army of Northeastern Virginia and Joseph E. Johnston commanded the Army of the Potomac at First Bull Run. A little over a year later it would be Lee's Army of Northern Virginia fighting elements of the Union Army of the Potomac at Second Bull Run, on nearly the same ground.

It was also during First Manassas or Bull Run that Jackson earned the famous nickname "Stonewall", but there is an enduring mystery over the origin of his nickname. What is known is that during the battle, Jackson's brigade arrived as reinforcements at a crucial part of the battlefield on the Confederate left. Confederate Brigadier General Barnard Bee, commanding a nearby brigade, commanded his men to reestablish their battle line next to Jackson's brigade, shouting, "There is Jackson standing like a stone wall. Rally behind the Virginians." General Bee was mortally wounded shortly after that command and died the following day. Thus, it remains unclear whether Bee was complimenting Jackson's brigade for standing firm or whether he was criticizing Jackson's brigade for inaction. Without Bee around to explain his command, nobody will ever know for certain. However, that has not stopped people from debating Bee's comment. Regardless, the nickname Stonewall stuck, and Jackson was henceforth known as Stonewall Jackson. His brigade also inherited the title, known throughout the war as the Stonewall brigade.

Stonewall Jackson

Arriving just as the Union Army was in full retreat, Confederate President Jefferson Davis was unaware of how instrumental Johnston had been to the Confederate victory, and Beauregard took advantage by claiming full credit for the victory and subsequently receiving the majority of public admiration. Given his fame for the success at Fort Sumter, Beauregard was already well-positioned to be cast as the hero of this major battle.

For his role in the Confederacy's first significant victory of the Civil War, Johnston was promoted to the rank of full general. Johnston, however, was personally displeased that he ranked fourth in overall seniority in the Confederate Army with three others, including Lee, having been promoted ahead of him. As the most senior officer of the U. S. Army to have sided with the South, he felt slighted that he was not made ranking general, as protocol would have suggested. In September 1861, Johnston wrote Davis, "It [the ranking of senior generals] seeks to tarnish my fair fame as a soldier and a man, earned by more than thirty years of laborious and perilous service. I had but this, the scars of many wounds, all honestly taken in my front and in the front of battle, and my father's Revolutionary sword. It was delivered to me from his venerated hand, without a stain of dishonor. Its blade is still unblemished as when it passed from his hand to mine. I drew it in the war, not for rank or fame, but to defend the sacred soil, the homes and hearths, the women and children; aye, and the men of my mother Virginia, my native South."

Davis was so taken aback by the letter that he actually brought it up amongst his Cabinet. For his own part, Davis argued that Albert Sidney Johnston and Lee had been full colonels in the U.S. Army, whereas Johnston had been only a lieutenant colonel in battle. Since Johnston's rank of brigadier general was for a staff position, Davis asserted it should be given less credence among battlefield commanders. Before too much credit is given to Davis, however, it must be noted that historians have strongly criticized him for notoriously playing favorites with his generals during the war. Some of his friends before the war, including Braxton Bragg, Albert Sidney Johnston and Robert E. Lee, were no doubt given preferential treatment throughout the war, while generals like Beauregard and Joseph Johnston found themselves on the outside.

Furthermore, although he strongly desired and intended to lead the South to a decisive victory, Johnston believed that Jefferson Davis's solution to the shortage of men, that of shuttling troops back and forth between theaters as needed, had no chance of actually working. Tensions then further escalated when his suspicions were confirmed. Johnston would continue to lose faith in the president's overall strategy, as well as respect for Davis himself, as Davis continued to promote an aggressive war that "took the action to the enemy." To Johnston, this strategy was ignorantly oblivious to the reality that the South was short of both manpower and supplies, and that a defensive war was the only logical one to fight.

Chapter 6: The Peninsula Campaign

After First Manassas, Johnston and his army stayed camped near the outskirts of Washington D.C., while the North reorganized the Army of the Potomac under Johnston's acquaintance, George B. McClellan. McClellan was widely considered a prodigy for his West Point years, his service in Mexico, his observation during the Crimean War, and his oft-forgotten campaign in Western Virginia against Robert E. Lee in 1861. Though he is best known for his shortcomings today, McClellan had nearly ended Lee's Civil War career before it started, as General Lee was blamed throughout the South for losing western Virginia after his defeat at the Battle of Cheat Mountain. Lee would eventually be reassigned to constructing coastal defenses on the East Coast, and when his men dug trenches in preparation for the defense of Richmond, he was derisively dubbed the "King of Spades". That Lee was even in position to assume command of the Army of Northern Virginia the following year during the Peninsula Campaign was due more to his friendship with Jefferson Davis than anything else. The fact Davis played favorites with his generals crippled the South throughout the war, but it certainly worked in the South's favor with Lee.

As he was reorganizing the Army of the Potomac, McClellan vastly overestimated the strength of Johnston's army, leading him to plan an amphibious assault on Richmond that avoided Johnston's army in his front. In response, Johnston moved his army toward Culpeper Court House, which angered President Davis because it signified a retreat. For that reason, Davis brought Lee to Richmond as a military adviser, and he began to constrain Johnston's authority by issuing direct orders himself.

However, Johnston's movement had disrupted McClellan's anticipated landing spot. McClellan had already faced a number of issues in planning the campaign even before reaching the jumpoff point. The first option for the landing spot (Urbana) had been scrapped, and there was bickering over the amount of troops left around Washington without the Army of the Potomac fighting on the Overland line. Finally, in March of 1862, after nine months in command, General McClellan began his invasion of Virginia, initiating what would become known as the "Peninsula Campaign." Showing his proclivity for turning movement and grand strategy, McClellan completely shifted the theater of operations. Rather than march directly into Richmond and use his superior numbers to assert domination, he opted to exploit the Union sea dominance and move his army via an immense naval flotilla down the Potomac into Chesapeake Bay and land at Fort Monroe in Hampton, Virginia, at the southern tip of the Virginia Peninsula. In addition to his 130,000 thousand men, he moved 15,000 thousand horses and mules by boat as well. There he planned for an additional 80,000 men to join him, at which time he would advance westward to Richmond. One of the European observers likened the launch of the campaign to the "stride of a giant."

McClellan's Peninsula Campaign has been analyzed meticulously and is considered one of the grandest failures of the Union war effort, with McClellan made the scapegoat. In actuality, there was plenty of blame to go around, including Lincoln and his Administration, which was so concerned about Stonewall Jackson's army in the Shenandoah Valley that several Union armies were left in the Valley to defend Washington D.C., and even more were held back from McClellan for fear of the capital's safety. The Administration also micromanaged the deployment of certain divisions, and with Stanton's decision to shut down recruiting stations in early 1862, combined with the Confederacy concentrating all their troops in the area, the Army of the Potomac was eventually outnumbered in front of Richmond.

At the beginning of the campaign, however, McClellen had vastly superior numbers at his disposal, with only about 70,000 Confederate troops on the entirety of the peninsula and fewer than 17,000 between him and Richmond. McClellan was unaware of this decisive advantage, however, because of the intelligence reports he kept receiving from Allen Pinkerton, which vastly overstated the number of available Confederate soldiers.

As Johnston marched his army to oppose McClellan, he was fully aware that he was severely outnumbered, even if McClellan didn't know that. For that reason, he was in constant communication with the leadership in Richmond, and in April he continued trying to persuade Davis and Lee that the best course of action would be to dig in and fight defensively around Richmond. President Davis would have none of it.

From the beginning, McClellan's caution and the narrow width of the Peninsula worked against his army. At Yorktown, which had been the site of a decisive siege during the Revolution, McClellan's initial hopes of surrounding and enveloping the Confederate lines through the use of the Navy was scuttled when the Navy couldn't promise that it'd be able to operate in the area. That allowed General John Magruder, whose Confederate forces were outmanned nearly 4-1, to hold Yorktown for the entire month of April. Magruder accomplished it by completely deceiving the federals, at times marching his men in circles to make McClellan think his army was many times larger. Other times, he spread his artillery batteries across the line and fired liberally and sporadically at the Union lines, just to give the impression that the Confederates had huge numbers. The ruse worked, leaving the Union command thinking there were 100,000 Confederates.

As a result of the misimpressions, McClellan chose not to attack Yorktown in force, instead opting to lay siege to it. In part, this was due to the decisive advantage the Union had in siege equipment, including massive mortars and artillery. The siege successfully captured Yorktown in early May with only about 500 casualties, but Magruder bought enough time for Johnston's army to confront McClellan on the Peninsula.

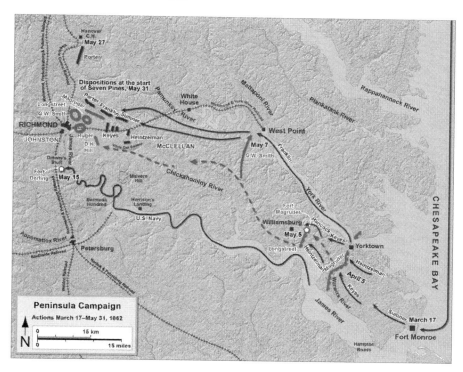

After withdrawing from Yorktown, McClellan sent Stoneman's cavalry in pursuit and attempted to move swiftly enough to cut off Johnston's retreat by use of Navy ships. At the battle of Williamsburg, which the Confederates fought as a delaying action to retreat, the South lost 1600 and the Union lost 2200 soldiers, but McClellan labeled it a "brilliant victory" over superior forces. Even then, the Union success was owed to Brigadier General Winfield Scott Hancock, who had disregarded orders to withdraw from corps commander Sumner and repulsed a Confederate attack. For the action, which McClellan described as "superb", Hancock had earned his nickname "Hancock the Superb".

Hancock the Superb

After Williamsburg, the Union army still had a nearly 2-1 advantage in manpower, so Johnston continued to gradually pull his troops back to a line of defense nearer Richmond as McClellan advanced. In conjunction, the U.S. Navy began moving its operations further up the James River, until it could get within 7 miles of the Confederate capital before being opposed by a Southern fort. McClellan continued to attempt to turn Johnston's flank, until the two armies were facing each other along the Chickahominy River. McClellan's Army of the Potomac got close enough to Richmond that they could see the city's church steeples.

By the end of May, Stonewall Jackson had startlingly defeated three separate Northern armies in the Valley, inducing Lincoln to hold back the I Corps from McClellan. When McClellan was forced to extend his line north to link up with troops that he expected to be sent overland to him, Johnston learned that McClellan was moving along the Chickahominy River. It was at this point that Johnston got uncharacteristically aggressive. Johnston had run out of breathing space for his army, and he believed McCellan was seeking to link up with McDowell's forces. Moreover, about a third of McClellan's army was south of the river, while the other parts of the army were still north of it, offering Johnston an enticing target. After a quick deluge turned the river into a rushing torrent that would make it impossible or the Union army to link back up or aid each other, Johnston drew up a very complex plan of attack for different wings of his army, and struck at the Army of the Potomac at the Battle of Seven Pines on May 31, 1862.

Like McDowell's plan for First Bull Run, the plan proved too complicated for Johnston's army to execute, and after a day of bloody fighting little was accomplished from a technical standpoint. At one point during the Battle of Seven Pines, Confederates under General James Longstreet marched in the wrong direction down the wrong road, causing congestion and confusion among other Confederate units and ultimately weakening the effectiveness of the massive Confederate counterattack launched against McClellan. Johnston wrote in his memoirs, "The operations of the Confederate troops in this battle were very much retarded by the dense woods and thickets that covered the ground, and by the deep mud and broad ponds of rain-water, in many places more than knee-deep, through which they had to struggle."

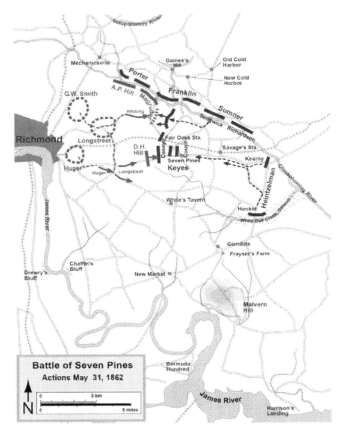

By the time the fighting was finished, nearly 40,000 had been engaged on both sides, and it was the biggest battle in the Eastern theater to date (second only to Shiloh at the time). However, McClellan was rattled by the attack, and near the end of the fighting that night Johnston had attempted to rally his men by riding up and down the battleline only to be nearly blown off his horse by artillery fire and having to be taken off the field. Johnston explained, "About seven o'clock I received a slight wound in the right shoulder from a musket-shot, and, a few moments after, was unhorsed by a heavy fragment of shell which struck my breast. Those around had me borne from the field in an ambulance; not, however, before the President, who was with General Lee, not far in the rear, had heard of the accident, and visited me, manifesting great concern, as he continued to do until I was out of danger." Having been seriously wounded, Johnston's command was given the following day to military advisor Robert E. Lee.

Johnston would later remark ruefully:

"I was eager to fight on the 31st, from the belief that the flood in the Chickahominy would be at its height that day, and the two parts of the Federal army completely separated by it: it was too soon, however. We should have gained the advantage fully by a day's delay. This would also have given us an accession of about eight thousand men that arrived from the south next morning, under Major-General Holmes and Brigadier-General Ripley; they had been ordered to Richmond without my knowledge, nor was I informed of their approach.8 After this battle of Seven Pines-or Fair Oaks, as the Northern people prefer to call it-General McClellan made no step forward, but employed his troops industriously in intrenching themselves.

I had repeatedly suggested to the Administration the formation of a great army to repel McClellan's invasion, by assembling all the Confederate forces, available for the object, near Richmond. As soon as I had lost the command of the Army of Virginia by wounds in battle, my suggestion was adopted. In that way, the largest Confederate army that ever fought, was formed in the month of June, by strengthening the forces near Richmond with troops from North and South Carolina and Georgia. But, while the Confederate Government was forming this great army, the Federal general was, with equal industry, employed in making defensive arrangements; so that in the "seven days fighting" his intrenchments so covered the operation of "change of base," that it was attended with little loss, considering the close proximity and repeated engagements of two such armies. Had ours been so strengthened in time to attack that of the United States when it reached the Chickahominy, and before being intrenched, results might and ought to have been decisive; still, that army, as led by its distinguished commander, compelled the Federal general to abandon his plan of operations, and reduced him to the defensive, and carried back the war to Northern Virginia."

Johnston's comments were in response to the results of the final fighting of the Peninsula Campaign, commonly referred to as the Seven Days Battles. Although the Battle of Seven Pines was tactically inconclusive, McClellan's resolve to keep pushing forward vanished. He maneuvered his army so that it was all south of the Chickahominy, but as he settled in for an expected siege, Lee went about preparing Richmond's defenses and devising his own aggressive attacks.

With more Confederate troops swelling the ranks, Lee's army was McClellan's equal by late June, and on June 25, Lee commenced an all-out attempt to destroy McClellan's army in a series of fierce battles known as the Seven Days Battles. After a stalemate in the first fighting at Oak Grove, Lee's army kept pushing ahead, using Stonewall Jackson to attack McClellan's right.

Although Stonewall Jackson was unusually lethargic during the week's fighting, the appearance of his "foot cavalry" spooked McClellan even more, and McClellan was now certain he was opposed by 200,000 men, more than double the actual size of Lee's army. It also made McClellan think that the Confederates were threatening his supply line, forcing him to shift his army toward the James River to draw supplies.

On June 26, the Union defenders sharply repulsed the Confederate attacks at Mechanicsville, in part due to the fact that Stonewall Jackson had his troops bivouac for the night despite the fact heavy gunfire indicating a large battle was popping off within earshot. When the Confederates had more success the next day at Gaines' Mills, McClellan continued his strategic retreat, maneuvering his army toward a defensive position on the James River and all but abandoning the siege.

McClellan managed to keep his forces in tact (mostly through the efforts of his field generals), ultimately retreating to Harrison's Landing on the James River and establishing a new base of operation. Feeling increasingly at odds with his superiors, in a letter sent from Gaines' Mills, Virginia dated June 28, 1862, a frustrated McClellan wrote to Secretary of War Stanton, "If I save the army now, I tell you plainly that I owe no thanks to any other person in the Washington. You have done your best to sacrifice this army." McClellan's argument, however, flies in the face of common knowledge that he had become so obsessed with having sufficient supplies that he'd actually moved to Gaines' Mill to accommodate the massive amount of provisions he'd accumulated. Ultimately unable to move his cache of supplies as quickly as his men were needed, McClellan eventually ran railroad cars full of food and supplies into the Pamunkey River rather than leave them behind for the Confederates.

Despite the fact all of Lee's battle plans had been poorly executed by his generals, particularly Stonewall Jackson, he ordered one final assault against McClellan's army at Malvern Hill. Incredibly, McClellan was not even on the field for that battle, having left via steamboat back to Harrison's Landing. Biographer Ethan Rafuse notes McClellan's absence from the battlefield was inexcusable, literally leaving the Army of the Potomac leaderless during pitched battle, but McClellan often behaved cooly under fire, so it is likely not a question of McClellan's personal courage.

Ironically, Malvern Hill was one of the Union army's biggest successes during the Peninsula Campaign. Union artillery had silenced its Confederate counterparts, but Lee still ordered an infantry attack by D.H. Hill's division, which never got within 100 yards of the Union line. After the war, Hill famously referred to Malvern Hill, "It wasn't war. It was murder." Later that evening, as General Isaac Trimble (who is best known for leading a division during Pickett's Charge at Gettysburg) began moving his troops forward as if to attack, he was stopped by Stonewall Jackson, who asked "What are you going to do?" When Trimble replied that he was going to charge, Jackson countered, "General Hill has just tried with his entire division and been repulsed. I guess you'd better not try it."

After Malvern Hill, McClellan withdrew his army to Harrison's Landing, where it was protected by the U.S. Navy along the James River and had its flanks secured by the river itself. At this point, the bureaucratic bickering between McClellan and Washington D.C. started flaring up again, as McClellan refused to recommence an advance without reinforcements. After weeks of indecision, the Army of the Potomac was finally ordered to evacuate the Peninsula and link up with John Pope's army in northern Virginia, as the Administration was more comfortable having their forces fighting on one line instead of exterior lines. Upon his arrival in Washington, McClellan told reporters that his failure to defeat Lee in Virginia was due to Lincoln not sending sufficient reinforcements.

By the time Johnston was recovered and able to reassume command five months later in November of 1862, Lee's Army of Northern Virginia had scored a decisive victory at Second Manassas, and Lee was clearly not going to be replaced. Johnston was subsequently relegated to the Western Theatre.

Chapter 7: Vicksburg

While the Confederates had been mostly successful in the Eastern theater, the Union had made steady advances across the Western theater. Ulysses S. Grant had captured Fort Henry and Fort Donelson in early 1862, the Union had been victorious in the Battle of Shiloh and the Siege of Corinth, and the Union navy had taken New Orleans. By the beginning of 1863, as Grant reassumed command of most of the Western theater, the Union forces were still intent on taking control of the entire Mississippi River, which would have the effect of cutting the Confederacy in two. With Grant's early victories in the war and the Union capture of New Orleans, Grant was reinstated to command at a time when the Confederates' last stronghold on the Mississippi River was at Vicksburg.

Grant's eventual capitulation of Vicksburg is considered one of the turning points of the Civil War, but his initial attempts to advance towards Vicksburg met with several miserable failures. First, Grant's supply base at Holly Springs was captured. Then an assault launched by General Sherman at Chickasaw Bayou was easily repulsed by Confederate forces with serious Union casualties. Grant then attempted to have his men build canals north and west of the city to facilitate transportation, which included grueling work and disease in the bayous.

Finally, on April 30, 1863, Grant finally launched the successful campaign against Vicksburg, using a strategy that even Sherman was doubtful about. Grant's army marched down the western side of the Mississippi River while the navy covered his movements, then crossed the river south of Vicksburg and quickly took Port Gibson on May 1, Grand Gulf on May 3, and Raymond on May 12. Realizing Vicksburg was the objective, the Confederate forces under the command of Pemberton gathered in that vicinity, but instead of going directly for Vicksburg, Grant took the state capital of Jackson instead, effectively isolating Vicksburg. Pemberton's garrison now had broken communication and supply lines.

Pemberton

In May 1863, General Johnston had been given command of the Confederacy's Department of the West, placing him under control of most of the Confederate forces in that theater. Johnston was almost immediately forced to fight a delaying rear guard action in the capital of Jackson against Grant, even while insisting he was physically unfit for field command. After that retreat, his most pressing concern was Pemberton and the Confederate forces in Mississippi, which were under direct threat from General Ulysses S. Grant's advance against Vicksburg.

Recognizing the critical nature of the situation, Johnston advised General Pemberton to immediately evacuate the city or risk being trapped by Grant's superior forces, further informing the general that he lacked the manpower to relieve him. Pembleton, however, was ordered by Confederate President Jefferson Davis to ignore Johnston and hold the city at all cost. Johnston began moving his forces west in an attempt to link up with Pemberton, but after Grant's victories at Champion Hill (May 16) and Big Black River Bridge (May 17), Pemberton was firmly entrenched in Vicksburg, and the nearly 25,000 men under Johnston had no way of relieving Grant's siege.

Completely choked off, the people of Vicksburg began to starve, with many eating rats to survive. Jefferson Davis and his top military brass were unable to determine how best to relieve Vicksburg and Pemberton, who was widely viewed as an abject failure. The end finally came on July 4, 1863, with Pemberton surrendering Vicksburg and its nearly 35,000 man garrison.

Coincidentally, the surrender of Vicksburg came a day after the Army of the Potomac scored a critical victory at the Battle of Gettysburg in the East, which has widely overshadowed the Vicksburg campaign in Civil War history. Despite the dazzle of Gettysburg, Union forces in the West had just cut the Confederacy in half.

When Vicksburg fell on July 4, 1863, Johnston was bitterly criticized by President Davis for his inaction and was nearly stripped of his commission. For his own part, Johnston heavily criticized Davis. In his memoirs, Johnston ridiculed Davis for giving him what he considered contradictory orders that would've forced him to coordinate the actions of armies across the Western theater even while at the head of an army in the field:

"I maintain that, however the order of May 9th may have been intended, it dissolved practically my connection with General Bragg and his army. For it is certain that while commanding one army in Mississippi, in the presence of the much more powerful one of General Grant, it was impossible for me to direct the operations of another far off in Tennessee, also greatly outnumbered by its enemy. That a general should command but one army, and that every army should have its general present with it, are maxims observed by all governments-because the world has produced few men competent to command a large army when present with it, and none capable of directing the operations of one hundreds of miles off; still less one capable of doing both at the same time. My interpretation of the order in question was the only one consistent with the respect I entertained for the President's knowledge of military affairs, and therefore did not make me obnoxious to the rebuke expressed in every part of this letter. My belief that he was incapable of an absurdity too gross to have been committed by the government of any other civilized nation, certainly should not have brought upon me his harsh censure."

The antagonistic relationship between Davis and Johnston was so public at this point that it was noted by the famous Southern diarist Mary Chesnut, who kept perhaps the most famous civilian diary of the war. In one entry, Chesnut wrote, "The President detests Joe Johnston for all the trouble he has given him, and General Joe returns the compliment with compound interest. His hatred of Jeff Davis amounts to a religion. With him it colors all things."

Grant and Sherman had received much of the acclaim out West in 1862 and 1863, but it was Sherman's friend George H. Thomas's turn at the Battle of Chickamauga. On September 19-20, 1863, the Confederate Army of Tennessee under Braxton Bragg decisively defeated General Rosecrans' Army of the Cumberland at the Battle of Chickamauga. Rosecrans committed a blunder by exposing a gap in part of his line that General James Longstreet drove through, sending Rosecrans and nearly 20,000 of his men into a disorderly retreat. The destruction of the entire army was prevented by General George H. Thomas, who rallied the remaining parts of the army and formed a defensive stand on Horseshoe Ridge. Dubbed "The Rock of Chickamauga", Thomas's heroics ensured that Rosecrans' army was able to successfully retreat back to Chattanooga.

Grant

Once the Union forces reached Chattanooga, however, it was the Confederates' turn to lay siege, with Bragg's army mostly encircling the city. On October 17, 1863, Grant was given command of the Military Division of the Mississippi which included the departments of Ohio, Cumberland, and Tennessee, and instructed to relieve Chattanooga. That promotion put Grant in command over the entire West, requiring Sherman to take command of the Army of the Tennessee.

What followed were some of the most amazing operations of the Civil War. Grant relieved Rosecrans and personally came to Chattanooga to oversee the effort, placing General Thomas in charge of reorganizing the Army of the Cumberland. Meanwhile, Lincoln detached General Hooker and two divisions from the Army of the Potomac and sent them west to reinforce the garrison at Chattanooga. However, Grant instead used Hooker's men to establish the "Cracker Line", a makeshift supply line that moved food and resources into Chattanooga from Hooker's position on Lookout Mountain.

In November 1863, the situation at Chattanooga was dire enough that Grant took the offensive in an attempt to lift the siege. By now the Confederates were holding important high ground at positions like Lookout Mountain and Missionary Ridge. First Grant ordered General Sherman and four divisions of his Army of the Tennessee to attack Bragg's right flank, but the attempt was unsuccessful. Then, in an attempt to make an all out push, Grant ordered all forces in the vicinity to make an attack on Bragg's men.

On November 24, 1863 Maj. Gen. Hooker captured Lookout Mountain in order to divert some of Bragg's men away from their commanding position on Missionary Ridge. Sherman's army was supposed to be one of the main assaulting forces, but it was repulsed and separated from Union forces near the base of Missionary Ridge. Once again, it was George H. Thomas's day.

The victory at Chattannooga is best remembered for the almost miraculous attack on Missionary Ridge. General Thomas's Army of the Cumberland singlehandedly delivered the stunning victory by storming over Missionary Ridge, and forcing the Confederate army into a disorganized rout. In doing so, the men had actually defied Grant's orders. Grant, initially upset, had only ordered them to take the rifle pits at the base of Missionary Ridge, figuring that a frontal assault on that position would be futile and fatal. The Army of the Cumberland had essentially conducted the most successful frontal assault of the war spontaneously. While Pickett's Charge, still the most famous attack of the war, was one unsuccessful charge, the Army of the Cumberland made over a dozen charges up Missionary Ridge and ultimately succeeded. A Southern writer of the time wrote, "Calamity, defeat, utter ruin. Unless something is done . . . we are irretrievably gone."

In the aftermath of that fighting, Bragg was so thoroughly reviled by some of his senior officers and had proven so incompetent that he was compelled to resign his command. Davis brought him to Richmond to make him a military advisor, and he asked Lieutenant General William J. Hardee, the senior corps commander, to take command. When Hardee refused, Davis considered Beauregard and even Robert E. Lee for the position, who refused it. Ultimately, despite serious reservations about his command style, on December 27, 1863 Davis placed General Johnston in charge of the Army of Tennessee. Davis hoped Johnston would demonstrate more aggressiveness than he had in the past.

Chapter 8: The Atlanta Campaign

Although the Army of the Potomac had been victorious at Gettysburg, Lincoln was still upset at what he perceived to be General George Meade's failure to trap Robert E. Lee's Army of Northern Virginia in Pennsylvania. When Lee retreated from Pennsylvania without much fight from the Army of the Potomac, Lincoln was again discouraged, believing Meade had a chance to end the war if he had been bolder. Though historians dispute that, and the Confederates actually invited attack during their retreat, Lincoln was constantly looking for more aggressive fighters to lead his men.

With Lee continuing to hold off the Army of the Potomac in a stalemate along the same battle lines at the end of 1863, Lincoln shook things up. In March 1864, Grant was promoted to lieutenant general and given command of all the armies of the United States. His first acts of command were to keep General Halleck in position to serve as a liaison between Lincoln and Secretary of War Edwin Stanton. And though it's mostly forgotten today, Grant technically kept General Meade in command of the Army of the Potomac, even though Grant attached himself to that army before the Overland Campaign in 1864 and thus served as its commander for all intents and purposes.

Before beginning the Overland Campaign against Lee's army, Grant, Sherman and Lincoln also began devising a new strategy that would eventually implement total war tactics. Grant aimed to use the Army of the Potomac to attack Lee and/or take Richmond. Meanwhile, General Sherman, now in command of the Department of the West, would attempt to take Atlanta and strike through Georgia. In essence, having already cut the Confederacy in half with Vicksburg campaign, he now intended to bisect the eastern half. On top of all that, Grant and Sherman were now intent on fully depriving the Confederacy of the ability to keep fighting. Sherman put this policy in effect during his March to the Sea by confiscating civilian resources and literally taking the fight to the Southern people. For Grant, it meant a war of attrition that would steadily bleed Lee's Army of Northern Virginia. To take full advantage of the North's manpower, in 1864 the Union ended prisoner exchanges, in an attempt to ensure that the Confederate armies could not be bolstered by paroled prisoners.

By 1864, things were looking so bleak for the South that the Confederate war strategy was simply to ensure Lincoln lost reelection that November, with the hope that a new Democratic president would end the war and recognize the South's independence. With that, and given the shortage in manpower, Lee's strategic objective was to continue defending Richmond, while hoping that Grant would commit some blunder that would allow him a chance to seize an opportunity.

Sherman united the armies for the Atlanta Campaign, which in essence formed the biggest army in American history. Sherman set his sights on the Confederacy's last major industrial city in the West and the General Joseph E. Johnston's Army of Tennessee, which aimed to protect it. After detaching troops for essential garrisons and minor operations, Sherman assembled his nearly 100,000 men and in May 1864 began his invasion of Georgia from Chattanooga, Tennessee, where his forces now spanned a line roughly 500 miles wide. The right wing and the cavalry, under General Oliver O. Howard, was directed to Jonesboro, Milledgeville, and then Atlanta; the left wing under General Henry W. Slocum was sent to Stone Mountain and then on to threaten Augusta before ultimately meeting up with Howard's forces. The 60,000 strong Army of the Cumberland, under General George H. Thomas, formed the backbone of Sherman's forces.

Johnston immediately understood his army's dilemma, and it naturally colored his generalship. He explained in his memoirs:

"My own operations, then and subsequently, were determined by the relative forces of the armies, and a higher estimate of the Northern soldiers than our Southern editors and politicians were accustomed to express, or even the Administration seemed to entertain. This opinion had been formed in much service with them against Indians, and four or five battles in Mexico-such actions, at least, as were then called battles. Observation of almost twenty years of service of this sort had impressed on my mind the belief that the soldiers of the regular army of the United States--almost all Northern men — were equal, in fighting qualities, to any that had been formed in the wars of Great Britain and France. General Sherman's troops, with whom we were contending, had received a longer training in war than any of those with whom I had served in former times. It was not to be supposed that such troops, under a sagacious and resolute leader, and covered by intrenchments, were to be beaten by greatly inferior numbers. I therefore thought it our policy to stand on the defensive, to spare the blood of our soldiers by fighting under cover habitually, and to attack only when bad position or division of the enemy's forces might give us advantages counterbalancing that of superior numbers. So we held every position occupied until our communications were strongly threatened; then fell back only far enough to secure them, watching for opportunities to attack, keeping near enough to the Federal army to assure the Confederate Administration that Sherman could not send reenforcements to Grant, and hoping to reduce the odds against us by partial engagements. A material reduction of the Federal army might also be reasonably expected before the end of June, by the expiration of the terms of service of the regiments that had not reinlisted. I was confident, too, that the Administration would see the expediency of employing Forrest and his cavalry to break the enemy's railroad communications, by which he could have been defeated."

In keeping with the Union strategy, Grant ordered Sherman to hit Confederate armies at will, keeping them too busy to form a united front, while continuing his "total war," slash-and-burn tactics of destroying crops, homes, and cities in his path. Grant knew that without Johnston's army, Lee had no real chance at victory. During the opening weeks of the Atlanta Campaign, the aggressive General Sherman was decidedly cautious of Johnston after having a wing of his army effectively clipped by Johnston at Bentonville. Meanwhile, General Johnston began gradually retreating in the face of Sherman's forces, despite repulsing them in initial skirmishes at Resaca and Kennesaw Mountain. Aside from Kennesaw Mountain, where a frontal assault incurred serious casualties, Sherman continued to eschew full-scale attacks in favor of strategic movements designed to continue moving toward Atlanta. Although Johnston's tactics were by all accounts "brilliantly planned and executed," Sherman's refusal to give battle foiled the strategy Johnston hoped to use (as outlined in his memoirs).

Throughout May 1864, Lee skillfully stalemated Grant in a series of battles known as the Overland Campaign, inflicting nearly 50,000 casualties on the Army of the Potomac. The casualties were so staggering that Grant was constantly derided as a butcher, and his lack of progress ensured that anti-war criticism of the Lincoln Administration continued into the summer before the election. The Democrats nominated George McClellan, the former leader of the Army of the Potomac. McClellan had not been as aggressive as Lincoln hoped, but he was still exceedingly popular with Northern soldiers despite being fired twice, and the Democrats assumed that would make him a tough candidate against Lincoln. At the same time, Radical Republicans were still unsure of their support for Lincoln, and many begun running their own campaign against Lincoln for not prosecuting the war vigorously enough, urging Lincoln to withdraw from the campaign. It would fall upon Sherman's forces in the West to deliver the necessary victory.

As Johnston continued moving steadily back toward Atlanta, President Davis grew more impatient. Fearing Johnston would give up Atlanta without a fight, Davis telegraphed Johnston to ask what he planned to do to stop Sherman. Already cultivating a decidedly hostile attitude toward the misguided Davis, a thought came to mind that spurred further distrust from Johnston. Earlier in the war, when General "Fightin' Joe" Wheeler had confided his battle strategy to Davis, it appeared verbatim in the Richmond newspapers the next day. Thus, Johnston was intentionally evasive, responding that he would fight Sherman whenever he saw a chance to do so with advantage. Upset with the response, Davis began to plan Johnston's dismissal.

By late May, Atlanta residents began to assume the fall of their beloved city was inevitable, and prepared to evacuate. Then in mid-July after Johnston had been pushed back nearly to

Atlanta, despite the fact that he had retreated and fought skillfully, Davis summarily fired Johnston and replaced him with General John Bell Hood on July 17, 1864. Hood had been an effective division commander in General Longstreet's corps of Lee's Army of Northern Virginia, and he had a reputation for aggressiveness. Confederate leadership sent Johnston a telegram informing him, "Lieutenant-General J. B. Hood has been commissioned to the temporary rank of general, under the late law of Congress. I am directed by the Secretary of War to inform you that, as you have failed to arrest the advance of the enemy to the vicinity of Atlanta, far in the interior of Georgia, and express no confidence that you can defeat or repel him, you are hereby relieved from the command of the Army and Department of Tennessee, which you will immediately turn over to General Hood."

Johnston immediately fired back with a retort that pointed out that in actuality, General Sherman had come no closer to Atlanta than Grant had come to Richmond, adding, "Your dispatch of yesterday received and obeyed. Command of the Army and Department of Tennessee has been transferred to General Hood. As to the alleged cause of my removal, I assert that Sherman's army is much stronger compared with that of Tennessee, than Grant's compared with that of Northern Virginia. Yet the enemy has been compelled to advance much more slowly to the vicinity of Atlanta, than to that of Richmond and Petersburg; and penetrated much deeper into Virginia than into Georgia." Johnston now realized that if he were to be of service to the South, it would be in spite of Davis.

Hood

Johnston would later sum up his view of the Atlanta Campaign while he was in command:

"No material was lost by us in the campaign, but the four field-pieces exposed and abandoned at Resaca by General Hood. The troops themselves, who had been seventy-four days in the immediate presence of the enemy; laboring and fighting daily; enduring toil and encountering danger with equal cheerfulness; more confident and high-spirited even than when the Federal army presented itself before them at Dalton; and, though I say it, full of devotion to him who had commanded them, and belief of ultimate success in the campaign, were then inferior to none who ever served the Confederacy, or fought on this continent."

Taking command in early July 1864, Hood lashed out at Sherman's armies with several frontal assaults on various portions of Sherman's line, but the assaults were repulsed, particularly at Peachtree Creek on July 20, where Thomas's defenses hammered Hood's attack. At the same time, Sherman was unable to gain any tactical advantages when attacking north and east of Atlanta.

In August, Sherman moved his forces west across Atlanta and then south of it, positioning his men to cut off Atlanta's supply lines and railroads. When the Confederate attempts to stop the maneuvering failed, the writing was on the wall. On September 1, 1864, Hood and the Army of Tennessee evacuated Atlanta and torched everything of military value.

On September 3, 1864, Sherman famously telegrammed Lincoln, "Atlanta is ours and fairly won." Two months later, so was Lincoln's reelection.

Sherman has earned fame and infamy for being the one to bring total war to the South, and it started at Atlanta. Once his men entered the city, Sherman ordered the 1,600 citizens remaining in Atlanta to evacuate the city as he, in Grant's words, set out to "destroy [Atlanta] so far as to render it worthless for military purposes," with Sherman himself remaining a day longer to supervise the destruction himself "and see that it was well done." Then on November 14, 1864, Sherman abandoned the ravaged city, taking with him thirteen thousand mules and horses and all the supplies the animals could carry.

One of the most famous movies of all time, *Gone With The Wind*, depicts the burning of Atlanta after Sherman occupied it in 1864. Over time, history came to view Sherman as a harbinger of total war, and in the South, Sherman is still viewed as a brutal warmonger. Considerable parts of Atlanta and Columbia did burn when Sherman occupied them in 1864 and

1865 respectively, but how responsible was Sherman for the initial fires? The answer is unclear.

As part of its retreat out of Atlanta, Confederate forces were ordered to burn anything of military value to keep it from falling into the hands of Sherman's army. Inevitably, those fires did not stay contained, damaging more than their intended targets. In November, preparing for the March to the Sea, Sherman similarly ordered everything of military value burned. Those fires also spread, eventually burning much of Atlanta to the ground. When Sherman's men left, only 400 buildings were left standing in the city.

After the war, Hood and Johnston would duke it out in print, and much of their memoirs are defenses of their actions and attacks on each other. Today most historians consider Hood's generalship in 1864 disastrous, and Johnston called Hood out for the Atlanta Campaign:

"General Hood, in his report of his own disastrous operations, accused me of gross official misstatements of the strength of the army and of its losses-asserting that I had "at and near Dalton" an available force of seventy-five thousand men, and that twenty-two thousand five hundred of them were lost in the campaign, including seven thousand prisoners. He recklessly appealed for the truth of these assertions to Major Kinloch Falconer, assistant adjutant-general, by whom the returns of the army were made, which were my authority for the statement attacked by General Hood. At my request, made in consequence of this attack, Major Falconer made another statement25 from the official data in his possession, which contradicts the appellant. By that statement, the effective strength of this army "at and near Dalton" was forty thousand four hundred and sixty-four infantry and artillery, and twenty-three hundred and ninety cavalry. The prisoners of war taken since the organization of the Army of Tennessee, in 1862, were always borne on its returns. In 1864 there were not quite seven thousand of them. More than two-thirds26 of the number reported by General Hood; the remainder27 by General Hardee; none by Polk, whose corps had not belonged to this army before 1864. To swell the list of my losses, General Hood asserted that the prisoners taken by the enemy at Shiloh, Murfreesboroa, Chickamauga, Missionary Ridge, and in the intermediate skirmishes, were lost by me in the campaign in Georgia The only prisoners taken from us during this campaign, that I heard of, were a company of skirmishers of Hardee's corps, and an outpost of Hood's (some two hundred men), captured about the middle of June, and a few taken from the right of Walker's and left of French's skirmishers on the 27th. As we usually fought in intrenched lines which were always held, the enemy rarely had an opportunity to make prisoners. The fact that those referred to by General Hood belonged to his corps and Hardee's only, which were the old Army of Tennessee, while none were reported in Polk's corps, which had never before belonged to that army, indicates clearly that those prisoners were captured in operations previous to this campaign.

Besides the grounds of my removal alleged in the telegram announcing it, various accusations were made against me subsequently. Some were published in newspapers appearing to have official authority; others were circulated orally, and referred to General Bragg's authority. The principal were: That I persistently disregarded the President's instructions.

That I would not fight the enemy.
That I refused to defend Atlanta.
That I refused to communicate with General Bragg in relation to the operations of the army.
That I disregarded his entreaties to change my course, and attack the enemy.
And gross exaggerations of the strength and losses of the army.

The President did not give me the benefit of his instructions in the manner of conducting this campaign, further than a brief telegram received early in July, in which he warned me against receiving battle with the Chattahoochee behind the army and near it. But as Lieutenant-General Pemberton's retreat from the Tallahatchie to the Yallobusha, in December, 1862, before an army which he thought not quite double his own; and General Bragg's, first from Murfreesboroa to Tullahoma, then from Tullahoma beyond the Tennessee River, and afterward the rout on Missionary Ridge and flight to Dalton, apparently had not lowered the President's estimate of the military merit of those officers, I supposed that my course would not be disapproved by him; especially as General Lee, by keeping on the defensive, and falling back toward Grant's objective point, under circumstances like mine, was increasing his great fame. I believed then, as firmly as I do now, that the system pursued was the only one at my command that promised success, and that, if adhered to, it would have given us success.

In the course so strongly condemned by the President, our troops, always fighting under cover, had losses very trifling compared with those they inflicted; so that it was not unreasonable to suppose that the numerical superiority of the Federal army was reduced daily, nor to hope that we might be able to cope with it on equal ground beyond the Chattahoochee, where defeat would be its destruction. The Confederate army, on the contrary, if beaten there, had a place of refuge in Atlanta, too strong to be taken by assault, and too extensive to be invested. I also hoped to be able to break, or to procure the breaking of, the railroad by which the invading army was supplied, and thus compel it to assail ours on our own terms, or to a retreat easily converted into a rout."

Chapter 9: The Last Confederate in the

Field

Johnston had headed to South Carolina after being removed from command, believing his Civil War career was over, but as it turned out, the war would follow him there. After the Atlanta Campaign, Sherman left Thomas's Army of the Cumberland to deal with Hood while he conducted his infamous March to the Sea, capturing Savannah, Georgia in time to offer it to Lincoln as a Christmas present. Meanwhile, Thomas had virtually annihilated Hood's army in the Franklin-Nashville campaign at the end of 1864.

By the beginning of 1865, the Confederacy was in utter disarray. The main Confederate army in the West under John Bell Hood had been nearly destroyed by General Thomas's men at the Battle of Franklin in late 1864, and Sherman's army faced little resistance as it marched through the Carolinas. Although Confederate leaders remained optimistic, by the summer of 1864 they had begun to consider desperate measures in an effort to turn around the war. From 1863-1865, Confederate leaders had even debated whether to conscript black slaves and enlist them as soldiers. Even as their fortunes looked bleak, the Confederates refused to issue an official policy to enlist blacks. It was likely too late to save the Confederacy anyway.

In January of 1865, Union Maj. General William T. Sherman advanced north from Savannah, Georgia, through the Carolinas, destroying everything of military value along the way as he had done in Georgia. He eventually intended to link up with Union forces in Virginia. With Sherman marching virtually unopposed through Georgia and now the Carolinas, a concerted clamor arose within the Confederate Congress, demanding that Davis restore Johnston's command. In January 1865, Congress passed a law giving Lee the powers of general-in-chief and suggesting that Johnston be reinstated as the commander of the Army of Tennessee. Davis gave Lee the position but would not budge regarding Johnston, privately writing in an unpublished memorandum, "My opinion of General Johnston's unfitness for command has ripened slowly and against my inclinations into a conviction so settled that it would be impossible for me again to feel confidence in him as the commander of an army in the field."

With Davis proving obstinate, Confederate politicians tried to circumvent him, including his own Vice President, Alexander Stephens. Stephens and nearly 20 Confederate senators personally petitioned Lee and asked him to use his newly acquired powers to appoint Johnston over Davis's head. Not surprisingly, Lee refused, but he passed along a personal recommendation to Davis that Johnston be reinstated. Given the mess, it's small wonder diarist Mary Chesnut sardonically remarked in her diary, "We thought this was a struggle for independence. Now it seems it is only a fight between Joe Johnston and Jeff Davis."

Finally, after General Lee added his personal recommendation, Davis relented, reinstalling Johnston as commander of the Department of South Carolina, Georgia, and Florida, and the Department of North Carolina and Southern Virginia in March. Altogether, this put Johnston in command of only about 25,000 soldiers, and even then they were deficiently equipped with supplies and ammunition. Once again, Johnston was tasked with stopping Sherman, despite the fact that his theater's forces were but a fraction of Sherman's horde. Johnston tried to persuade Lee to send parts of his army to help Johnston defeat Sherman, which would then allow Johnston to help Lee defeat Grant, but Lee disagreed with the plan. Lee's siege lines were already severely strained around Petersburg, and they would be broken less than a month after Johnston had been reinstated.

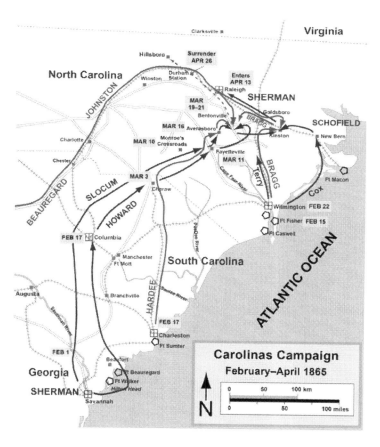

Resuming command, General Johnston concentrated the various remnants of the Army of Tennessee under Lt. General Alexander P. Stewart, Maj. General Robert Hoke's division from the Army of Northern Virginia, units from the Departments of South Carolina, Georgia, and Florida under Lt. General William J. Hardee, and cavalry under Lt. General Wade Hampton in North Carolina. This ragtag collection was dubbed the "Army of the South."

Following erroneous reconnaissance information reporting that the two Union wings of Sherman's army (one under Maj. General Henry W. Slocum, the other under Maj. General Oliver O. Howard) were twelve miles apart, Johnston planned to concentrate his entire army on General Slocum's wing, quickly defeat it and destroy its transport trains before it could reunite with the remainder of the Union column. In actuality, the armies were much closer together. As Slocum's men marched along Goldsboro Road on March 19, 1865, about a mile south of Bentonville, North Carolina, the Confederates under General Johnston attacked.

On the first day of the battle, the Confederate Army attacked Slocum's flank and managed to rout two divisions of the Union Army, but they could not successfully push the remainder of the army off the battlefield. The following day, additional Union forces arrived unexpectedly, resulting in skirmishing that lasted for the next two days, during which Johnston's supplies and manpower reached the critical point. Recognizing that his only option was to abort the assault and withdraw, during the night of March 21 Johnston withdrew his army across Mill Creek and burned the bridge behind him. Failing to detect the Confederate retreat until it was over, the Union lost the opportunity to achieve a decisive victory over Confederate forces. Johnston was both praised and harshly criticized for retreating.

After months of staring at each other from a distance during the Siege of Petersburg, on March 24, 1865 Lee prepared to break out of Fort Stedman and join up with the only other Confederate army left. Instead, Grant's full-out counterattack against Lee's weakened armies resulted in 4,000 new Confederate fatalities, essentially crippling what remained of Lee's battered troops.

On April 1, 1865, at the Battle of Five Forks, Philip Sheridan provided Union forces an extraordinary advantage by locating a weak point in General Lee's right flank and then breaking through, all while cutting off rail supplies to Lee. The critical encounter at Five Forks is best remembered for General George Pickett enjoying a cod bake lunch while his men were being defeated. Historians have attributed it to unusual environmental acoustics that prevented Pickett and his staff from hearing the battle despite their close proximity, not that it mattered to the Confederates at the time. Between that and Pickett's Charge at Gettysburg, Pickett and Lee were alleged to have held very poor opinions of each other by the end of the war, and there is still debate as to whether Lee had ordered Pickett out of the army during the Appomattox campaign.

The following day, Generals Grant and Meade ordered a general assault against the weakened

Petersburg lines by the Second, Ninth, Sixth, and Twenty-fifth Corps. That day, April 2, 1865, Lee abandoned Petersburg, and thus Richmond with it. Quickly dispatching a communique to President Jefferson Davis, Lee stated, "My lines are broken in three places. Richmond must be evacuated this evening." Lee still maintained hope of joining up with Johnston.

Lee's battered army began stumbling west toward a rail depot in the hopes of avoiding being surrounded by Union forces and picking up much needed food rations (which would not arrive on time, fittingly). While Grant's army continued to chase Lee's retreating army westward, the Confederate government sought to escape across the Deep South. On April 4, President Lincoln entered Richmond and toured the home of Confederate President Jefferson Davis.

Fittingly, the food rations did not arrive as anticipated. On April 6, 1865, Major General Sheridan played a principle role in the defeat of Confederate forces at Saylor's Creek, after which he then raced to block the "Rebels" at the Appomattox Court House. On April 7, Sheridan's report read, "If the thing is pressed I think that Lee will surrender," prompting Lincoln to send an immediate dispatch to Grant saying, "Let the *thing* be pressed."

With Lee now nearly trapped and running out of provisions (his manpower reduced to fewer than 30,000), on April 7, 1865, Grant sent Lee the first official letter demanding Lee's surrender. In it Grant wrote, "The results of the last week must convince you of the hopelessness of further resistance on the part of the Army of Northern Virginia in this struggle. I feel it is so, and regret it as my duty to shift myself from the responsibility of any further effusion of blood by asking of you the surrender of that portion of the Confederate States army known as the Army of Northern Virginia."

When Lee proposed to hear the terms, the communications continued until April 9, when the two met at Appomattox Court House.

When Lee and Grant met, the styles in dress captured the personality differences perfectly. Lee was in full military attire, while Grant showed up casually in a muddy uniform. The Civil War's two most celebrated generals were meeting for the first time since the Mexican-American War.

The McLean Parlor in Appomattox Court House. McLean's house was famously fought around during the First Battle of Bull Run, leading him to move to Appomattox.

The Confederate soldiers had continued fighting while Lee worked out the terms of surrender, and they were understandably devastated to learn that they had surrendered. Some of his men had famously suggested to Lee that they continue to fight on. Porter Alexander would later rue the fact that he suggested to Lee that they engage in guerrilla warfare, which earned him a stern rebuke from Lee. As a choked-up Lee rode down the troop line on his famous horse Traveller that day, he addressed his defeated army, saying, "Men, we have fought through the war together. I have done my best for you; my heart is too full to say more."

Appomattox is frequently cited as the end of the Civil War, but there still remained several Confederate armies across the country, mostly under the command of General Joseph E. Johnston, who Lee had replaced nearly 3 years earlier.

Although Appomattox was not technically the end of the Civil War, it was apparent to seemingly everyone but Jefferson Davis that the war was over. Johnston was now the last hold-out and hope of the Confederacy. As made clear in his memoirs, given the surrender of Lee's army and his hopeless position in the Carolinas, Johnston proposed to negotiate terms of surrender with Sherman, against Davis's explicit orders.

"Mr. Mallory came to converse with me on the subject, and showed great anxiety that negotiations to end the war should be commenced, and urged that I was the person who should suggest the measure to the President. I, on the contrary, thought that such a suggestion would come more properly from one of his "constitutional advisers," but told Mr. Mallory of my conversation with General Breckenridge.

That gentleman fulfilled his engagement promptly; and General Beauregard and myself were summoned to the President's office an hour or two after the meeting of his cabinet there, next morning. Being desired by the President to do it, we compared the military forces of the two parties to the war: ours, an army of about twenty thousand infantry and artillery, and five thousand mounted troops; those of the United States, three armies that could be combined against ours, which was insignificant compared with either-Grant's, of a hundred and eighty thousand men; Sherman's, of a hundred and ten thousand, at least, and Canby's of sixty thousand-odds of seventeen or eighteen to one, which in a few weeks could be more than doubled.

I represented that under such circumstances it would be the greatest of human crimes for us to attempt to continue the war; for, having neither money nor credit, nor arms but those in the hands of our soldiers, nor ammunition but that in their cartridge-boxes, nor shops for repairing arms or fixing ammunition, the effect of our keeping the field would be, not to harm the enemy, but to complete the devastation of our country and ruin of its people. I therefore urged that the President should exercise at once the only function of government still in his possession, and open negotiations for peace.

The members of the cabinet present were then desired by the President to express their opinions on the important question. General Breckenridge, Mr. Mallory, and Mr. Reagan, thought that the war was decided against us; and that it was absolutely necessary to make peace. Mr. Benjamin expressed the contrary opinion. The latter made a speech for war, much like that of Sempronius in Addison's play. The President replied to our suggestion as if somewhat annoyed by it. He said that it was idle to suggest that he should attempt to negotiate, when it was certain, from the attempt previously made, that his authority to treat would not be recognized, nor any terms that he might offer considered by the Government of the United States. I reminded him that it had not been unusual, in such cases, for military commanders to initiate negotiations upon which treaties of peace were founded; and proposed that he should allow me to address General Sherman on the subject. After a few words in opposition to that idea, Mr. Davis reverted to the first suggestion, that he should offer terms to the Government of the United States--which he had put aside; and sketched a letter appropriate to be sent by me to General Sherman, proposing a meeting to arrange the terms of an armistice to enable the civil authorities to agree upon terms of peace. That this course might be adopted at once, I proposed that he should dictate the letter then to Mr. Mallory, who was a good penman, and that I should sign and send it to the Federal commander immediately. The letter, prepared in that way, was sent by me with all dispatch to Lieutenant-General Hampton, near Hillsboroa, to be forwarded by him to General Sherman. It was delivered to the latter next day, the 14th, and was in these terms: "The results of the recent campaign in Virginia have changed the relative military condition of the belligerents. I am therefore induced to address you, in this form, the inquiry whether, in order to stop the further effusion of blood and devastation of property, you are willing to make a temporary suspension of active operations, and to communicate to Lieutenant-General Grant, commanding the armies of the United States, the request that he will take like action in regard to other armies — the object being, to permit the civil authorities to enter into the needful arrangements to terminate the existing war."

Sherman

Ironically, what followed would result in both Johnston and Sherman being subjected to ludicrous charges of treason. As soon as Lee surrendered on April 9, 1865, Ulysses S. Grant dispatched a boat from his headquarters at City Point, Virginia with a message to Sherman announcing the surrender and authorizing him to offer the same terms to Johnston. On April 18, Sherman entered into an agreement with Johnston which addressed political and military considerations *conditionally*, the understanding being that the armistice was subject to approval by superior authority. Moreover, Sherman drafted the terms of surrender consistent with what he thought Lincoln had conveyed to Grant and him at City Point in March. General Sherman sent a staff officer to Washington to hand-deliver the terms of the agreement to Grant, which reached him on April 21.

However, Lincoln was assassinated by John Wilkes Booth on April 14, throwing the government into a state of shock and flux. And upon examination of the document, Grant realized that the terms of the agreement had left out certain key military considerations, and so suggested to Secretary of War Edwin Stanton that the matter be referred to President Andrew Johnson (who'd been in office just a matter of days) and his cabinet for their action. Subsequently, a cabinet meeting was called and a unanimous decision was made that Sherman's offer was far too lenient and the agreement should be disapproved, with an order issued directing Grant to proceed to Sherman's headquarters and personally assume operations against the enemy general.

Rather than recognize Sherman's misstep as an honest mistake and not an intentional exceeding of his authority -- after all, he'd had no experience in drafting a terms of surrender document -- both Johnson and Stanton characterized his actions as "akin to treason", with Secretary Stanton calling for official action to be taken by the War Department. And though Grant quickly came to Sherman's defense, arguing that Sherman's extraordinary military record greatly contradicted the charge, the War Department's public announcement succeeded in arousing great distrust in Sherman among the people of the North, a sentiment that would follow him for years.

When Grant arrived at Raleigh on April 22, 1865 to assume operations, he explained the new developments to Sherman and directed him to annul the truce with Johnston and demand that he surrender his army under the same terms accorded Lee. But rather than execute these actions himself, Grant opted to handle the matter in a way that wouldn't rob Sherman of the thunder he very much deserved. Intentionally remaining behind the scenes at Raleigh, Grant instructed Sherman as to how to proceed, making certain the surrender was promptly concluded, while allowing Sherman the formalities of this momentous event.

Sherman wasn't the only one running afoul of superiors. As Davis and the Confederate Cabinet fled, Johnston asked for instructions, only to receive orders suggesting that he disband his army, have it melt away back into the South, and then rendez vous at a predetermined point to reinitiate hostilities. Johnston explained his opposition:

"The substance of these dispatches was immediately communicated to the Administration by telegraph, instructions asked for, and the disbanding of the army suggested, to prevent further invasion and devastation of the country by the armies of the United States. The reply, dated eleven o'clock P. M., was received early in the morning of the 25th; it suggested that the infantry might be disbanded, with instructions to meet at some appointed place, and directed me to bring off the cavalry, and all other soldiers who could be mounted by taking serviceable beasts from the trains, and a few light field-pieces. I objected, immediately, that this order provided for the performance of but one of the three great duties then devolving upon us — that of securing the safety of the high civil officers of the Confederate Government; but neglected the other two--

the safety of the people, and that of the army. I also advised the immediate flight of the high civil functionaries under proper escort.

The belief that impelled me to urge the civil authorities of the Confederacy to make peace, that it would be a great crime to prolong the war, prompted me to disobey these instructions — the last that I received from the Confederate Government. They would have given the President an escort too heavy for flight, and not strong enough to force a way for him; and would have spread ruin over all the South, by leading the three great invading armies in pursuit. In that belief, I determined to do all in my power to bring about a termination of hostilities. I therefore proposed to General Sherman another armistice and conference, for that purpose, suggesting, as a basis, the clause of the recent convention relating to the army. This was reported to the Confederate Government at once. General Sherman's dispatch, expressing his agreement to a conference, was received soon after sunrise on the 26th; and I set out for the former place of meeting, as soon as practicable, after announcing to the Administration that I was about to do so.

We met at noon in Mr. Bennett's house, as before. I found General Sherman, as he appeared in our previous conversation, anxious to prevent further bloodshed, so we agreed without difficulty upon terms putting an end to the war within the limits of our commands, which happened to be coextensive-terms which we expected to produce a general pacification:"

Thus, on April 26, 1865, after all the confusion, General Johnston ignored President Davis's orders and surrendered his army and all the Confederates under his command in the Carolinas, Georgia, and Florida. However, even as Johnston's surrender was secured, Secretary Stanton continued to denounce Sherman, calling for his formal "dressing down." And although Sherman was never officially charged with treason and the public finally came to understand the circumstances of Sherman's so-called "act of treason," the riff between Sherman and Stanton continued throughout Stanton's tenure as Secretary of War until 1869.

Johnston telegrammed Southern leaders to explain his surrender. "The disaster in Virginia, the capture by the enemy of all our workshops for the preparation of ammunition and repairing of arms, the impossibility of recruiting our little army opposed to more than ten times its number, or of supplying it except by robbing our own citizens, destroyed all hope of successful war. I have made, therefore, a military convention with Major-General Sherman, to terminate hostilities in North and South Carolina, Georgia, and Florida. I made this convention to spare the blood of this gallant little army, to prevent further sufferings of our people by the devastation and ruin inevitable from the marches of invading armies, and to avoid the crime of waging a hopeless war."

In his surrender address, General Order Number 22, Johnston exhorted his men: "Comrades: In terminating our official relations, I earnestly exhort you to observe faithfully the terms of pacification agreed upon and discharge the obligations of good and peaceful citizens, as well as you have performed the duties of thorough soldiers in the field. By such a course, you will best secure the comfort of your families and kindred and restore tranquility to our country. You will return to your homes with the admiration of our people, won by the courage and noble devotion you have displayed in this long war. I shall always remember with pride the loyal support and generous confidence you have given me. I now part with you with deep regret – and bid you farewell with feelings of cordial friendship and with earnest wishes that you may have hereafter all the prosperity and happiness to be found in the world."

After Johnston surrendered, Sherman made the magnanimous decision to give 10 days' rations to the Confederate soldiers, as well as horses and mules that they could use for farming. Sherman even distributed foodstuffs to civilians across the South. Though this is all forgotten in the name of demonizing Sherman across the South even 150 years after the start of the Civil War, Johnston was both impressed and exceedingly grateful. Johnston wrote to Sherman that his generosity "reconciles me to what I have previously regarded as the misfortune of my life, that of having you to encounter in the field.

In the immediate aftermath of Johnston's surrender, the remaining Confederate forces would surrender or quit. The last skirmish between the two sides took place May 12-13, ending ironically with a Confederate victory at the Battle of Palmito Ranch in Texas. Two days earlier, Jefferson Davis had been captured in Georgia.

Although many Confederate generals were highly critical of Johnston after the close of the War, the memoirs of both Sherman (*Memoirs of General William T. Sherman: By Himself*) and Grant (*Personal Memoirs of Ulysses S. Grant*) present Johnston in a favorable light. Sherman described Johnston as a "dangerous and wily opponent", while criticizing Johnston's Confederate nemeses, General Hood and Confederate President Jefferson Davis. Grant fully supported Johnston's military decisions in the Vicksburg Campaign, stating, "Johnston evidently took in the situation, and wisely, I think, abstained from making an assault on us because it would simply have inflicted losses on both sides without accomplishing any result." Commenting on the Atlanta Campaign, Grant wrote, "For my own part, I think that Johnston's tactics were right. Anything that could have prolonged the war a year beyond the time that it finally did close, would probably have exhausted the North to such an extent that they might then have abandoned the contest and agreed to a settlement."

Meanwhile, after the war Johnston couldn't help but continue to take digs at Davis. "I know Mr. Davis thinks he can do a great many things other men would hesitate to attempt. For instance, he tried to do what God failed to do. He tried to make a soldier of Braxton Bragg and you know the results. It couldn't be done."

Chapter 10: Life after the Civil War

After the Civil War, Johnston at first struggled to make a living to support himself and his wife, who, like him, was suffering ill health. From 1866 to 1867, he served as president of a small railroad, the Alabama & Tennessee River Rail Road Company, during which time he renamed it the Selma, Rome and Dalton Railroad. By the end of 1867, the railroad would go bankrupt, though apparently by no fault of Johnston.

Leaving the railroad business (but only temporarily), in 1868 Johnston established an insurance company in Savannah, Georgia, acting as an agent for the Liverpool & London and Globe Insurance Company. Within 4 years it had a network of more than 120 agents across the South, a testament to his organizational skills. The income from this venture afforded him time to tend to his dying wife and pen his Civil War memoirs.

In 1874, Johnston published *Narrative of Military Operations During the Civil War, a highly detailed account of the events of the Civil War that sharply attacks Davis's handling of the Confederate military and the mistakes of other Confederate generals. Many viewed Johnston's memoirs as an obvious attempt to justify his Civil War career, which had been plagued by charges of being overly cautious. Of course, Johnston was hardly the only Civil War general to author self-serving memoirs; in fact, that was standard fare for the period. But unlike those of Sherman and Grant, Johnston's autobiography sold poorly, with its publisher and Johnston failing to even make a profit.*

In the winter of 1876–77, Johnston moved from Savannah, Georgia to Richmond, Virginia. From 1879 to 1881, Johnston served in the 46th Congress as a Democratic congressman but was not supported for renomination in 1880. During the Grover Cleveland administration (1885–1889), due to Johnston's prior railroad experience, he was appointed a Commissioner of Railroads.

After his wife Lydia Mulligan Sims McLane died in 1887, Johnston spent his remaining years traveling to various veterans' gatherings, where he was often greeted with cheering crowds. Clearly, his perceived shortcomings and perceived military incompetence were seemingly forgiven or forgotten by many, and like many other key figures of the Civil War, his celebrity grew over time.

As a testament to his character, Joseph Johnston never forgot the magnanimity of the man to whom he surrendered at Bennett Place that day in April of 1865, and he never permitted an unkind word to be said in his presence about Sherman. Sherman and Johnston corresponded regularly, as did Johnston and Grant, and Sherman and Johnston frequently met for cordial dinners in Washington, D. C. whenever Johnston visited.

So close had the two men grown that when Sherman died on February 14, 1891, Johnston served as head pallbearer at his funeral. Ironically, during the official procession held in New York City on February 19, 1891, Johnston, described as small and graying with a distinct military bearing at this stage of his life, refused to wear his hat despite frigidly cold, rainy weather, stating emphatically, "If I were in his place and he were standing here in mine, he would not put on his hat." Consequently, Johnston caught a cold that day which quickly developed into pneumonia.

On March 21, 1891 at the age of eighty-four, Joseph Eggleston Johnston died in Washington, D. C. He was buried next to his wife Lydia Mulligan Sims McLane Johnston in Green Mount Cemetery, Baltimore, Maryland.

In 1912 a public monument to General Joseph Johnston was erected in Dalton, Georgia.

During World War II, the United States Navy named a Liberty Ship in honor of Johnston.

On March 20, 2010, a bronze statue of Johnston was dedicated at the site of the Battle of Bentonville in North Carolina.

Today, Johnston's personal papers are held by the "Special Collections Research Center" at the College of William & Mary, in Williamsburg, Virginia.

Chapter 11: Johnston's Legacy

General Joseph Eggleston Johnston was in command of Confederate forces during the South's first major victory (First Bull Run/Manassas in July 1861) and at the last desperate battle fought (Bentonville in April 1865). He was the senior ranking Confederate at the beginning of the Civil War, and he was the one whose surrender truly ended the war. His commitment to the Confederate cause was both instrumental and indisputable.

Many of his contemporaries, even those who questioned his intestinal fortitude for offensive warfare, considered the short, balding general with the bristling white side whiskers and grizzled goatee one of the greatest Southern field commanders of the Civil War, with some going so far as to rank him perhaps second only to Robert E. Lee. Modern military strategists agree that at a minimum, no matter how heavily-scrutinized and second-guessed he was, Johnston had a better understanding of what it would take for the Confederacy to survive long enough to achieve victory than his critics, and that perhaps he should have been heeded more often.

Still, while Johnston should be commended for having never suffered a direct defeat during the entirety of the Civil War, the fact remains that his battlefield victories were never decisive either. That is a fact that cannot and should not be ignored.

Today, as then, opinions concerning Johnston's leadership abilities as a commanding general in the Confederate Army are mixed. On one hand, he was one of the Confederacy's most sensible and intelligent military leaders; careful and crafty, he never sent his men into battles they had no chance of winning. But the arrogance with which he took it upon himself to determine which battles were winnable kept him at constant odds not only with Confederate President Jefferson Davis (and behind-the-scenes politicians) but a considerable number of his own men. Johnston's strategy also bothered soldiers who preferred battle to the seemingly endless game of dodge-and-run that brought neither glory nor decisive results. In a letter written by one of Johnston's men at the front to his wife, the soldier wrote, "The truth is we have run until I am getting out of heart, and we must make a stand soon or the army will be demoralized."

On the occasion that Johnston did order offensive operations, they were often characterized as too complex tactically to execute. But if anything, his record paradoxically indicates that Johnston was much less one-dimensional than he is remembered. While seemingly a defensive fighter by nature (taking a subordinate role at First Bull Run, retreating at Yorktown in 1862, methodically avoiding a confrontation with General Grant at Vicksburg in 1863, and then retreating to the outskirts of Atlanta rather than being drawn into open battle with General Sherman), he nonetheless took the offensive at the Battle of Seven Pines in 1862, and even entrenched at Atlanta—in seeming contradiction to his stance earlier that year when he stated emphatically that it's better to conduct a campaign of maneuver rather than "hunker down and wait for the "Bluecoats" to strike at the time and place of their choosing." One can't help but wonder how the constant conflict with Davis may have affected his reasoning and resolve.

Further examination indicates that while fellow officers and troops initially responded well to his leadership style, his decision to evacuate Harpers Ferry during his first command of the Civil War alienated a portion of his men and may well have tainted the opinions of his superiors. Subsequent retreats convinced Jefferson Davis that Johnston simply could not effectively lead a charge. Had Johnston not been severely wounded at Seven Pines, historians speculate that his actions there would most likely have fallen under Congressional scrutiny, and it's hard to imagine that he would've struck out at McClellan's army like Lee did during the Seven Days Battles. It's easy to imagine Johnston fighting a battle like Fredericksburg, but hard to imagine him fighting a battle like Second Manassas or Gettysburg. Clearly, as the Confederate results of those battles indicate, that could be both a good thing and a bad thing.

Perhaps the best way to characterize Johnston's war record is to look at him as an old-style Southern soldier fighting in a new-style war to the very best of his abilities. Even those who did adapt to the new strategies made necessary by the Civil War's technological advances did not do so until the middle of the war.

During the Civil War and its immediate aftermath, many other names were applied to America's bloodiest conflict, including "The War Against Northern Aggression" and "The Second American Revolution". For his part, Johnston preferred "The War Against the States," the implication being a war waged by the federal government against Southern states and states' rights. Thus, by this preference, Johnston removed any ambiguity as to his definition of the cause; by his support, he declared his unwavering commitment.

Yet, while other Confederate leaders were publicly lauded for their efforts, some for their mere presence, for some reason the South would not or could not bring itself to credit fairly a man who even at his weakest moments, enabled the South to survive long enough to fight another day. Indeed, had the South at-large been permitted to write his epitaph in 1891, his headstone might well state: "Here lies Joseph E. Johnston, the man who most disappointed us." Despite being one of the senior commanders of the Confederacy, Johnston is one of the South's least commemorated or recognized leaders.

Quite strikingly, a perusal of the many articles, books, and references carrying his name reveals a glaring lack of childhood information. Johnston's family life, education, anecdotal references into his character, and the like are all eschewed in favor of immediate focus on his military record, though it should be noted Johnston himself took the same approach As if to obscure any hint of humanity or the man inside the uniform, Johnston has been systematically reduced to a mere caricature; a template of how to alienate one's nation and be robbed of glory.

From many historians' perspective, Johnston should be one of the most celebrated Confederate generals of the Civil War, and yet the number of memorials in the entire South dedicated to him can be counted on one hand. It's difficult to know with any certainty whether this says more about Joseph Eggleston Johnston or the cause to which he devoted his considerable industry.

Bibliography

Bennett Place State Historic Site website: http://www.bennettplacehistoricsite.com/history/gen-joseph-e-johnston/ accessed 8.13.2012.

Catton, Bruce. *Grant Takes Command*. New York: Little, Brown and Company, 1968.
    This Hallowed Ground. Great Britain: Wordsworth, 1998.

Davis, Kenneth C. *The Civil War: Everything You Need to Know About America's Greatest Conflict but Never Learned*. New York: William Morrow and Company, Inc., 1996.

Eicher, John H., and David J. Eicher. *Civil War High Commands*. CA: Stanford University Press, 2001.

Gaffney, P., and D. Gaffney. *The Civil War: Exploring History One Week at a Time*. New York: Hyperion, 2011.

Govan, Gilbert E., and James W. Livingood. A *Different Valor: The Story of General Joseph E. Johnston, accessed via GoogleBooks: http://books.google.com/books/about/A_different_valor_the_story_of_General_J.html?id=v5EsA AAAMAAJ 08.14.2012.*

Lanning, Michael Lee. *The Civil War 100*. Illinois: Sourcebooks, Inc., 2006.

McPherson, James M. *Ordeal by Fire: The Civil War and Reconstruction*. New York: McGraw- Hill, 2001.

Sell, Bill. *Civil War Chronicles: Leaders of the North and South*. New York: MetroBooks, 1996.

Stevens, Joseph E. *1863: The Rebirth of a Nation*. New York: Bantam Books, 1999.

Nathan Bedford Forrest
Chapter 1: Forrest's Family Lineage

Of all the men who participated in the Civil War, Nathan Bedford Forrest has been universally acknowledged as one of the toughest and most courageous. To understand how Forrest became that man, a look at his childhood goes a long way toward providing an explanation.

Nathan Bedford Forrest was born near Chapel Hill, Bedford County, Tennessee on July 13, 1821, the first of 12 offspring to hardscrabble farmer-blacksmith William Forrest and his wife Miriam Beck. William Forrest's family had moved from Virginia to North Carolina, where various family members would fight in the Revolutionary War, and later to Tennessee during the second half of the 18th Century, while the Beck family moved from South Carolina to Tennessee a few years before them.

Heirs to English, Scottish, and Irish yeomen, the Forrests scraped by along the western frontier of America, trading in cattle, mules and horses for a century or so before the first of their family found prominence. Shadrack Forrest was identified in the 1800 North Carolina census as owning 780 acres of land and one slave. In 1806, Shadrack moved his family to Sumner County, Tennessee near Nashville, where they bought property.

In 1810, Shadrack's son, Nathan Forrest, bought 150 acres of land, and the following year, he and his father jointly purchased 470 more acres, making them substantial land owners. Eleven years later, in 1821, Miriam, the wife of Nathan's eldest son William, gave birth to Nathan Bedford, apparently named after his grandfather and the county in which he was born. A recollection from a neighbor from that time describes the Forrest family as, "all energetic, high-minded, straightforward people. I have never heard of any of them being dissipated or connected with anything that was disreputable."

Of Scotch-Irish decent, the Becks emigrated to South Carolina sometime during the 1700s and then moved to Bedford County, Tennessee, where they acquired considerable land and were known to be a vigorous, tough-minded, and prolific family.

Surviving documents describe Nathan's mother, Miriam Beck, as a woman who stood five feet ten inches in height, weighed one hundred eighty pounds, had grey eyes, and was known to be so religious that she observed the Sabbath by cooking Sunday dinners on Saturday; a woman so stern and righteous that she once gave her son a serious thrashing with a peach-tree switch, even though he was 18 years old at the time.

In fact, vigorous might be selling Miriam short. After having 12 children by her husband William, she remarried after his death and produced four more.

Chapter 2: Early Life, 1821-1841

Born into poverty in the backwoods of Tennessee in 1821 and raised without formal education, Forrest and his family were "inured to hardship by seemingly endless labor," but that hard work would help Forrest establish himself as a prominent plantation owner and slave trader in the antebellum South.

By all accounts, Nathan's father could hardly be considered "accomplished" by any measure. The log cabin Nathan was born in belonged to the Beck family, William's work as a blacksmith seems to have been sporadic at best, and his father owned no land until six years after he and Miriam married, when in 1826 he somehow acquired 50 acres at a place called Spring Creek for a nominal fee of $1. A short time later, however, William sold those fifty acres for $400 which he applied to the purchase of 181 acres.

One of the factors thought to have shaped young Nathan's personality and worldview was the fact that he had survived when several of his sibling had not; two of his eight brothers and three of his sisters all died during childhood of typhoid fever. This in itself seems to have instilled in Nathan a particular passion for life that made him unlike other boys of his time and place.

The central factor, of course, was the frontier, and young Nathan was a frontier boy in every sense of the word. Known to many primarily by his various exploits and boyhood adventures, one often-told tale relates how Nathan single-handedly killed a large timber rattler while on a blackberry picking mission. Other stories tell how Nathan once dived repeatedly into a creek to recover a pocketknife for a friend, refusing to give up until he retrieved it; how when thrown from his horse into a pack of wild dogs he managed to frighten the dogs away, sending them howling into the woods; and of rushing a group of drunken loiterers with a pair of shears when they refused to vacate from in front of his uncle's tailor shop. Indeed, even before he'd reached his teens, Nathan showed signs of the indomitable traits and mastery of the backwoods he would later put fully on display as a general in the Confederate Army.

In 1834, Nathan's family gave up their plot in Spring Creek and moved to the "wilds" of Tippah County, Mississippi (now Benton County), where Nathan spent most of his youth helping out on the small hill farm his father leased from the Beck family (but never owned).

Although Nathan is said to have been an avid reader, he attended less than six months of formal school, and it's unlikely that even *subscription* schools, those paid for by the community, were established in what was still considered the "wilderness". Furthermore, after his father died in 1837, the 16 year old Forrest became head of the family as the eldest son.

Obliged to support his widowed mother and eleven siblings with no resources other than their meager plot of land, he devoted the next five years of his life to this work, neglecting his own education. As head of household, however, he did see to it that his brothers and sisters were provided as fine an education as was available in that place and time. He and his younger brothers cleared more land and continued the cultivation begun by their father, growing corn, wheat, oats, and cotton). Together the Forrests gradually increased their cattle, horses, and mules, eventually becoming one of the more prosperous families in the area.

Another incident that speaks of the inimitable character that would come to define Nathan occurred in 1838, not long after his father's death.

On a return trip from welcoming a new neighbor, a trip requiring his mother and her sister Fanny to cover ten miles through the wilderness on horseback (for which they were rewarded a basket of chicks), within one mile of home they were attacked by a mountain lion which had apparently caught scent of the chicks. Though sustaining severe claw marks to her neck and shoulders, an attack which left their horse dead, Miriam refused to forfeit the basket of chicks. Afterwards, the bloodied women proceeded home on foot.

Immediately after dressing his mother's wounds, Nathan took a flintlock musket, rounded up the family's hounds, and disappeared into the night. By midnight, the dogs had the cat treed, but Nathan didn't have sufficient light to shoot the animal. Waiting at the foot of the tree until sunrise, he killed the animal and by 9:00 a.m. returned home carrying the cat's scalp and ears. After this event, Nathan had earned a fearless reputation within the area, with exploits American schoolchildren have come to associate with frontier icons like Daniel Boone and fellow Tennessean Davy Crockett.

By February 1841, the younger Forrest brothers - John, William, Aaron, Jesse, and Jeffery - were old enough to maintain the farm on their own so Nathan, now nearly 20 years of age, decided to enlist in a Mississippi volunteer army unit under Captain Wallace Wilson. This unit, and others like it across the South, intended to deal with Mexico's attempts to reclaim Texas, which had just years earlier won its independence and would not become a U.S. state for several more years.

Due to Wilson's poor management of the unit, however, it was forced to disband even before it set off for Texas, as a result of being unable to book steamer passage; the unit simply didn't have the money. But while most of the volunteers simply went home, Nathan paid his own way and finally arrived in the new settlement of Houston only to find his services unneeded. As it turned out, Mexico was making no advances, and it would be another five years before the Mexican-American War. Broke and disappointed, Nathan took a job splitting rails to obtain enough money to get back home.

Chapter 3: Personal Life, 1840-1861

Little has been written about the childhood and early years of Nathan Bedford Forrest, in part because his lack of education made him incapable of writing well, and there is no indication he kept a journal. Thus, historians rely upon a few surviving accounts to piece together the picture of a man known primarily through his actions beginning at about the age of forty, at the start of the Civil War.

One very insightful and often-told anecdote illustrating Nathan's enigmatic character involves two stranded young ladies and two less-than-chivalrous young men the 24 year old Nathan encountered in 1845 along the road near his house. As the story goes, one late summer day Nathan came upon a black carriage driver struggling to free a coach stuck in a mud hole at a creek ford not far from his home near Hernando, Mississippi. Inside the coach were the widow Elizabeth Montgomery and her 18 year old daughter Mary Ann, two "proper" ladies who were new residents of the area.

As Nathan approached and assessed the scene, he saw that the two young men on horseback seemed perfectly willing to let the slave struggle on his own to free the carriage, apparently offering no assistance whatsoever. Pulling to one side of the road, Nathan hitched his horse to a fence and waded out to the carriage through the mud, introduced himself, and obtained the women's permission to carry them one at a time to dry ground. Afterwards, he waded back into the mud to help the unfortunate driver free the now-lightened coach.

As he lifted the two women back into the coach, Nathan harshly chastised the two young men for their uselessness, and then proceeded to threaten them with physical harm if they didn't leave immediately, which they did. With what would later be recognized as typical Forrest boldness, just before the ladies pulled away, Nathan asked permission to formally call upon them at their home. In light of the chivalry he'd shown, they consented.

While this had been the first time the two women had met Nathan, considering the notoriety that already surrounded the brash and often volatile young man, it seems likely they had at least *heard* of him prior to that encounter; perhaps even read about him in the local newspapers. In a front page story appearing in the Memphis-based *American Eagle* a few months earlier, it was reported that in what was termed a "most bloody affray," Nathan had apparently intervened on his uncle's behalf (one Jonathan Forrest) when the Matlock brothers shot his uncle during a business deal gone awry. As the story was reported, Nathan stepped forward, drew his two-shot pistol and shot the younger Matlock (known as T. J.) through the shoulder, and then fired on the elder Matlock, shooting him through the arm (which later had to be amputated). Then when the other two Matlock brothers lit upon him, he took a knife tossed to him by someone in the crowd and proceeded to stab them mercilessly. Nathan was also wounded in the encounter. Incredibly, one of the Matlock brothers would serve under Forrest during the Civil War.

Local legend says this was not the first or last time Nathan was involved in such an incident, and obituaries would later note, "He was known to his acquaintances as a man of obscure origin and low associations, a shrewd speculator, negro trader, and duelist, but a man of great energy and brute courage."

Just prior to the Civil War, Nathan Bedford Forrest was known to many as a Memphis speculator and Mississippi gambler, and his volatility had a penchant for getting him in duels. But when he came calling on the Montgomery ladies in the summer of 1845, he presented himself as a young, successful mercantile dealer with an office on the public square of their mutual county, DeSoto.

As he approached the Montgomery home, Nathan found the two "useless" young men he'd met that day on the muddy road sitting on the front porch. Upon recognizing that they too were prospective suitors, he immediately handed them their hats (despite one being a minister) and ordered them to leave the premises, which they quickly obliged. Once invited inside, Nathan wasted no time in proposing to Mary Ann, presenting his case succinctly as to why he would make the ideal husband: he cleverly argued that if Mary Ann were to accept as a suitor one of the two boys he'd so tactfully dismissed, she could expect to frequently find herself as helpless as she did that day at the creek, whereas, he and his profitable business could support her securely and comfortably. She told him she would have to consider it.

Upon his second visit, Nathan arrived with marriage license in hand, assuring her that he intended to marry her; and on his third, she finally accepted. On September 25, 1845, the two were married, but if Mary Anne's uncle and guardian, the Reverend Samuel Montgomery Cowan had gotten his way, the wedding would never have taken place. According to a classmate of Mary Ann who happened to be visiting the Montgomerys, when Nathan approached the Reverend Montgomery Cowen for his blessing (and to officiate the ceremony), the reverend is said to have stated emphatically, "Why, Bedford, I could never consent! You cuss and gamble, and Mary Ann is a good Christian girl." To this the clever Nathan countered, "I know that, reverend! And that's just why I want her!"

The newlywed Forrests set up housekeeping in a relatively simple Hernando home constructed of two log cabins built side-by-side, then covered with clapboards to form a single house. As far as lodgings went, it was above average for the Southwest frontier, but hardly what Mary Ann expected from such a *successful* entrepreneur. What Nathan had neglected to tell Mary Ann was that the death of his uncle Jonathan, who had been his partner in many business dealings, had left him in considerable debt. In fact, although he owned a home, five slaves, five horses, twenty head of cattle, fifteen sheep, two oxen, a wagon, and seventy-five barrels of corn, he was tens of thousands of dollars in debt. This would, of course, change considerably over the course of the next 15 years, but that would have been no comfort to Mary Ann at the time. The Forrests would have at least two children: William Montgomery Bedford, born in 1845, and a daughter, Fanny, who died when she was five years old.

Over the course of the next two decades, Forrest was extremely active in several endeavors. He captained a boat which ran between Memphis, Tennessee and Vicksburg, Mississippi, he profitably engaged in plantation speculation, and he became the nominal owner of two plantations not far from Goodrich's Landing near Vicksburg, where he had 100 or more slaves toiling for him. Given his status as a prominent slaveowner and trader, acclaimed writer Shelby Foote would later try to soften contemporary criticism of Forrest's slavetrading by noting he "avoided splitting up families or selling to cruel plantation owners."

Regardless, by the time the Civil War broke out, Forrest had made himself one of the richest men in the South.

Chapter 4: The Civil War

By the time the Civil War started in 1861, Nathan Bedford Forrest was one of the richest men in the South, with income from cotton, livestock, real estate, and slaves accruing a personal fortune estimated at $1.5 million. Although major planters were exempt from military service, when Nathan heard that his native Tennessee had voted to secede from the Union and join the Confederacy, he couldn't wait to volunteer. On July 14, 1861, Nathan, along with his youngest brother Jeffery and fifteen-year-old son William, enlisted as a private, joining Captain Josiah White's Company "E" Tennessee Mounted Rifles. His superior officers, as well as Tennessee state governor Isham G. Harris, were surprised to find someone of Forrest's wealth and prominence amongst the ranks.

Forrest may have been a common soldier but for the fact that local officials wished to utilize his wealth and status. In October 1861, Governor Harris authorized Nathan to raise and fund his own cavalry regiment, which he quickly accomplished by posting ads inviting "men with good horse and good gun" to join his regiment "if you wanna have some fun and to kill some Yankees.")

Impressed with his natural leadership and ability to train men (despite having no training himself), the governor commissioned him Lieutenant Colonel Nathan Bedford Forest and directed him to prepare his troops for action. It also helped that Forrest was a commanding 6'2, 210 pounds, truly the "most man", as Shelby Foote later put it.

From the beginning of the war, Forrest displayed quick and sound judgment, with a gift for executing tactics that often succeeded due to their sheer boldness. With his own unit, known as "Forrest's Cavalry Corps", he immediately organized a raid to confiscate Union equipment, and he even took two Union sympathizers hostage, hoping to exchange them for two Southern compatriots the Union was holding.

Despite the loss of Fort Sumter in April 1861, the North expected a relatively quick victory, and their expectations weren't unrealistic, given the Union's overwhelming economic advantages over the South. At the start of the war, the Union had a population of over 22 million. The South had a population of 9 million, nearly 4 million of whom were slaves. Union states contained 90% of the manufacturing capacity of the country and 97% of the weapon manufacturing capacity. Union states also possessed over 70% of the total railroads in the pre-war United States at the start of the war, and the Union also controlled 80% of the shipbuilding capacity of the pre-war United States.

But while the Lincoln Administration and most Northerners were preoccupied with trying to capture Richmond in the summer of 1861, the most decisive actions early in the Civil War took place in the Western theater. At the beginning of the fighting, Confederate forces had occupied both Fort Henry on the Tennessee River and Fort Donelson on the Cumberland River in Tennessee, affording them strategic control of Western Kentucky and the primary water routes from the Ohio River into Tennessee. At the time, both sides were hoping border states like Kentucky that had not yet picked a side would join theirs. Lincoln himself famously quipped, "I hope to have God on my side, but I must have Kentucky."

In January 1862, an unheralded general in command of the District of Southeast Missouri persuaded his superior to allow him to launch a campaign on the Tennessee River. At the time, Ulysses S. Grant owed his position more to politics than any demonstrable military skill, but he would prove to be the North's greatest general, beginning with this campaign. As soon as his superior, General Henry "Old Brains" Halleck acquiesced, Grant moved against Fort Henry, in close coordination with the naval command of Flag Officer Andrew Hull Foote. The tag team of infantry and naval bombardment helped force the capitulation of Fort Henry on February 6, 1862.

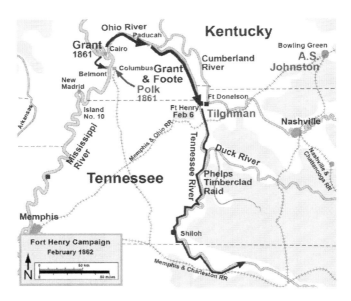

On February 14, Lieutenant Colonel Forrest's cavalry unit was attached to the Confederate garrison manning Fort Donelson, a strategically important position. After forcing the surrender of Fort Henry, Grant and Foote immediately followed it up with an attack on Fort Donelson on the Cumberland River, which earned Grant his famous nickname "Unconditional Surrender".

With the help of the naval forces, Grant's soldiers enveloped the Confederate garrison at Fort Donelson, which included Confederate generals Simon Buckner, John Floyd, and Gideon Pillow. In one of the most bungled operations of the war, the Confederate generals tried and failed to open an escape route by attacking Grant's forces on February 15. During the fighting, Forrest's men captured a Union battery, and although the initial assault was successful, General Pillow inexplicably chose to have his men pull back into their trenches, ostensibly so they could grab more supplies before their escape. Instead, they simply lost all the ground they had taken, and the garrison was cut off yet again.

During the early morning hours of February 16, the garrison's generals held one of the Civil War's most famous councils of war. The three generals agreed to surrender their army, but none of them wanted to be the fall guy, so Floyd, Pillow, and Buckner bickered among themselves as to who would officiate the surrender, and who would be allowed to execute a timely escape. With an unmistakable and comically inflated sense of self-importance, General Floyd (who had a history of retreating from battles and feared he'd be executed if captured) relinquished command to Pillow (who thought he served the greatest loss to the Confederacy if captured), who then relinquished command to Buckner, the least senior officer. At that council, Forrest strongly protested the plan to surrender the garrison and insisted everyone could escape. But Forrest was still only a no-name cavalry officer, and he was dealing with some of the Confederacy's most vainglorious leaders.

Upon conveying their intentions to Forrest, Pillow immediately crossed the Cumberland in a skiff, while Floyd prepared to escape with his two regiments (about two thousand men) via two approaching steamers. At the boat landing, Floyd ordered the men of the 20th Mississippi to form a barricade to prevent the remainder of the fort's garrison from deserting while he and his men boarded and escaped across the Cumberland to Nashville. Realizing that like Buckner's eleven thousand men, his men were to be sacrificed, Forrest refused to make it so easy for the enemy.

With no attempt to conceal his anger at the cowardice displayed by his commanding officers, Forrest announced, "I did not come here to surrender my command!" He then proceeded to round up his own men and rallied nearly 4,000 total before leading them on a daring and dramatic escape under the cover of darkness through the icy waters of Lick Creek to escape the siege and avoid capture. Ultimately, this spawned a loyalty from his men that few Confederate leaders enjoyed; becoming the first notch in the belt for the general who would come to be known as "The Wizard of the Saddle."

Despite all of these successful escapes, General Buckner still decided to surrender to Grant. As a long-standing legend describes, when asked for terms of surrender, Grant sent a letter stating, "No terms except an unconditional and immediate surrender."

Floyd

Buckner

Pillow

Grant's campaign was the first major success for Union forces in the war, which had already lost the disastrous First Battle of Bull Run in July 1861 and was reorganizing the Army of the Potomac in anticipation of the Peninsula Campaign, which would fail in the summer of 1862. The capture of Fort Donelson by the Union army accomplished several significant objectives: it ensured that Kentucky would remain in the Union, set the stage for the invasion (and subsequent occupation) of Tennessee, secured the Tennessee and Cumberland Rivers for Union Army transportation of troops and supplies, and led to the eventual control of the Mississippi River, initially recognized by Union war planners like Winfield Scott as the key to winning a protracted war.

Fort Donelson also elevated Ulysses S. Grant from an obscure and largely unproven leader to the rank of major general, while both the Union and Confederacy got their first real taste of Forrest's tenacity. It wouldn't take long for Forrest to display it again.

Grant

A replica of Shiloh Church. The original was ruined during the battle.

Grant had just secured Union command of precious control over much of the Mississippi River and much of Kentucky and Tennessee, but that would prove to be merely a prelude to the Battle of Shiloh, which at the time was the biggest battle ever fought on the continent.

After the victories at Fort Henry and Fort Donelson, Grant was now at the head of the Army of the Tennessee, which was nearly 50,000 strong and firmly encamped at Pittsburg Landing on the western side of the Tennessee River. The losses had dismayed the Confederates, who quickly launched an offensive in an attempt to wrest control of Tennessee from the Union.

At the head of the Confederate army was Albert Sidney Johnston, President Jefferson Davis's favorite general, and widely considered the South's best general. On the morning of April 6, Johnston directed an all out attack on Grant's army around Shiloh Church, and though Grant's men had been encamped there, they had failed to create defensive fortifications or earthworks. They were also badly caught by surprise. With nearly 45,000 Confederates attacking, Johnston's army began to steadily push Grant's men back toward the river.

As fate would have it, the Confederates may have been undone by friendly fire at Shiloh. Johnston advanced out ahead of his men on horseback while directing a charge near a peach orchard when he was hit in the lower leg by a bullet that historians now widely believe was fired by his own men. Nobody thought the wound was serious, including Johnston, who continued to aggressively lead his men and even sent his personal physician to treat wounded Union soldiers taken captive. But the bullet had hit an artery, and Johnston began to feel faint in the saddle. With blood filling up his boot, Johnston unwittingly bled to death.

Johnston

Johnston's death was hidden from his men, and command fell upon P.G.T. Beauregard, who was the South's hero at Fort Sumter and at the First Battle of Bull Run. General Beauregard was competent, but Johnston's death naturally caused a delay in the Confederate command. It was precious time that Grant and General Sherman used to rally their troops into a tight defensive position around Pittsburg Landing.

That night, nearly 20,000 soldiers from Don Carlos Buell's Army of the Ohio began streaming in under the cover of darkness to back up Grant, but their arrival was noticed by Colonel Forrest's well-placed scouts. Forrest attempted to take the news to General Beauregard, but Beauregard was nowhere to be found. With Forrest unable to rouse and sufficiently organize the troops himself, when Grant attacked at dawn with his army now totaling nearly sixty thousand men, the South's thirty-five thousand battle-worn soldiers simply couldn't withstand the onslaught.

The following morning, Grant's army, now reinforced by Don Carlos Buell's 20,000 strong Army of the Ohio, launched a successful counterattack that drove the Confederates off the field and back to Corinth, Mississippi. And Forrest was in the thick of it. Forrest was instrumental in protecting the Confederate rear guard with his cavalry, securing their retreat south. Grant's army had just won the biggest battle in the history of North America, with nearly 24,000 combined casualties among the Union and Confederate forces.

The following day, April 8, Forrest nearly changed the course of history. After the victory at

Shiloh, Grant ordered Sherman to advance some men south down the road to Corinth to determine whether the Confederates were regrouping or retreating. As they did so, Sherman came upon a Confederate field hospital, which was fiercely protected when Forrest ordered a bold cavalry charge. The skirmish, known as the Battle of Fallen Timbers, nearly resulted in Forrest's 300 cavalry chargers capturing Sherman himself, and Forrest led from the front, to the extent that he got out ahead of his own men and began shooting and using his saber before realizing he was alone and surrounded by Union troops, one of whom cried out, "Kill that goddamn Rebel! Knock him off his horse!" In the melee, a nearby Union soldier put his musket to Forrest's side and fired, nearly blowing him out of his saddle. Incredibly, Forrest continued to fight, grabbing a Union soldier and pulling him into the saddle to use him as a human shield. Forrest spun his horse around and galloped off bleeding, making his escape despite having a bullet lodged near his spine. A week later, it would be removed without the benefit of anesthesia.

By now, it was becoming clear to the Union that Forrest was competent in conducting traditional cavalry roles like reconnaissance and screening an army, and he was a "devil" while fighting. Sherman himself would later label Forrest "the most remarkable man our Civil War produced on either side." One of Grant's friends noted Forrest "was the only Confederate cavalryman of whom Grant stood in much dread."

With Union armies now occupying middle Tennessee, Colonel Forrest executed a series of brilliant cavalry maneuvers within that territory that quickly made his name known across America and earned him promotion to Brigadier General on July 21, 1862. His crack cavalry brigade then hung onto Union general Buell's flank during his march into Kentucky, protected General Bragg's retreat from Tullahoma to the Tennessee River, and that winter, while the army was in winter quarters, vigorously covered the Union front at Nashville, continually stinging the enemy at every opportunity.

By December of 1862, Union forces were amassing two huge, independent armies. On the Mississippi, General Ulysses S. Grant was preparing to threaten Vicksburg, while at Nashville, Maj. General William Rosecrans' Army of the Cumberland was setting-up to drive southward toward Chattanooga. And with neither commander appearing to be willing to wait until spring to initiate their offensives, a Confederate winter strategy was urgently needed.

Confederate President Jefferson Davis sat in on closed-door discussions as Western Theater commander General Braxton Bragg decided that General Forrest would establish operations in west Tennessee to frustrate Grant, while Brig. General John Hunt Morgan and his Army of Tennessee would sweep north around Rosecrans' base at Nashville and attempt to sever Union supply lines by destroying key railroads and bridges in Kentucky. For his part, Forrest and his men had already destroyed nearly sixty miles of train track, greatly frustrating Grant. This set the stage for Forrest to play a critical role in numerous cavalry operations, his primary mission to torment Union forces by striking at their most vulnerable points.

In December 1862 and again in January 1863, Forrest led a raid into west Tennessee which ultimately contributed to Grant's abandonment of his initial campaign in central Mississippi. Then in February, Forrest and General Joseph Wheeler attacked Fort Donelson in a skirmish known as the Battle of Dover but were readily repelled by the relatively small Union garrison, which Forrest blamed on Wheeler. Infuriated, Forrest told him in no uncertain terms, "Tell [General Bragg] that I will be in my coffin before I will fight again under your command!"

In early 1863 Forrest was ordered to conduct extensive raids in an effort to sever the communication lines of Union General William Rosecrans' Army of the Cumberland, Forrest entered Tennessee with less than one thousand men and managed to capture McMinnville. He then took the Union garrison of 2,000 men at Murfreesboro by surprise, capturing all the survivors, including Union Major General Thomas L. Crittenden. The quick moving Forrest proved impossible to trap for the Union, and by the time he finished his series of raids, he actually returned to Mississippi with more men under his command than he started with.

One of Forrest's greatest accomplishments came at the end of April. On April 30, Forrest confronted cavalry led by Union General Able Streight, who had launched a cavalry raid from Rome, Georgia that became known as "Streight's Raid". Forrest harassed Streight's troopers at Sand Mountain throughout April, and in May he tricked Streight into thinking he had a larger force by making his men parade in plain sight of the enemy, giving the impression he had many more men than he actually had. When Streight surrendered his nearly 3,000 strong force, it turned out he had so many more men than Forrest that that Forrest had to enlist local civilians to guard them.

In the summer of 1863, Forrest was again assigned by General Braxton Bragg to serve under General Joseph Wheeler. Considering their history, Forrest demanded that he be transferred to west Tennessee, and was subsequently dispatched there with a pitifully small force (perhaps as a form of reprimand). Not to be deterred, Forrest recruited additional men from the area and soon had a force large enough to give Union commanders ongoing headaches.

On September 19-20, 1863, the Confederate Army of Tennessee under Braxton Bragg decisively defeated General Rosecrans' Army of the Cumberland at the Battle of Chickamauga. Rosecrans committed a blunder by exposing a gap in part of his line that General James Longstreet drove through, sending Rosecrans and nearly 20,000 of his men into a disorderly retreat. Forrest commanded the cavalry of the right wing, and he led a charge during the battle that picked up hundreds of retreating Union stragglers. The destruction of the Union army was prevented only by General George H. Thomas, who rallied the remaining parts of the army and formed a defensive stand on Horseshoe Ridge. Dubbed "The Rock of Chickamauga", Thomas's heroics ensured that Rosecrans' army was able to successfully retreat back to Chattanooga.

Still, the Confederates had a great chance to strike a fatal blow to Rosecrans' army, and Bragg was strongly urged by some of his subordinates, including Forrest and General James Longstreet, to follow up the success at Chickamauga with a decisive advance on Chattanooga. Bragg's failure to do so left both Forrest and Longstreet incredulous. Longstreet would constantly feud with Bragg over the next few months, while Forrest openly asked, "What does he fight battles for?" In one of the most famous confrontations of the Civil War, Forrest threatened Bragg's life during a heated exchange, telling his commanding officer, "I have stood your meanness as long as I intend to! You have played the part of the scoundrel, and are a coward! If you were any part of a man, I would slap your jowls and force you to resent it! You may as well not issue orders to me, for I will not obey them! And I say to you that if you ever again try to interfere with me or cross my path, it will be at the peril of your life!"

Forrest was so dissatisfied with the incompleteness of the victory and ineptness of his superiors that he tendered his resignation from the army. Of course, no matter how often he feuded with other generals, the Confederacy realized he was indispensable. As the commanding officer, Bragg used his power to remove Longstreet from his presence by giving him an independent command, and Bragg gave Forrest an independent command in Mississippi.

Despite these arguments, by the end of 1863 Forrest had earned himself accolades for his strategy, tactics, courage, and fighting, earning a promotion to major general. But it was also apparent that his volatile temperament hurt his relationship with fellow officers, especially those he deemed incompetent. Ironically, he almost never had the chance to feud with Bragg because he was convalescing in the run up to the Battle of Chickamauga as a result of an infamous encounter earlier that month. In early September, Forrest famously feuded with Lieutenant Andrew Wills Gould, an artillery officer under his command, after an ambush during Streight's Raid that resulted in Forrest's men losing two cannons. Forrest accused Gould of cowardice for the loss of the guns and attempted to transfer Gould, leading the young headstrong officer to confront Forrest personally. The confrontation got more heated, when Gould allegedly shouted, "No man can accuse me of cowardice and both of us live!" As Forrest reached for a penknife, Gould reached for his gun, and in the scramble Forrest was shot in the abdomen. Somehow, the injured Forrest managed to subdue Gould and stabbed him, causing a severe wound.

Incredibly, the fight was still not over. Gould rushed out of the room gushing blood, and he was quickly taken to a field hospital. Meanwhile, Forrest thought he had been mortally wounded and became blind with rage, shouting, "Get out of my way! I am mortally wounded and will kill the man who has shot me!" Forrest grabbed pistols and headed to the hospital to finish off Gould, but Gould made a mad dash out of the hospital when he saw Forrest coming. When Forrest fired a shot at Gould, it ricocheted off a wall and struck another soldier in the leg. Gould didn't get far before fainting, which pleased Forrest, who reportedly stuck him with his boot. Forrest would later learn to his great surprise that his wound was not serious, and Gould would die a few weeks later of his wound.

Forrest was proving to be a pain to some powerful Confederate generals, but the South was acutely aware that Forrest was an even bigger pain to the North. At the end of 1863, Forrest began operations in west Tennessee with a small unit, but he managed to recruit several thousand volunteers, including a number of veteran soldiers, and he whipped them into shape so that they were combat ready before their first confrontation. Upon hearing of Forrest's growing aptitude for adaptive warfare, General Sherman wrote to Union Commander-in-Chief Henry Halleck that men like Forrest are "men that must all be killed or employed by us before we can hope for peace. They have no property or future, and therefore cannot be influenced by anything except personal considerations." Sherman repeatedly ordered his Memphis commanders to catch "that devil Forrest", essentially putting a bounty on his head.

Forrest already had a controversial Civil War record entering 1864, but he was about to participate in perhaps the most controversial battle of the war. After functioning as an independent raider for the next several months, on April 12, 1864, units of Forrest's cavalry surrounded Fort Pillow on the Mississippi River, north of Memphis. Ironically, the fort had been built in 1861 and named after General Gideon Pillow, the same General Pillow who proved wildly incompetent at Fort Donelson and ignored Forrest's suggestion to escape the siege instead of surrendering to Grant.

As far as skirmishes go, Fort Pillow was a completely unremarkable fight. Before attacking, Forrest demanded the unconditional surrender of the Union garrison, a normal custom of his, and he warned the Union commanding officer that he would not be responsible for his soldiers' actions if the warning went unheeded. What made Fort Pillow markedly different was that a sizable amount of the Union garrison defending the Fort was comprised of black soldiers, which particularly enraged Confederate soldiers whenever they encountered those they viewed as former slaves in the field.

It is still unclear exactly how the fighting unfolded, but what is clear is that an unusually high percentage of Union soldiers were killed, and the Confederates were accused of massacring black soldiers after they had surrendered. Primary sources tell conflicting accounts of what happened at Battle of Fort Pillow, leaving scholars to piece together the battle and determine whether Confederate soldiers purposely shot Union soldiers after they had surrendered..

News of the "Fort Pillow Massacre" quickly spread across the country, and it enraged the North. Black soldiers across the country began wearing patches that simply read, "Remember Fort Pillow", and the outrage was instrumental in forcing the Union to threaten to execute Confederate prisoners of war if the Union's black soldiers were not treated properly when captured themselves. Arguments over whether a massacre actually occurred, and what role Forrest played in it, continue to this day. Recent Forrest biographer Brian Steel Wills, taking his subject's past into account, labeled evidence of Forrest's participation in a massacre at Fort Pillow "circumstantial or questionable," claiming Forrest's war record "does not substantiate this charge." Fort Pillow historian Richard Fuchs charges Forrest with full complicity in the massacre, arguing that pro-Forrest arguments appear "designed to prevent any distraction from the hero worship" of Forrest. Author Shelby Foote credited Forrest for "doing all he could to end" the slaughter, while author Robert Browning Jr. argued that since Forrest "lost control of his men," he "shoulders the responsibility for the unnecessary deaths."

While General Forrest conceded that unarmed Blacks were indeed killed, he would not specify whether this had taken place during or after the battle, either upon his orders or from one of his field commanders. All Forrest confirmed in his report was that "the river was dyed with blood of the slaughtered troops for two hundred yards." Forrest also noted in the report, "The approximate loss was upward of five hundred killed, but few of the officers escaping. My loss was about twenty killed. It is hoped that these facts will demonstrate to the Northern people that negro soldiers cannot cope with Southerners."

By May 1864, the Fort Pillow affair became a matter of congressional enquiry, with many leaders from both Union and Confederate camps anxious to condemn Forrest simply on principle alone. Certainly those who had personally experienced his temper and knew of his volatile reputation could easily imagine him capable of a massacre. Somewhat surprisingly, one of the men who believed Forrest was not guilty of an intentional massacre was General Sherman, who by 1864 begrudgingly admired his troublesome adversary. Based on statements taken from many of his own men who had been taken prisoner by Forrest and attested that "he was usually very kind to them," Sherman stated, "No doubt Forrest's men acted like a set of barbarians, shooting down the helpless negro garrison after the fort was in their possession; but I am told that Forrest personally disclaims any active participation in the assault. I also take it for granted that Forrest did not lead the assault in person, and consequently that he was to the rear, out of sight if not of hearing at the time."

Regardless, Fort Pillow permanently marred Forrest's reputation for the rest of his life, and it was featured prominently in his obituaries throughout the North in 1877.

By late spring of 1864, General Sherman was preparing his armies for an invasion of Georgia that came to be known as the Atlanta Campaign. Combined, Sherman's armies formed the biggest army in American history, and Sherman set his sights on the Confederacy's last major industrial city in the West and the General Joseph E. Johnston's Army of Tennessee, which aimed to protect it. Johnston was hopelessly outnumbered, and he would spend much of the summer retreating closer and closer to Atlanta, but in the meantime, the Confederates recognized Napoleon's famous maxim that an army marches on its stomach. To lead such a gigantic force, Sherman needed to have secure supply lines and communication lines, relying heavily on railroads. Major General Forrest understood this as well, and he fully exploited it, resulting in his greatest victory.

On June 1, Forrest led his men from their supply base at Tupelo, Mississippi, intending to raid Sherman's railroad supply line in Tennessee. As fate would have it, however, on that very same day, Union Maj. General Samuel D. Sturgis marched out of Union headquarters near Memphis with about 8,000 men headed for Tupelo in search of Forrest. Following several days of miserable weather that brought troops and artillery movement to a virtual crawl, on June 7, Sturgis called a staff meeting to discuss the possibility of a new strategy; possibly going back to base and choosing an alternate approach. Under his command were cavalry commander Brig. General Benjamin H. Grierson, infantry commander Colonel William L. McMillen, and 93rd Indiana Infantry commander Colonel De Witt Thomas. Colonel McMillen convinced Sturgis to continue on rather than turn back in disgrace.

Unbeknownst to Sturgis, Confederate intelligence reports had alerted Confederate leaders of Sturgis' movement, and Forrest was sent to intercept his men. However, even though Forrest knew precisely where Sturgis would be (by June 9, the Union column would reach Brice's Cross Roads), he didn't have enough men to mount an offensive alone, so he set out to beef-up his cavalry with men gleaned from various scattered army camps along the Mobil & Ohio Railroad, planning to meet up with the enemy at the crossroads with more intimidating numbers.

Ultimately mustering three mounted units under Colonel W. A. Johnson and H. B. Lyon, Colonel Edmund Rucker, and Colonel Tyree Bell, Forrest's strategy was to obliterate Sturgis' cavalry which, by his estimation, would reach the crossroads three hours before his infantry. As he told Colonel Rucker that morning, "[Brice's Cross Roads] is densely wooded and the undergrowth so heavy that when we strike them they won't know how few men we have. In this heat, and coming on at a run five or six miles over muddy road, their infantry will be so tired we will ride right over them!"

The next day, June 10, Forrest's 4,800 men engaged Sturgis' 8,000, with Forrest successfully executing some of the most brilliant military tactics used in the Civil War. Utilizing horses to move his men quickly from one point to another, he instructed them to dismount and concentrate their firepower at key positions--then remount and move the action to another location; stinging, moving, and stinging again. At times during the fighting, fierce hand-to-hand combat ensued, with the struggle so close at some points that weapons couldn't be reloaded and were instead used as clubs.

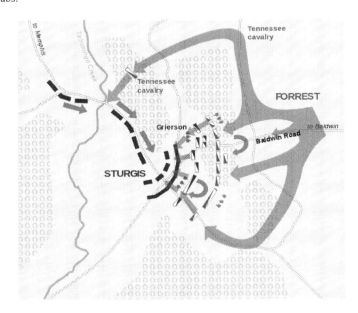

So fast and furious was Forrest's all-out assault that General Grierson became convinced he was facing far superior numbers, and finally requested that he be allowed to withdraw his entire cavalry. Union commander Colonel De Witt Thomas recorded this incident, writing, "One of the hardest battles I have ever witnessed! The enemy flanking me every few moments and my men charging their front, contesting for every foot of ground . . . I pressed again upon the enemy . . . was again outflanked and had to again give back, which I did by retreating and firing . . . ."

About 4:00 that afternoon, Forrest was seen racing up and down the front line on horseback, shouting encouragement to his men, just prior to ordering another charge along the line and doubling-up of troops at the Union crossroads position. At his signal, the Confederates then began a furious barrage of small arms and artillery that stunned Union officers who were convinced that Forrest's artillery was heavily supported by a line of riflemen, which they were not.

Sending the 59th Colored Regiment to hold off the Confederates with bayonets and muskets for clubbing, the Union troops initiated retreat, leaving confusion and pandemonium in their wake. It was reported that some of the black soldiers discarded their "Remember Fort Pillow" badges, worried that Confederate soldiers spotting them would kill them or treat them more harshly, and after the battle, Union leaders again accused Forrest of massacring unarmed and helpless black soldiers. Whether that was true or not, the extent of the damage to Sturgis's force was clear to everyone, including the general himself. In his official report, Sturgis wrote, "The enemy pressed heavily on the rear, so there was nothing left but to keep in motion. The artillery and train have already gone to hell! My soldiers are nothing but a mob!"

That night in the darkness, the retreating Union column took the wrong road across Hatchie Swamp, resulting in wagons, artillery, and ambulances sinking into the deep mud. Sturgis was resigned to simply abandon them where they stood. When Forrest reached the swamp at 3:00 a.m., he found dozens of drowned and dying horses and mules, a mile-long caravan of burning wagons, numerous cannon and other artillery, and a row of abandoned ambulances filled with wounded men begging for medical attention, all buried in the bog.

As Forrest sent his men to continue the harassment of the retreating Union soldiers, they discovered thousands of rifles and cartridge boxes as well as hundreds of straggling comrades too weak to keep up with the fleeing Union troops. Still Forrest pursued. By the end of June 11, 1864, Sturgis' army was without food and ammunition, and the infantry had begun abandoning their shoes; their feet too blistered and bloody to cover them.

The Battle of Brice's Cross Roads cost the Union forces over a quarter of their strength, with Forrest inflicting nearly 5 times as many casualties as he suffered. Additionally, all the Union's artillery, ambulances, wagons, ammunition, camp equipment, 184 horses and mules, and over 2,000 rifles were now in the hands of Confederate forces, all due to Forrest's brilliant strategy and relentless pursuit. This extraordinary victory demonstrated not only what inferior numbers could accomplish under the right command, it showed what Forrest himself was capable of achieving.

While the Atlanta Campaign was still in full swing, Forrest was involved in a clash at the Battle of Tupelo from July 14-15. Once again, it was brought about by Union forces intent on pinning down Forrest and keeping him at a safe distance from Sherman's lines. Having already obliterated one Union army at Brice's Cross Roads, Sherman feared Forrest might move into Tennessee and damage Union supply lines that were already going to be extended as his army pushed its way into Georgia. Sherman ordered Union Major General A. J. Smith to march south from Memphis and "follow Forrest to the death, if it costs 10,000 lives and breaks the Treasury."

After maneuvering for several days, General Smith found himself confronted at Tupelo by Forrest and his commanding officer, Major General Stephen D. Lee. Fully aware of the inherent danger of fighting the crafty Forrest on the open battlefield, Smith ordered his men to dig in and wait for the Confederates to come to them. Left with no alternative but assault the fortified

Union positions, Forrest and Lee unleashed a series of vicious attacks against the Union lines, but they were made in unsupported, piecemeal fashion. The attacks seemed uncharacteristically ill-conceived for the usually methodical Forrest, who would later assert that the Union's defenses were unassailable.

Handily resisting Forrest's haphazard attacks, Smith managed to turn the tables on Forrest and deliver the first significant beating Forrest suffered. After two days of fighting, Forrest's troopers had been defeated, and Forrest was wounded in the foot in the process. Smith eventually withdrew his forces to Memphis, convinced that Forrest's men wouldn't be taken, much to the chagrin of Union leaders who hoped to permanently sideline him.

Although Smith had not succeeded in stopping Forrest to the extent Sherman had hoped for, he had delivered Forrest a staggering blow and severely damaged his ability to impede Sherman's campaign. Historians acknowledge that the Battle of Tupelo (and Forrest's defeat) significantly contributed to Sherman's ability to seize Atlanta and the momentum his army picked up there after.

Throughout the summer and fall of 1864, Forrest led numerous raids, including a well-documented one straight into the heart of downtown Memphis in August 1864 while it was occupied by Union forces. He also raided a Union supply depot at Johnsonville, Tennessee, on October 3, 1864 (the Battle of Johnsonville), which caused millions of dollars in damage.

However, the Confederacy was in its death throes. When General Joseph Johnston retreated to within 3 miles of Atlanta, President Jefferson Davis replaced him with John Bell Hood, an aggressive general who had served effectively as a division commander at places like Gettysburg and Chickamauga but was now being promoted a station too high. Hood lost Atlanta after a series of attacks on Sherman's larger army before heading north, hoping to bring the fighting back into Tennessee.

In early December, Forrest's men fought along with Hood's Army of Tennessee in the Confederacy's most decisive, and disastrous, campaign. At the end of 1864, Hood effectively destroyed his army in a series of vicious but futile frontal assaults against General George H. Thomas's well-entrenched Army of the Tennessee. At the Battle of Franklin, Hood managed to lose over a dozen field generals, including half a dozen killed, among them Patrick Cleburne, the "Stonewall of the West". Weeks later, Hood was routed in similar fashion at the Battle of Nashville. At the Battle of Franklin, Hood detached Forrest with a command in a diversionary method, hoping to draw Thomas's army out of its entrenchments. The ruse failed, but Hood attacked anyway, despite having less men when they left with Forrest. Once again, Forrest chafed under what he viewed as incompetent leadership, arguing with Hood that he should be allowed to use his force to cut off a potential escape route in the case of victory. When Hood refused Forrest's advice, Forrest did so anyway.

On December 5, 1864, Forrest then engaged Union forces near Murfreesboro (where his army was effectively repelled at what would be known as the Third Battle of Murfreesboro), and on December 25, a portion of his army was taken totally by surprise and captured in their camp at Verona, Mississippi during a raid of the Mobile & Ohio Railroad by a division of Union Brig. General Benjamin Grierson.

Despite those setbacks, Forrest distinguished himself once again while covering the rear of the retreating Army of Tennessee after Franklin, earning him further recognition. In February 1865, Forrest was promoted to Lieutenant General and given the duty of guarding the frontier from Decatur, Alabama to the Mississippi River, where he continued his bold, relentless raids. With worn-out horses and dwindling manpower, he attempted to cut off an advance of three divisions led by Union Maj. General James H. Wilson south of Tennessee near Selma, Alabama, one of the South's last remaining centers of war-supply manufacturing. Although he was initially able to resist the Union advance, on April 2, his weakened troops were eventually forced to retreat, leaving Selma to the Union army.

Forrest continued to fight on until hearing news of Lee's surrender of his Army of Northern Virginia at Appomattox, which took place on April 9, 1865. Appomattox is widely remembered today as the end of the Civil War, but there still remained several Confederate armies across the country, mostly under the command of General Joseph E. Johnston. On April 26, Johnston surrendered all of his forces to General Sherman, and over the next month, the remaining Confederate forces would surrender or quit. The last skirmish between the two sides took place May 12-13, ending ironically with a Confederate victory at the Battle of Palmito Ranch in Texas. Two days earlier, Jefferson Davis had been captured in Georgia.

Forest maintained limited field operations until May 9, when he finally decided to quit the war. He had suffered several war wounds, and was legendarily credited with killing 31 Union soldiers and having 30 horses shot out from under him. Forrest is said to have quipped, "I was a horse ahead at the end,"

Whether that is true, what is certain is that Forrest gave a rousing farewell address to his soldiers before quitting the war:

"Civil war, such as you have just passed through naturally engenders feelings of animosity, hatred, and revenge. It is our duty to divest ourselves of all such feelings; and as far as it is in our power to do so, to cultivate friendly feelings towards those with whom we have so long contended, and heretofore so widely, but honestly, differed. Neighborhood feuds, personal animosities, and private differences should be blotted out; and, when you return home, a manly, straightforward course of conduct will secure the respect of your enemies. Whatever your responsibilities may be to Government, to society, or to individuals meet them like men.

The attempt made to establish a separate and independent Confederation has failed; but the consciousness of having done your duty faithfully, and to the end, will, in some measure, repay for the hardships you have undergone. In bidding you farewell, rest assured that you carry with you my best wishes for your future welfare and happiness. Without, in any way, referring to the merits of the Cause in which we have been engaged, your courage and determination, as exhibited on many hard-fought fields, has elicited the respect and admiration of friend and foe. And I now cheerfully and gratefully acknowledge my indebtedness to the officers and men of my command whose zeal, fidelity and unflinching bravery have been the great source of my past success in arms.

I have never, on the field of battle, sent you where I was unwilling to go myself; nor would I now advise you to a course which I felt myself unwilling to pursue. You have been good soldiers, you can be good citizens. Obey the laws, preserve your honor, and the Government to which you have surrendered can afford to be, and will be, magnanimous."

Chapter 5: The Postwar Years

Forrest after the Civil War

Forrest may have given one of the most magnanimous farewell addresses of the Civil War, which is ironic on several levels. After all, literally nobody had fought harder than Forrest for the cause, which he was personally and financially heavily invested in, and the volatile Forrest had a legendary stubbornness and tenacity. Furthermore, in the decade after the Civil War, "Fort Pillow Forrest", as he was known in the North, would become the most notorious unreconstructed rebel and one of the most controversial men in America.

When Forrest finally gave up the fight and returned to Memphis, he found that his plantation had been leveled, his slaves freed, and his vast fortune confiscated. Financially wiped out, he resumed planting and sometime later became the president of the Selma, Marion & Memphis Railroad, which he helped promote. Forrest also became active in Democratic Party politics.

However, all of Forrest's postwar activity pale in comparison to his reputed involvement with another organization. Near the end of the 1860s, Forrest also reportedly became instrumental in the organization of what would become the Ku Klux Klan, and according to some accounts, may have been its first Grand Dragon. In fact, although no source has ever completely substantiated the rumors, Forrest has become widely recognized as the founder of the Ku Klux Klan, and whether the rumors are true or not, the rumors themselves have played a principal role in the shaping of Forrest's image, starting with the Klan's inception. Forrest never openly admitted nor denied the extent of his involvement, but reports state that while Forrest was a K.K.K. founder (and even took part in lynching), he also sought to have it disband in 1869 (both of which may be true).

As the Klan became a growing source of frustration for the North, Forrest was called before a Congressional Committee to give testimony about the Klan. While refusing to admit that the Klan existed, Forrest nonetheless justified subversive actions by vigilante groups, arguing that they were defending against Northern Republican aggression. When asked about the size of the Klan, Forrest estimated that the number of vigilantes was in the hundreds of thousands, although he "could not speak of anything personally" and got all his "information from others." Forrest was clearly refusing to directly answer the questions, but it was true that the Klan, even by the early 1870s, was not centrally controlled or even completely identifiable. If the Klan connections attributed to Forrest did exist, Forrest was now powerless to control or stop the terrorism being attributed to the Klan

During the last two years of his life, it seems quite likely that Nathan Forrest experienced what can best be termed a "change of heart," perhaps attributable to his wife Mary Ann. Although history would ultimately not credit him with much more than an indomitable, even ruthless method of warfare that proved remarkably effective, in his mid-50s, documents indicate that he not only ordered the dissolution of the Ku Klux Klan branch he headed, but went on to repeatedly disavow the race hatred it promoted, railed against racial discrimination, and even publicly appealed for social and political advancement for Blacks.

Throughout the mid-1870s, Forrest's health began to fail him, brought about in part due to the many serious wounds he had suffered during the Civil War. Travelling to different parts of the country failed to help him, and Forrest died in Memphis, Tennessee on October 29, 1877 at the age of 56, probably of diabetes. Papers in the North were extremely critical of Forrest in obituaries. The *Boston Globe* sardonically referred to Forrest as "General Napoleon Bonaparte Forrest." The New York Times, while lauding "dignified" and "gallant soldiers" like Lee, criticized "Fort Pillow Forrest" for his "ruffianism" and "cut-throat daring." Meanwhile, those same qualities were being celebrated by Southerners. The *Memphis Daily Appeal* exhorted Forrest for "the courage of his heart, the valor of his principles, and the energy of his character," comparing his tactics to "the methods of the Crusaders." The *Charleston News and Courier* simply labeled Forrest the "hero of Tennessee."

Nathan Bedford Forrest's fighting tradition was also passed down in the family. Forrest's great-grandson, Nathan Bedford Forrest III (April 7, 1905--June 13, 1943) was a brigadier general in the United States Army Air Forces who died in service to his country, the first American general to be killed in battle in Europe.

Although Nathan Bedford Forrest had virtually no formal education and no military training to speak of, he advanced from private to lieutenant general at an unprecedented rate - the first and only man to do so - during the Civil War, and he earned a reputation as one of the finest cavalry leaders ever in the field. Perhaps more than any other general in the Civil War, he instilled fear in his enemies, drew anger from his superiors, and garnered as much respect from his men as any officer of the war on either side of the conflict.

As his record demonstrated time and again, Forrest's personal bravery and capacity for fighting were nearly matched by his abilities as a battlefield tactician. Wounded no fewer than four times, records show that he also had at least twenty-nine horses shot out from under him or wounded beneath him. And while many in authority initially thought that an uneducated, untrained soldier who hadn't attended West Point would never be effective, let alone attain greatness, his personal toughness and dedication were never in question, and always amply evident. His often-repeated motto regarding battle was: "I always make it a rule to get there first with the most men. War means fighting, and fighting means killing. Get them scared and keep the scare on them."

He despised cowardice, remained fully committed to the cause even after everyone else had abandoned it, and had no tolerance for incompetent leadership. This is well exemplified by his reaction to General Braxton Braggs' refusal to pursue the Union Army at Chickamauga, He punctuated his stance by taking his cavalry to Texas without official authorization, never fighting under Bragg again. And while many would see this as a blatant act of insubordination, Forrest clearly saw himself as loyal to a *cause*--not the whims of those who prove ineffectual at championing that cause.

For all the reasons Northern commanders found Forrest an incessant thorn in their sides and Southern commanders found him a difficult man to swallow, and even harder to command. It is a testament to how effective Forrest was that a man who gave several commanding officers major headaches was eventually promoted to the highest rank the Confederacy had to offer.

Unlike most of the principle leaders of the Civil War who received the country's best military training at West Point and "cut their military teeth" on the Mexican-American War, Forrest never aspired to a career in the military and thought it hardly worthwhile to squabble with Mexico over land. Indeed, his momentary foray into military life in 1841 was precipitated on the idea that Mexico may not stop at Texas but invade the United States.

He did, however (at least momentarily), consider conquering Mexico himself, and told friends he could do so in six months with 30,000 men and 20,000 rifles. Ever the businessman, he said he would then confiscate the country's mines and considerable Church assets, set himself up as ruler, and then open up the country to the two hundred thousand Southerners he expected to flock there. Forrest was always a man of big ideas, but he didn't engage in idle bragging either. Had the Civil War not interrupted his ambitions, and had he lived longer, who knows what he may have accomplished. He had already gone from broke to being extravagantly wealthy by the time he reached 40.

Forrest's lack of formal education is well reflected in his writing (once likened to that of a child for whom English was his second language) as this correspondence to onetime business associate Minor Meriwether demonstrates: "All diferances [sic] between us air satisfactory setled [sic] and I asure [sic] you that thair [sic] is no unkind feling [sic] towards you from me. I have . . . never felt unkindly to wards your Self only when I felt you was using your influence [sic] against my Intrest [sic]." Even so, Forrest is said to have developed an emphatic knack for oral sentence structure, which effectively served to counterbalance his illiteracy. Thus despite his lack of proper schooling, he clearly understood the need to communicate explicitly, and taught himself to do so.

His farewell address to his troops makes clear that, even if he had help writing and articulating his ideas, he was capable of stirring thoughts.

While Forrest's detractors found much to fault in his personality, those who knew him best describe a man whose virtues outweighed his vices. Perhaps it should be expected of a rough and tumble man of the frontier that he often spoke profanities and had an admitted fondness for gambling, including reportedly gambling very large sums of money when he was wealthy. At the same time, Forrest had some "Southern Gentleman" attributes to his personality as well, exhibiting perfect manners for women and clergy. Forrest never drank or used tobacco, and he openly showed delight in the presence of children.

He was known for his love of horses and known to race on more than one occasion, despite suffering chronic boils. And despite his lack of education, he was witty, often with a knack for humor. At a dinner party held during the Civil War, a woman of high social status Forrest why his hair had turned gray while his beard remained dark, to which he replied, "Because I tend to work my brain more than my jaws!"

Forrest was clearly graying even during the Civil War

Forrest's legacy will almost certainly be marred permanently by Fort Pillow, his slave trading, and his well documented disdain of African Americans. Even in his own day, he was one of the most hated men in America, and everything evil that could be alleged about Forrest eventually was.

For example, one oft cited but almost certainly apocryphal story involves an incident reported by Union private William J. Mays, who claims to have witnessed Forrest approach two Negro women with their three children and say, "Yes, damn you. You thought you were free, did you?" as he shot them all dead. Then of course, there were the alleged atrocities against black soldiers at Fort Pillow. Of the alleged massacre, a story in *Harper's* stated, "The annals of savage warfare nowhere record a more inhuman, fiendish butchery than this, perpetuated by the representatives of the 'superior civilization' of the States in rebellion."

Although much has been made of Forrest's questionable conduct at Fort Pillow, some historians have argued Forrest had a genuine sense of humanity concerning his slaves, one that became more prominent with age. Of course, that does not seem to square with what Forrest did or wrote, leaving some biographers to suggest it may have been as much a matter of good business as humane treatment.

In the field, as well as on his own plantation, Forrest had a reputation for not separating members of black families, and made it a habit of providing hygienic care and clean clothes to his slaves. He even offered 45 of his own slaves their freedom if they would agree to serve as teamsters to his Confederate troops, which they did and were rewarded as promised. And as several newspaper accounts note, there were hundreds of African Americans among the thousands of Whites at Forrest's funeral, indicative, perhaps, of an understanding they possessed about the enigmatic Forrest that many others did not.

Forrest frequently argued the hypocrisy of those who professed to be outraged by slavery's inhumanity, particularly what he viewed as jealousy of the economic advantage slavery afforded slaveholders. He noted that while there was considerable favor by Northerners to grant the land of Southern slave owners to their former slaves after the Civil War, there was no interest whatsoever in providing freed slaves Northern land and protecting their civil rights and safety by bringing them North. Forrest asserted that few Northern states even permitted Blacks. Thus, Forrest was quick to lend his respect for Southerners who stood by their beliefs (regardless of what those beliefs entailed) and were willing to fight for them, but withhold it from those Northerners who engaged in war without honor or conviction of purpose.

Biographers describe Forrest as standing 6'2 and weighing 210 pounds, a powerful and dominant build. At the same time, Forrest was described as remarkably agile, with steady, piercing eyes. No matter what anyone thought of the man, there was no doubt that he possessed a commanding presence.

Of course, Forrest is also described as a violent, passionate man who struggled with emotions his entire life and for whom discipline and order were essential to his stability. Naturally intimidating, he used his skills as a hard rider and fierce swordsman to great effect, both on and off the field, and was even rumored to sharpen both the top and bottom edges of his saber and wield it with particular zeal.

In his popular novel about the Battle of Shiloh, Shelby Foote, in covering the battle, wrote Forrest's sword "looked ten feet long." Foote probably wouldn't have gotten much of an argument out of the Union soldiers who had the misfortune of fighting him.

Chapter 7: The Relationship between Society and Civil War History

Historian Georg G. Iggers, in analyzing the formation of history and historiography, once wrote that there were two "dominant traditions" in the practice of writing history. Ac-cording to Iggers, the first tradition was "predominantly learned and antiquarian" while the other was "literary." Thus, Iggers argued, the writing of history is inevitably subjective. Other historians believe the issue of subjectivity was a factor in precipitating Enlightenment. In *Telling the Truth About History*, Appleby, Hunt and Jacob note that during the Enlightenment, thinkers began to believe that science could be objective, and that science could build a "platform upon which all knowledge could rest." This idea was extrapolated to the field of history through the belief that objectively studying history could ultimately help to explain it.

After the Enlightenment, it was believed that the specialization of history as a "professional discipline" could be done objectively. Historiography as a profession and subject matter came into being because it was believed that history itself could become a profession and subject matter. According to Iggers, historiography was borne out of the notion that history "needed" to be written by professional historians not just for each other, but for society as a whole, arguing that the public "turned to the historians in search of their own historical identity." In that manner, history would be "both a scientific discipline and a source of culture."

Therein lay a paradox that Iggers himself realized. It's impossible for something to be both scientific and cultural, since the "scientific ethos of the profession" necessitates objectivity and the cultural function of the profession is inherently subjective. In this sense, historiography could not merely be the study of history; historiography naturally affects history as well.

While Iggers focused on historiography's influence on cul-ture and society, his description of historiography failed to account for society's influence on historiography. This has only recently begun to be expounded upon by historians and applied to the Civil War. In New Perspectives on Historical Writing, historian Peter Burke notes that history "is now viewed as a cultural construction, subject to variation over time..." Thus, the idea of objective history becomes "unrealistic." In a recent dissertation, one scholar defined public memory, a "constant series of rememberings and forgettings which, more often than not, are prompted or privileged in order to legitimize social and political orders." They argue that historiography, far from being a professional subject detached from the public, has actuallybeen directly affected by the public's perception of history.

Despite the fact that the Civil War ended over 140 years ago, it remains a polarizing topic for the country to this day. Thomas Pressly, author of Americans Interpret Their Civil War, believes the "continued appeal of Civil War themes...can be explained in part by the opportunity such themes have afforded...for escape from present reality into a past that was ap-pealingly pictured as colorful and idyllic." Pressly further notes the Civil War "involved vital issues of lasting significance," thus the war "enlisted not only the interest of successive generations but also their loyalties and their emotions." Far from being a 20th or 21st century phenomenon, David Blight notes the "troubled career of Civil War memory began well before the conflict ended." Americans have been dealing with these emotions and memories since the 1860s, and it became the principal driving force of Civil War history and historiography. The shaping of Civil War history and historiography is a very poignant example of the influence of memory.

In *Race and Reunion*, Blight describes Civil War historiography as a "story of how in American culture romance triumphed over reality." Moreover, scholarship discussing social influences on Civil War historiography has only recently come about. Civil War historiographical trends had always been neatly divided along established lines, which may explain why historians took so long to thoroughly analyze the formulation of those trends.

Studying the historiography of Forrest's legacy since the 1860s provides a perfect glimpse into how social memory shapes historiography.

Born into poverty in the backwoods of Tennessee in 1821 and raised without formal education, Forrest and his family were "inured to hardship by seemingly endless labor," but that hard work would help Forrest establish himself as a prominent plantation owner and slave trader in the antebellum South. When the war broke out, Forrest enlisted in the army and was instructed to raise a battalion of cavalry. Forrest spent the entire war fighting in the Western theater, becoming the only individual in the war to rise from the rank of Private to Lieu-tenant General. By the end of the war, Forrest was known throughout the South as the "Wizard of the Saddle," and anec-dotes of his prowess in battle were legendary. In addition to being injured multiple times in battle, Forrest has been credited with having killed 30 Union soldiers in combat and having 29 horses shot out from under him.

History has properly accorded Forrest his place as one of the most courageous soldiers of the Civil War, and Forrest at-tained a number of command successes in the Western theater of the war. But Forrest was also a rough and tumble frontiers-man who became a prominent slave trader, an overt racist, and likely a leader of the Ku Klux Klan after the Civil War. John E. Stanchack, an editor of the Civil War Times Illustrated, aptly noted in 1993, "Everything...about [Forrest] is bent to fit some political or intellectual agenda." Ashdown and Caudill, authors of The Myth of Nathan Bedford Forrest, write that the story of Forrest "embraces violence, race, realism, sectionalism, politics, reconciliation, and repentance. It is a story about the fall and redemption of the darker side of the American dream."

With these characteristics, it has proven almost impossible for any American to have a neutral view of Forrest, and it has been even harder to ignore him. Subsequently, Forrest's image has vacillated from celebrated to reviled, sometimes both at once, over the last 140 years, as the numerous and notable as-pects of Forrest's life and legacy were considered by different people at different times.

What makes the study of Forrest's legacy even easier from the standpoint of history and historiography is the fact that he wasn't much of a writer, and thus he personally did not write anything that could shape his own legacy. Thus, all of the perception of Forrest and his legacy have come from the public and interested outsiders, making it possible to measure historiography and popular memory influence and interconnect with each other. The study of Nathan Bedford Forrest's legacy, within the public's perception of the Civil War as a whole, indicates that society's collective perceptions of history have often been fueled by sectionalism, racism and nationalism, and that society's views strongly influence the formation of historiography itself. This can be seen in the way historiography eflects and perpetuates those sentiments.

Chapter 8: Forrest's Legacy in the 1860s and 1870s

In 1865, the South was a "bleak landscape of destruction and desolation," and the Southern Confederacy had just lost its rebellion with its military defeat. Renowned Civil War historian James McPherson described the region as a "vacuum of devastation and chaos." Fearing lawlessness in the South and seeing the need to rebuild its infrastructure, the federal government, headed by Northern Republicans, believed it was necessary to impose a military subjugation of the South to restore order, placing the rebellious states under martial law. But the sectional animosity that originally led to secession still remained, leaving the country as politically fractured as it was in 1861. And though the South may have been physically subdued, the rebellion was spiritually alive for many Southerners.

As McPherson noted, the Southerners "were a proud people who had staked all and lost all," and Southern contempt for the North was just as strong among noncombatants as it had been amongst soldiers. Reconstruction historian Eric Foner wrote that "from the moment the Civil War ended, the search began for legal means of subordinating a volatile black population that regarded economic independence as a corollary of freedom and the old labor discipline as a badge of slavery."

Though the Confederacy was "decisively defeated," David Blight writes that Reconstruction would "determine just how defeated the South really was..." To continue their resistance, Southerners simply dropped the gun and picked up the pen, intending to project the history of their failed rebellion as a just and heroic cause doomed to failure because of the North's large advantage in military resources. Writing after the war, former Confederate General Jubal Early described the Confederates as "patriots...vindicating the true principles of the government founded by our fathers."

In 1867, Edward Pollard, an editor for a Richmond newspaper, published *The Lost Cause*, championing his voluminous book as a "New Southern history" of the war. Pollard's work poignantly reflected the sentiments of unrepentant rebels clinging to their ideology. Pollard explicitly explained the motivation behind what he termed the "Lost Cause." Although the South had lost the Civil War, he argued that the South could still wage and win the "war of ideas." Conceding that the South's loss meant "restoration of the union and the excision of slavery," Pollard was still defiant, writing that "the war did not decide Negro equality." Taking that into account, historian David Blight noted, "Reconstruction was at once a struggle over ideas, interests, and memory." These Southerners vowed to defy the North, the Republicans and

Reconstruction, and "Lost Cause" sentiments began to quickly spread across Southern white society.

Though he was uninterested in reinterpreting Southern history, one of the most renowned "unrepentant" rebels during this period was Nathan Bedford Forrest. Forrest had already become one of the most controversial soldiers during the war, and Forrest's individual exploits had reached a "mythic stature" by war's end. In a letter after the war, Forrest wrote that he could sense he was "regarded in…the North, with abhorrence, as a detestable monster…guilty of unpardonable crimes…" For the most part however, due to his frontier background and lack of education, Forrest wrote and spoke very little regarding his own legacy before or after the war, even if he was aware of it. While other major generals of the war wrote memoirs and often argued over the Civil War (with the exception of Lee, who died in 1870), Forrest did not. This left his legacy destined to be shaped largely by others, in the form of public perception and historiography. As a result, it is easier to understand how and why Forrest's legacy has been molded and changed over time.

While Forrest is almost universally regarded as a courageous and capable cavalry officer, agreements over his legacy end there. As Jay Winik aptly put it, Forrest was an "incongruous amalgam of the proudest and the darkest sides of the Confederacy, walking…boldly and comfortably in hand." Forrest was known as one of the most obstinate and toughest men of the war, and he made no apologies for his very stark views and controversial war record, including the allegations of massacre at Fort Pillow. As a result, "issues of race and racism tended to frame conflicting interpretations of Forrest's image" in the first few decades after the war, and these conflicting interpretations understandably divided between North and South.

During this time, Forrest was celebrated throughout the South, but he was concurrently notorious and controversial in the North. The New York Times referred to Forrest as "Fort Pillow Forrest," referring to allegations that his soldiers massacred a Union garrison, a sizable portion of which was black, after it had surrendered at the Battle of Fort Pillow in 1864. With such a legacy, Forrest was viewed in the North as the living embodiment of the Lost Cause and unreconstructed Southern white males.

During the beginning of Reconstruction, authors such as Pollard and Early were busy reinterpreting the Civil War and posing the Confederate soldier as a superior embodiment of the Southern males' "martial perfection." Instead of attempting to rewrite the South's past, Forrest was more interested in affecting the South's future. Having spent his own money to finance his soldiers, Forrest spent the first few years of Reconstruction involving himself in failed business ventures and Democratic politics, even traveling to New York for the Democratic convention. In an open letter printed in the New York Times in May 1868, Forrest noted that Southerners "barely live under the accumulated weight of disfranchisement and oppression." Forrest's letter aptly described Southern white Democrats' infuriation with Reconstruction. Through their writings about "Negro Rule" "carpetbaggers" and Southern white Republican "scalawags," the perception of Reconstruction as unusually and unnecessarily harsh took hold throughout the country. This interpretation of Reconstruction would remain the standard view until the 1960s, at the height of the Civil Rights Movement.

Given these Southern sentiments about Reconstruction, Forrest and many others began to join groups "pledged to protect the weak and innocent and to keep order." Prevailing rumors surrounding Forrest's activities within a new secret society in Tennessee ensured that his legacy would forever remain controversial.

Although no source has ever substantiated the rumors, Forrest has become widely recognized as the founder of the Ku Klux Klan. Whether true or not, the rumors themselves have played a principal role in the shaping of Forrest's image, starting with the Klan's inception. The Klan was loosely centralized, with David Mark Chalmers describing Forrest's group as an "anarchic local autonomy." According to Chalmers, Forrest was the "Imperial Wizard," and he credits Forrest with attempting to disband the Klan by 1869, with the original Klan supposedly dispersed by 1871.

Whatever Forrest's ties to the KKK were in the 1860s, vigilante groups which increased violence against blacks throughout the South during the late 1860s were collectively grouped together and branded the Ku Klux Klan. Since "martial law and the large-scale use of troops seemed to be the only answer to Klan violence," the Federal government focused on cracking down on the Klan. Forrest himself was called to testify about his connections with the Klan before a United States Senate Select Committee, which published his testimony in 1872.

Forrest, as resolute as any Confederate in confronting armed Northern soldiers, could not have been more irresolute in confronting unarmed Northern politicians. While refusing to admit that the Klan existed, Forrest nonetheless justified subversive actions by vigilante groups, arguing that they were de-fending against Northern Republican aggression. When asked about the size of the Klan, Forrest estimated that the number of vigilantes was in the hundreds of thousands, although he "could not speak of anything personally" and got all his "information from others." Though Forrest's testimony on the Klan was deliberately shifty and non committal, there were elements of truth to the testimony in that the Klan, even by the early 1870s, was not centrally controlled or even completely identifiable. If the Klan connections attributed to Forrest did exist, Forrest was, in effect, powerless to control or stop the terrorism being attributed to the Klan.

1877 would mark the end of both political Reconstruction and Forrest's life, and public perception greatly influenced the initial legacies of both subjects. McPherson writes that the end of Reconstruction ultimately was brought about by the "wavering commitment" of Northern Republicans. Due in part to Southern castigation of Reconstruction, Northern society had become disillusioned with carpetbaggers and was not committed to black rights. The war's "revolutionary achievements" had thus been based more on pro-Union and anti-Southern motivations than pro-black sentiment.

To "emancipationist" writers, most notably Frederick Douglass and W.E.B. DuBois, "Reconstruction required a full accounting of the past," an accounting that was not coming in the foreseeable future. Though they appealed to people to remember the necessity of Reconstruction for black Americans, their vision would be obscured in the North out of political expediency. It would take another 80 years before historians started to challenge the view of Reconstruction as being a harsh and detrimental occupation of the South.

Forrest's health had been rapidly declining throughout 1877, in conjunction with the end of political Reconstruction. In October 1877, he died in Memphis at the age of 56. Conflicting opinions of Forrest were palpable throughout the coun-try in the wake of his death. Papers in the North were extremely critical of Forrest in obituaries. The Boston Globe sardonically referred to Forrest as "General Napoleon Bonaparte For-rest." The New York Times, while lauding "dignified" and "gallant soldiers" like Lee, criticized "Fort Pillow Forrest" for his "ruffianism" and "cut-throat daring."

Meanwhile, those same qualities were being celebrated by Southerners. The Memphis Daily Appeal exhorted Forrest for "the courage of his heart, the valor of his principles, and the energy of his charac-ter," comparing his tactics to "the methods of the Crusaders." The Charleston News and Courier simply labeled Forrest the "hero of Tennessee."

Forrest remained unreconstructed to his death, but society around him was in a state of flux. As a result of the 1877 Compromise and the end of political Reconstruction, "reconciliation seemed to sweep over the country's political spirit," and sectional reconciliation became politically expedient in the North. This gave embittered Southerners a chance to influence the national perception of Civil War memory, leading Blight to note that "those who own the public memory…will achieve political and cultural power."

Chapter 9: Sectional Reconciliation and Its Effect on Forrest's Legacy

The Southerners had already influencing the legacy of the Civil War with the concrete beginnings of Pollard's "Lost Cause," which was already finding its way into Southern writing, most notably in the Southern Historical Society. Described by Blight as "the vehicle for presenting the Confederate version of the war to the world," Civil War historiography originated with the papers published by the Society. Written mostly by unreconstructed veterans aiming to relate and rewrite the history of the Civil War, the Society's papers became the most important driving force for Southern revisionism, dedicated to making their vision of Civil War history the dominant one. The Society would prove to be extremely successful at this. Commenting on Forrest's legacy, historian Mark Grimsley wrote that the "truth behind the legend matters less than the legend's sheer existence, its power, its pervasiveness." Grimsley's description just as accurately reflected the aims of the Society.

The Society's stated aim was the homogenization of Southern white males, but longstanding feuds between former generals found their way into the papers, and the feuds were frequently based on regional differences. These former Confederates looked to their idealized war heroes as symbols of their suffering and struggle. Based in Richmond, the Society's ideal Southern white male embodied the "Virginian" essence of aristocracy, morality and chivalry. The Society's ideal male, of course, was Robert E. Lee. David Blight credits the Society for creating a "Lee cult" that dominates public perception to this day. Writing about this perception of Lee, Charles Osbourne described the perception as "an edifice of myth built on the foundation of truth…the image became an icon."

The writings of these unreconstructed Lost Cause advocates were instrumental in creating a market for literature and memoirs written by Civil War veterans in the 1880s, and those works would ironically became the principal driving force toward sectional reconciliation. "Sentiment" would be "achieved…in a resurgent cult of manliness and soldierly virtues recycled in…veterans' papers, speeches, and reminiscences." Often written with profit in mind, veterans' memoirs tended to focus on the anecdotes and courage in battles that they experienced. According to Blight, this had the effect of "disembodying" the soldiers' courage from the war's causes, allowing soldiers and citizens of both the North and South to celebrate the Civil War without facing its divisive roots. Though Forrest never wrote memoirs, he was consulted by Thomson Jordan and J.P. Pryor for a book detailing the "remarkable achievements" of his military campaigns. Jordan's book on Forrest's war record, published in 1868, was comparable to the 1880s influx of veterans' memoirs.

Civil War literature in the 1880s was not restricted solely to veterans' writings. An increased sense of sectional reconciliation, fostered by Northern prejudices and Southern intolerance, manifested itself in a flood of literature that worked to obscure minorities' visions of the war. According to Blight, "Americans needed another world to live in" outside of Reconstruction. Southerners found that world in the "sacred remembrances of the grace and harmony of the Old South." As a result, literature across the country focused on the "romantic" memory of the Civil War era and antebellum society, frequently including literature about loyal slaves and benign masters.

In his dissertation, Lance Allen Rubin noted that memory could be "embodied in a public site as opposed to existing in an unspoken context." Given the heightened sense of reconciliation and the desire to recognize and glorify Civil War soldiers, states throughout the North and South recognized Memorial Days, and monuments began to be erected across the nation in the 1890s. An equestrian statue of Robert E. Lee that was unveiled in Richmond in 1890 sparked an outburst of sentimentality in the North as well as the South. Reporting on the unveiling of the Lee statue, the New York Times referred to the memory of Lee as a "possession of the American people" and called the monument a "National possession." As far west as Minnesota, it was noted that the "Lee cult" was "in vogue." Of course, not all Northerners shared the sentimental appreciation of the Lee cult. Frederick Douglass found that he could "scarcely take up a newspaper…that is not filled with nauseating flatteries of the late Robert E. Lee."

Sectional reconciliation was also bolstered by pervasive racism across the entire nation. Historian David Blight credited a higher rate of immigration and the Spanish-American War for the increased racism. While old Southern codes and the Lost Cause found even more national support, blacks were "bystanders," and their "emancipation" was "invisible." This doomed the efforts of black emancipationists and black veterans to have both the causes of the war and black experiences in the war included in its historiography.

Their loss would be Forrest's gain. Court Carney described the effect of racism as "breathing new life" into Forrest's image. By the turn of the century, Forrest's legacy, instead of being controversial, became celebrated nationally. With the extension of Jim Crow and racism, Forrest's connections to the original Klan became both prevalent and glorified. Weeks before an equestrian statue of Forrest was to be unveiled, a writer for the *Memphis News-Scimitar* could not help but compare the veil to a Klan robe. Sentimentality had completely "replaced lingering sectional hostility," and the Memphis Commercial Appeal could correctly claim, "Those who saw nothing specially brilliant in [Forrest's] record before are beginning to acknowledge him one of the greatest generals that fought on either side." When Memphis unveiled an equestrian statue of Forrest in 1905, the New York Times, which had 30 years earlier dubbed him "Fort Pillow Forrest," now wrote that Forrest "won quite as much appreciation in the North as in the South, though in the former, of course, the appreciation was a little slow in finding expression."

At the same time, Forrest, who had been viewed as the ultimate frontier tough guy in life, got the dignified Virginian Robert E. Lee treatment, as the Lost Cause view of the Civil War took hold. The Lost Cause sentiment was clearly discernible in the Memphis News Scimitar's description of the Forrest statue as an "emblem of a standard of virtue." By the turn of the century, President McKinley praised all Civil War soldiers for displaying "American valor." Sectional reconciliation, initiated largely by unreconstructed Southerners and accepted by Northerners disillusioned with Reconstruction, was "politically complete" and now totally controlled the course of the Civil War's legacy, continuing to do so until the 1960s. Republican Reconstruction was viewed negatively and sectional reconciliation was embraced.

During that same period of time, Forrest's legacy was further influenced by current events, public perception and historians. In the case of Forrest's legacy, public perception and historiography would influence each other. Though a couple of books about Forrest's war record had already been published, the first comprehensive biography on Forrest's life was written in 1899 by John Allen Wyeth. The effects of sectional reconciliation and the domination of the Lost Cause are discernible throughout the book, and Wyeth lauded Forrest in every possible manner with those in mind. Wyeth wrote that Forrest's "strict morality was evident in every particular." "Forrest was by nature deeply reverent and religious." Despite his "terrible temper and violent language," Forrest had a "natural simplicity and tenderness." Wyeth celebrated both Forrest's military genius and his courage in battle. Forrest's frontier background and lack of education belied a "remarkable intellect." Forrest, while having an "extraordinary capacity for war" and a "genius for strategy," was also "distinctively aggressive" in battle. Forrest's war achievements and successes were due to his "spirit of devotion to the cause...to which all else was a secondary consideration."

It is clear that for Wyeth, Forrest embodied the rough and tumble frontiersman and the chivalrous Lee at the same time. Put simply, Wyeth's Forrest was all things to all Southerners. Racial issues inherent in telling Forrest's life story were either ignored or blamed on blacks, who are at one point deemed "creatures" in the book.

Chapter 10: The Impact of the World Wars on Forrest's Legacy

Similar to the effects of the Spanish-American War, the nation's participation in World War I against a common, foreign opponent ensured a heightened sense of American nationalism. In addition, more war solidified Forrest's image as an American military hero. Both the New York Times and New York Tribune published articles praising Forrest's military prowess, neglecting any mention of race issues. The Tribune labeled Forrest the "most extraordinary cavalry leader of the Civil War." Civil War historiography and Forrest's legacy would remain unchanged heading into the 1920s.

World War II also shined the spotlight on Forrest's war record. When the Nazis used blitzkrieg warfare across Europe during World War II, Forrest was compared with Hitler for the first time, and it was a positive comparison. The Memphis Commercial Appeal observed, "Hitler, more than anyone else, is applying Forrest's methods." Speculation abounded that Nazi generals had studied Forrest's tactics, leading Lawrence Wells to write a fictional tale about Erwin Rommel traveling to America to study Civil War battlefields in *Rommel and the Rebel*. Another biography on Forrest was published by Robert Selph Henry in 1944. *First With The Most*, titled after Forrest's famous military maxim, focused almost exclusively on Forrest's war record and attributes in battle. Pointing out that "no book had to teach Forrest" how to successfully conduct war, Henry wrote, "Forrest has become part of the American fighting tradition."

The perception of Forrest as a war hero was also strengthened during this period of time by historically based narratives. Forrest appeared in numerous Civil War narratives by renowned Southern writers William Faulkner and Shelby Foote. Their narratives branded Forrest as a rough, rugged and courageous soldier with almost immortal qualities in battle. In one fictional short story, Faulkner's narrator and his grandmother assist "big, dusty" General Forrest in his efforts to attack Union positions at Hurricane Creek. Forrest then leads his forces to a decisive victory at "Harrykin Creek." Embracing Forrest's rugged, frontier characteristics, and emphasizing Forrest's lack of education, Faulkner's narrator tells readers it does not matter how one speaks "when you fought battles like he did."

Foote in particular idolized Forrest in his writing. In his popular 1952 narrative *Shiloh: A Novel*, Foote glorifies Forrest's uneducated background and courage in battle, writing in the novel that Forrest's sword "looked ten feet long." Foote also distances Forrest from the "Lost Cause" sentiments, crediting Forrest for being a harbinger of total warfare more in the mold of Sherman. By the time Foote finished his three volume *Civil War: A Narrative*, Court Carney wrote that Volume Three "undeniably displayed Foote's passionate admiration" of Forrest. That observation is hard to dispute. In the final volume, Foote writes that Forrest was "much feared" for his "unorthodox methods" and Forrest "believed that boldness and the nature of the terrain…would make up for the numerical odds he faced." Foote would continue to defend Forrest during the second half of the 20th century, and, in doing so, he would become the most prominent pro-Forrest figure in America, often making himself a lightning rod for criticism.

Chapter 11: Progressivism Reshapes Forrest's Legacy

Although sectional reconciliation helped unite the nation, it could not paper over the fact that the transformation of the nation from an agrarian society to an industrial one was rooted in the Civil War, with the Industrial North facing the Agrarian South. Moreover, that economic transformation could not eradicate the old Agrarian values that many people still clung to, especially Southerners along the frontier. These people formed the backbone of a new political movement, Progressivism, which aimed to establish individualism. Economic problems suffered by agrarians in the late 19th century led "Progressive" writers to split from the standard viewpoints regarding the Civil War, its history, and its causes. Posing the war as a clash between the "old agrarian" culture versus the "new industrial" one, these authors resoundingly reshaped the legacy of the Civil War and some of its most famous generals, including Forrest.

By the 1920s, in conjunction with continued economic problems, some writers questioned the primary tenet of slavery being the sole cause of war, choosing instead to focus on economic factors. Historian Richard Hofstadter noted, "Almost every aspect of American life…was being reconsidered" during the Progressive Era in the early 20th century. One scholar who had immersed himself in the Progressive movement was Charles Beard. Charles and his wife Mary published a seminal, two volume history of the country that depicted the war as a clash of different classes, with slavery being the primary difference between Northern industrialists and Southern agrarians. The Beards, while acknowledging the Civil War was an "irrepressible conflict," described it as a "social war" in which "the main economic results…would have been attained had there been no armed conflict."

In the wake of this agrarian thesis, other historians began to question the war's origins further.

Though the Beards believed the war was "irrepressible," some historians began to openly question whether the war was even necessary in the first place, blaming the war on "extremists" and arguing that slavery was a "non issue" that would have naturally gone extinct. Since this viewpoint "belittled" slavery's importance in starting the war, it also rejected the "moral superiority of the Northern cause."

One of the individuals who supported the Beard thesis was Andrew Nelson Lytle, who wrote that the origins of the war were based on the fact that the "agrarian tradition, South and West, was in danger." Seeking "epic Southern heroes who could illustrate the virtues of the Old South," Lytle published a biography on Forrest in 1931 that portrayed him as an agrarian farmer fighting for "plain people" to preserve an archaic way of life against the Northern industrialists. One scholar described this vision of Forrest as a "Southern Horatio Alger parallel."

The difference between Wyeth's Forrest in 1905 and Lytle's Forrest in the 1930s was quite stark. Lytle cast Forrest as a "son of gods," and a "hero who could save absolutely." While Wyeth lamented that Forrest's authorities "were slow to appreciate...his wonderful ability," Lytle argued that Forrest could have won the war. And whereas Wyeth's biography ties Forrest's legacy to Lee's, Lytle's biography emphasizes the separation between the two, blaming Jefferson Davis, Lee and other educated West Pointers for not realizing Forrest's inherent greatness and for not being able to properly comprehend strategy necessary for a Confederate victory. Instead of glorifying Forrest's morality, Lytle gave Forrest a more defiant characteristic, portraying him as a warrior who would not hesitate to kill his own men if they attempted to flee. Forrest's reputation as the rough and tumble frontiersman was reestablished.

Dealing so heavily with agrarian topics, Lytle excuses Forrest's slave trading by noting that he was benign to his slaves and "burdened by appeals from them to be bought." And while there were "extraordinary" casualties at Fort Pillow, Lytle blamed the insults of "former slaves" in the Union army as enraging the Confederates. Lytle's portrayal of Forrest completely reshaped the course of Forrest's legacy, and Lytle's depiction of a tough, partisan, no-holds-barred warrior continues to be the dominant perception of Forrest today.

The agrarian version of Forrest has remained since it was resurrected 80 years ago, but the Progressives' interpretation of the Civil War was mostly disregarded after World War II. When the United States entered World War II, the questioning of the Civil War's necessity came to a relatively abrupt end, and Beard's interpretation of the war was strongly challenged. "Instead of ignoring and belittling wars," historians could find "that war has been an inescapable aspect of the human story." Moreover, after World War II, the Cold War was mostly viewed by Americans as "antagonism of irreconcilable ideologies." Refuting the economic interpretation of the Civil War's origins, Henry Seidel Canby noted Americans "had seen in their own time...economic interpretations bombed into cellars by a war where ideologies have been more significant than potential profits."

Thus, present realities pointed historians to a "new nationalist tradition," which interpreted the Civil War as a conflict over different ideologies, and a sense of right and wrong were discernible between the North and South once again. Pressly pointed out that none of the proponents of this interpretation "was born in or had lived in the one-time Confederate states." The "new nationalist tradition" viewpoint culminated with Allan Nevins' enormous Ordeal of the Union, a multivolume history of 19th century America. Writing that the "main root of the conflict...was the problem of slavery," Nevins interpreted the Civil War as a "war over slavery and the future position of the Negro race in North America."

Chapter 12: The Civil Rights Movement and Its Effect on Forrest's Legacy

In the 1950s, the issue of desegregation stirred racial discord and sectional antagonism across the country. In response to the changing landscape, Southern whites further embraced Forrest as a representative symbol of their frustration with desegregation. Meanwhile, African Americans began to challenge the national adulation of Forrest. The sectional antagonism would spill into the 1960s, fostering a social Civil Rights movement on a national level. The Civil Rights movement was so nationally divisive during the 1960s that it was termed a "second Civil War," a "second Reconstruction," and a second "War of Northern Aggression" by different groups. It also happened to coincide with the centennial of the Civil War, an irony not lost on many. As the country became more divided over race, the Civil War Centennial Commission hoped to establish national unity by ignoring the divisive nature and origins of the war. One brochure referred to the military forces as "starting lineups," and the Commission director specifically referenced the "outstanding story" that many Southern blacks were loyal to their masters.

The Commission was fighting a losing battle. The Civil Rights movement served as a visual reminder of the "diversity, conflict and discontinuity" that brought about the Civil War to begin with. At the height of the Civil Rights movement, the Civil War was once again viewed largely as as a conflict over freedom and even a "revolution." The narrative espoused by African American emancipationists like Douglass and Du Bois resurfaced during the political movements. And though their voices had been previously obscured by mainstream perception, Blight noted that blacks had retained a collective memory of hate crimes and the Klan, all of which "reflected a legacy of violence that began during Reconstruction."

With the Civil Rights movement bringing racial issues to the fore, the experiences of African Americans and other minority groups gained national prevalence, and historians began to reinclude them in the narrative of the Civil War. The inclusion of African American experiences in the Civil War reaffirmed slavery as its primary cause, but more notably, it had a critical impact on public perception of the Reconstruction Era, which had been almost universally viewed as harsh and overbearing. Taking Southern institutions like Jim Crow and the Ku Klux Klan into account, Reconstruction historians since the 1960s have viewed Republican

Reconstruction in a considerably more positive light. Directly answering some of the commonly held views of Reconstruction, McPherson argued "the postwar era…affected the South as it affected the rest of the country." Southerners had cast a pall over "Negro Rule" Reconstruction in their writings and memory, despite the fact that blacks never held more than 20% of offices in the South.

With the inclusion of African American participation in the Civil War narrative, racial issues reemerged as an important topic for both historians and society as a whole. Naturally, this greatly affected Forrest's legacy. The Battle of Fort Pillow, perhaps the most controversial battle involving black soldiers during the Civil War, became a topic of dispute during the 1960s. While historians began to argue about Fort Pillow within academic circles, racial issues as a whole had a very polarizing affect on society and non-academic writing.

Regardless of what actually occurred, the studies and literature regarding Fort Pillow often devolve into an indictment or acquittal of Forrest himself. Forrest demanded the unconditional surrender of the Union garrison, a normal custom of his, and he warned the Union commanding officer that he would not be re-sponsible for his soldiers' actions if the warning went unheed-ed. Recent Forrest biographer Brian Steel Wills, taking his subject's past into account, labeled evidence of Forrest's par-ticipation in a massacre at Fort Pillow "circumstantial or ques-tionable," claiming Forrest's war record "does not substantiate this charge." Fort Pillow historian Richard Fuchs charges For-rest with full complicity in the massacre, arguing that pro-Forrest arguments appear "designed to prevent any distraction from the hero worship" of Forrest. While Foote credited For-rest for "doing all he could to end" the slaughter, Robert Browning Jr. argued that since Forrest "lost control of his men," he "shoulders the responsibility for the unnecessary deaths."

Fort Pillow and racial atrocities became a big interest for non academic writers as well. Perry Lentz, noting that Fort Pillow "seemed to have slipped from the American imagination," wrote *The Falling Hills*, a fictional narrative about Fort Pillow. Lentz describes Forrest as "wrathful and animal-like," clearly considering Forrest guilty of a massacre. In addition to Lentz's novel, Ashdown and Caudill note a handful of other stories about Fort Pillow that are based more on "Agrarian" or sectional biases than strict historical interpretations of the battle.

Chapter 13: Arguments over Forrest's Legacy Harden

Aside from the inclusion of racial issues in public perception of the Civil War, there were no major studies of Forrest and thus no additions to the historiography of his legacy in the 1970s or 1980s. During that same period of time, however, the public perception of Forrest became more polarized than ever before. Court Carney noted that the continued focus on Forrest's frontier characteristics throughout the 20th century had the affect of "attracting the attention" of Southern men, while "women seemed more comfortable with the gallant image of Lee." In the 1980s, Forrest was still regarded by many Southerners as "exemplifying the outlaw rebel spirit." In explaining that fact, Mark Grimsley noted that Southern society still admired the old code that tied honor to "violence, swagger and reckless courage."

Conversely, African Americans "failed to see anything positive in the continued commemoration" of Forrest. Contesting the popular perceptions of Forrest during the Civil Rights movement, African Americans continued to dispute Forrest's legacy. In the late 1960s, Tennessee's state legislature removed Forrest's birthday from the list of state holidays, and Middle Tennessee State removed Forrest's silhouette as its logo. By the 1980s, Forrest was "an obvious target for African American anger and contempt," and Forrest's equestrian statue in Memphis "became a focal point for attacks by African Americans incensed by a public memorial to a notorious Klansman." There was a large outcry in 1988 after Shelby Foote said that blacks had "overlooked the facts about Bedford Forrest. He was certainly not the villain they perceive him to be." In response, the executive director of the Memphis chapter of the Congress of Racial Equality called for the removal of Memphis' Forrest equestrian statue, by which time Forrest had been reinterred and buried underneath it. An African American published newspaper, the Memphis Tri-State Defender, compared Forrest to Jack the Ripper, Charles Manson and Adolf Hitler, calling him a "whore-mongering mass murderer."

Nevertheless, Shelby Foote remained undeterred in defending Forrest throughout the 1980s, and that defense of Forrest, emphasizing the same aspects Lytle did, continues to reflect the public perception of Forrest today. In an interview with the Memphis Commercial Appeal, Foote defended the controversial aspects of Forrest. Arguing that the Ku Klux Klan was "not a hate group when Forrest knew it," Foote alleged Forrest was "not a Klu [sic] Kluxer in the way we know them today." Calling Forrest "the most man," Foote also tried to assuage Forrest's slave trader image by claiming that Forrest "avoided splitting up families or selling to cruel plantation owners."

In making those arguments, Foote clearly felt the need to deflect criticisms of Forrest's controversial characteristics, specifically the issue of race. Foote and other defenders of Forrest did so by arguing that Forrest was merely "a product of his time and place," and that it was unfair "to judge people of the past by the standards of the present." According to Foote, people "have to take the past as it is." Richard Fuchs, who held Forrest responsible for Fort Pillow in his book, counters that viewpoint, arguing that historians should not "be guided by the attitudes of Southern society in antebellum America."

Foote would make Forrest an even more recognizable Civil War figure by appearing in Ken Burns' Civil War documentary in 1990. Foote's defense and praise of Forrest in the documentary made Forrest a more central and popular figure in the Civil War, and Forrest's reputation "got a significant boost." Ashdown and Caudill noted that the documentary "made Foote a national celebrity and Forrest one of the most vividly imagined figures of the war."

Chapter 14: Forrest's Legacy in the 21st Century

Foote's influence is apparent in the two biographies published about Forrest in the 1990s, which remain the only two that have been written since the Civil Rights movement. Though both are comprehensive and more evenhanded than their predecessors, the two biographers, in trying to explain away Forrest from a 19th century perspective, come across as sympathetic toward him. One of the most recent works on Forrest is Robert M. Browning Jr.'s *Forrest: The Confederacy's Relentless Warrior*, published in 2004. Despite focusing mostly on military matters (due to being part of a military series of books), Browning's book is perhaps the most evenhanded work to date. Browning covers Forrest's overt racism. In addition to considering blacks "deluded," Forrest's Fort Pillow report is noted, in which he mentioned "Negro soldiers cannot cope with southerners." Browning also considers Forrest responsible for the massacre at Fort Pillow. At the same time, Browning writes, "Historians who have closely scrutinized Forrest…have absolved him of villainy." And in the spirit of Foote and Lytle, Browning believes "the roots of Forrest's rise to greatness…go back to his childhood on the frontier." Browning's book appeals in some regard to every conceivable viewpoint of Forrest.

In some sense, the fact that Forrest remains the most controversial man of the Civil War continues to boost his image in the South, especially among Southern white males who embrace Forrest as the symbol of Southern manhood even tighter in response to the racial blowback over his legacy. Over time, Tennessee erected more monuments to Forrest than Illinois and Virginia did for Lincoln and Washington respectively, including a Forrest monument in the state's Capitol building. Like the debate over the use of the Confederate flag, controversy has ensued over monuments, streets, schools and buildings dedicated to or named after Forrest across the South. Forrest's name has been removed from a street in favor of a civil rights advocate, and there was also an attempt to remove his name from a predominately black school in Alabama.

Meanwhile, Forrest's supporters continue to stand defiantly behind him stronger than ever. Even while debates persisted over monuments, another Forrest equestrian statue was erected in 1998. The statue's sculptor described Forrest as a "true chivalric hero" and an "innovator" of war, a fitting allusion to the dichotomy of Southern historiography between the Lost Cause and the Agrarians that had such a large impact on interpretations of Forrest's image. Analyzing the continued debate, Court Carney quipped that some support "raising" monuments to Forrest, and others support "razing" monuments to Forrest.

Matthew Grow noted that even as late as the 1980s, the Lost Cause was still the most written about topic regarding Civil War history. If anyone had mistakenly thought the Lost Cause was a thing of the past, the Southern Partisan, in response to efforts aimed at removing Forrest's name from mon-uments, wrote that Forrest "may just come roaring out of the grave one day…you will see…black men run like you haven't seen in years." As far as perception of Forrest is concerned, there is no reason to believe that these two sides will ever find a middle ground. However, at least one Civil War writer found evidence that Forrest's image continues to grow more popular with Southern whites. Tony Horwitz, author of the critically acclaimed *Confederates in the Attic: Dispatches from the Unfinished Civil War*, met a Georgian memorabilia salesman who stated Forrest had "eclipsed Lee fivefold" in sales of T-shirts in recent years. Horwitz attributed this finding to "a hardening ideological edge to Confederate remembrance," while Ashdown and Caudill attribute Forrest's growing popularity to his "spirit of resistance" and the South's "swelling racial pride."

The manner in which interpretations of Forrest's legacy have swung wildly depending on the political climate of the time makes clear the strong correlation between public perception and the writing of history. Additionally, it is clear that public perception and historiography were and continue to be influenced by sectional, racial and gender biases, which at times left Forrest's legacy nationally celebrated and at other times made him among the most hated men in America.

Influenced by these factors, society's role in crafting history becomes obvious. It is apparent in looking at Forrest's legacy and the legacy of the Civil War as a whole that public perception and interpreations of the Civil War greatly influenced historians' interpretations of the Civil War. The Lost Cause clearly influenced Wyeth's biography of Forrest in 1905, much the same way Progressivism influenced Lytle's biography of Forrest in the 1930s. In turn, what these men wrote about Forrest took root in public perceptions, creating a circular cause-and-effect result. Thus, historiography, instead of being the professionally objective study of history that Iggers and others envisioned, is subjective by nature and inherently influenced by society's collective perception of its own history.

Bibliography

Joyce Oldham Appleby , Lynn Hunt , Margaret Jacob Telling the Truth About History New York: W. W. Norton & Company, 1995.

Ashdown, Paul., and Caudill, Edward. The Myth of Nathan Bedford Forrest (The American Crisis Series) Lanham, MD: Rowman & Littlefield, 2005.

Beard, Charles A., and Beard, Mary. The Rise of American Civilization Vol. II. New York: Macmillan Company, 1927.

Blight, David. Race and Reunion : The Civil War in American Memory Cambridge, MA: Harvard University Press, 2001.

--------. "Epilogue: Southerners Don't Lie, They Just Remember Big." Where These Memories Grow: History, Memory, and Southern Identity
Edited by W. Fitzhugh Brundage . Chapel Hill , NC : University of North Carolina Press, 2000.

Boston Globe. October 30, 1877 .

Browning, Jr., Robert M. Forrest: The Confederacy's Relentless Warrior (Military Profiles)
Washington D.C: Brassley's Inc., 2004.

Burke, Peter. "Overture. "The New History: Its Past and its Future." New Perspectives on Historical Writing Edited by Peter Burke. 2nd ed.
University Park, PA: Pennsylvania State University Press, 2001.

Canby, Henry Seidel. Walt Witman an American Boston : Houghton Mifflin

Company, 1943.

Carney, Court. "The Contested Image of Nathan Bedford Forrest." Journal of Southern History, 67 (3), 601-630.

Chalmers, Mark David. Hooded Americanism: The History of the Ku Klux Klan New York: F. Watts, 1981.

Charleston News and Courier. November 1, 1877 .

Davis, William C. "Behind the Lines." Civil War Times 18 (1979), 50.

Faulkner, William. "My Grandmother Millard and General Bedford Forrest and the Battle of Harrykin Creek," Collected Stories New York, Random House, 1950.

Fehrenbacher , Don E. "Disunion and Reunion." The Reconstruction of American History. Edited by John Higham . New York: The Humanities Press, 1962.

Foner , Eric. Reconstruction: America's Unfinished Revolution, 1863-1877 New York: Harper and Row, 1989.

Foote, Shelby. Shiloh: A Novel; New York: Dial, 1952.

Fuchs, Richard L. An Unerring Fire: The Massacre at Fort Pillow. Rutherford, N.J.: Fairleigh Dickinson University Press, 1994.

Grimsley , Mark. "The Life of Nathan Bedford Forrest." Civil War Times Illustrated, 32 (1993), 58-73.

Grow, Matthew J. "The Shadow of the Civil War – A Historiography of Civil War Memory," American Nineteenth Century History, 4 (2, 2003) 77-103.

Henry, Robert Selph . As They Saw Forrest: Some recollections and comments of contemporaries. Jackson, T.N.: McCowat -Mercer Press, Inc., 1956.

--------. "First With the Most:" Forrest. Indianapolis , I.N.:Bobbs -Merrill Company, 1944.

Hofstadter, Richard. The Progressive Historians: Turner, Beard, Parrington . New York : Alfred A. Knopf, 1968.

Horwitz , Tony. Confederates in the Attic: Dispatches from the Unfinished Civil War. New York : Vintage Books, 1999.

Hurst, Jack. Nathan Bedford Forrest: a Biography,; New York: A.A. Knopf, 1993.

Iggers , Georg G. Historiography in the 20th Century From Scientific Objectivity to the Postmodern Challenge. London: Wesleyan University Press, 1997.

Isserman , Maurice., and Kazin , Michael. America Divided: The Civil War of the 1960s. New York: Oxford University Press, 2004.

Joint Select Committee to Inquire into the Condition of Affairs in the Late Insurrectionary States.
Ku Klux Conspiracy: Report of the Joint Select Committee to Inquire into the Condition of Affairs in the Late Insurrectionary States. Washington, D.C.: GPO, 1872.

Jordan, Thomson., and Pryor, J.P. The Campaigns of General Nathan Bedford Forrest. Foreword by Albert Castel (DaCapo Press, 1996).

Kolchin , Peter. Sphinx on the American Land: The Nineteenth-Century South in Comparative Perspective . Baton Rouge: Louisiana State University Press, 2003.

Lentz, Perry. The Falling Hills. New York: Charles Scribner's Sons, 1967.

Lytle, Andrew Nelson. Bedford Forrest: and His Critter Company (Southern Classics Series) New York: G.P. Putnam's Sons, 1931.

McPherson, James. Ordeal By Fire: The Civil War and Reconstruction New York: Alfred A. Knopp , Inc., 1964.

Memphis Commercial Appeal. May 31, 1901. July 13, 1940. July 13, 1985.

Memphis Daily Appeal. October 30, 1877. November 1, 1877.

Memphis News Scimitar. May 17, 1905.

Memphis Tri-State Defender. June 11, 1988.

Mendel-Reyes, Meta. Reclaiming Democracy: The Sixties in Politics and Memory New York: Routledge , 1995.

Murdoch, David. The American West: The Invention of a Myth. Reno & Las Vegas, NV, University of Nevada Press, 2001.

Nevins , Allan. Ordeal of the Union . Vol. IV. New York: Scribner, 1947-1950.

New York Times. May 24, 1868. September 13, 1868. October 30, 1877. May 30, 1890. May 12, 1905.

New York Tribune . May 27, 1918 .

"Old South Rears Its Head Along Interstate." American Enterprise. 1998. Vol. IX.

Osborne, Charles C. Jubal The Life and Times of General Jubal A. Early, CSA, Defender of the Lost Cause. Chapel Hill, N.C: Algonquin Books, 1992

Panabaker , James. Shelby Foote and the Art of History. Knoxville, T.N.: University of Tennessee Press, 2004.

Pollard, Edward. The Lost Cause: A New Southern History of the War of the Confederates. New York : E.B. Treat & Co., 1867.

Pressly , Thomas J. Americans Interpret Their Civil War. New York : Collier Books, 1962.

Rubin, Lance Allen. 'Remembering is Hell' William Dean Howells, Realism, and the American Memory Crisis. Ph.D. diss . University of Denver , 1997.

Stamp , Kenneth M. The Era of Reconstruction, 1865-1877. United States : Vintage Books, 1965.

Stanchack , John E. "Behind the Lines," Civil War Times Illustrated, 32, (September/October 1993), 14.

Steiner, Paul. Medical-Military Portraits of Union and Confederate Generals. Philadelphia: Whitmore Publishing Co., 1968.

Wyeth , John Allen. That Devil Forrest: Life of Nathan Bedford Forrest. New York: Harper & Brothers, 1959.

20376552R00264

Printed in Poland
by Amazon Fulfillment
Poland Sp. z o.o., Wrocław